FROM THE BALAWAT GATE. (BRITISH MUSEUM.)

ASSYRIAN ECHOES

OF

THE WORD.

BY REV. THOMAS LAURIE, D. D.

WITH ILLUSTRATIONS.

WIPF & STOCK · Eugene, Oregon

Wipf and Stock Publishers
199 W 8th Ave, Suite 3
Eugene, OR 97401

Assyrian Echoes of the Word
By Laurie, Thomas
Softcover ISBN-13: 978-1-7252-8991-8
Hardcover ISBN-13: 978-1-7252-8992-5
eBook ISBN-13: 978-1-7252-8993-2
Publication date 10/29/2020
Previously published by American Tract Society, 1894

This edition is a scanned facsimile of the original edition published in 1894.

PREFACE.

NEVER was antiquity so remote as now, and never were we better acquainted with it. It seems as though God had held back the knowledge of facts that men might give free scope to their unbelief, and then let the full flood of information sweep away the objections raised against his Word as the tide sweeps away the structures children had erected on the sand.

Never did so many books issue from the press, and if many assail the authority of Holy Scripture a larger number rally around it in loving loyalty. One who spent nearly 40 years in Bible lands has shown how those lands light up the pages of the Book. Nor the lands only; the languages that have been spoken there do the same: their ordinary style and their peculiar idioms we joyfully hail as old friends whose acquaintance we had formed in the sacred page.

This volume does not claim to march in the front ranks of Assyrian scholars. The writer has not excavated mounds hitherto unknown, and interpreted the tablets he found there, as our own "Wolfe expedition" has done so well. His has been the humbler aim of making a larger number acquainted with the work that has been done, and with some at least of the results obtained. He has sought to gather up the fragments, that nothing be lost; so that humble believers who have been startled by the noise of the battle now raging round the Word may have their hearts reassured by the corroborations of the truth that lie stored up in every ancient mound and are brought to light by the pick of the explorer.

Not that Scripture is dependent on any endorsement from without, for, as the sweet singer of Olney says,

> " It gives a light to every age ;
> It gives, but borrows none."

In a glorious sense it can say with its Author, "The witness which I receive is not from man," for testimony from without only answers objections raised from outside. The true evidence that Scripture is from God is in itself, and in the work which it begins and carries on in the hearts of men.

Yet it is very pleasant to find God using the common language of ordinary men to convey his revelation of the truth; and as the old familiar phrases of Scripture have met our eye in the Assyrian monuments we confess to having hailed them with peculiar joy. And this may account for the presence of some things in this volume which establish no truth, only look out on us as old acquaintances, all the more welcome that we were not looking for them in so strange a place.

Then obscure phrases are made clear, as, *e. g.*, "The mount of the congregation." Isa. 14:13. Old words are filled with new meaning, as, *e. g.*, the Hebrew word for Temple. Historical difficulties are removed; *e. g.*, we can point those who charged Isaiah with inventing a Sargon who never existed to the palace which he built and to his name repeated so often on its walls. The Belshazzar whom Daniel is accused of creating out of his own fancy is found in an inscription of his father, Nabonidus, acknowledged as his eldest son.

Many facts of history in the royal inscriptions, many incidents of daily life recorded on the tablets, illustrate and confirm the Scripture record. It may be that many would be of little value if they stood alone, but taken together they form a delightful corroboration of the truth.

One object of these pages has been to give a general idea of the progress that has been made in this interesting department of archæology; and if sometimes an Egyptian voice is heard among the Assyrian echoes, that may be more readily forgiven since the two are blended together in the original sources of information.

The reader will naturally ask, How have these inscriptions been deciphered, and what progress has been made in their interpretation?

Until near the close of the last century they were regarded more as curiosities than as veritable records. On the rock of

Behistun Sir Robert K. Porter thought he saw Tiglath Pileser and the ten tribes, and Keppel found in them Queen Esther and her maidens, so wide were their guesses from the truth. The writer remembers how Mons. Botta, as late as 1843, used to puzzle over the records of Sargon at Khorsabad, wondering what language they represented, whether they were alphabetical or syllabic, and whether they were to be read from left to right or the opposite.

But to go back to 1801. In that year Grotefend, then a student at Bonn, noticed that the Persepolitan inscriptions began with three or four words, one variable, the others unchanged, and thought the variable one must be a proper name, and others royal titles. One of the names, too long for Cyrus and too short for Artaxerxes, might be Darius. This gave him conjecturally six letters. Another name of the same length might be Xerxes, and the letter r occurred according to his guess. The third name was much longer, and that he put down as Artaxerxes, and here also the second letter was r and the end of the name Xerxes. He now had quite an alphabet, and he enlarged it by putting the Zend word for king, Khshaya Thiya, after the proper name, and that also turned out to be correct; so a beginning was made, and an alphabet of forty letters. This was the foundation of the decipherment of the Persian cuneiform. Later Prof. Lassen, of Bonn, translated all the Persian inscriptions that were accessible, and at the same time Colonel, now Sir Henry, Rawlinson, who was British Resident at Bagdad while the writer was in Mosul, copied the inscriptions at Hamadan and Behistun, and though entirely ignorant of the work of Prof. Lassen made out an alphabet that differed from his in only one letter.

More than one language, however, was spoken in Persia, and as in the days of Esther the king's scribes wrote to every people in their own language, Esther 8:9, so in those records on the rocks other languages were used, and engraved alongside of the Persian. These were much more complex and involved, as the characters were not alphabetic but syllabic, and the languages quite diverse in words and grammatical forms. Here, too, however, the proper names were of great service, and the discoveries of Botta and Layard not only greatly increased the material to be studied, but the library of Asshurbanipal in Nineveh furnished grammars and syllabaries that aided very much in the decipherment of the old agglutinative language of the Accadians. The Assyrian resembles the Hebrew, and so these two languages throw light on each other.

The work is slow, but continually becomes more accurate and reliable, for the use of a term in new connections gives fixity to what was known before, and enlarges the number and variety of renderings. Even in Hebrew the meaning of some words is not yet settled. A Jewish Rabbi visited the writer one day in Mosul to inquire how we understood some words in the Old Testament of whose meaning he was not sure; but our knowledge of the Assyrian promises to be as much more thorough as the mass of original material is now more varied and extensive. The oil furnished by the rocks lights up the recesses of the mine, and it is very abundant.

While these words are being written comes a notice of one hundred and twenty-four out of six hundred epistles published by Prof. R. T. Harper of the University of Chicago, whose aim is to publish all of the eight thousand now in the British Museum. And how much more is to come after that?

The alphabetic arrangement has been adopted in this volume, partly because of the miscellaneous character of the facts and partly for convenience of reference by the reader.

Assyrian prices have been given in sterling money because at the present writing the prospect for the stability of our own money values is not so promising as it might be.

The great thesaurus of Assyrian literature is "The Cuneiform Inscriptions of Western Asia," edited by Sir Henry Rawlinson and others, five volumes, folio; but as these are within the reach of few, other works are also quoted when the passage occurs in them.

In the frequent references to these works the following abbreviations are used to save space:

A. D. denotes Assyrian Discoveries. By George Smith. New York.

PREFACE. 7

A. L. and S. Lectures on Assyrian Languages and Syllabary. By Prof. A. H. Sayce, LL. D. London.

A. M. Assyrian Manual. By Prof. G. D. Lyon of Harvard, University. Chicago.

Ass'l. Asshurbanipal. By George Smith.

B. L. Lectures on Babylonian Literature. By Prof. Sayce, London.

B. and N. Babylon and Nineveh. By A. H. Layard, M. P. London.

Bib. Sac. Biblia Sacra. By Prof. D. G. Lyon.

C. G. Chaldean Genesis. By George Smith. Revised edition. New York.

C. and S. Travels in Chaldea and Susiana. By W. K. Loftus, F. G. S.

D. L. Assyrische Lesestücke. By Prof. Friedrich Delitzsch, LL. D. Leipzig.

H. L. Hibbert Lectures for 1887. By Prof. Sayce, LL. D. London.

K. A. T. Keilenschriften und das Alte Testament. Von E. Schrader. Geissen.

L. N. Nineveh and its Remains. By A. H. Layard, M. P. Two vols. New York.

P. and C. History of Art in Chaldea and Assyria. By Perrot and Chipiez. Two vols. London.

R. Inscriptions of Western Asia. Five vols. London.

R. of P. Records of the Past. Old and new series. Twelve and six vols. London.

S. Sargon. By Prof. D. G. Lyon. Leipzig.

Senn. Sennacherib, History of. By George Smith. London.

NOTE.—If the reader finds occasional repetition in this volume, it is to spare him from cross references, which often cause more search than satisfaction.

ASSYRIAN ECHOES OF THE WORD.

ABEDNEGO.

It seems to be the general opinion that this is an error, and that it should read Abed Nebo, servant or worshipper of Nebo, Dan. 1:7, but it is not so easy to determine how the mistake occurred, if indeed it is a mistake; some future discovery may bring to light an Abednego among the Assyrian records. The Assyrian character *bu* would seem much more likely to be mistaken for *gu* than the Hebrew ב for ג, but we cannot suppose that Daniel would make such a blunder. It may be that some zealous Hebrew copyist purposely misread the name, as a token of his displeasure because Azariah consented to be known as the worshipper of an idol. The name **Zikar, or Arad, Nabu,** the man or servant of Nebo, occurs in R., vol. III., p. 46, col. 1, l. 82.

Another instance of a change of names such as was made in the case of Azariah and his companions is Psammeticus II., son of Pharaoh Necho, king of Egypt. He was made ruler of **Bukkunnanni'pi** (Athribis) under the name of **Nabu** Shezibani, and afterwards became king of Egypt under his original name. (Trans. Soc. Biblical Archæology, II. x. 364.)

ABRAHAM.

It was very pleasant to read the familiar name of Abram in characters whose earlier forms were familiar to his own eye. The Assyrian form is **Abramu,** and means exalted, or honored, father. It occurs in R. II. 69. No. 3 reverse. 4. 20.

Some may think of him as an illiterate country boor; but he lived in the capital of a nation which, though it had a cumbrous way of writing by syllables instead of letters, and had clay tablets instead of books, yet had made wondrous advancement in literature. Works abounded on grammar, astronomy, mathematics, jurisprudence, poetry, history, and *belles lettres.* Many towns had libraries well patronized by the citizens. The men of this region were the source of civilization in Western Asia. Art, science, and philosophy came from them. The Assyrians were like the Romans, a nation of soldiers, but their literature was from Chaldea, translated from its ancient language. We know not when or where their first library was founded. The Chaldean Noah is said to have buried his inscribed tablets at Sippara (Sepharvaim) before the flood, and dug them up again after leaving the ark; and the epic of **Izdubar** containing the story of the flood came from Erech, now Warka. The great work on astronomy in 72 books was prepared for the library of Agane, or Accad, near Sippara. The catalogue of this library requests the reader to write the number of the tablet he wishes and it will be furnished, for every tablet had its number and its place. The library of Assurbanipal at Nineveh was composed mainly of translations from these Accadian tablets. See B. L. pp. 6–13.

As Abraham occupied a respectable position at least in such a community he must have been a man of much intelligence, and it is interesting to note how in all ages God honors intelligence. When he selected an apostle to carry the gospel into Europe as far as Rome, and perhaps even into Spain, he chose one educated in the schools of both Tarsus and Jerusalem. When he wanted one to lead his people out of Egypt he chose one learned in all the wisdom of the Egyptians; and it was not otherwise when he selected the founder of his ancient church. Not only was Abraham strong in faith himself, not only did he so train his children that they kept the way of the Lord, but, occupying the position he did in society, he must have been an educated man in that intelligent city of Ur.

ADRAMMELECH.

2 Kings 17:31. "The Sepharvites burnt their children in fire to Adrammelech and Anammelech, the gods of Sepharvaim."

Adrammelech is the same as **Adarmalku** (Adar is king); Anammelech is **Anamalku** (Anu is king). Sepharvaim is Sippara. The word is dual in the Hebrew because there were two cities, one on each side of the river. One of these worshipped **Anunit,** the wife of **Anu**, the god of the sky, and they exalted Anu as the king of the gods. The other was devoted to the service of the sun god, and contained the ancient temple of **E Babara** (the house of lustre) round which sun-worship chiefly centred. Indeed the fragment of a geographical tablet seems to speak of four Sipparas—Sippara proper, Sippara of the desert, Sippara the ancient, and Sippara of Shamshu. One of them has been discovered by Mr. Hormuzd Rassam in Abu Habba, and another by our own Dr. W. Hayes Ward in Anbar, an hour's distance from Sufeirah and the Euphrates (H. L. 169). Why the votaries of the sun god named their object of worship Adrammelech is hard to see, but it is in keeping with the mystery of the name of Adar, who is now called **Ninip** and again **Uras**, so that scholars are at a loss to know what his true name is. It is possible that the two names in the text may be the war-cries of a local rivalry that survived even transportation to Palestine (H. L. 7. 47. 151–3), each city insisting on the supremacy of its own God.

AHAB.

This well known king of Israel, husband of the noted Jezebel, is mentioned by Shalmanezer II., B. C. 860–825, as **Akha abbu mat Sirlaa**, Ahab of the land of Israel, R. III. 8. 91 and 92; and the same text speaks of Benhadad of Damascus as **Rimmon adar** or **idri**.

The fact mentioned by Shalmanezer, that in his campaign against them both he captured 1,200 chariots, 1,200 horsemen, and 20,000 footmen from Rimmon idri, and 2,000 chariots and 10,000 men from Akha abbu, R. III. 8. 90 and 91, R. of P. III. 99, and new IV. 70, lets us into the secret of the covenant which Ahab and Benhadad made together, as recorded in 1 Kings 20:31–34. Ahab might not have felt so brotherly towards Benhadad, with whom he had some old scores to settle, had they not suffered so much from their common enemy the king of Assyria; and it was the hope of securing his help to avenge the injuries inflicted by Shalmanezer that made him so complaisant to Benhadad now.

According to our received chronology Ahab would have been dead before the great battle of Karkar, when Shalmanezer gained such a victory, B. C. 853, but the Assyrian dates are uniformly 40 years behind ours.

ALPHABET.

There have been many theories of the origin of alphabetical writing. It has been held that the Hebrew was the original alphabet, but certainly the Hebrew letters now in use are of a comparatively modern origin. Then the Phœnician has been credited with being the original from which all others were derived. Other theories have obtained more or less currency. The present drift of opinion, in the light of the monuments, is that the Hebrews and other nations derived their letters from the Phœnicians, and that the alphabet of the latter is of Egyptian origin. In the earliest period of Egyptian history we find both syllabic hieroglyphics and 21 letters of an alphabet. There were so many Phœnician settlers in the delta of the Nile that it was known as Keft-ur (greater Phœnicia). They were a thrifty race of traders, and with their practical business instincts chose the simpler letters and passed by the hieroglyphics, and thus alphabetical writing found its way to their native cities on the coast of Syria. The reader will recognize in Keft-ur the Caphtor from whence came the Philistines (Amos 9:7). See "Fresh Light from the Monuments," pp. 71 and 72.

ALTAR.

This was known in Hebrew as *mizbeakh*, in Chaldee, *madbukh*, in Arabic, *madbakh*, and in Syriac, *madbakho*. Along with this similarity of sound was an identity of meaning, for in them all the altar was the place of sacrifice or, more precisely, of slaughter.

That there were altars in Babylonia and Assyria is beyond all question. Specimens of both are given in the American edition of Smith's Large Bible Dictionary, p. 77. The writer has also in his possession a photograph of the small temple of Makhir, the god of dreams, explored by Mr. Hormuzd Rassam at Balawat near Mosul, and in that appears a marble altar ascended by steps. He saw also the stone altar, triangular in form, with a round flat top, when it was first brought to light by Mons. Botta at Khorsabad. See P. and C. I. 255 and 256, as well as p.

77 of Smith's Bible Dictionary already quoted. Also Layard's "Nineveh and its Remains," II. 355. A similar one is depicted in Layard's "Babylon and Nineveh," opposite p. 351.

So we know they had the thing, but unfortunately we do not know the name they gave it; for where we speak of the altar they spoke of the sacrifice offered upon it, and made that the object of their thought.

In his "Elementary Grammar," see Syllabary, 144, Prof. Sayce renders the word **kisallu** altar, and other writers have done the same; but in his "Hibbert Lectures" (p. 410, note) he says that the term is borrowed from the Accadian **kizal,** place of oil, or anointing, and represents the upright object with a top like an extinguisher so frequent in the bas reliefs. I suppose he speaks of the two objects standing before the bas relief in the niche of the wall in figure 70 of P. and C. Art of Chaldea, etc., I. 196; and Prof. Lyon in his "Manual," p. 75, says that the ideogram read **kisallu** is variously translated as floor, platform, and altar, but should probably be read **samnu,** oil, whenever it occurs in connection with the verb **pashashu,** to anoint. In my perplexity I wrote to Prof. Lyon to ascertain the Assyrian term corresponding to the Hebrew mizbeakh, and when he replied, "I ought to know it, but I do not," the writer is not ashamed to confess his own ignorance in the matter, though it is a point that cannot long remain unsolved.

Nothing has been found so far in Babylonia or Assyria corresponding either in form or size to the great altar of burnt-offering before the Tabernacle or the still larger one before the Temple. This seems as though in these lands an ox was never burned whole on their altars; even the Jews burned the flesh of the bullock for the sin-offering in a place without the camp. And, though oxen in Eastern lands are not at all so large as with us, yet they must always have been cut in pieces before being consumed even on the largest altar. See Lev. 9:13, also verses 19–21. At any rate, in Assyria emphasis was laid on the slaying of the victim, not on its burning.

Prof. Sayce gives the term *arel* for altar (H. L. 57) but that word is not Assyrian but Moabitish, being taken from the Moabite stone of King Mesha.

In the "tent of meeting" before the veil, Exod. 40:26, was the golden altar (of incense), and (verse 29) the altar of burnt-offering was at the door of the tabernacle of assembly. So Herodotus in describing the great temple of Belos in Babylon (H. L. 93), says, "Outside the shrine" containing the great golden statue of the god, seated in a golden chair by a golden table, "is a golden altar. There is also another great altar on which full-grown sheep were sacrificed, for on the golden altar only sucklings were allowed to be offered. Upon the larger altar also," unlike the Jewish custom, "the Chaldeans burn every year 1,000 talents of frankincense when they keep the festival of the god."

ANGEL, DESTROYING.

2 Sam. 24:15, 16. "So the Lord sent a pestilence upon Israel from the morning even to the time appointed: and there died of the people from Dan even to Beersheba seventy thousand men. And when the angel stretched out his hand toward Jerusalem to destroy it, the Lord repented him of the evil, and said to the angel that destroyed the people, It is enough; stay now thine hand."

That was a terrible infliction, for a fraction over one in every eighteen of the people perished. But there was this consolation: the people knew that there was a reason for it in the deliberate and persistent transgression of a divine command; and, far better than that, it was not the work of an enemy but of their Father in heaven: "Jehovah; a God of compassion, and gracious, slow to anger and plenteous in mercy and truth" (Exod. 34:6), who out of the fulness of his own grace kept mercy for thousands, forgiving iniquity and transgression and sin (v. 8).

Far different was it in Babylonia, for there not only calamities of even greater extent occurred, but these calamities they supposed were the work of malevolent deities, from whom the gods whom they served had no power to protect them.

Thus **Nergal** (the great Ner) who among the Assyrians was the god that had the power of death and was called the great warrior, always making war on and overcoming the human race, is charged to "strike the people of the black heads (*i. e.* the non-Shemitic population of Babylonia) with the destruction of the god Ner. Let thy weapons be their sword of destruction, and make thy hands move." C. G. 127.

Then Bil, or **Mullil,** the god of Sheol, looks on and says in his heart, " Ner is crouching at his city gate (the city of the dead) among the corpses of the noble and the slave." C. G., 128. " In the city to which I send thee, thou shalt fear no man, small and great slay together, and save not the smallest of that evil race ;"—" like the pouring down of the rain shalt thou throw down their dead bodies in the squares of the city " (p. 129. 16-18 and 24). The reader must bear in mind that Mullil, as the lord of Hades, is the master whom Nergal is bound to obey. It must have been terrible to feel that they were helpless victims in the hands of such merciless and malevolent powers, without a friend that had power to help them. How different from the condition of Israel in the hands of their covenant God, who saith (Isa. 54:7), "For a small moment have I forsaken thee, but with great mercies will I gather thee." "For the mountains shall depart and the hills be removed, but my kindness shall not depart from thee, neither shall my covenant of peace be removed, saith the Lord that hath mercy on thee " (v. 10).

ANOINTING.

In our estimate of the religion of the Old Testament the idea of sacrifice seems to have attained a degree of prominence that overshadows other truths, or puts them in the background. And it may be questioned whether anointing with oil has that measure of prominence in our thoughts which it possesses in the record. It was an act of very frequent occurrence in the Hebrew ritual.

Jacob poured oil upon the stone which he set up in Bethel, Gen. 28:18. It was also poured upon the meal-offering, Lev. 2:1. Anointing and consecration were inseparable, in the case of the priests, Exod. 28:41; 30:30; 40:15, and of the ark, Exod. 30:26, the altars, the candlestick, and the table for the showbread, vs. 27-29, and of the laver and its base, 40:11. The king also was set apart to his office by anointing, 1 Sam. 10:1; 16:1; 1 Kings 1:39; 2 Kings 9:1. The official name of our

Saviour is not the sacrifice, but Messiah, the anointed one. Dan. 9: 25, 26; John 1: 41 and 4: 25.

In like manner anointing is mentioned with great frequency in the inscriptions. It is always a part of the programme in rebuilding a palace and renewing its inscriptions, if with Prof. D. G. Lyon (Manual, p. 75) instead of **kisallu** we read **samnu lipshuush,** let him anoint with oil. See R. V. 62, 25 and Manual 24, 16; R. V. 64, 45 and Manual 37, 21; R. V. 64 3, 9 and Manual 38, 15, and R. V. 64 3. 46 and Manual 39, 17.

Another passage (R. V. 61. No. 1. 25) is rendered by Prof. Sayce (Hib. Lect. 527, 251), "May he pour out the oil of thy wants like water, the oil may he rain on thy threshold abundantly." Prof. Lyon renders it "May he pour oil over thy bolts (**sigarika**) like water, in fulness of oil may he cause thy threshold to abound." Either way it shows how freely oil was used, and what an important place it held in their religious ceremonies.

APPAREL, ROYAL.

As far back as the entrance of Israel into Canaan we read of "a goodly Babylonish mantle," Josh. 7: 21. "Esther put on her royal apparel," and royal apparel was brought to Mordecai, and worn by him. Esther 5: 1, 6: 8, 8: 15.

All these passages lead us to expect something very splendid in the royal apparel, and the splendor set forth in the bas-reliefs amply justifies the language of Scripture. The dress of King Sennacherib (B. and N. 150) is exceedingly elaborate. Some of the representations of Sargon discovered by Mons. Botta in Khorsabad are no less magnificent (P. and C. 97). The same is true of the statue of Asshurnatsirpal, found by Mr. Layard in the N. W. Palace at Nimrood (L. N. II. 12).

But the clearest conception of the elaborate splendor of the royal apparel may be obtained from the figures 253 and 254 in vol. II. of P. and C., pp. 365 and 367. These represent the embroidery on the upper part of the king's mantle; and while it may be rash to say that it has never been equalled, it seems safe to assert that it has never been excelled. The rosettes, guilloches, trees of life, hunting scenes, scenes of worship, winged men and winged monsters, must be seen to be appreci-

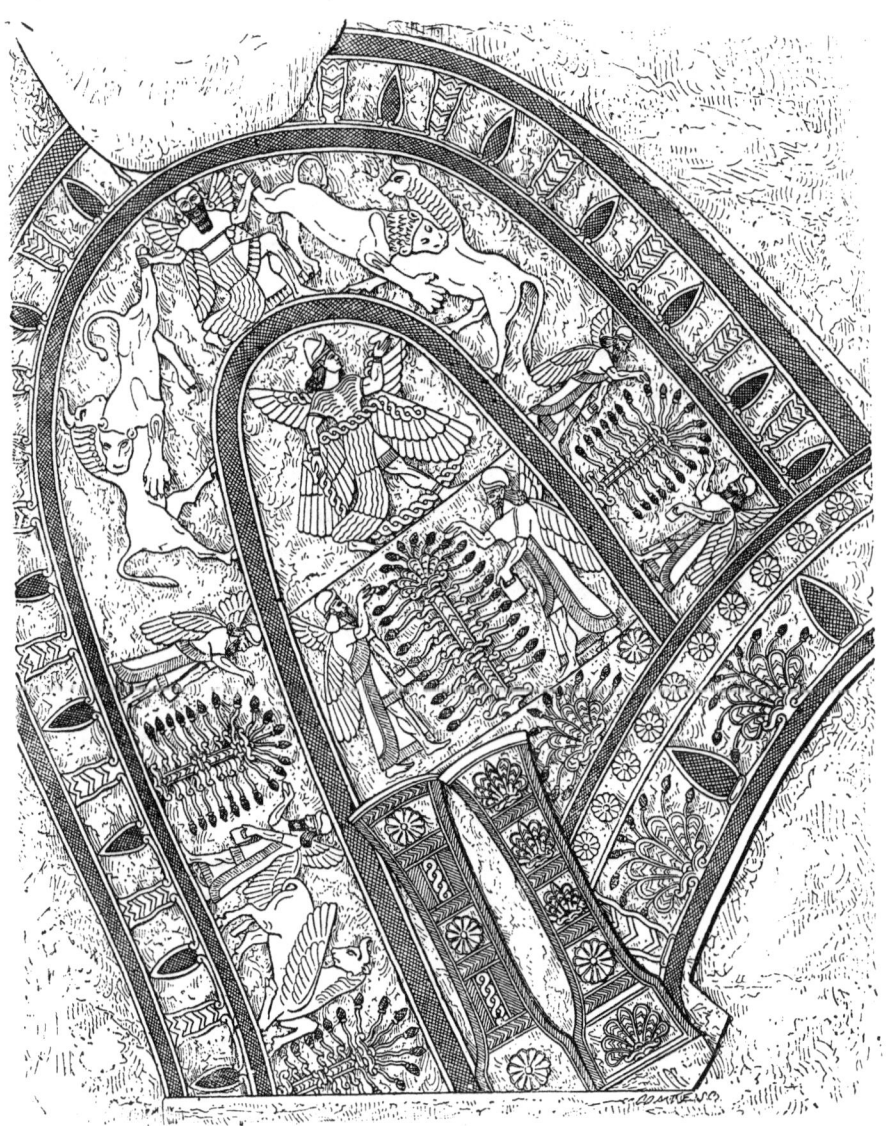

EMBROIDERY ON UPPER PART OF THE KING'S MANTLE. (From Layard.)

ated; no mere description could do them justice. So a portion of one is here inserted, that the reader may note the excellent handiwork of that early day.

APPIRYON.

Sometimes even the Cappadocian species of the cuneiform throws light on an obscure word in Scripture. In Cant. 3:9 we read that "King Solomon made for himself a palanquin of the wood of Lebanon." The old version read "chariot." The Hebrew is אַפִּרְיוֹן, *appirion*, and it occurs nowhere else in the whole range of Semitic literature. Some scholars had derived it from the Greek, which has Φορεῖον in the same sense; but in looking over some tablets found in Cappadocia, near Kaisariyeh, belonging to a Russian gentleman, Mr. Golennischeff, Prof. Sayce found the word **aparne** in the same sense, showing that the word had come from that elevated mountainous region where, if anywhere, such means of conveyance would be needed, and whence the word had been adopted, with various modifications, into other languages, just as the word palanquin itself has come to us from the East Indies. R. of P. new VI. 118.

APPLE OF THE EYE.

In Deut. 32:10 we read that the Lord kept his people "as the apple of his eye," בְּאִישׁוֹן עֵינוֹ. *Ish* is a noun meaning a man, and אִישׁוֹן, *ishon*, perhaps peculiar form of that noun, perhaps a diminutive—meaning "the little man," as in looking into the eye of another one sees a diminutive image of himself. The same expression occurs in Psa. 17:8, where the Psalmist prays to be kept (literally) as the little man, the daughter of the eye; and also in Prov. 7:2, "keep my law as the little man of the eye." Gesenius observes that in the pupil of the eye, as in a mirror, one sees his own image reflected in miniature, and that this pleasing idea is found in the Arabic, Greek, Latin and Persian.

The idea is something very precious, for the writer speaks of an object to be kept with special care. It will be observed, however, that the idea of something to be kept with especial care is true, however we define the word *ishon;* in other words, this idea is quite independent of the meaning we attach to that word.

Now in the Assyrian inscriptions is a corresponding term, written sometimes **nishit,** and sometimes more fully **nishit ena.** Nis or **nish,** like *ish* in Hebrew, means a man, or, as Friedrich Delitzsch says, folk. Either way will do. The little folk of the eye is as expressive as the little man of that organ, for of course as one man sees himself in it so does another, and the same mirror answers for all.

Asshurnatsirpal, King of Assyria B. C. 885–860 (Layard's Standard Inscription, I. 1., and D. G. Lyon's Assyrian Manual, 5. 1 and 2), calls himself the favorite, **nishit,** of **Bil** and **Adar,** and the beloved, **naram,** of **Anu** and **Dagan** (Dagon).

Sargon, King of Assyria B. C. 722–705 (Layard 33 and Lyon's Manual 9. 1), calls himself the favorite, **nishit ini,** of **Anu** and **Bil,** and so in other instances.

Prof. G. D. Lyon, following the lead of Prof. Friedrich Delitzsch, gives a different shade of meaning to the expression **nishit ena,** making it mean the *lifting up* of the eye, that peculiar elevation and brightening up that takes place when the object of affection comes within the field of vision. So understood, it corresponds to the Levitical benediction, Num. 6 : 26, "The Lord lift up his countenance upon thee," and to the prayer of the Psalmist (4 : 6), " Lord, lift thou up the light of thy countenance upon us." The Hebrew extended the sphere of affectionate recognition over the whole face, the Babylonian concentrated it in the eye, as its most expressive feature, and this beaming of the eye in love lifting it to a higher plane of expression is certainly a worthier idea, and one more fitting for a being created in the image of God, than an apple or an image of a man on the retina of the eye. Prof. Lyon quotes a line from the Izdubar Legend, R. IV. 48. 1. 6: **Ana duunki sa ilu Iztubar, ina attasi rubuut Istar** ("for the favor of the divine Izdubar the Lady Ishtar lifted up her eyes"); and though in this case the character of the agent is not fitted to give elevation to the thought, yet the meaning—and that is all we care for—is even more expressive, for it denotes not only affection going out towards another, but also the desire of a response of love from the object of regard, and thus becomes a most admirable description of prayer to God, as in the expression,

"Unto thee do I lift up mine eyes, O thou that sittest in the heavens!" Ps. 123 : 1.

ARIOCH.

Arioch, King of Ellasar, is introduced to us in Gen. 14:1 as one of the four kings from the region of Babylonia that invaded Canaan in the days of Abraham.

Ellasar is identified with Larsa, a city on the east of the Euphrates, a little further north than Ur on the west of that river, and represented by the modern Senkereh. It was noted for its library, which was especially rich in works on mathematics. Here Lig Bagas, cir. B. C. 3000, built the Temple of the Sun, called **Bit** (or **E**) **Parra.** R. of P. V. 64-68 and R. I. 5–16. For an interesting account of the present condition of Senkereh, see W. K. Loftus' Chaldea and Susiana, chap. 20., pp. 240–263.

So much for the place; as for Arioch, he is probably to be identified with **Rim Agu** or **Eri Aku**—the name appears in both forms, the same as **nabu** or **nabium, tamti** or **tamtim**—the son of **Kudur Mabuk,** the king of Elam. He was made king of Larsa while his father was yet living, and claimed to be also king of Shumir (Shinar) and Accad. He embellished the city of Ur, encircling it with the wall called **Harris galla,** and erecting in it a strong tower. He is called also the **mizkin** of Eridu, whatever that means, and ruler of Nipur (Niffer).

He was evidently a mighty man in his generation, and famous through all the region. His taking of the city of Karrak was an event of such note that it formed an era from which other events were dated, as occurring in such and such a year after the capture of Karrak. After that he ruled the whole region from Nipur to the Persian Gulf. He dug the channel Udkasnun (?) from the Tigris to the sea, and built the great wall of Bellu. He was attacked in turn by Khammuragas (Khammurabi, some read it), who reigned from B. C. 2290–2235, and founded Babylon; and though at first he seems to have repulsed him, in the end Eri Aku was conquered, and Babylon rose to supremacy. R. of P. V. 64-68.

The fact most interesting to us, however, is that his father,

Kudur Mabuk, styles himself "Father of Phœnicia, or Palestine" (Prof. Sayce's "Ancient Empires of the East," p. 111), and Gen. 14 only shows how he followed in his father's footsteps. If it was the attack of Khammuragas that hindered his taking vengeance for that midnight surprise near Damascus, it only shows us how God protected his servant Abraham from the wrath of those who were stronger than he.

ARK.

In ancient Egypt the images of the gods were carried in arks shaped like Nile boats (Smith's Large Bible Dictionary, Amer. Ed., p. 156), and though the platforms on which the Assyrian gods were carried in procession had not that form in later times (see P. and C., Art in Chaldea, etc., I. 75 and 76) yet the name continued ship (**elip,** Accadian **ma**) to the end.

A poetical description of one is given in R. IV. 25. 9-32, reminding one somewhat of the beautiful picture of the ships of Tyre in the 27th chapter of Ezekiel. For the translation see Hib. Lect., 67 and 527. The first-mentioned page says R. II. by mistake; it should be R. IV.

> Its helm is of cedar wood . . .
> Its serpent-like oar has a handle of gold,
> Its mast is pointed with turquoise.
> Seven times seven lions of Eden occupy the deck.
> The god Adar (Kudur) fills the cabin constructed within.
> Its side is of cedar from the forest;
> Its awning is the palm wood (leaf?) of Dilmun;
> The canal bears away its heart;
> The sunrise rejoiceth its spirit.
> Its house, its elevation is a mountain giving rest to the heart.
> The ship of the god of Eridu (Ea) is fate.

> Ningal the princess (Davkina) is the goddess whose word is life.
> Merodach is the god who pronounces the good name.
> The god who blesses the house, makes it move in Eridu.
> Nin Nangur, the bright one, the mighty worker of heaven,
> With pure and blissful hand, has pronounced the word of life.

> May the ship cross the canal before thee,
> May the ship cross its mouth behind thee,
> May the glad heart make holiday within thee.

ARPAD.

Two errors concerning this city call for correction. One is found in Young's Concordance, which says that "perhaps it is the same as Arvad, now Ruad;" but that is an island on the coast and this is a city in the interior, for it is mentioned along with Hamath and Damascus. Jer. 49:23; 2 Kings 18:34 and 19:23; Isa. 10:9, 36:19 and 37:13.

While the American revision of Smith's Bible Dictionary, like Gesenius, distinguishes Arpad from Arvad, it says, "No trace of its existence has yet been discovered, nor any mention of the place outside of the Bible;" but in the list of the eponyms during the reign of Sennacherib the eponym for B. C. 692 is "Zazaa, prefect of Arpadda" (Senn. 16). Also in the great inscription of Sargon on the wall of his palace at Khorsabad the names of Arpad, Simyra, Samaria and Damascus occur in line 12; also in the third tablet of room II. in the plan of Mons. Botta. G. Smith, in A. D. p. 274, finds it in line 17 of a fragment of the annals of Tiglath Pileser II., and in his History of Assyria, p. 81, says that this king captured the city only after a siege of two years, B. C. 740. Prof. Sayce describing this campaign says, "Arpad, now Tel Erpad, near Aleppo, was the first object of attack. It held out for three years, and did not fall till B. C. 740." (Fresh Light from the Inscriptions, 102.)

ARROWS.

David says, Psa. 45:5, "Thine arrows are sharp in the heart of the enemies of the king." Thus expressing his confidence in the active protection of God at the moment when he wrote. And as in water face answereth to face, so also the feelings of an idolater towards his idol sometimes resemble the feelings of the good man towards God. Asshurbanipal writes of the god Adar, the great son of Bil (R. V. 9. 85 and A. M. 33. 1): **Ina utstsishu zaqti uparii napishtim** *amilu* **nakrutiya**: with his sharp arrows he destroyed the lives of my enemies. This, however, is only one of many gods whom he describes as engaged to help him. He says (R. V. 9. 75 seq. and A. M. 32, 37 seq.): "Beltis, the beloved (consort) of **Bil** the conqueror, the mighty one among the goddesses, who sits enthroned with **Anu** and Bil, pierced my enemies with her powerful horns. Ishtar, who dwells in Arbela clothed in fire and raised aloft in brilliance, upon the Arabians rained destructions. Dibbara (the god of pestilence), the warrior, overcame all opposition and transfixed my foes. Adar with his great strong spear, the son of Bil with his sharp arrows, destroyed the life of my enemies."

ASHERAH.

The word אשרה has been unfortunately mistranslated in our English Bibles. It has been rendered "groves," and yet, even though nothing were known about Assyrian, one would think that the statement that King Josiah "brought out the grove from the house of the Lord" would have led the translators to suspect that something was out of the way. 2 Kings 23:6. So also, in verse 7, the account of the women weaving hangings for the groves ought to have awakened suspicion that all was not right. It would be a formidable undertaking to weave draperies for one grove, much more for groves in general. Assyrian discoveries teach us that Asherah is a goddess. That is her proper name, just as Aristu, Beltis, and Ishtar are the names of other goddesses. She has been designated as the goddess of fertility. The name also is applied to certain cones or phallus-like images made of wood, that were used as symbols of this goddess, or in some way connected with her worship. In such passages as 2 Kings 23:4, which tells of vessels made for Baal and for Asherah, the goddess herself is obviously referred to; vessels would not be made for a god and for groves, but for a god and a goddess they would be appropriate, at least in the estimation of their worshippers. So in 2 Chron. 24:18. Serving groves and idols sounds like a strange mingling of things unsuitable, but to worship images of Asherah and other idols is precisely such an association of things as we should naturally expect. So also erecting altars for Baal and making either images or symbols of the goddess (2 Chron. 33:3) fit very well together. Such passages as Exod. 34:13; Deut. 7:5 and 12:3; Judg. 6:25-30 obviously refer to the wooden symbols, which could be set up or cut down or burned in the fire. See R. of P. new III. 71, note 2, also V. 97, note 3.

ASSES.

With us the horse is prominent among domestic animals employed for work, but in the Old Testament the horse was chiefly used for war. That grand description of this animal in Job 39: 19–25 is the description of a war horse.

In the inventory of the possessions of Abraham is no mention of horses, while asses are very prominent. The same is true of the possessions of Job, 42:12, and of Jacob, Gen. 30:43. It was on one of those animals that Abraham rode when he went to sacrifice Isaac, Gen. 22:3 and 5. Balaam also rode on an ass when on a visit to a king, Num. 22:21–33. Men of rank rode on white asses, Judg. 5:10. It was the asses of his father that Saul went to seek, 1 Sam. 9:3. And while the Mosaic law has not a word to say about horses it provides for the redemption of the firstling of an ass, Exod. 13:33. It was the stray ass of his enemy that the Israelite was to bring back, Exod. 23:4; and the next verse required him, if he saw the ass of him that hated him lying under his burden, to be sure and help him up. So also ver. 12. The people of God were to rest on the seventh day, that their ox and ass might rest, and they were forbidden to yoke these two different animals into the same plough, Deut. 22:10. Nor can we forget how the Lord of all rode as it was foretold of him, Zech. 9:9, on an ass, and on a colt the foal of an ass, Matt. 21:5. All these things shut us up to the conclusion that the ass was the domestic beast of burden among the Jews.

In beautiful conformity with this, the cuneiform inscriptions make the ass the representative animal of this class. It stands forth in them as the animal par excellence, and the horse, the mule, and the camel are distinguished from it by marks peculiar to themselves.

To make this understood it must be borne in mind that there are two classes of signs in Assyrian—one to express the sound of a syllable, and another standing for an idea, and hence called an ideograph. Now the ideograph **Tum** represents the ass. This forms as it were the foundation. The horse is represented by **Tum** with the addition **mat-ra,** east country or east mountain. The horse, then, in Assyria was "the ass of the east country," showing that the horse originally came from the mountainous regions of the East, which were Persia and Media. The mule (?) was distinguished by signs which are read **paru**, *i. e.*, it was the **paru** ass, and our interrogation point denotes that the meaning is disputed, some reading bullock instead of mule. The camel was marked by **Tum** with other signs, which are read **Gammalu**, and sometimes that term was written phonetically, hence our word camel. Taken all together it is a most interesting confirmation of the accuracy of Holy Scripture in little things—the same domestic situation of things extending through Palestine which existed in Babylonia and Assyria."

ASSES, WHITE.

Judg. 5:10. "Speak, ye that ride on white asses."

In early times a white breed of asses was raised at Zobeir, now known as Bassora, near the mouth of the Euphrates, but at present they are known under the name of Baghdad donkeys. They are larger than the common breed and more costly. In size they might be located about half-way between an ass and a horse. They are used by the rich and by civil dignitaries. In the early occupation of Mosul by our mission one of them was used by Mrs. Hinsdale, as better suited for her needs than any other animal for riding. They are much better looking than the ordinary ass, and their motion is very easy.

ASSYRIAN, THE.

We read in Isa. 52:4: "My people went down at the first into Egypt to sojourn there, and the Assyrian oppressed them without cause."

We have here, according to some, a statement of the earliest oppression of Israel, and an allusion to a much later oppression by the Assyrians, and Commentators up to this day have interpreted this passage in that way, and found no difficulty. See Alexander, Cowles, and The Speaker's Commentary. Lately it has been said that the first clause merely states the going down of Israel into Egypt, and the last one tells us that at that time the Assyrian, in the person of Pharaoh, oppressed them without cause. A full presentation of this last view may be found in a very interesting article in the Century Magazine for May, 1887, by the learned Orientalist, John A. Paine. This, however, bases the explanation given of the word Assyrian (1) on the idea that Teie, the mother of Amenophis III., was the daughter of **Duisratta,** king of **Mitauni,** which is **Naharaina** or Mesopotamia, and (2) on the features of **Ramses II.** as transmitted on the monuments, together with photographs of his embalmed body, which is still extant in the Museum at Boolak in Egypt. These facial resemblances are in the nature of the case uncertain ; where one sees them very clearly another does not detect them at all, perhaps because his eye is not trained to the work. And the first basis turns out to be a mistake. Teie was not the name of the Mesopotamian queen, but **Tadukhepa.**

Still it might be equally premature to decide against this explanation of the word Assyrian, for as queen **Neferari,** wife of **Ramses II.,** had two names, so **Tadukhepa** may have also had one to spare. It is a very interesting fact, if it can be established, that the Pharaoh of the Exodus was by descent on his mother's side an Assyrian, but we must wait till the genealogy is fully made out before giving our adhesion to it; and the progress of discovery is now so rapid that we may not have to wait long. This is only a hint of other discoveries equally interesting that may await us in the near future, when Tel el hesy (Lachish), Kirjath-Sepher, and other ancient depositories, shall have yielded up their priceless treasures.

ASSYRIAN LANGUAGE.

The Assyrian language is writen in cuneiform characters which do not represent an alphabet but syllables, and names, or words. The Babylonian cuneiform is more elaborate and complicated than the Assyrian. It is also more ancient. One may read Assyrian with ease and yet be unable to decipher the Babylonian. The Akkadians are supposed to have invented this mode of writing, and used it first for their own language.

Its earliest specimens date from the era of Sargon of Agade, circa 3800 B. C., and it was used till about the beginning of the Christian era. The Persians used similar forms, which in their hands became an alphabet.

The cuneiform was originally picture-writing, but assumed its present wedge form from using a square iron rod to mark the characters in the soft clay. In inscriptions on stone they were formed with a chisel. The Assyrian belongs to the northern group of the Semitic, along with the Hebrew and Aramaic. It has a much more intimate relation to the Hebrew than to the Arabic. It is written from left to right with nothing to distinguish the ends of either words or sentences. Only very rarely does a word pass from one line into another.

The same character may represent several syllabic values, besides more than one ideogram, and the reader must determine from the context which is the one intended.

BALAK AND BALAAM.

These names are suggestive. Balak means the spoiler, and "son of Zippor" (the little bird or sparrow) reminds us of Oreb (the raven) and Zeeb (the wolf), names of Midianites who were neighbors of Moab. Balaam (a stranger) was the son of Beor (a torch or lamp).

They lived about 1452 B. C., or not far from 3,000 years ago. For the home of Balaam, see under "Pethor."

The inspired writer shows us what good reason Balak had to fear the approach of Israel. The report of the miracles wrought in Egypt, the destruction of Pharaoh and his army in the Red Sea, and the continuous miracle of the manna in the wilderness were all well fitted to fill him with evil forebodings; but why should he send for Balaam to curse them? Or why should he expect that his curse should avail for the deliverance of Moab? The Assyrian monuments furnish a satisfactory answer to these enquiries. According to them the sorcerer (**ashipu**) had power to utter a spell or curse which even the gods were powerless to resist. If the ceremonies were rightly performed, if the knots were tied in the right manner and order, and if the utterance of the invocation was in all respects according to rule, no power on earth or heaven could stand before it. This spell was called **Mamit.** In the Accadian, **Mami** was a goddess, also written **Mammetu,** who was called "the maker of fate," and who "has fixed the destinies" of men. She corresponded to the Fate of the Romans, and the Ate of the Greeks. Now Balaam was a noted **ashipu** and at the same time an acknowledged prophet of the same God whom Israel served. Indeed he uses the name of Jehovah frequently, see Num. 22:8, 13, 18, 19; 23:3, 8, 12, 21, 26; 24:6, 13. And Balak fully recognizes Balaam as his prophet, 23:17; 24:2.

This fact and the Babylonian belief in the **mamit** make the reason very plain why Balak was so eager to have Balaam pronounce it against Israel, for he thought that, once pronounced, no power in heaven, earth, or hell could hinder its fulfilment.

BANKS.

Luke 19:23. Then wherefore gavest thou not my money into the bank? The question naturally arises, When did banks begin to exist? If by that we mean when did such institutions as are now known by that name originate, the origin of modern banking may be traced to the money-lenders of Florence in the 14th century; but they were not introduced into England till the 17th century. Still the simple table of the money-changer and money-lender dates very far back, and the word is τραπεζαν (table), in the text quoted above.

The Sons of Egibi, a banking firm in Babylonia, carried on business, from an unknown period previously, down to the 4th century B.C. There are a number of tablets relating to them and their affairs dated in the reigns of different kings, and showing that they transacted an extensive business of exchange abroad as well as money-lending at home. R. of P. XI. pp. 85-99.

BATTLEMENTS.

Deut. 22:8. When thou buildest a new house, then thou shalt make a battlement for thy roof, that thou bring not blood upon thine house, if any man fall from thence.

In Syria the battlement around the flat roof is often wanting, and again it is so low as to be practically worthless for protection. In the house occupied for a time by the writer, in a Moslem suburb of Beirut, the wall was carried up less than a foot above the roof.

In Assyria we can only infer the kind of roof that covered

the palace from the débris that fills the chambers, and the roofs of the houses of the common people can be seen only in the imperfect pictures of them in the bas reliefs, for the originals long centuries ago disappeared; but the modern houses in Mosul may retain some tradition of former days, and their battlements are higher than in Syria. In the first house occupied by our mission they rose as high as the neck of one standing on the roof, and in the last house we had, over some of the rooms they were much higher even than that. Indeed one of them looked like a room with the roof gone, the walls were so high.

The view of Sidon in Alexander's Kitto, p. 1160, repeated in the American Edition of Smith's "Dictionary of the Bible," p. 3626, gives a general idea of the roofs of Syria.

BEASTS, WILD.

Both Holy Scripture and the cuneiform inscriptions, when they would describe the utter desolation of a city, picture it as the home of wild beasts.

Zephaniah thus describes the desolation of Nineveh (2:14): "Herds shall lie down in the midst of her; all the beasts of the nations, both the pelican and the porcupine, shall lodge in the capitals (of the columns) thereof, their voice shall sing in the windows, desolation shall be in the thresholds, for he hath laid bare the cedar work."

Compare Isa. 34:13-15; and also 13:21, 22.

Asshurbanipal, king of Assyria B. C. 668–626, says of Elam, R. V. 6. 100-106, and Smith's Asshurbanipal, 234. 5-9: "**rikim amiluti, kibiis alpi u tsiini shisiit alala, tabu utsaam maa agarishu imiri tsirna (purimi) tsabati umaam tsir mala bashuu parganis usharbitsa kirib shuun.**" The voice of men, the treading of oxen and sheep, the sound of pleasant music I caused to cease (dried up) in its fields; wild asses, gazelles, every kind of wild beast of the desert I caused to dwell in them safely. The rendering of **parganis** is doubtful, and some copies add **ugalkhu** to **purimi,** which seems to be the name of some great bird.

The Scripture speaks of wild beasts also as beasts of the field, Psa. 80:13; Deut. 7:22, "lest the beasts of the field increase upon thee." Now the increase of domestic cattle is not something to be feared. 1 Sam. 17:44, "I will give thy flesh to the beasts of the field," but cattle do not eat human flesh. The inscriptions also speak of the beasts of the field or plain (**bool tsir**), but it is in sharp distinction from wild beasts, as where **Khasisadra** speaks of taking **bool tsir oo umaam tsir,** "beasts of the field and wild beasts of the desert," into the ark (ship). R. IV. 50. col. 2. 29. Assyrian Manual 57. 20, and Prof. Delitzsch's Lesestücke, 103. 81.

BEFORE, STAND.

God said to Abram, Gen. 17:1: "Walk before me, and be thou perfect." Elijah said to Ahab, 1 Kings 17:1: "As Jehovah, God of Israel, liveth, before whom I stand," etc. See also 18:15; 2 Kings 3:14, and 5:16. The psalmist also speaks, 123:2, of the eyes of a servant being on the hand of his master.

And Asshurbanipal speaks of servants **dagil paniya,** "looking on my face." R. V. 1. 70 and 76. Now a servant who stands before his master as in the East, with his eyes watching for the slightest indication of his will, that he may run and do it, is exactly in the attitude described by the expression, "looking upon his face." So also **ushadgilu pani** is to cause one to be looked on as a master, or to entrust one with authority. Sennacherib says, R. I. 41. 17 and 18, and A. M. 14, 16 and 17, "The people of Babylon for his unfitness seated him on the throne, and entrusted to him the lordship of **Shumir** and **Akkad.**"

BEL BOWETH DOWN.

Isa. 46:1. Bel (**Bil**) boweth down. Nebo (**Nabu**) stoopeth. Their idols are upon the beasts and upon the cattle. The things that ye carried about are made a load, a burden to the weary beast. Verse 7, They bear him upon the shoulder, they carry him, and set him in his place. If the reader will turn to Layard's Nineveh and its Remains, II. 342, or his Monuments of Nineveh, first series, plate 65, or Perrot and Chipiez' History of Art in Chaldea, I. 75 and 76, he will find a beautiful illustration of verse 7, where a sort of dress parade of the gods is represented, with their images upright and in a majestic attitude. And if he will imagine the same images securely strapped to

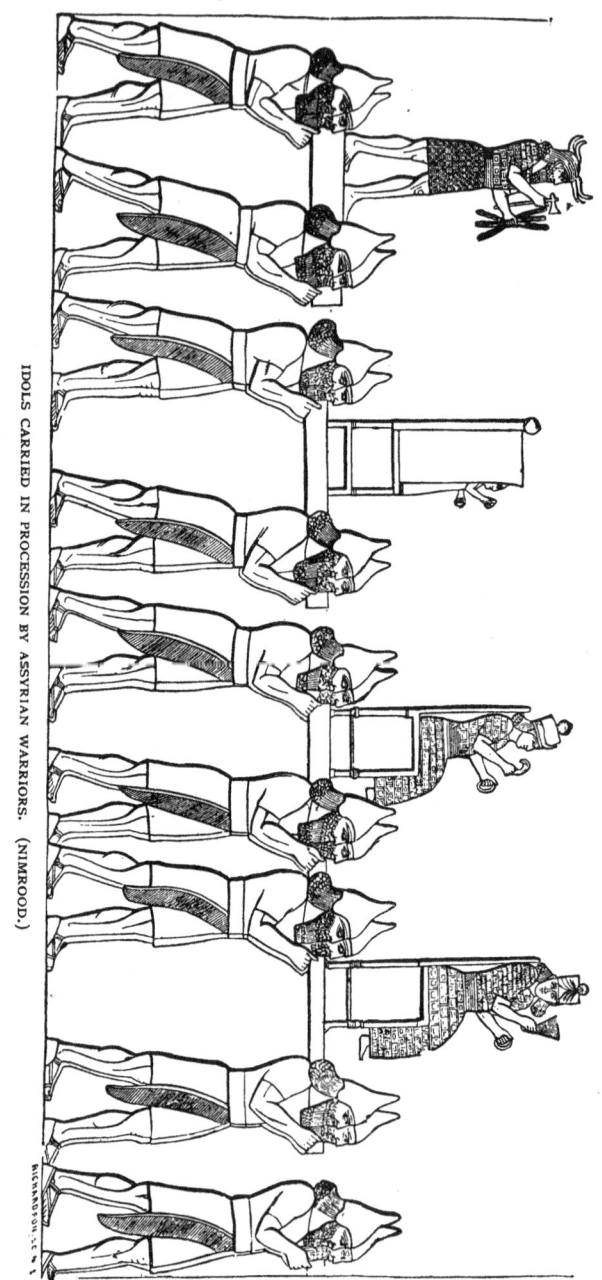

IDOLS CARRIED IN PROCESSION BY ASSYRIAN WARRIORS. (NIMROOD.)

the pack-saddles of mules and so carried over rough roads on a long journey, and in attitudes corresponding to the tired aspect of the brute bearers, he will have a very vivid illustration of the language of the prophet.

THE BEAUTIFUL GATE OF THE TEMPLE.

The lame man was "laid daily at the gate of the temple which is called Beautiful." Acts 3:2. One would hardly expect to find the name given by universal consent to that splendid entrance of the temple of Herod duplicated in a Babylonian temple; yet Nebuchadrezzar, in the large India House inscription, so called, col. 2. 51-53. R. of P. new III. 108. 51-53, says:

> The gate **Khilisu,** even the beautiful gate,
> And the gate of **E Zida** (and) **E Sagilla**
> I had them made brilliant as the sun.

E or **Bit Zida** was the chief temple of **Borsippa,** dedicated to Nebo; and **E** or **Bit Sagilla,** the temple of **Bil Marduk** in Babylon, built by a previous king, was repaired and embellished by Nebuchadrezzar, so that it owed more to him than to the original builder.

BELSHAZZAR.

Dan. 5 : 1 and 30 declares that Belshazzar the king was slain on the night of the capture of Babylon by the Medes and Persians, but it has been objected that other historians affirm that Nabonidus (**Nabunahid**) was at that time king of Babylon and therefore Daniel was mistaken. In seeking to vindicate the prophet some have tried to identify Belshazzar with Evil Merodach, and others with Nabonidus, but without success. Sir Henry Rawlinson, however, has solved the difficulty by means of an inscribed cylinder found in the great temple of the moon god at **Ur** (Mugheir.) This temple was built by **Uruch,** the earliest known king of a united Babylonia, and then repaired by Nabonidus who deposited a copy of this cylinder in each of the four corner-stones, and in it he speaks of **Bil** (or **Marduk**) **Shar Utsur** (**Bil Shar Utsur** is manifestly Belshazzar, and the Bil of Babylon was Merodach, often called for that reason **Bil Marduk**) as his oldest son, whom he had admitted to a share in the government. The cylinder inscription is given in R. I. 68. col. I.

and the fact is mentioned by Loftus in his Chaldea and Susiana," p. 131; and so, while Belshazzar died, as described by Daniel, Nabonidus escaped to Borsippa and at length died in Caramania. Thus also we see how Belshazzar promised to make Daniel the *third* ruler in the kingdom if he could read and interpret the handwriting on the wall, 5: 16—he could not make him the second, for he himself held that position. So beautifully do the monuments corroborate the written word.

BETHEL, PILLAR.

Gen. 28: 18 and 19. And Jacob rose up early in the morning, and took the stone that he had put under his head, and set it up for a pillar, and poured oil upon the top of it, and he called the name of that place Bethel, *i. e.*, the house of God.

In like manner when **Izdubar** left **Khasisadra,** and his sickness had been removed by the waters of the sea, "he bound together heavy stones and, offering an animal in sacrifice, poured over it the libation of an homer," and having thus secured the favor of the gods set out for home.

There was this difference, however, between the Babylonian and the Hebrew: the former found a spirit already dwelling in the stone, and so recognized its inherent sanctity: the latter sanctified what was before a common thing by pouring on it oil that dedicated it to God. So among the Arabs were sacred stones, like the black stone of the Kaaba, and three similar stones at the gates of Mecca, known by the names of Hobbul, Lâta and Uzza. At Medain Saleh, the burying-place of the ancient Nabatheans, are niches in the rock containing sacred stones. Above one is the inscription, "This is the place of prayer which Seruh, son of Tuka, erected to Auda of Bostra, the great god, in the month Nisan, of the first year of King Malkhos;" but Auda had previously dwelt there. Compare also the meteoric stone that represented Artemis at Ephesus, and the conical stone in the Adytum of Aphrodite at Paphos. H. L. 408–10.

BINDING AND LOOSING.

These words of Christ to his disciples (Matt. 18:18), "Whatsoever ye shall bind on earth shall be bound in heaven, and whatsoever ye shall loose on earth shall be loosed in heaven," are somewhat peculiar. They refer to the government of the church and the binding comes first, as the principal thing; the loosing seems to follow as a sort of corollary, for he who has power to do one can also do the other.

In this connection it is interesting to note that a very common name for ruler in Assyria is **Pikhatu,** literally "binding," from the verb **pikhu,** to bind, or shut—though we would expect the word binder rather than binding. The idea seems to have been, "he who has power to bind in fetters and shut up in prison," or to bind duties and obligations upon his subjects. It may be said that the same term is used to denote the province that is governed, and so the original idea may have been the families or communities bound together as a satrapy; but, even so, the idea of binding is very prominent. The other, however, is more likely to have been the original idea, for in ancient times the ruler was more thought of than the people whom he ruled, and binding in chains or "binding heavy burdens" on men were much more prominent acts of rulers than more amiable exercises of authority. Any way, this Assyrian title of the ruler gives new significance to the words of Christ.

BODY FASTENED TO CITY WALL.

1 Sam. 31 : 10 tells us that the Philistines fastened the body of Saul to the wall of Bethshan. The Hebrew verb rendered "fastened" means to fasten by driving (a nail), and this passage is quoted by Gesenius as an instance of that meaning. But we can hardly form a conception of a whole body being thus fastened to a wall. It would have required very large spikes to do this, and then verse 9 informs us that the head had already been severed from the trunk, so that the whole body could hardly have been treated in this way. Still we are told that after the men of Jabesh Gilead had taken down the body (ver. 12) they burned his bones (ver. 13).

May it not be that only the prominent members of the body were dealt with in this way? We are all familiar with the ancient custom of fastening the heads of great offenders over the city gate. The first time that the writer passed through the gate of Mardin, in Turkey, several heads of Kûrdish rebels, cut off the day before, looked down on him from spikes overhead.

Some things in the Assyrian monuments may throw light on the subject. Men were impaled and their bodies left on the stakes whereon they were put to death. A bas-relief in Layard's Nineveh (II. 283) shows three bodies hanging limply on stakes that entered the breast just below the ribs; the arms hang down in front, and the position of the head indicates that life has departed. These stakes seem to have been set up outside the wall of a city.

Again, some of the kings of Assyria, after flaying men alive, fastened the skin on the city wall. It is quite possible that the head, hands and feet were also fastened along with the skin, each in its proper position, so that the whole body thus represented may have been spoken of as fastened to the wall. The verb used is **khalib,** to cover, or be covered. See R. V. 2. 4, and A. M. 48. 5; also R. I. 19. 90–93, 110. The translation may be found in R. of P. new II. 143, 144 and 145.

BOUND HAND AND FOOT.

Matt. 22:23. Bind him hand and foot.

John 11:44. Lazarus came forth from the grave bound hand and foot.

In R. V. 9. 22, also A. M. 31. 17 and Ass'l. 273. 123, Asshurbanipal says of **Abiyati** and **Amu,** Arab chiefs, **Qati u shipi biritu parzilli addishunuti.** (Their) hands and feet I placed in fetters of iron.

In R. V. 1. 131, A. M. 47. 30, and Ass'l. 26. 21, he says of the rebellious kings of Egypt, **Ina biriti parzilli, ishqati parzilli utammikhu qati u shipi.** In bonds of iron, fetters of iron, they bound (them) hands and feet.

BOW DOWN.

Isa. 51:23. Bow down that we may go over.
Isa. 55:12. Ye shall all bow down to the slaughter.
Rom. 11:10. Bow down their back alway.
Tiglath Pileser, R. I. 16. 82 and 83, and Prof. Sayce's Gram-

mar 113. 82 and 83, prays that **Anu** and **Ramanu** may cause those who destroy his monumental records to dwell bowing down (**kamis**) in the presence of their enemies.

Nebuchadrezzar describes the other gods in the temple of Bil Marduk (Merodach) in Babylon as standing around him listening reverently and bowing down before him. India House Inscription, col. II. 62, and R. of P. III. 108. 60–62.

There is a marked difference, however, between Scripture and the inscriptions, in that while the former often speak of others being delivered from their enemies, as Gen. 22 : 17, 2 Sam. 7 : 1, 1 Chron. 22 : 9, Prov. 16 : 7 and Heb. 10 : 13, the latter almost uniformly confine such blessings to the royal writers themselves, and ask for the destruction of their enemies.

BOWELS, COMETH FORTH OUT OF.

Gen. 15 : 4. He that shall come forth out of thine own bowels shall be thine heir.

Compare 2 Sam. 7 : 12 and 16 : 11, 2 Chron. 32 : 21.

This form of expression is as frequent in the Assyrian as in the Hebrew. Asshurbanipal, R. V. 2. 56 and Ass'l. 59. 91, speaks of the daughter of Baal, king of Tyre, as **tsiit libbi shu**, proceeding from his body. R. V. 2. 62 uses the same expression concerning his son. The passage reads **aplu** (Ass'l.) **tsiit libbi shu utir ma adin shu,** the son proceeding from his body I restored and gave him. The phrase occurs again, R. V. 3. 22 and Ass'l 61. 105.

Libbi is the Assyrian for the Hebrew Leb or Lebab, and Arabic Lib, meaning heart. Though in R. V. 1. 5 and Ass'l 4. 5 **lib ummi shu** means the womb of his mother, it seems to be a general term for all the internal organs of the body.

BRASS, DOORS OF.

In Isa. 45 : 2 God saith to Cyrus, " I will go before thee and make the rugged places plain, I will break in pieces the doors of brass." (נחושה). Gesenius defines the kindred word נחשות as "copper, mostly as hardened and tempered, and so used for arms and other instruments."

In 1878 Mr. Hormuzd Rassam discovered at Balawat, a

mound five hours east of Mosul, bronze bands about ten inches wide, with a row of rosettes at top and bottom, and another in the middle separating two rows of repoussé relief work each three and a half inches wide. Archæologists determined that they had covered a wooden door about twenty-seven feet in height and three inches thick. See Transactions of the Society of Biblical Archæology Vol. VII. Part 1. pp. 83–118, and P. and C. Art in Chaldea and Assyria I. 194, 242 and II. 210–217, where two engravings of these bands are given, one colored to represent the metal as it now appears.

A beautiful and permanent historical representation of the victories of Shalmanezer II. (B. C. 862–825) seems to have been the object in encasing the wood with bronze rather than merely to impart additional strength to the door.

The upper bas-relief in the colored plate of P. and C., represents a sacrifice made by the king on the shore of Lake Van, and the lower one a *tête du pont* and the progress of chariots along a difficult road, calling not only for a tight rein on the part of the charioteer but for another man to hold the horse's head.

In the other plate the upper portion shows chariots picking their way carefully up the bed of a mountain torrent and the lower one contains a row of captives approaching the king and bowing down even to the dust at his feet, presumably the act described so often in the inscriptions as "kissing his feet." It also illustrates the phrase, "Ummanigus surely (?) kissed the ground." Ass'l. 160. 79.

BRAZEN SEA.

In the Temple court stood a Brazen Sea, 2 Kings 25 : 13. Circular in form, it was about fifteen feet across and seven and a half feet in height. It rested on the hind-quarters of twelve oxen, three of them looking towards each point of the compass.

One scarcely expects to find the counterpart of this in Assyria, but in the seventh Izdubar tablet, col. 4, lines 10–18, **Heabani** says, "In the house, O my friend, which I must enter, *i. e.*, Hades, for me is laid up a crown (compare 2 Tim. 4 : 8) among those who wear crowns, who have ruled the earth from days of old, to whom **Anu** and **Bil** have given names of renown. Glory have they given to the shades of the dead. They drink the bright waters. In the house, O my friend, which I must enter, dwell the lord and the **lagaru,** dwell the soothsayer and the great one, dwell the anointing priest **(pashishu)** of the abysses (or deeps) of the great gods." H. L. 63.

The deeps of the great gods were large tanks of water in the Babylonian temples used for purposes of purification. In the main building of the Yezidee temple of sheikh Adi the writer saw one large enough for a swimming bath, filled with translucent water. It was no doubt used for the same purpose as the brazen sea of Solomon.

BREACHES.

Isa. 58 : 12. Thou shalt be called the repairer of the breach. Compare 1 Kings 11 : 27 and 2 Kings 12 : 5, 6, 12.

This is a very unusual expression, and one that we would hardly expect to find repeated in any language, and yet this identical phrase occurs in the inscriptions of Sargon, builder of the first Assyrian palace discovered at Khorsabad by Mons. Botta, the pioneer in Assyrian discoveries.

Sargon claims to be **shakin shubare Sippar Nipur Babilu,** the repairer of the breaches of Sippar (Sepharvaim) Nipur (Niffer) and Babylon. Prof. Lyon's Sargon Cylinder Inscription, line 4. The idea is, he who had restored whatever had become broken down or decayed in those cities, whether buildings and monuments or institutions and laws ; and it is pleasant among so many records of destruction to find some that commemorate restoration, though both the original builders of noted structures and subsequent repairers took good care to immortalize their works.

BRIDLE.

The Lord said to Sennacherib (B. C. 705-681) by the mouth of Isaiah (19 : 28) : " Because of thy raging against me, and for that thine arrogancy is come up into mine ears, therefore will I put my hook in thy nose, and my bridle into thy lips, and I will turn thee back by the way by which thou camest."

It may seem absurd to speak of putting a bridle into the

lips of any one, but in these words the Lord may be using figures of speech that were perfectly intelligible to all who heard them, and if there was such a thing as a literal insertion of a bridle or cord into human lips practised by the Assyrians that fact would give to these words peculiar force. Now the father of this same Sennacherib built a splendid palace at **Dur Sargina.** It was the first of the Assyrian palaces brought to light in modern times. Mons. Botta sent his workmen there March 20, 1843, and immediately both sculptures and inscriptions rewarded their search. Among the sculptures of this palace at Khorsabad was one representing the king putting out the eyes of a prisoner with the spear in his right hand, while his left hand holds one end of a cord inserted at the other end into the flesh of the lower lip of his victim. His hand grasps two similar cords inserted in like manner into the lower lips of two others who are thus held waiting their turn to undergo the same fate. Would not the son of Sargon recall that bas-relief on the walls of the palace in which he was born, when God said to him, "I will put my bridle into thy lips, and turn thee back by the way by which thou camest"? See Smith's Assyria, p. 169, and Rawlinson's Anc. Mon., I. 243 and III. 7.

BRIGHTNESS.

One is hardly aware how often this term is applied to persons in Scripture till he traces out the use of the word. In Dan. 2:31 we read that the brightness of an image was excellent. 4:36, Nebuchadrezzar says, "My majesty and brightness returned unto me." 5:6 and 9, the Hebrew reads, "The king's brightness was changed," and Isa. 46:11 speaks of being delighted with the abundance of the brightness of Israel.

It may be that such expressions were originally borrowed from the Babylonians; at any rate they occur with great frequency in the inscriptions. A very common phrase in those of Sennacherib is **pulkhi milammi bilutiya iskhupu shu:** The fear of the brightness of my lordship overwhelmed him. He says this of Hezekiah. R. I., 39. 30 and Senn. 63. 30. Also of Eluloeus, king of Tyre. R. I., 38. 35 and 36 and Senn. 53. 35, 36. Another phrase of like import is **milammi sharutiya iktumshu.**

Asshurbanipal says this of **Tarquu** (Tirhakah) king of **Kuusi** (Cush) R. V. I, 85. Ass'l. 19, 87 and 88. and A. M. 44. 8 and 9.

The same term is also used concerning God, Ezek. 1:4 and 27, Hab. 3:4, and in Heb. 1:3 it is spoken of Christ. Psa. 18:12 speaks of the brightness that is before God, and so does Ezek. 10:4.

This idea of brightness in connection with God is illustrated in an inscription of Asshurbanipal, who describes his favorite goddess "Ishtar, who dwells in Arbela," as **ishati litbushat**, clothed in fire, and **milammi nishaata**, exalted in brightness, and adds that she rained destruction upon the land of Arabia. R. V. IX. 80, and Ass'l. 278. 62 and 63.

The Psalmist says, 104:2, "Thou coverest thyself with light as with a garment," and Sargon (Lyon's Sargon 40. 11) speaks of himself as **khalib namurrati**, clothed in brightness.

A hymn to the god **Adar** or **Uras** says, "On the throne of the shrine supreme, even on his seat, is a brilliant light when he kindles it." Hib. Lect. 479.

BRINGING BACK.

That was a glad day in Jerusalem when David and all the house of Israel brought in the ark of the Lord with shouting, and with the sound of the trumpet, 2 Sam. 6:16. The white-robed Levites, the singers and musicians, the glittering mail of the captains, the bronzed faces of the common soldiers, and the jubilant monarch, with the many-colored oriental garments of the rejoicing multitude, must have made a picture never to pass from the memory of those who witnessed it.

Babylonia however could match it with a similar gladness, for this is one of those things in which heathen may stand along with the chosen people. The joy may not be so spiritual, but that is not strange, for it does not belong to the things of the Spirit.

The image of the goddess **Nana**, who by many is identified with Ishtar, had been held captive in Elam for 1,635 years, having been carried there by **Kudur Nankhundi** about 2280 B. C., and during all those centuries her people in Erech (Warka) had remained loyal in their devotion. Generation followed generation to the grave. Events of history might fade from memory, but still they stood steadfast in their allegiance; they did not change their god, though she was no god. Jer. 2:11. Asshurbanipal says, "At that time she and the gods, her fathers, mentioned my name as the coming ruler over the nations, and entrusted to me the return of her deity to her own land, saying, 'Asshurbanipal, take me away from wicked Elam and bring me into **Bitanna,**' (name of her temple). This command, which their deities had uttered from remote times, again they made known to a later age, and the hand of her great deity I laid hold of, and the straight road to Bitanna she took with joyful heart. On the first day of the month Chisleu I brought her into Erech into the **Bitkhiliana** (another name of her temple) which she loved. I caused her to dwell in an enduring sanctuary." Ass'l. 235, 236.

We may doubt whether **Nana** really foretold the royal name, but his people did not doubt it, and from the prominence given to the event in the records of the monarch there is no question but there was a joyous celebration on the day when the goddess who had been absent more than sixteen centuries was brought home again. See "Change Gods," and as an illustration the musical procession, under "Music."

BROTHER.

Amid the mass of evil in the inscriptions—and there is no lack of it—it is pleasant to light now and then on something kind and genial.

The Bible makes much of human relations. God is called our Father who is in heaven, and speaking of men Isaiah says (41:6) "every one said to his brother, Be of good courage," thus recognizing the brotherhood of men. See Zech. 11:14; Judg. 21:6; Prov. 18:24, and especially in the New Testament: see Acts 21:20; Rom. 16:23; 1 Cor. 5:2; 6:6; 7:12, 15.

In the Izdubar legend of the deluge, R. IV. 50. 3. 4, and A. M. 58. 24, also D. L. 104, 106, it is said that so dark was the storm that brother did not see his brother, **ul immar akhu akhashu.** And Asshurbanipal, R. V. III. 108 and Ass'l. 155. 39, says that the people of Babylon, Borsippa and Kutha **iprusa akhuut,** broke off the brotherhood. **Iprusa** corresponds to Hebrew פרס.

So even amid the darkness of Babylonia now and then shine out glimpses of the glory to come, when the gospel shall have filled the earth as the waters cover the sea.

BUILDING ON THE SAND.

Our Saviour says, Matt. 7 : 24-27, " Every one therefore who heareth these words of mine and doeth them shall be likened unto a wise man who built his house upon a rock : and the rain descended, and the floods came, and the winds blew and beat upon that house, and it fell not, for it was founded upon the rock. And every one that heareth these words of mine and doeth them not shall be likened unto a foolish man who built his house upon the sand: and the rain descended, and the floods came, and the winds blew and smote upon that house, and it fell, and great was the fall thereof."

We find no repetition of these words, or anything resembling them, in Assyria, but her palaces furnish a striking object-lesson illustrating these words of the Lord. No doubt they were often destroyed by the hand of violence, and the mark of fire is on many of their ruins, but their material and manner of constructing furnish a very striking confirmation of this teaching of Christ.

Strictly speaking, they were without a foundation ; nor that only, they were erected on mounds of earth or unburned bricks high above the level of the surrounding surface. P. and C., I. 127, say that they stood so high above the soil that the ground line of the palace " leaves the roofs of ordinary houses, and even the summit of the tallest palms, far below." Then " the whole interior was composed of crude brick, and if they were not thoroughly dry the shrinkage in dessication must have injured the structure, especially as the different positions and exposures of the bricks must have caused an inequality in the process, and settlements would occur compromising the equilibrium of the higher portions, and preparing for the destruction of the whole building" (p. 133), for though the walls were faced with burned bricks carefully set, yet in a storm the water would pour over the whole surface and strike violently against every angle, till some bricks would be detached and the water would reach the soft core within. So the process of disintegration would advance from year to year till the mounds assumed their present appearance.

Nabopolassar had to rebuild nearly all the palaces and temples from their foundations in his day, and his distinguished son Nebuchadrezzar seemed to do nothing else but build during his long reign. Herodotus (456. B. C.) appears to have seen the great temple of Bel Merodach while it was still practically intact, but Diodorus (60 B. C.) speaks of it as a structure "which time had caused to fall," and it was a complete ruin in the time of Strabo, who was born 60 B. C.

Asshurnatsirpal (885–860 B. C.) built a palace in Nineveh, and Sennacherib (B. C.) 705–682, rebuilt it and restored the one built by Rimmon Nirari (812–783 B. C.) in the same city at Nebby Yunus.

So also Asshurnatsirpal erected a palace at **Calah** (Nimrood) and Sargon (722–705 B. C.) restored it.

This frequent reconstruction was made necessary by the fact that these structures were built on the sand.

BUTTER AND HONEY.

Isa. 7 : 15. Butter and honey shall he eat; ver. 22. To us this seems a strange juxtaposition of things; we can hardly understand it; and commentators have explained the incongruousness of the mixture by saying that the prophet speaks of the condition of the country when the fields, instead of being cultivated as usual, were devoted to pasturage.

But the people of Mesopotamia seem to have recognized no incongruity in the association. They speak of it as an every day custom in which they see nothing that calls for explanation, any more than in the butter and sugar we compound for pudding sauce.

There is a cuneiform tablet in the British Museum, numbered K. 48, a portion of which is thus translated by Prof. Sayce, in H. L., p. 301., note: "Offer sacrifices, lay reeds which have been cut up, offer food and oil. Let the hand of the prince take honey, **dishpu**, and butter, **khimitu**, the food of the god of revelations, **Bar-bar**, and recite as follows," etc.

CAPPADOCIA.

In R. IV. 25. 2. 28, is another mention of these two articles. The first half of the line speaks of bringing dates and **kuatir**, which some interpret pine cones, but the last half is very plain. That says, " Place " *i. e.* as an offering on the altar, "honey and butter," precisely the same words as before; showing how familiar the association of these two articles of food was in Babylon and Nineveh. In R. IV. 25. 4. 45, is a line that seems to make these the food of paradise. " He (Ea) will place thee in the midst of honey and butter." See also R. of P. XI, 162. 7. Other quotations might be made, but these are sufficient to prove the custom.

If any one is curious to look further into the matter, let him consult Hib. Lect. 529. 28. and 530. 7.

CAPPADOCIA.

Cappadocia, or, to give the ancient spelling, Kappadokia, is mentioned twice in the New Testament: once among the countries represented at the feast of Pentecost when the Spirit descended on the Apostles, Acts 2:9, and once among the countries to which Peter addressed his first epistle. 1 Pet. 1:9.

Its eastern boundary was the Euphrates, from the vicinity of Malatia as far north as nearly to Erzingan. On the south it took in the northern part of the province of Marash along the ridge of Mt. Taurus as far west as the neighborhood of ancient Derbe, thence it ran some distance to the west of Kaisariyeh as far as the boundary of Ancient Phrygia, and thence returned through the centre of the Pashalic of Sivas to the Euphrates at Kemakh. It was known to the Assyrians as **Khani Rabbat.** Asshur Muballid, king of Assyria 1400–1370 B. C., writes to Amenophis IV. of Egypt concerning it, R. of P. new III. 62, and Asshurnatsirpal (885–860 B. C.) tells of Shalmaneser I. the builder of Calah (1300–1271 B. C.) having sent Assyrian colonists to the east of it, at **Khalzilukha** (or Dibkha). This colony imported many things from home. They had inscriptions in which is mentioned their tartan (**Turtanu**) their chief judge (**Rab Zikitum**), and so on. They even had their annual eponym (**Limmu**). We find also the names of many Assyrian gods, as **Asshur, Anu, Ishtar, Bil, Nabu, Nana, Shamsu** and **Zu,** and some others besides, as **Babu, Basku, Tarku,** and people were named from the gods, as **Nanas** from **Nana, Nineps** from **Ninip,** and **Nenaris** from **Nannaru,** a title of Sin. (R. of P. new IV. 121, 122.)

It is interesting to see how they were discovered. Mr. Pinches, of the British Museum, had noticed two tablets in an unusual script and apparently in a strange language. Finding the word **kudina** (mules) in one of them, he remembered that a tablet from Nineveh spoke of mules being obtained from Cappadocia, and at once associated the two together. Then Prof. W. M. Ramsay bought five more tablets at Kaisariyeh, and Mr. Golennischeff's large collection of them furnished abundant material to Prof. Sayce for study and comparison, as witness his interesting article, R. of P. new VI. 115–131.

CAULS.

The word in the original is *shibisim*, שׁבִיסִים Isa. 3:18, and is rendered nettings: caps of network, in Gesenius.

They were just such things as are worn by young women to-day to confine the hair, and it shows the antiquity of this fashion when we find no less than ten of them worn by the younger members of the musical procession. See "Music." One or two of the wearers, however, are grown up women. Frequently one of the monuments illustrates several scriptures in matters that have no necessary connection with each other.

CEDAR, THE.

No king of Assyria or Babylonia came as far west as Syria without carrying back beams of cedar, either from Lebanon or Amanus, and they are enumerated along with the other precious things carried away as tribute to the capital. It may seem as though it would be impossible to convey such huge spars so great a distance, but the soldiers were subsidized as carriers, and such labor was cheap as well as abundant; nor did those who had the management of the matter think much of the toil and suffering that might be involved. There were few palaces of any note in the valleys of the Tigris and Euphrates that could not boast their beams of cedar for the support of the roof, and boards of cedar for their doors.

As a specimen of these royal records concerning cedars we quote some passages from the India House inscription of Nebuchadrezzar, R. I. 53–58 and R. of P. new III. 101–123.

Col. 2. 30–39, he says, "Silver, gold, brightness of precious stones, copper, **mismakanna** wood, cedar, whatever is precious in large abundance, the produce of mountains, the fulness of seas, a rich present, a splendid gift to my city of Babylon, into his presence (*i. e.*, of Merodach) I brought."

And again, in col. 3. 18–32 : " To build **E Saggilla** my heart lifted me up, the chief thing have I regarded it, the choicest of my cedars which I brought from the noble forest of Lebanon for the roof of **E Kua,** the sanctuary of his lordship (Merodach). I looked them out and my heart set them apart. The huge beams of cedar I covered with shining gold for the roof of **E Kua.** The panels under the cedar of the roof I made bright with gold and precious stones."

Compare also col. 3. 38–53, col. 6. 8–15, where he says, " I laid on (it) strong beams of cedar for the roof, doors of cedar I set up in its gates (*i. e.*, the openings for the doors) (covered) with plates of bronze and with bolts* and hinges of copper work."

Having procured their cedar from such a distance, and with so much labor, no doubt it was finished very elaborately, for their work in stone and metal evinces no lack of skill.

David speaks of dwelling in a house of cedar, 1 Chron. 17 : 1, and Asshurnatsirpal, L. N. I. 18, A. M. 6. 20, speaks of a palace of cedar, also of cypress, of juniper, of **urkarini,** of palm-tree, etc.; not that the entire structure was composed of these woods, but only those portions that are usually constructed of wood. Cedar wood was valued for its compact grain, its size, its durability and its fragrance.

There was another use of cedar wood in Babylonia which is also mentioned in Scripture. Cedar twigs were used in connection with sacrifice. Compare Lev. 14 : 4, 6, 49, 51, 52 ; also Num. 19 : 6.

When **Khasisadra** came out of the ship after the deluge and built an altar on the mountain of **Nitsir** he arranged the sacred

---

* Probably let into the lintel overhead and the threshold beneath for the doors to revolve on.

vessels by sevens, and placed cedar wood, cane and **riggir** underneath. D. L. 105, 149, 150. A. M. 60, 17 and 18. So also the directions for a religious ceremony, R. IV. 62. No. 2, obverse, 154 seq., also H. L. 539, 540, speak of cedar wood, sherbin wood, scented reed, palgrass, etc. The fragrance of the cedar seems to be the reason for its use in religious services.

CEMETERIES.

The twenty-third chapter of Genesis contains the account of the purchase of the field and cave of Machpelah by Abraham from the sons of Heth in Hebron for the possession of a burying-place, and all the ages have been moved by the sight of the bereaved patriarch buying a place for the burial of his beloved Sarah.

The limestone of Palestine furnished many caves suited for this purpose, catacombs already prepared for such a use, but the level and stoneless plain of Babylonia offered no such facilities. There was no rock out of which to hew a tomb for the dead any more than stones wherewith to build houses for the living, and yet it is strange that in Assyria, that land of rock and mountain, so few sepulchres have been found, while every mound between Niffer and Mugeyer is a place of graves. Arrian, *De Expeditione Alexandrou*, VII. 22, says that most of the sepulchres of the Assyrian kings were in the region south of Babylon. The most important of these is Erech (Warka), where the accumulation of human remains is enormous. One can hardly convey any idea of it. The area of the ruins is nearly six miles in circumference, and almost the whole of it is filled with the bones that were buried there for many centuries. At first they may have buried in the earth, but later on the coffins were laid side by side and end to end, and one on top of the other, like bricks in a wall or strata in a cliff. The Persians of to-day in carrying their dead to be buried in Kerbela and Meshed Ali seem only to be keeping up the practice of many centuries. Probably no other place on earth can compare with Warka. Even Thebes does not contain such a mass of mortality. For 2,500 years after it was founded by Urukh it seemed to be the favorite graveyard of all the region. Mr. Loftus dug in many places to the depth of thirty feet, when the safety of his workmen forbade him to go farther in the loose, treacherous soil, and he found nothing but clay coffins and dead men's bones. He was satisfied that it was the same to the base of the broad mound, which was sixty feet in height.

The earliest form of the coffin is the "Babylonian urn," so-called, shaped like a pear, and lined with bitumen. Another form is like an oval dish-cover, sloping outwards towards the base; but the kind most in use was a slipper-shaped, glazed earthen one, with an oval opening near the head for the admission of the body, and a hole near the foot for the escape of gas. The whole was coated with rich enamel, green without and blue within. After the body was placed within, the large opening was closed with a lid and hermetically sealed. Loftus, Travels in Chaldea and Susiana, chap. xviii.

The annexed representation is reproduced from p. 204 of that volume. It shows a side and a front view of the same coffin.

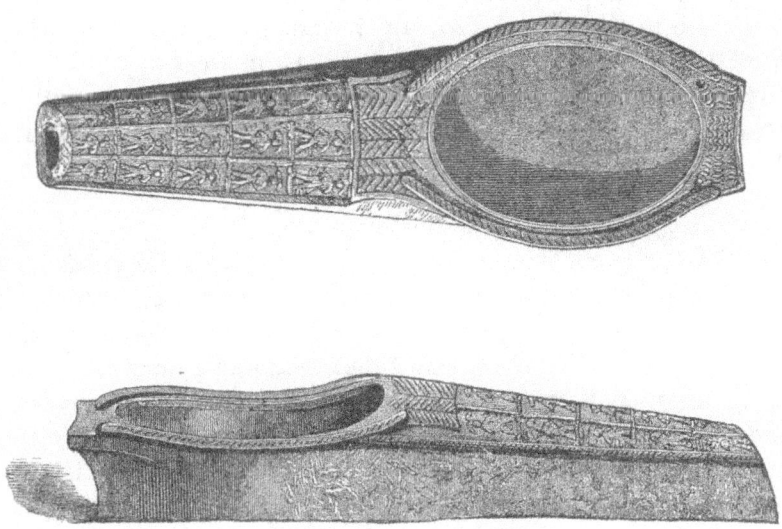

GLAZED CLAY COFFIN, FROM WARKA.

CHAIN OF GOLD.

This seems to have been a favorite form in which gold was used as an ornament, and it was worn about the neck. We find it in places and at periods far apart. Pharaoh, King of Egypt, arrayed Joseph in garments of byssus, or fine linen, and put a chain of gold about his neck, Gen. 41 : 42; and Belshazzar said to the wise men of Babylon, "Whoever shall read this writing, and show me the interpretation thereof, shall be clothed with purple, and have a chain of gold about his neck." Dan. 5 : 7, also 16 : 19.

It will be noticed that in both cases honor is conferred in two ways: *a*, by dress, in the case of Joseph of fine linen, and in the case of Daniel of purple, and *b*, by hanging a chain of gold about the neck.

We find the same twofold expression of honor in the monuments. When Asshurbanipal would show his regard for Pharaoh Necho, one of the kings of Egypt, he clothed him in **birmi,** whatever that was; some render it linen, which would be appropriate in Egypt, but Prof. Lyon translates, "a kind of clothing," without specifying what, and then, as in both these Scripture examples, he adds, " A chain of gold, the insignia of his royalty, I made for him." R. V. 2. 10, 11, and A. M. 48 and 49 14-16. It also was doubtless hung about his neck.

CHANGING GODS.

The prophet Jeremiah asks (2 : 11), "Hath a nation changed their gods, which yet are no gods?" as though such a thing had never been known. What is the testimony of the inscriptions on this point? In answering this question we must be careful to distinguish between progress and change. By progress is meant a natural development, as the germ develops into a plant, and the plant again develops first leaves, then blossoms, and, last of all, the ripened fruit. Change is where one god is arbitrarily set aside and another substituted for it. If, for example, Babylon had renounced Bel Merodach and taken Asshur in his stead, that would be such a change as Jeremiah intimates had never taken place.

The religion of early Babylonia was the lowest Shamanism. Everything that moved was credited with life, and as injury to man often resulted from the movements of bodies, charms and incantations were depended on for deliverance. They had sorcerers but not yet priests. Gradually, however, living beings outside of the human 'race were divided into benevolent and malevolent, or good and evil, and this opened the way for the charm to turn into a prayer and the enchanter into a priest. The first gods were objects close at hand, like **Gibil,** the fire god; for fire was recognized as a fruitful source of both good and evil. Then, as the area of thought and observation enlarged, the worship once rendered to **Gibil,** or to fire and flame near at hand, was gradually transferred to **Shamash** or the sun-god, who was regarded as the great source of fire, and hence of life and light as well as of scorching heat and drought; but this was not a change of gods, it was only progress in the same direction, movement along the same line.

Other causes intensified this result. In Babylonia the Shemite appeared, and his ideas modified those of the Accadian who had previously stood alone. It may have been progress or compromise, or both together, but the result was modification, not change in the proper sense of that term.

Another cause affected the relative importance of different gods. When a city or tribe attained political supremacy, through war or otherwise, the gods of that city or tribe shared in that supremacy, and the gods of the conquered town or province occupied a lower place than before. Still they were not changed for others, they were only subordinated. This is illustrated in the case of Nabonidus, king of Babylon; previous to his day the gods of surrounding cities had shrines in **E Saggil,** the great temple of Bel Merodach at Babylon, where they rendered homage to the great god of the capitol; but Nabonidus gave great offence, both to the priests of the other cities and to the priests of Merodach, by transferring the gods themselves from their temples in other cities to Babylon. The anger of the priests whose idols were removed needs no explanation. That of the priests of Merodach was occasioned by the worship of the others detracting from the sole supremacy that had previously belonged to their god; now others also were objects of worship in the place that of right belonged to him alone. So bitter was this feeling that Cyrus, by taking sides with the offended priests, captured Babylon without a battle, as he himself records (R. V. 35. 7-35, especially line 17, and A. M. 39. 23-41. 34, especially 40. 18-21; see also R. of P. new V. 164. 1-168. 36, especially 166. 17), and Nabonidus fell before the hatred of the priests rather than by the arms of Cyrus.

The practice of the Assyrian kings in carrying off the gods of conquered people may seem to conflict with the immutability of idolatrous attachments, but it only shows that the kings of Assyria knew how to distress those whom they subdued, for the removal of an idol by no means involved the cessation of its worship, as the following facts may show: **Kudur Nankhundi,** king of **Elam,** conquered **Erech** and carried off the image of **Nana,** its tutelary goddess. Did the men of Erech forsake the service of Nana and turn to another god? Instead of that, for 1,635 years they remained faithful to their absent idol, until Asshurbanipal conquered Elam and restored Nana to her faithful votaries. See H. L. 261, R. V. 6. 107-124, R. of P. I. 90. 9-24.

The spirit that maintained steadfast devotion for 1,635 years to one who was no god gives great force to the question of the prophet, and is a sharp rebuke to Israel for forsaking the fountain of living waters, and hewing out broken cisterns that can hold no water. Jer. 2:13.

On a fragment of a tablet published in R. IV. 19. No. 3, is a threnody, and what remains of it is translated by Mr. T. G. Pinches in R. of P. new I. 85 as "An Erechite Lament." It seems well named, and the worshippers of the captive Nana, as they chanted it by the moonlight under the feathery palm-trees, must have presented an impressive spectacle of loyalty to their long-absent idol. This pleasant picture, however, dissolves in air when we remember that Nana was only another name for Ishtar, the Babylonian Aphrodite, and that Erech was the city of "the choirs of the festival girls and consecrated maidens of Ishtar," with all their abominations; represented in our day by the dancing-girls connected with the temples of Hindostan. H. L. 184. See "Bringing Back."

CHARIOTS.

One is struck with the prominence given to chariots in the Old Testament accounts of wars. Exod. 14:7 tells that Pharaoh took 600 chosen chariots, and all the chariots of Egypt, and captains over all of them; and not till verse 9 are we told that he took his horsemen and his army. So God declares that he will get honor first of all upon his chariots, v. 17, and then we are informed that the waters covered all the chariots, v. 28, and—after that—also all the host. And the song in chapter 15:4 was, "Pharaoh's chariots"—first of all—"and his host hath he cast into the sea."

This peculiarity runs through all the subsequent history; we are even told that the chariots of God are 20,000. Psa. 68:17.

Precisely the same prominence is given to chariots in the inscriptions.

Tiglath Pileser I., in Assyrian **Tukulti apali sharra**, B. C. 1120–1100, R. I. 9. 71 and A. M. 1. 7, says, " By the help of Asshur, my lord **narkabati u ummanatiya luptikhir,**—the chariots and my army I assembled;" as though the chariots were the principal thing. Again, R. I. 10. 6 and A. M. 2. 5, **narkabati u quradiya,** the chariots and my soldiers I took, etc. Again, he says that the enemy collected their chariots and their armies, R. I. 12. 84 and A. M. 3. 15. Sennacherib calls his war chariots the casters down of the evil and the good, R. I. 41. 82 and A. M. 16. 11, and again he speaks of his lofty war-chariots which prostrated his enemies, R. I. 41. 56 and 57 and A. M. 15. 23, showing how much he depended on them for victory.

Shalmanezer II. took from Hazael of Damascus 1121 chariots, but only 470 horsemen, R. III. 5. No. 6. 11 and 12 and A. M. 8. 19, though perhaps the chariots could not get out of his way so easily as the horses without such incumbrances.

The figure on the following page is taken from Nineveh and its Remains, II., 269. The bas relief was found in the southwestern palace at Nimrood, built by Esarhaddon 681–668 B. C., but originally belonged to the northwestern palace of Asshurnatsirpal 885–860 B. C., and, little as either of those kings may

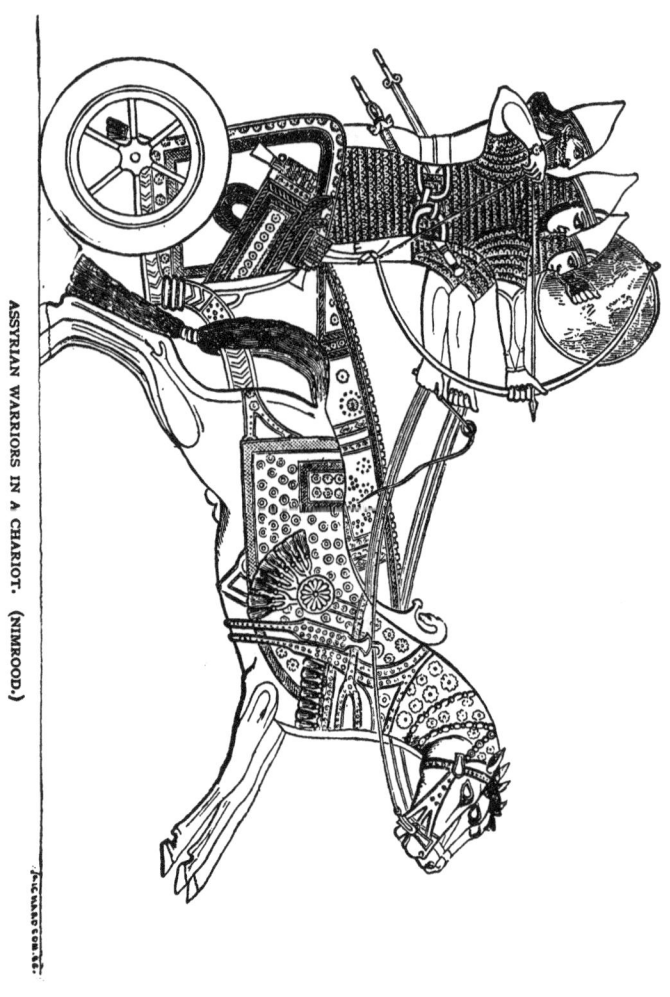

ASSYRIAN WARRIORS IN A CHARIOT. (NIMROOD.)

have intended it, it furnishes a beautiful illustration of the words of Nahum concerning the chariots of Nineveh. He wrote in the days of Hezekiah, while Nineveh was yet in the full tide of her prosperity.

He speaks of the noise of a whip, and the noise of the rattling of wheels and of prancing horses and jumping chariots (3:2). We can almost see and hear the picture, it is so vivid. First of all is the sharp lashing of the whip as the charioteer mercilessly urges the horses to their utmost speed, and in the bas-relief the whip is very conspicuous. Perhaps rumbling would be a better word than rattling, for that suggests something loose and out of order; but here all is firm and strong. There is the whir of the spokes as they rapidly beat the air, the rush of the whole mass through the atmosphere—horses and harness, men and their armor, and the various parts of the chariot itself—all accentuated, as a musician would say, by the regular stroke of the hoofs on the road. The expression "jumping chariots" is not only picturesque but accurate, for the pole of the chariot bends at such an angle, it is fastened so firmly, and so strengthened by the ornamented board that joins the upper part of the body with the front end of the pole, that when the wheel strikes an obstacle the whole stiff machine is jerked from the ground by the impetuous steeds and carried forward through the air till it strikes the road again some distance in advance. Well may the prophet say in one place (2:3) that it flashes with steel—either its polished surfaces glittering in the sunlight or the sparks flying as it strikes the stones; and again (2:4) it flames like a torch, it flashes like the lightning. How expressive, too, of their headlong rush are the words "they rage on the streets"—like living monsters seeking whom they may devour; and then that other dash of the pencil: not only in the narrow oriental streets, where such a thing might be expected, but even in the broad ways, or, as we would say, the wide squares, they jostle one against another. A glance at the bas-relief at once explains this. There is not a moveable joint in their entire construction, not a coupling-pin round which as a fulcrum the horses may be turned to one side; but the entire body, horses and chariot, moves in straight lines, and so they cannot but jostle for they cannot bend out of the way.

ASSYRIAN ECHOES OF THE WORD.

The construction of the chariot without either horses or men may be seen more clearly in Rawlinson's Anc. Mon. I. 412, and the changes in form at different periods may be seen (do. 413) P. and C. II. 76. L. N. II. 272. B. and N. 447.

CHEDORLAOMER.

This is the name of the king of Elam who went with Amraphel, king of Shinar, Arioch, king of Larsa, and Tidal, king of Goiim, (**Gutium,** Ass'n.) on a campaign into the land of Canaan. It is to be expected that the monuments will throw some light on this episode of antiquity, but while some inscriptions lift this account of Chedorlaomer from the sphere of the mythical into that of actual occurrence and others shed light on the narrative, still we have not that complete illustration of this incursion into Canaan that we hope to have when the monuments are more fully brought within the reach of scholars.

It would appear from the order of the names in Gen. 14:1, that Amraphel was the leader of the expedition, as he is mentioned first. Shinar is also written Shungir, and as we see the g elided in Lagamaru, so here as in the Hebrew שער it is changed into *ayin*. Amraphel is read by some Amarphel. (See Sayce's Anc. Emp. of East, 111).

Various fanciful derivations of the name Chedorlaomer have been given in our Bible Dictionaries, as in Smith, *Kuduret el ghomer*, handful of sheaves, though that would make it part Arabic and part Hebrew, and also *Kudur el akhmar* (the red), but these have been set aside by the discovery of an Elamite god named **Lagamaru** (R. III. 22. 77, also V. 6. 33, and Ass'l. 228, 77), and Chedor (**Kudur**) means servant, or one devoted to the service of, and so this king calls himself the servant of Lagamaru. One of the sons of **Ummanaldas,** a king of Elam in the days of Asshurbanipal, was called **Kudurru.** Ass'l. 106. 78 and 116. 88. Another king of Elam was named **Kudur nankhundi** (Ass'l. 250. 12); still another is **Kudur mabuk** (R. I. 2. No. 111, and R. of P. III. 19).

Then if Kudur is so common a name among the Elamites, and Lagamaru is one of their gods, even though the name has not yet been discovered we may confidently expect to find it hereafter.

It has been intimated by some that this episode is mythical, but the cuneiform inscriptions found at Tel el amarna, written in the Babylonian language and script, cumbersome as it was, show that the Babylonian power was no myth in Southern Palestine in the days of **Burna Buriyas** and **Asshur yuballidh**, B. C. 1400–1370, for it formed a portion of their empire, nor in the light of those despatches to Amenophis IV., or Khu en Aten, son of Amenophis III. and the Mesopotamian princess Tadukhepa, can the victory of Abraham over those confederate kings be anything else than an actual occurrence. See R. of P. new V. 62. The tide of battle and conquest seems to have ebbed and flowed between Egypt and Babylonia all through the centuries from Abraham to Amenophis IV., or from *circa* 1900 B. C. to 1400 B. C. Meanwhile we must wait patiently for the greater light on this portion of inspired history that is sure to come.

CHILDREN, DESIRE FOR.

Gen. 30:1. And when Rachel saw that she bare Jacob no children, Rachel envied her sister, and said unto Jacob, Give me children, or else I die.

1 Sam. 1:8. Then said Elkanah her husband to Hannah, Why weepest thou? and why eatest thou not? and why is thy heart grieved? Am I not better to thee than ten sons?

These instances reveal the intensity of the desire for children on the part of the Jewish women. One reason why the desire was so strong was the national expectation of the Messiah. Each woman hoped that she might be privileged to bring him into the world, and hence her intense desire for offspring.

The Assyrians had no expectation of a Messiah. Did they also prize the gift of children? We have no direct record of the fact, for their histories deal chiefly with war and conquest, and give little insight into popular sentiment aside from these things. Still, the very names of some of her noted kings, as **Sennacherib**, Sin, the moon god, has increased brothers, **Asshurbanipal**, Asshur has created a son, **Asshuryuballidh**, Asshur giveth life, **Ea mukin ziri**, Ea establishes a seed, **Nabuyusabsi**, Nebo caused to exist, all bear witness to a desire for children, and to the feeling that for such gifts they were dependent on the favor of the gods.

R. of P. XI. 75. 11, gives the prayer of **Arad Nabi**, that **Asshur, Shamash, Bil, Zirbanitu, Nabu, Tasmitu, Ishtar** of Nineveh, and **Ishtar** of Arbela, may give old age and offspring to King Asshurbanipal.

CHILDREN EATEN.

There is a dreadful picture of fathers and mothers driven to the extremity of eating their own children, Deut. 28:53-57. Nor is this the only one. We have glimpses of the same in 2 Kings 6:28 and 29, and also elsewhere; and the same horrible practice is brought before us again and again in the monuments. When Asshurbanipal seized the wells of the Arabians under Vaiteh the suffering people were guilty of this unnatural crime. The record is very brief. It reads simply, "**Ana buri shunu ikulu shir apli shunu:**" for their food they ate the flesh of their children, R. V. 9, 59; A. M. 32, 14, and Ass'l. 276, 43, but it tells a terrible story of suffering on the part of both parents and children. On a previous page we are told that those who fled for refuge into Babylon, and were shut up there, endured the horrors of famine till **ikulu shir akhamis,** they ate the flesh of one another. R. V. 8. 37; A. M. 29. 6. and Ass'l 263. 27. Again, **binuti shunu,** their daughters, are added to the victims that furnished this cannibal feast in R. V. 4. 44, and A. M. 26. 1. Other quotations might be added but it is too distressing, for, though the events occurred millenniums ago, still the truth remains that we are not reading fiction but a record of actual occurrences.

But even this is not the worst. There is, if possible, a still lower depth. Jews built the high places of Tophet in the valley of the son of Hinnom, to burn their sons and daughters in the fire, Jer. 7:31. Still we might hope that the fire had not been used in a way to destroy life, did we not read again, Jer. 19:5, "They built the high places of Baal to burn their sons in the fire for burnt offerings unto Baal," and the accounts furnished by history of the manner of the offering make it horrible enough.

CISTERN.

Isa. 36: 16. Drink ye every one the waters of his own cistern. In 30 : 14, the word is גבא and in Jer. 14 : 3, גבים.

The inscriptions carefully discriminate between fountains of water, **ina,** and cisterns **guubbu.** Asshurbanipal, R. V. 8. 102, and A. M. 30. 20, also Ass'l. 269, 88, tells us that he pitched his camp at Laribda, in Arabia, by the cisterns, **guubbaani,** of water.

And it is worthy of note that while God promised to Israel, Deut. 8:7, a land of brooks, of water, of fountains and depths springing out of valleys and hills, the envoy of Sennacherib promised to allow the citizens of Jerusalem only (2 Kings 18:31, and Isa. 36: 16) to drink every one the waters of his own cistern; he makes no allusion to either fountain or well of living water: showing how thoroughly the plan of Hezekiah had been carried out to stop all the fountains, and the brook that flowed through the midst of the land, so that the Assyrians should find no water. 2 Chron. 32: 3, 4. Rabshakeh, the chief officer, thought they had none, and were wholly dependent on rain water.

CITIES, ANCIENT AND MODERN.

When a traveller describes a city he mentions those things which distinguish it from every other. Is the scenery picturesque? Is it noted for wealth, manufactures, commerce, or general intelligence? These are brought out with great distinctness. So also the difference between ancient and modern types of thought is brought out in the contrast between ancient and modern descriptions of cities.

That the ancients were perfectly aware of the distinguishing peculiarities of different cities is manifest from the Assyrian bas-reliefs. In the palace of Asshurbanipal on the large mound of Koyunjik, opposite Mosul, the Elamite city of **Madaktu** is represented with its walls and rivers, its houses and palaces, its palm and other trees, and a triumphal march is portrayed, with instruments of music, both male and female singers, and great rejoicing. P. and C. I. 331. Also, the city of Lachish is set before us in the bas-reliefs of Sennacherib from the same mound, presenting an entirely different landscape, with its vines and fig-trees, the royal throne and tent, and the king deciding the fate of the prisoners brought before him. B. and N. 149-151, and frontispiece Smith's Hist. of Senn.

Yet, notwithstanding this confessed appreciation of the facts, in the written inscriptions they are entirely ignored. Sidon is mentioned by name in the records of Sennacherib, but there is nothing to tell us whether it stood on a mountain or a plain, on the sea shore or on an island. Jerusalem also is mentioned, with its walls and gates, but though the temple of Solomon was then standing there is not the slightest allusion to it. In the mind of the Assyrian king it was only a strong city to be subdued and plundered; and some parts of the Old Testament in this respect very much resemble Assyrian inscriptions.

One thing relating to ancient cities was very prominent both in Hebrew and in Assyrian thought. Prominent cities were each dedicated to some god. Jerusalem was *par excellence* "the city of God," Psa. 46:4; 48:1, or "the city of Jehovah," as the only true God, Psa. 101:8; Isa. 60:14.

In like manner the old Assyrian city now known as Kalah Shergat was named by its founder the city of the god Asshur, and when the capital was removed to Nineveh the tutelar deity went with it. H. L. 124.

Babylon also was the city of Bel Merodach. See R. V. 35. 15, 17; A. M. 40. 14, 19. A hymn to that god says, "May thy city speak to thee of a resting-place; it is thy house." "May Babylon speak to thee of a resting-place; it is thy house." R. IV. 18. 3, 4. Again, "Look down upon thy temple; look down upon thy city, O lord of rest." "Look down upon Babylon; look down upon (the temple of) **E Saggil** (*i. e.*, the lifter up of the head), O lord of rest." H. L. 489. Marduk is called king of Babylon and lord of **E Saggil**. R. IV. 29. 9. So a hymn to the god Nebo says, "O lord of Borsippa, no city can compare with thy city Borsippa." R. IV. 20, No. 3. 1, 11. Nergal also is addressed thus: "O Lord of Kutha." R. IV. 26. 5; compare 2 Kings 17:30. Nusku is called "the god of Nipur, who giveth rest to the heart." R. IV. 26. 3. And to Shamash (the sun-god) it is said, "O Lord of **E Babara** (*i. e.*, house of brightness, the name of his temple in the city of Sippara, called Sepharvaim in 2 Kings 18:34, and Isa. 36:19), in **E Babara** (is) the seat of thy sovereignty." H. L. 513, 168. The more familiar examples of Artemis (Diana) of Ephesus and Pallas Athene of Athens, with many more, hardly need to be mentioned. The Old Testament also speaks of the "Holy City." Neh. 11:1; Isa. 48:2; 58:1; Dan. 9:24; Matt. 4:5; 28:53. But heathenism only can speak of cities dedicated to some deity, and that dedication sometimes, instead of holiness, involved unspeakable pollution and abomination.

The Old Testament also speaks of cities as "strong" (Heb. מָעוֹז, fortified). Isa. 17:9; 23:11; Judg. 6:26; see also Psa. 31:22; 60:11. Every reader of Assyrian is familiar with the phrase **alani dannuti** (strong cities). R. I. 38, 41. will give the Assyrian characters.

Where small cities are mentioned we would naturally expect large cities to be the correlate, but instead of that we have **dannuti u bit durani** (strong and walled) in the annals of Sennacherib, where he says: "And of **Khazaqiahu*** the Jew (**Yaudana**), who had not bowed to my yoke, I took forty-six of his *strong, walled* cities and *small* cities in their environs without number," etc. R. I. 39. 11-17; compare I. 40. 64, 65, 66. Walled or fenced cities are also mentioned in the Hebrew מְצֻרוֹת, fenced, or inaccessible, Num. 13:28; Deut. 1:28; 3:5; Jos. 14:12; Isa. 25:2, and the occurrence of the term in Assyrian is too common to need reference.

These things show very clearly how men's views of places are moulded by the prevailing practices of the times. Neither Hebrew nor Assyrian asked whether a city was flourishing and prosperous, but only, Is it so fortified as to be able to resist attack? A sad comment on the violence and insecurity of ancient days, before the gospel brought peace to the world.

CITY AND COUNTRY.

The inscription of Cyrus brought from Babylon some nine years ago is unfortunately in some places unreadable, but one sentence in it may furnish a text for a short discourse. He says,

---
* Hebrew חִזְקִיָּהוּ, Hizqiahu.

"**Ilu Sin shar ilani sha shamii u irtsitim sha ullanuush shu alu u matu la innamduu.**" The god Sin, king of the gods of heaven and earth (during) whose absence (lit. distance) the city and country were not established, *i. e.*, not prosperous. R. V. 64. 26, 27. A. M. 37. 4, 5. Nabonidus had collected the other gods of Babylonia into the capital, much to the disgust of the priests of Bil Marduk, whose income was thus diminished, and as a result Marduk and the other gods quitted Babylon. But I wish to speak not of the history, but of the expression "city and country." A similar phrase occurs in the inscription of Asshur-natsirpal (L. N. I. 13, A. M. 6. 5) that reads "**alani u khurshani,**" cities and wooded mountains. We find also "**ali u tsiri,**" cities and plains, R. V. 3. 133 and A. M. 24. 27, also Ass'l. 158. 59, which is evidently equivalent to "city and country."

In Mark 5:14 and Luke 8:34 we find "they fled and told it in the city and country." In Luke 23:26 we have the phrase coming out of, or from, the country, and in Mark 6:56, "wheresoever he entered, into villages or city or country." Here the small towns are distinguished from the cities and the country.

In 1 Sam. 6:18 כפר הפרזי is rendered by Gesenius and by our versions "country villages." In this passage they are contrasted with fenced cities, and both together include the whole land; for in the interior of the old Bible lands the rural population dwell not every man on his own farm, but each district builds its houses close together for mutual protection. In Kurdistan the writer has seen them built in a hollow square, with only one entrance for the entire village. Such a thing as a house standing alone and far from neighbors is there unheard of. It would not be safe.

Now if in California Chinamen find gold in the refuse thrown away by Anglo Saxons, the writer may feel emboldened to question whether the Hebrew שדה, rendered by Gesenius field, country, should not in many places be translated country instead of field, although even the new revision retains the other rendering. We do not say "city and field," but "city and country." A few examples may be quoted: would not Deut. 28:3 read better "Blessed shalt thou be in the city and blessed shalt thou be in the country"? Also verse 16, where "cursed" occurs instead of "blessed." 1 Kings 14:11 would be more perspicuous if it read, "Him that dieth (of Jeroboam) in the country shall the fowls of the air eat." So also 1 Kings 16:4; 21:24, where the same thing is said of Baasha and of Ahab. In 1 Chron. 27:25 both our old version and the new revision translate a Hebrew singular בשדה (in the country) by an English plural (in the fields) as indeed they were compelled to do to be consistent; for the treasuries were not in any one field, but in the country, in many places, wherever it was convenient to store up grain. For at that time the government of David was so strong and so firmly established that it was safe to deposit stores in the open country.

It is significant of this security that the inspired writer here discribes the land as in four divisions: the country, the cities, the villages, and the castles, or forts, that held violence of all kinds in check.

The complaint of Jeremiah, 14:18, would be much more intelligible to modern ears if it read thus: "If I go into the country, then behold the slain with the sword," because there they were without protection, "and if I enter into the city, then behold them that were sick with famine," because the country was so unsafe it could not be cultivated, and the roads were so dangerous that men did not dare to bring in supplies; and the same things might be said of a similar lament by Ezekiel, (7:15.)

One wonders why the revisers did not change the awkward rendering "field" for "country" in all these places, when it is of equal authority according to the best lexicographers, and expresses the meaning much more clearly. A revision of a translation should give the exact meaning of the original in the language of the present, and no other word can take the place of "country" in these Scriptures, bringing out the meaning of the original Hebrew in the English of to-day.

CITY, THY.

Dan. 9:16. O Lord, according to all thy righteousness let thine anger and thy fury be turned away from thy city Jerusalem, thy holy mountain; because for our sins and for the iniquity of our fathers Jerusalem and thy people are become a reproach to all that are round about us. v. 17. Cause thy face to shine upon thy sanctuary that is desolate, for the Lord's sake. v. 18. Behold our desolation and the city that is called by thy name. v. 19. O Lord, hear; O Lord, forgive; O Lord, hearken and do; defer not, for thine own sake, O my God: because thy city and thy people are called by thy name.

On the night of the first day of the new year the priest who watched in the temple of **Bil Marduk** in Babylon chanted a hymn of which these words form a part:

> O Bil, lord of the world, who dwellest in the temple of the sun,
> Reject not the hands that are lifted to thee.
> Show mercy to thy city Babylon.
> To E Saggil,* thy temple, incline thy face.
> Grant the prayers of thy people, the sons of Babylon.

H. L. 81. 483, 489, 491, also R. IV. 46 and 47.

One cannot but wish that this last prayer had been offered to the living God, who redeems his people from their sins, and not to an imaginary being, who had no real existence and therefore could not help his worshippers. Reading such words one is reminded of the address of Paul to the men of Athens: "What therefore ye worship in ignorance, this set I forth unto you."

CITY AND TOWER.

Gen. 11:4 tells how men proposed to "build a city and a tower whose top might reach to heaven," and commentators have straightway dreamed of an insane ambition that would scale the skies, or an equally insane presumption that would assault omnipotence; but the men of that day had actual sins enough without our adding any imaginary ones to the list, and the true reason is that assigned in the same passage from their own lips: "Lest we be scattered abroad on the face of the whole earth." Other cities had also towers, as the tower of Penuel, Judg. 8:17; Shechem, Judg. 9:51; Edar, Gen. 35:21; Siloam, Luke 13:4; Syene, Ezek. 30:6. When Asa built cities in Judah, besides walls and gates he built in them towers as a thing of course,

---

* Or **Bit Saggil,** an Accadian term, meaning, "The house of the raising of the head."

2 Chron. 14:7. And if these men after the flood proposed to build a tower that would reach to heaven it was because the memory of that terrible destruction was so fresh in their minds, because the world around them seemed so large and empty and those who were to occupy it so few, that they felt bound to keep them together. The same instinct that now draws youth from the country into the city was stronger then than now, for violence was more rife and insecurity greater, so a tower was then more indispensable than pavements and gas-lights are to-day.

In Babylonia and Assyria the **ziggurat** (tower) was the most conspicuous part of their temples, and served the ends of astronomy as well as of religion. Men of rival cities boasted of the height and strength of their towers as they now do of their splendid structures or extensive manufactures, and we can readily see that even in that early time after the flood anything that made men proud of their city would tend to prevent the segregation which they dreaded.

CLEAN.

The distinction between animals as clean or unclean dates back as far as the flood, Gen. 7:2, and seems to have been then not a new idea but a well-known fact. It also came down even to gospel times, as appears from the words of Peter in Acts 10:14, 15.

The same distinction appears to have existed in Assyria, for we read (R. IV. 32. 1.3) of a gazelle clean or without blemish, **ellu**, and in 62. No. 2. 55 of a pure lamb, **ibbu**, and clean herbs; so also a pure strong sheep (64. 2. 22). The hog, Heb. *chazir*, is not mentioned in the Semitic inscriptions, either Babylonian or Assyrian (H. L., 83), and reptiles were counted unclean as among the Jews. One of the penitential psalms expresses sorrow for having eaten the forbidden thing. These things seem to indicate that the Babylonians, like the Jews, divided animals into two classes, one the clean, lawful to be eaten, and the other the unclean, which might not be eaten. Still the certainty is not absolute, for each of these texts may be explained without such a distinction as existed between the clean and unclean animals in Scripture.

CLOTHED WITH CURSING.

Psa. 109:18. As he clothed himself with cursing like as with his garment, so let it come into his bowels like water, and like oil into his bones.

It would seem as though such words could hardly find a parallel in any language, and yet on boundary stones in Babylon and Assyria may be found such sentences as these, invoking curses on any invader of the rights of the owner: " May the bright Sin (moon god) who dwells in the sacred heavens clothe him with leprosy as with a garment." R. of P. IX. 96. 100, 106. " May Gula, the great queen, the wife of Ninip, infilter into his bowels a poison that cannot be got rid of, and may he micturate blood and pus." R. of P. IX. 96. 101, 107. These are only specimens of a long list of like punishments to be inflicted by other gods.

COLORS: BLUE, VERMILION.

Ezekiel 23:5, 6, describes Israel as doting on the Assyrians, "who were clothed with blue, governors and rulers, all of them desirable young men, horsemen riding upon horses," and adds that Judah also did the same, vs. 12, 14, 15, for "she saw men portrayed upon the wall, the images of the Chaldeans portrayed with vermilion, girded with girdles upon their loins, exceeding in dyed attire upon their heads, all of them princes to look upon, after the likeness of the Babylonians in Chaldea, the land of their nativity."

The prophet had evidently visited the palaces of Assyria and wandered through their many halls bordered with the monumental bas-reliefs that record the triumphs of her kings. We now can look on many of the same sculptures, and no one can gaze on the figures of the monarch, his court and his generals without feeling that they are "all of them princes to look upon," and also being impressed with the fact that there is not an old man to be seen among them, but they are all, in the words of the prophet, "desirable young men," vigorous, energetic, and impressing the spectator with a feeling of respect for their manifest executive ability.

As for the colors mentioned by Ezekiel, we can hardly expect that after they have gone through all the rough handling and friction of a voyage to Europe, and then for so many years been exposed to the dampness of an English or even a French climate, we should find the freshness of color which showed itself to their first discoverers.

Mons. Botta tells us, P. and C. II. 247, "The band about the head of the king or vizier is often colored red, as well as the rosettes, which in other figures sometimes decorate the royal tiara. The same tint is used upon fringes, baldricks, sandals, earrings, parasols and fly-flappers, sceptres, the harness of horses, and the ornamental bosses with which it was covered, and the points of weapons. In some instances blue is substituted for red in these details." Could there be a more complete endorsement of the prophet who says that Israel saw the Assyrians "clothed with blue," and Judah saw the same personages "portrayed with vermilion"? We might have feared that Ezekiel had been careless, to say the least, in allowing the diversity of statement, but here we find in the seeming discrepancy an exact transcript of the facts.

Mons. Place, the successor of Mons. Botta, L. N. I. 58, says that on one of the fragments unfortunately lost in the Tigris the colors were more brilliant than usual. The fan of peacocks' feathers in the king's hand was the brightest mineral blue.

Mr. Layard says, L. N. II. 238: "There were fewer remains of color at Nimroud than in the ruins explored by M. Botta. I could distinguish them on the hair, beard and eyes, on the sandals and bows, on the tongues of the eagle-headed figures, and very faintly on the garland round the head of a winged (figure), and on the representation of fire in the bas-relief of a siege . . . At Khorsabad the remains of paint were far more general, being found on the draperies, the mitre of the king, the flowers carried by the winged figures, the harness of the horses, the chariots and the trees. In the bas-reliefs of a siege, the flames issuing from the houses and the torches of the assailants were invariably red."

Then quoting Ezek. 23: 14, 15, he says, p. 240, "The prevalence of a red color, shown by the remains at Khorsabad, and the elaborate and highly ornamented head dress of the Khorsabad and Koyunjik kings are evidently indicated;" p. 241 he adds: "On the sculptures I have only found black, white, red and blue, and these colors alone were used in the painted ornaments of the upper chambers at Nimroud—at Koyunjik there were no traces of color." "The Assyrian red exceeds in brilliancy that of Egypt, which was merely an earthy bole. It approaches nearly to vermilion on the sculptures at Khorsabad, and has a bright crimson or lake tint on those of Nimroud."

In a note on p. 243 he adds: "The following were the parts of bas-reliefs on which colors were found at Nimroud and Khorsabad. The hair, beard, eyebrows, eyelids and eyeballs, black; the inner part of the eye, white; the king's mitre, principally red; the crests of helmets, blue and red; the heads of arrows, blue; the bows, red; the handles of maces, red; the harness of horses, blue and red; sandals in oldest monuments, black, edged with red; in those of Khorsabad, striped blue and red; the rosettes in the garlands of winged figures, red; trees at Khorsabad, a bluish green; flowers, green, occasionally red; fire, always red."

It may be worth while to add that the Hebrew חקק, which is translated "portray," means literally to cut or engrave; as though the prophet intended to convey the idea that the bas-reliefs were cut in the stone slabs that served to wainscot the halls, as well as colored with paint, so accurate are his statements respecting the things which he had seen in Assyria.

COMMANDMENT, SECOND.

Exod. 20:4. Thou shalt not make unto thee a graven image, nor *the likeness of* any form that is in heaven above, or that is in the earth beneath, or that is in the water under the earth, etc.

It may seem strange that this threefold specification should be made, of things in heaven above, the earth beneath, and the water under it; but precisely this was needed to make—according to the old saying—"the plaster as large as the sore." The gods of Egypt were drawn from these three departments. There the fowls of heaven were represented, among others, by the ibis, the hawk, and the goose. Among

CONCUBINE.

animals we need only mention Apis, the sacred bull, though even the jackal is among the list of the gods. Then Pharaoh was the living image of the sun-god upon the earth, and from the waters under the earth among others was the crocodile. Renouf's Religion of Ancient Egypt 167-74, 245-9.

These three departments also found a place in the Assyrian Pantheon. In that, the birds of heaven were represented by the god **Zu,** the divine storm bird, corresponding to the Prometheus of Greek mythology (H. L. 224-9), and bird-headed figures abound on the monuments. See P. and C. I. 63. The earth was represented by the **Shidi,** or winged bulls, that guarded the gates of Assyrian palaces. See frontispiece in L. N. and B. and N., also B. and N. 360. Here also kings were received into the number of the gods, as was the case with **Naram Sin,** son of Sargon of Accad. H. L. 31 and Trans. Soc. Biblical Archæology, 1877. And the waters under the earth produced **Ea,** the god of ancient **Eridu,** who is figured sometimes as clothed in the skin of a fish (B. and N. 350 and P. and C. I. 64) and again as having a human bust joined to the body of a fish. L. B. and N. 343, Smith's Dict. of Bible 528. So perfectly do the prohibitions of the second commandment fit in to the idolatrous practices that called for the enactment of the law.

CONCUBINE.

It is worthy of note that when a Hebrew had occasion to make mention of a concubine he could find no word in his own language to express the idea, but had to use an exotic term concerning the origin of which scholars are not agreed to this day. That term פילגש occurs in Judg. 19:2; but the Assyrian has a word of its own to denote the idea, only scholars are not agreed about its pronunciation, and concubinage was denoted by the addition of **uti,** the regular termination of abstract nouns. Prof. Delitzsch in his Lesestücke seems to analyze the term for concubine into two ideograms, one the determinative for female and the other the ideogram for **tukulti,** help, or service. Still he gives no pronunciation.

The difference between the Hebrew and Assyrian in this respect represents the different status of women in the religion of the Bible and in heathenism. In the one her position is that of virtue and honor, and any deviation from that is a degradation induced from without; in the other degradation is the rule rather than the exception. It is the inevitable working of the system. Asshurbanipal in his inscriptions boasts that Baal, king of Tyre, **Yahimelek,** his son, and **Yakiinlu,** king of **Arvad,** sent each a daughter and the daughters of their brothers to be his concubines, and that **Ningallu,** king of **Tabalu,** and **Saandasharmi,** king of **Khilakaa** (Cilicia), sent each a daughter with large dowries for the same purpose. R. V. 49–80 and A. M. 21–24.

COPIED OUT.

Prov. 25 : 1. "These also are proverbs of Solomon which the men of Hezekiah, king of Judah, copied out." Hezekiah lived about 300 years after Solomon, and yet, instead of adding something new to the stock of human knowledge from the experience of those three centuries, the royal scribes are employed in transcribing the sayings of the wise king uttered so long before. This would not be the natural order of things to-day; but Assyria furnishes a perfect parallel to this procedure in the capital of Judea. In the lands watered by the Euphrates and Tigris civilization and culture began at the southern border and travelled northward. The Accadians were the source of all the literature both of Babylonia and Assyria. The hymns to the gods were originally written in Accadian, and from that translated into Assyrian. The same was true of the whole of the early literature of that region.

Sennacherib transferred a library from **Calah** to Nineveh in the latter part of his reign, but Asshurbanipal was the only Assyrian king who really cared for learning. When Babylonian cities were captured no spoil was so acceptable to him as some ancient tablet from Ur or Babylon, and a colophon at the end certified that it belonged to the Royal Library. One is sufficient for a specimen. At the end of the hymn to Sin (see "Moon") we read: "Like its old copy, copied and made public. Tablet of **Ishtar-shumeshesh,** chief scribe of Asshurbanipal, the king of all, the king of Assyria, and son of **Nabu-zir-esir,** chief of the penmen."

COUNT.

The frequent use of this verb is one of the peculiarities that constitute what is called a Scriptural style; *e. g.*, Psa. 44:20, "We are counted as sheep for the slaughter;" 139:22, "I count them mine enemies:" 1 Sam. 1:16, "Count not thine handmaid for a daughter of Belial." Compare Acts 20:24 and Philemon, 17.

The same use of this verb is characteristic of the inscriptions:

Ana shalati amnu, I counted as spoil, is a very frequent phrase. Asshurbanipal uses it, as in R. V. 2. 133 and Ass'l. 85. 54. So does Sennacherib, as in R. I. 39. 5., Senn. 60. 5 and A. M. 12. 2.

Shalati is from the verb **shalalu,** to carry off, and includes both captives and plunder, as in the above instances, where men or people are mentioned as well as horses, asses, oxen and sheep, and valuables of all sorts.

COVENANT.

The word covenant occupies a very prominent place in Scripture. The people of God are looked on as in covenant with him, and departure from him is transgressing the covenant: Josh. 7:11, 15; Hosea 6:7; 8:1, or forsaking it, Jer. 22:9; or breaking it, Deut. 31:20; Lev. 24:15; Jer 11:10; 31:32. Even sins against men are regarded as breaches of the covenant of God. Prov. 2:17.

The word occupies an equally prominent place in the Assyrian monuments. Asshurbanipal complains thus of the rulers in Egypt, R. V. I. 119, 120, Ass'l. 23. 124, A. M. 46. 9, 10: "Afterwards these kings, as many as I had appointed to office, **ina adiya ikhtuu,** transgressed against my covenant, and did not keep the oath (**mamit**) which they had made by the great gods."

R. V. 123, Ass'l. 24. 7 and A. M. 46:15, he says, "To Tirhaka, King of Kush, **ana shakan adii,** for making covenants, and alliance they sent their envoys." R. V. 1. 132, Ass'l. 26. 21, A. M. 46. 26, he says, "The oath of **Asshur,** king of the gods, captured those who had sinned against the covenants of the great gods." Compare R. V. 7. 18. 93, Ass'l. 238. 44 and 257. 106.

COVERING THE FACE.

When David heard of the death of Absalom he covered his face and cried with a loud voice, "O my son, Absalom! O Absalom, my son, my son!" It was the instinctive movement of sorrow that did not wish others to intrude on his grief, nor see anything that would call off his mind from his sore distress.

The Assyrians show us that they also recognized this spontaneous expression of mental anguish when they picture the gods as crouching down by the walls of heaven, dissolved in tears and with their lips covered, because so distressed by the destruction of the human race by the flood. So **Adrakhasis** describes to Izdubar the effect which the deluge produced in the Chaldean Olympus. A. M. 59. 13, D. L. 104. 120. See "Deluge." Covering the lips is equivalent to covering the face, for one cannot cover them without covering the most expressive portion of it.

CREATION.

It is an interesting inquiry how far the Chaldean account of Creation is in agreement with the Mosaic; but only a partial answer can be given to the question, the copies of the creation tablets are so imperfect. They are seven in number, corresponding to the seven days of the Mosaic creation, though, unlike that, the seventh Chaldean tablet is devoted to the creation of animals. The account of the creation of man is not yet recovered, only R. IV. I. I. 36, 37 speaks of "the woman brought forth from the man," but that is the work of evil spirits, not of the gods.

We have only the beginning of the first tablet, small fragments of the second and seventh, portions of the third, nearly the whole of the fourth, about two-thirds of the fifth, and none at all of the sixth. The first tablet speaks of "that time," corresponding to the "In the beginning" of Moses. Out of a watery chaos called **Mummu Tiamat** proceed both the gods and the world. This same **Tiamat**, Hebrew *Tehom*, the abyss, figures also as a dragon, the leader of the powers of evil, and is spoken of as "the wicked serpent."

The order of events is somewhat obscure; but first of all

are the original deities, **Lakhma** and **Lakhama**, then **Ansar** and **Kisar**, the sky and atmosphere, and last of all **Anu, Bil**, and **Ea**—the Zeus, Pluto, and Poseidon of Chaldea.

In connection with the chaos there seems to have been a host of imperfectly formed and malevolent creatures under **Tiamat**, and before creation could be a success **Tiamat** and her hosts must be overcome. This work devolved on Merodach, the son of **Ea**, who engaged in single combat with the dragon and overcame her. The sky was formed out of her skin and became the dwelling-place of the new gods. The earth seems not to have been made till after the institution of the heavenly bodies in the fifth book, and it is not very manifest just where the creation of the light comes in. A complete set of the tablets, however, may clear up that as well as other dark points and give us a more intelligent knowledge of their ideas. As it is, there appears a heaven-wide difference between the materialism and polytheism of Chaldea and the spirituality of the word of the living and true God. See under "Dragon."

One very noticeable thing in the Chaldean account of Creation is that the gods are created, as well as men and matter.

It would be interesting to see a skeptical scientist try to make the Chaldean record of Creation conform to the revelations of science on that subject. Before he could find any possible way to reconcile the two he might obtain a new conception of the truthfulness and accuracy of the Scripture record.

CREATOR, FATHER.

Peter 4:19. Wherefore let them also that suffer according to the will of God commend their souls in well doing unto a faithful Creator.

Some complain of this as wanting in comfort. They say, "If it had spoken of commending ourselves to 'a loving Father,' that had been genuine consolation; but 'a faithful Creator' is too cold and abstract an idea to cheer our sorrow." The question might be raised whether the Creator has not a purer and more tender affection for those whom he has formed in his own image, Gen. 1:27, than all the fathers that ever lived; but we do not need to press that point. The Scriptures use Creator and

Father as synonymous; for when carrying back the genealogy of Christ they do not stop with Adam, Luke 3:38, but carry it one step further, "Adam, the *Son* of God."

One would hardly look for help to the Assyrian on such a point, and yet we find it there; for Asshurbanipal, after saying, R. V. 1. 5. and A. M. 19, 20, that **Asshur** and **Sin** created him, **ibnuu,** calls Esarhaddon three lines after that **abu banuua,** "the father, my creator," and repeats the same in line 27.

It may be said this refers only to man, but in the account of the deluge the goddess Ishtar says, A. M. 59. 9 and 10, "I, the mother, did not bring forth, **ullada,** mankind that like the progeny of fishes they should fill the sea." This manifestly refers to the *creation* of the race. Is even Ishtar thus pictured by her worshippers as possessed of natural affection? and what shall we say of the true Creator, who asks, Isa. 49:15, "Can a woman forget her sucking child?—yea, these may forget, yet will I not forget thee"?

CRUELTIES.

2 Sam. 12:31. And he (David) brought (out) the people that were therein, and put them under saws and under harrows of iron, and under axes of iron, and made them pass through the brick kiln.

This would be branded as inhuman conduct to-day. Why was David so cruel? It was not the grace of God in him that yielded such fruit, but it was the cruel spirit of the nations round about that blinded him to its enormity, and made his heart callous to human suffering.

This may appear from a view of the cruelties inflicted by the kings of Assyria as set forth in their own annals. Asshurnatsirpal lived later than David, he was the cotemporary of Jehu, and he records in his annals (R. I. 21.72, R. of P. new II. 154.72) "Twenty soldiers I captured alive, in the wall of his palace I immured them." This was at **Ameka.** In **Suru** on the Euphrates above the mouth of the Balikh he built a pyramid at least in part of living men, then flayed alive the rebellious nobles, and covered the pyramid with their skins. Others he impaled alive on stakes inserted in the upper portion of the pyramid. He built eight such pyramids at different places. In one city he cut off the legs and arms of the leaders, and then flayed their king alive on his return to Nineveh (R. I. 19.89-93 and R. of P. new 143 and 144) and both these horrid cruelties are portrayed in the bas-reliefs of his palaces. B. and N. 456 and Kitto's Bible Illustrations, Isaiah, p. 232.

After that, in the city of **Tela,** he cut off the limbs of some of his captives, and the noses, ears, and fingers of others, put out the eyes of many, built one pyramid of living men, and another of human heads, and burned their young men and maidens in the fire. R. I. 19. 117, 118, and R. of P. new II. 146. 117, 118. Then at **Ipsilipria,** in the neighborhood of Lake Van, he built up a column of heads, and consumed their young men and maidens in the fire, R. I. 20. 19, and R. of P. new II.148, 149. In the city of **Pitura** (Pethor, Num. 21 : 5) also he burnt many soldiers in the fire, as well as young men and maidens, and built his two kinds of pyramids besides impaling 700 men in front of the city gate. R. I. 22. 108, 109, R. of P. new II. 159. 108, 109. At **Amida** (Diarbekir) he piled up a pyramid of 600 human heads and impaled 400 soldiers before the gates. R. I. 26. 107, 108, R. of P. new II. 174. 107, 108. One wonders how his soldiers could have endured for so long the sight of so much human suffering. It seems as though even the protracted monotony of so much misery must have palled on the senses. And what an education for the young men who were made to carry out such—shall I call it—refinement of torture? One is ready to question the utility of the history that compels us to dwell upon such horrors.

I have passed over several cases where a number were impaled, lest the reader should be surfeited with the monotony of misery, yet as some may turn to these pages for light on the statement that "the dark places of the earth are full of the habitations of violence," Psa. 74: 20, the case of the fortified city of **Kinabu** must be added, where he destroyed 3,000 captives by fire, besides burning their young men and maidens to ashes, building 600 bodies of slain soldiers into pyramids, and flaying alive **Khula** the ruler of the city. R. I. 19. 108-110. R. of P. new II. 145. 108-110.

This does not furnish very pleasant reading, and the worst thing about it is that it is not fiction, but the record of sufferings actually endured and of cruelties really inflicted by one who was not ashamed to record them on his monuments as a memorial of his glory. His full length statue is given in L. N. II. 12 from his palace at Nimrood, and it looks fully capable of such enormities. No wonder he styles himself "the unique monster .... the consumer of the strong. The hero who spares not" (R. I. 26. 126, 127, R. of P. new II. 176, 126, 127), adding another to the list of those whose glory is in their shame and showing us from what a horrible pit we have been lifted up by the grace of God in Jesus Christ our Lord ; for if Christ had not come to our earth what power had availed to check the perpetuation of such cruelties?

CUNEIFORM WRITING, EXTENT OF.

Cuneiform writing originated among the non-Semitic population of **Sumir and Akkad,** who spoke an agglutinative language like the Tatar and Turkish. From them it passed over to the Semitic Babylonians and Assyrians, who used its signs in writing their own language. In **Elam** or **Anzan** it was used to record their ideas and annals, and in the ninth century B. C. it was adopted by the annalists of Van and Ararat to express their Alarodian words. Cuneiform tablets mainly relating to business affairs have been found near Cæsarea in Central Asia Minor. A colony from Assyria introduced it there. A seal with cuneiform characters was found near Herat, and Sir Henry Rawlinson found an inscription in this character at Seri-pul (Siripool) forty-five miles southwest of Balkh. The tablets of Tel el Amarna in Egypt bear witness that it was the common medium of literary intercourse from Assyria as far west as Egypt (R. of P. new II. 55 seq., and VI. 115 seq.), even before the exodus of Israel from Egypt.

CURSE OF JERICHO.

The curse pronounced by Moses, Deut. 13 : 16, and by Joshua, 6 : 26, on the man who should rebuild Jericho finds a curious illustration in R. I. 14. 13-11. See also A. M. 4. 14-30 and the notes on 66.

Tiglath Pileser I. (**Tugulti apal i sharru**: servant of the son of the house of the firmament, B. C. 1120-1100), R. of P. new I. 90, after describing the capture and utter destruction of the city

Khunutsa, adds that over the shapeless mounds of rubbish he sowed **tsipa,** stones (see 1 Kings 3 : 19), and I made a **birik siparri** (literally, copper lightning)* from the spoils of the lands which I had captured through the help of my God and Lord, and I wrote upon it that that city should never be rebuilt nor its walls re-erected. A house of brick I built upon the ruins (lit. upon its head) and I placed within it that **birik siparri.**" The object was the preservation of that written prohibition from age to age so that it should never be transgressed. This is translated in R. of P. V. 20. 29, but the meaning is not fully brought out—as indeed it could not have been at that early date, 1875, even by the best scholars.

CURSING.

1 Sam. 17 : 43. And the Philistine cursed David by his gods.

We have a specimen of such cursing in the list of maledictions which Tiglath Pileser invokes on the heads of any who may in the future erase the inscriptions that set forth his mighty deeds. He says, R. I. 16. 74–88, "May the gods **Anu** and **Rammanu,** the great gods, my lords, exceedingly put him to shame and curse him with a grievous curse. May they overthrow his kingdom and forcibly remove the foundation of his throne, the armies of his lordship may they annihilate, his weapons may they break in pieces. May they bring about the defeat of his warriors. May they cause him to spend life bowing down (Rom. 11 : 10) before his enemies. May **Rammanu** with destructive thunderbolts dash his land in pieces. Want, hunger, and famine, dead bodies may he cast on his land. Against the lordship of his fulness may he pronounce. Let his name and his seed perish in the land." Other kings pronounce like maledictions on the destroyers of their records and their monuments. Indeed, such curses form a stereotyped portion of the contents of the inscriptions on every corner-stone (**Timin**) of temple and palace in Babylonia and Assyria. In this connection one cannot help thinking of those words of the Psalmist (109 : 17–19), " Yea, he loved cursing, and it came unto him, and he delighted not in blessing, and it was far from him. He clothed himself also with cursing as with his garment, and it came into his inward parts

* It would seem to be a curse engraved on copper.

76 ASSYRIAN ECHOES OF THE WORD.

MUSLIM DEVOTEE CUTTING HIMSELF LIKE THE PROPHETS OF BAAL. (1 Kings 18:28.)

like water, and like oil into his bones. Let it be unto him as the raiment wherewith he covereth himself, and for the girdle wherewith he is girded continually."

CUT THEMSELVES.

The priests of Baal, in their great contest with Elijah at Mount Carmel, "cried aloud, and cut themselves after their manner with knives and lances till the blood gushed out upon them." 1 Kings 8:28.

In their mourning for Tammuz (see under "Tammuz") the frenzied worshippers tore their hair, disfigured their faces, and cut their breasts with sharp knives in token of their deep distress. The wailing of the women mingled with the cries of the Galli, the emasculated priests of Ashtoreth. At Komana in Kappadokia 6,000 eunuch priests joined in the worship, and the Galli of Phrygia rivalled the priests of Baal and Ashtoreth in cutting their arms with knives, in scourging their backs, and in piercing their flesh with darts. H. L. 229, 267.

Nor is such worship yet obsolete; it is still practised in Western Asia. Modern dervishes sometimes cut themselves with knives and swords till the blood pours out, or pierce their naked flesh with iron spikes till they faint with pain and loss of blood. See "Bible Lands" by Rev. H. J. Van Lennep, D. D., p. 767; pp. 765 and 769 are sketches from life made by his facile pencil, and as one looks at them he is amazed that any man could suppose that in such ways he was rendering service to God. One of them is here reproduced.

CYRUS.

Isa. 45:1-4. Thus saith the Lord to his anointed, to Cyrus, whose right hand I have holden, to subdue nations before him; and I will loose the loins of kings, to open the doors before him, and the gates shall not be shut. I will go before thee, and make the rugged places plain: I will break in pieces the doors of brass, and cut in sunder the bars of iron: and will give thee the treasures of darkness, and hidden riches of secret places, that thou mayest know that I am the Lord who call thee by thy name, even the God of Israel. For Jacob my servant's sake, and Israel my chosen, I have called thee by thy name: I have surnamed thee, though thou hast not known me.

Isa. 41:2 also asks, "Who hath raised up one from the east, whom he calleth in righteousness to his foot? He giveth nations before him, and maketh him rule over kings; he giveth them as the dust to his sword, and as the driven stubble to his bow." Also Isa. 44:28: "That saith of Cyrus, He is my shepherd, and shall perform all my pleasure, even saying of Jerusalem, She shall be built; and to the temple, Thy foundation shall be laid."

The monuments of Babylonia furnish some remarkable coincidences with these words of Isaiah; but before quoting from them a few words of introduction are needed in order to make them understood. The reader already knows that, while Israel worshipped the one only living and true God, in Mesopotamia men worshipped gods many and lords many; but there was also a difference in Mesopotamia itself. While in Assyria religion was national, and the whole empire united to exalt Asshur as the father of the gods, in Babylonia each city had its own god, whom it preferred before all others. Thus Ur was devoted to **Sin**, the moon-god, **Sippara** (Sepharvaim) to **Shamash**, the sun-god, and Babylon to **Bil Marduk** (Merodach). More than that: the prosperity of each city and of its special cult went together. If the king of the city subdued his neighbors, not only did the government of the conquered city submit to the conqueror but its god became subordinate also. The worship of its special idol did not cease, but the god of the conquering city became *primus inter pares* among the gods of the tributary cities, who became the attendants of the god of the conqueror. Their shrines were arranged around his, in token of their inferiority; or, as Nebuchadrezzar, king of Babylon, expressed it when his victories had made his god Merodach supreme in Babylonia, "They stood around him listening in reverence, and bowed down before him. But Nabonidus (**Nabunahid**, Nebo is exalted), the last king of Babylon, B. C. 556–541, went a step further, which gave great offence both to the conquered cities and to the inhabitants of his own capital. He undertook to remove the idols of the various cities to Babylon, both them and their worship. This, of course, gave offence to the other cities, who were thus robbed of all the glory that remained to them after they had lost their liberty, and it also offended the Babylonians, because it brought in a host of other gods to divide with Merodach the honor that had up to this time belonged to him alone.

These statements may prepare us to appreciate some extracts from the Cylinder Inscription of Cyrus found in the palace of Babylon by Mr. Hormuzd Rassam in 1879, which is written in the Babylonian language by Babylonian scribes and for Babylonian readers. It may be found in R. V. 35, and also in A. M. 39-42. There is a good translation by Prof. Sayce in R. of P. new V. 165-168, and also one by Prof. H. V. Hilprecht of the University of Pennsylvania in the "Sunday-School Times," 1893, pp. 34 and 35. Throughout it speaks of Nabonidus as the enemy of Merodach, and of Cyrus as his favorite, and it is significant that as soon as Nabonidus suffered a reverse the whole population at once submitted. The unpopularity of Nabonidus may perhaps furnish an explanation of the way in which the gates of the city happened to be left unguarded on that night when Belshazzar was slain; for of course bars and gates were provided in order to be closed, and if they were left open there must have been some reason for the negligence, such a breach of military discipline outside being hardly accounted for by the revelry within the palace.

Unfortunately only 16 of the 45 lines of this Cylinder Inscription are legible, but these make us acquainted with several important facts. Because of the outcries of the Babylonians, **Marduk** and the gods deserted the city. All around was desolation till Marduk sought out a righteous king after his own heart, whom he took by the hand. (Comp. Isa. 41 : 2 and 13, and 45 : 1.) Cyrus, king of Anzan (Elam), he proclaimed his name for universal kingship. (Compare with this Isa. 45 : 3 and 4.) The country of **Quti** (Kûrdistan) and all the people of the nomads (**Mandu**)—Prof. Hilprecht says, "The tribes in the north and northwest of Assyria"—he made to bow at his feet. He caused the black heads (Accadians) to yield to him. In justice and righteousness has he cared for them. (Comp. Isa. 41 : 2.) Merodach, the great lord, the restorer (?) of his people, beheld with joy the works of him who was righteous in heart. To Babylon he caused him to march and take the road to that city, and as a friend and helper marched at his side. He marshalled the weapons of his extended army, countless as the waters of the river. Without a battle he caused him to enter Babylon, which he spared. In Shapsha (?) he gave Nabonidus the king, who did not worship him, into the hands of Cyrus. All the men of Babylon, all **Shumir** and **Akkad,** princes and **Sakkanakka** (high priest or chief) bowed before him and kissed his feet. They rejoiced in his dominion. Their faces shone. "I am **Kuraash,** the king of all, the great king, the mighty king, the king of **Tintir** (Babylon), the king of **Shumir** and **Akkad,** the king of the four quarters of the heavens, the son of **Kaambuzia** (Cambyses), the great king, the king of **Anzan,** the grandson of **Shiispiish,** the great king, the king of **Anzan,** of an ancient royal family, whose rule **Bil** and **Nabu** love, and whose dominion was the joy of their heart.

"When I entered Babylon graciously, with joy and rejoicing, in the palace of the kings I fixed the abode of my lordship. **Marduk;** the great lord inclined (?) the large (broad) heart of the sons of Babylon to me; daily I cared for his worship. My numerous (extended) troops march (?) peacefully in Babylon." The five lines following are imperfect.

"For these things **Marduk,** the great lord, rejoiced over me, King **Kuraash,** his worshipper, and **Kaambuzia,** the son of my body, and favored my whole army that in peace moved on prosperously before him. By his great command all the kings dwelling in palaces of all the regions from the upper sea (Lake Van) to the lower sea (Persian Gulf), indeed the dwellers in all lands, even the kings of the west land, dwelling in Sutari (?), all of them brought their great tributes to Babylon and kissed my feet. From —— to **Asshur** (Kalah Shergat) and **Shushinak** (?) (Susa) **Akkad, Eshnunak** (or **Abnunak**), **Zamban Mi turnu** (the river Tornadotos, near Bagdad) **Durilu** as far as the borders of **Quti** (Kûrdistan), cities beyond the Tigris, founded from ancient days. The gods who dwelt in them I restored to their places, and founded for them a permanent abode. All their inhabitants I gathered together and restored to their dwelling-places, and the gods of **Shumir** and **Akkad,** whom Nabonidus had brought into Babylon, thereby provoking the lord of the gods, by the command of **Marduk**, the great lord, I settled in their sanctuaries according to their desire."

And so the same Cyrus who was hailed as a benefactor in Jerusalem because he restored the vessels of the temple which Nebuchadrezzar had taken away was also hailed as the restorer of the gods of Babylon to their worshippers. Only in this last case it was not a follower of Zoroaster but a worshipper of Merodach honoring his own god, and Cyrus, according to his own annals, was not king of Persia, but king of Elam.

DAGAL רגל.

This verb has been derived from the noun רגל, a banner, and in Ps. 20:6 has been translated thus: "In the name of our God *we will set up our banners.*" There is another derivation, suggested by the Assyrian, that would be much more appropriate. In that language **dagala** means "to look to," and hence "to trust," "to confide in," and in the causative form, "to commit," "to entrust to the care of." Thus Asshurbanipal speaks of "servants looking to or beholding my face." R. V. I. 70, 76, also A. M. 42, 19, 25. So also he says that the gods **zanin ishriitishuun ushadgilu panuua,** the adorning of their shrines entrusted to me. The goddess Ishtar said to Esarhaddon (**Asshur akh iddina,** Asshur has given a brother), R. IV. 68. 2. 28 and 29, **Mutaakh enika, ana aashi dugulanni:** direct your eyes to me, look to me. A hymn to the sun god says, R. IV., 19. No. 2. 53–55, "Thou art the enlightener of the regions of the far-off sky, and of the great earth; their cynosure (**digilshina**) art thou." In the light of this meaning of the word that Psalm would read, "We will rejoice in thy salvation, and hold our eyes fixed upon the name of our God." So also Cant. 5: 10, is not "the standard bearer among ten thousand," but the one among them all who attracts our loving gaze. The Hebrew is דגול. See Bib. Sacra. 1884. p. 379. See "Look upon the face."

DAGON.

1 Sam. 5:4. And when they arose early on the morrow morning, behold Dagon was fallen upon his face to the ground

before the ark of the Lord; and the head of Dagon and both the palms of his hands *lay* cut off upon the threshold; only the stump of Dagon was left to him.

Dagon is generally regarded as the god of the Philistines. We read of the house (temple) of Dagon at Ashdod, 1 Sam. 5:2, and there seems to have been another at Gaza, Judg. 16:21, 23. The Philistines fastened the head of Saul in the temple of Dagon, 1 Chron. 10:10, but we are not told whether it was one of these two or another in some other city. A town in Judah bore the name of Beth Dagon, Josh. 15:41, and there was another of the same name in the tribe of Asher. Josh. 19:27.

There was also a Babylonian **Dagan, Da** in Accadian meaning a summit, and **gan** being the participle of the verb "to be" (H. L. 188. note), so that Dagan means "the exalted one." Asshurnatsirpal, B. C. 883-858, calls himself "the beloved of Anu and Dagon." R. I. 17. 10, 11, also R. of P. new II. 135, and A. M. 5. 2.

Sargon, B. C. 722-705, assumes the same title. See Prof. Lyon's Sargon I. 1 and 30. 1 and 31. 1. He also says, do. do. 13. 10 and 40. 10 and 41. 10, that "he has extended his protection over the city of Kharran and (as the warrior of, or) according to the ordinance of Anu and Dagan, had written down their laws." Now Kharran (way) was a sort of half-way house between Babylonia and Palestine, and so formed a connecting link between the Dagan of Assyria and his name-sake among the Philistines.

The general opinion has been that Dagon bore the form of a fish, but there is nothing to give rise to such an opinion either in the records of the Greeks or the Assyrians. The Scriptures certainly do not teach such an idea. The only ground for it is the fact that the Hebrew word דג means fish; but that is no sufficient basis. As well might we claim that Sharon meant the royal demesne because שר means prince in Hebrew and **shar** is king in Assyrian.

דגן (grain) is a much more likely derivation, as Philo Biblius of Gebal (Jebail) says in one place, "Dagon, who is Σιτων, "Siton," the god of grain, and in another, "Dagon, since he invented grain (siton) and the plough, is called Ζευς Αροτριος, *arotrios*. (Sanconiathon, ed. Orelli, pp. 26 and 32.) There is a seal of crystal in

the Ashmolean Museum at Oxford, England, inscribed in Phœnician letters "to Baal Dagon," but the symbol engraved on it is
not a fish, but a tree. (Prof. Sayce in S. S. Times, May 27, 1893.)

True, there is a fish god found on the Assyrian monuments,
but it has no connection with Dagon. It represents **Ea** or **Oannes,**
as Berossos calls him, the god of **Eridu** (Abu Shaherain), which
was once a seaport in the Persian Gulf. Berossos tells us that
he came out of the Erythrean Sea in the morning, instructed
men in useful arts all day, and then returned to his watery home
at night. Dagon, however, is not associated with **Ea,** but with
Anu, the god of the sky. See S. I. I. Still, even in the American edition of Smith's Dictionary, a copy of a bas-relief of
Oannes, or **Ea,** the god of pure life, is made to represent Dagon,
and the old definition of Gesenius, "diminutive of Dag, little
fish, or dear little fish," is given as the true etymology of the
term, and Alexander's Kitto argues very lamely against the derivation from dagan (grain).

It was not the body of a fish, but of a man, whose head and
hands were cut off that lay on the threshold of the temple of
Ashdod. The Septuagint adds "his feet" also, and a fish has
neither hands nor feet.

DARKNESS.

Job 10: 21. The land of darkness and of the shadow of
death. 22. A land of thick darkness, as darkness itself, a land
of the shadow of death, without any order, and where the light
is as darkness.

The writer of Ishtar's descent to Sheol, in Assyrian **mat la
nugaa** the land (whence is) no return, calls it **biti shu iribushu
zuummuu nuuru,** the house whose entrance is the taking away
of light. R. IV. 31. 7; also in D. L. 110. 7, and A. M. 52. 7.
Line 9 of the same reads as follows: **nuuru ul immaru, ina ituti
ashba:** the light is not seen; in darkness it dwells.

The ideas are alike in both Job and the Assyrian, but the
expression of them is immeasurably more poetic in the former.
There is a blackness of darkness, especially in the statement
that there the light is as darkness, compared to which the other
is tame and commonplace.

84   ASSYRIAN ECHOES OF THE WORD.

DEDICATION.

Neh. 12:27. To keep the dedication, חנכה, with gladness, both with thanksgivings and with singing, with cymbals, psalteries and with harps.

Under "Music" is given a bas-relief of a musical procession representing such a scene with great vividness.

And, R. V. 10. 106 and 107, Asshurbanipal tells us after describing his palace at Nineveh, which he was not ashamed to name **bit riduti** (domus coitionis), **sipir ipsiiti aqtsur niqani urri-ikhti aqqaa ana ilani biliya ina Khidaati risaati usharrishu**: the work of its construction I put together; willing * sacrifices I offered to the gods my lords; with joy and rejoicing I dedicated it.

DELUGE, THE.

Traditions of the Deluge exist in many lands, not in the old world only, but also in the new. It was to be expected then that among the old records of Babylonia we should find some account of an event that made so permanent an impression on the race. Nor are we disappointed. In the palace of Asshurbanipal, on the mound of Koyunjik, Mr. Layard found a chamber where clay tablets of all shapes and sizes had been stored away. The clay was very fine, the characters were formed on it while soft, and then it was burned, the tablets having been perforated with small holes to permit the escape of the gases in the fire, so that they should not crack or lose their shape. The inscriptions were in the cuneiform character which does not represent letters but syllables; many characters are used as ideograms, *i. e.*, each one represents a word or object. Thus the character **mat** represents also country, for **matu** is country; and **shu** stands also for **kishatu**, a multitude, or **shanitu**, repetition. Inscribed cylinders with from six to ten sides were deposited in the foundations of temples and palaces as we deposit documents in corner-stones. One was placed under each corner and contained the annals of the royal builder.

The early literature of Babylonia astonishes us by its

---

* Literally "hastened." I know not how sacrifices could be hastened, unless by the fact that the victims submitted without resistance to their fate.

amount and variety. Nor is it lacking in beauty or finish. They had works on grammar, mathematics, astronomy, geography, history, and jurisprudence. Bilingual lexicons also explained the obsolete Accadian in the spoken language, which was Shemitic. There were poems also, and mythological traditions. There were many copies made of important works, for though there was no press there were many scribes, and many cities had their libraries, so that we may perhaps handle the identical tablet that has been read by Daniel, Ezekiel, Nehemiah, or even Abraham.

Perhaps no Assyrian library was larger than that of Asshurbanipal already mentioned, and in examining a mass of broken fragments in the British Museum that once belonged to it George Smith discovered pieces that seemed to speak of the Deluge, and having put them together with great labor found an account of that event narrated by **Khasisadra,** or **Shamash Napishti,** the Chaldean Noah, to **Izdubar,** who is supposed by many to represent the Nimrod of Genesis. It forms the eleventh book of an epic in twelve books. Izdubar, suffering with painful disease, comes to his ancestor who dwells as a god at the mouth of the Euphrates, and learns from him the story of the flood.

It is vain to inquire which is the more ancient account, the Mosaic or the Chaldean, for just as these Izdubar tablets were copied by the royal scribes in Nineveh from much older ones brought from Babylonia, so it is probable that Moses also had very ancient records from which he was guided by the Spirit of God in writing a true history of the past. But which was the older, the tablets copied under the superintendence of **Ishtarshum-eshesh** or the records in the hands of Moses, who shall decide? The same providence of God may throw light on this question hereafter that has so wonderfully opened up the buried treasures of the past to us to-day; for the same God who has led us so far is able to lead us still further in our knowledge of ancient days.

It will doubtless be found, when we know exactly how many years transpired between the Deluge and the formation of the first Izdubar tablets in Chaldea, that the period was long enough to bring about many changes in the tradition before it was stereotyped in baked clay; and Moses may either have had access to earlier sources of information, or the Spirit of God may have guided him to reject the errors and follies which idolatry had already introduced into the record. No one who believes that "God has of old time spoken unto the fathers in the prophets by divers portions and in divers manners" (Heb. 1:1) can for a moment question the fact of such guidance. Nor can we call in question the antiquity of this inspiration when Zecharias was inspired to tell us (Luke 1:70) that "God spake by the mouth of his holy prophets which have been since the world began." The older writers, then, whom Moses followed may have been equally inspired of God with himself, at least so as to furnish a reliable basis for his record of the past.

We shall find the Chaldean tradition of the Deluge differing in many things from the inspired record, but in most of the points of diversity it will not require very long study to distinguish truth from error, though there is a morbid scrupulosity that may feel tempted to withhold approval from the inspired account because it is ours, and early associations have prejudiced us in its favor, and to look favorably on the other because it comes from another source, or even because it is the less credible of the two. The impulse that prompts to help the man who is under, or who has no friends, may be found operative here also.

And yet it may be well to remember that if both accounts had come to us from sources equally deserving of credit we must show them equal favor, but if one comes from a people noted for their immorality, if this immorality went on till just as their palaces were buried out of sight so they also sank into the grave that had been dug by their own vices, we may well question the account emanating from such a source wherever it differs from the other. In such matters moral character tells. One who knows affirms, "Either make the tree good and its fruit good, or make the tree corrupt and the fruit corrupt; for the tree is known by its fruit" (Matt. 12:33). If, now, the other comes from a different people, who, though also by nature children of wrath, were yet subjected to a moral discipline that lifted them steadily towards holiness, if, though at times this upward movement seemed irregular, yet it was moved forward by one who never faltered, and if the Scriptures given through that people are the source of all spiritual life in the most favored lands to-day, then may we expect to find truth in the line of this moral progress. At any rate we should not accept the latest novelty simply because it contradicts Holy Scripture. Scripture has more than a claim to inspiration. The Quran and the Book of Mormon have that, but the claim of the Bible is established by its fruits on a foundation that cannot be removed, but abideth for ever.

So far we have had reference to the character of the two nations and their Scriptures. Let us also glance at their contents. If anything is settled in religion it is that there is only one living and true God. What intelligent man believes that Noah was a polytheist? Yet the Chaldean account of the Deluge in connection with that event describes the acts and words of **Anu** and **Ea**, of **Bil** (Bel), and **Nabu** (Nebo), of **Ishtar** and **Rammanu** (Rimmon), besides goddesses and demigods without number. In such a pantheon Noah would never recognize the God with whom he walked. What would he say of gods who "huddled together in terror like dogs" or who "swarmed like flies over a dead carcase?" and yet, as we shall see, these words are used of the gods of Chaldea. If the record errs on a point so fundamental how can we trust it in other matters when it contradicts the Scriptures?

This early departure from monotheism is a proof of the inspiration of Holy Scripture with its revelation of one living and true God that has not yet received the attention it deserves. Genesis is more trustworthy than this Izdubar tablet because written under the inspiration of the Holy Spirit, and that guidance was given in a way that left Moses free to use every written help within his reach, and God took care that the result was in accordance with the facts. We know there are many different traditions. One where Noah is known as Ogyges; another in which he is called Deucalion. That of Apamea, where he and his wife are pictured standing inside the ark and the name Noe written on it in ancient letters. Besides these, Hierapolis and Samothracia, Megara and distant China had each its tradition, yea, even Mexico also, and other American nations. Then we are not to suppose that the patriarchs learned nothing from generation to generation, for they constantly received instruction from Him who was "the light of the world." Besides, the flood was not further removed from Abraham than the Reformation is from us, and an intelligent Christian in New England can appreciate that Reformation better than some learned German professors.

That the use of other records by the sacred writers is not inconsistent with inspiration is manifest from the number of ancient writings either quoted or referred to in the Old Testament; *e. g.*, the Book of Jasher, Josh. 10 : 13 ; the Book of the Wars of the Lord, Num. 21 : 14 ; the Book of Nathan the Prophet, 2 Chron. 9 : 29 ; the History of Shemaiah the Prophet, 2 Chron. 12 : 15 ; the History of Iddo the Seer, 2 Chron. 13 : 22 ; the prophecy of Ahijah the Shilonite, 2 Chron. 9 ; 29, etc. The inspired writer is not less under divine control in rejecting what is erroneous in previous records than in writing down a direct revelation of truths previously unknown. So we are not at all concerned to know how many previous records Moses had access to in performing the work assigned him.

One mode of attack on the book of Moses has been to deny the existence of writing at a period so early as that in which he lived ; but Egyptian research has shown that the great pyramids of Gizeh were in course of erection and hieroglyphic writing already fully developed at a time when, according to our chronology, the creation was taking place. H. L. 33. The statues also discovered at Telloh, on which an inscription tells us that the stone, a hard diorite, was brought from the land of Magan, (the Sinaitic peninsula) may be roughly dated at about B. C. 4000. H. L. p. 137. These, to say nothing of other discoveries, set that objection forever at rest.

Unexpected light on this point has also come from another quarter. In the winter of 1877 tablets covered with cuneiform characters were found among the mounds of Tel el Amarna, on the eastern bank of the Nile, half-way between Minieh and Siout. These were government despatches from rulers in Assyria, Babylonia, Kappadokia, Syria, and elsewhere, to the kings of Egypt, Amenophis III. and his son Amenophis IV., on public affairs, and as Asshur Yuballidh of Assyria and Burna Buriyas of Babylonia were among the correspondents the date of the despatches must be *circa* B. C. 1430. So here we have, not copies of, but the identical letters, written at least 100 years before the exodus of Israel from Egypt, showing that writing was then practised all over Western Asia.

It would be very unsatisfactory to give the whole of this eleventh Izdubar tablet as we now have it, there are so many imperfect lines, and so many lacking altogether, but portions can be selected which will convey a good idea of the thread of the story. At the outset we read:

> The divine **Gisdubar** (or Izdubar) said to **Khasisadra** the far away,
> Do I really behold thee? Thy form has not changed. As I am, so art thou.

A few lines later **Khasisadra** replies:

> "Let me unfold to thee the story of the preservation,
> And the decree of God let me relate to thee.
> Thou knowest the city of **Surippak** on the banks of the Euphrates.
> It is an ancient city, and the great gods
> To the production of a deluge gave their minds."

Then, after mentioning several things, the god **Ea** says:

> "O dweller in **Surippak,** son of **Ubaratutu,**
> Leave thy house, build a ship, gather into it the chief (heads) of living creatures,
> For they will destroy the seed of life, both of cattle and of wild beasts.

Passing now over more than 50 fragmentary lines it proceeds:

All that I had I gathered together. All that I had of silver and gold I gathered together.
All that I had of every kind of seed of living creatures I gathered together.
I put on board the ship all my family and near kindred.
Cattle of the field, wild beasts of the field, and all the workmen I put on board.
The god Shamash (the sun) issued a command.
A voice cried, In the evenings
The heavens will rain down destruction.
Enter into the ship and shut the door.
That command was urgent.
Four days I turned imploringly to his face,
Till I feared to look one day longer.
(Then) I entered the ship and shut the door.
I committed the great structure and its contents to **Buzurkurgal** the mariner.
Then the goddess named **Shalmu Sheri ina namari** (the water of dawn at daybreak)
Rose from the horizon (foundation of heaven) as a black cloud.

In it **Rammanu** (Rimmon, god of the air) thundered.
The gods **Nabu** (Nebo) and **Sharru** (the king) went on before.
The throne-bearers (compare Ezek. 1) bore it over mountain and plain.
The **Targulli** (servitors ?) of the great god of pestilence filled all with confusion.
The god **Ninip** marched in advance, causing the streams to flow.
The **Annunaki** (spirits of earth, demons) carried blazing torches.
In their brightness the earth shimmered;
The rushing roar of **Rammanu** reached the skies;
All brightness was turned into darkness.
They laid waste the earth like (an invading army ?)
Swiftly sped the winds, charging on men like the shock of battle;
Brother saw not brother. In all the heaven one could not discern another.
The gods were terror-stricken by the storm.
They sought shelter. They went up to the heaven of **Anu** (highest heaven),
Like dogs the gods huddled together. They crouched down by the walls.
Ishtar cried out like a mother in her pangs.
Thus spake the great goddess (god) of kindly speech :
That race is verily turned to clay;
A calamity which I had plainly foretold to the assembled gods.
I proclaim war for the destruction of my people.
I, their mother, did not bring men forth that they should fill the sea like the spawn of fishes.
The gods as well as the **Annunaki** joined in her weeping;
The gods sat in their places dissolved in tears;
They covered their lips, mourning the flood so near at hand.
Six days and seven nights the storm advanced, the flood and the tempest destroyed.
At the dawn of the seventh day the storm slackened its fierce attack. It was calm;
The sea went down, the evil wind and flood abated.
My eyes were fastened on the sea; I lamented aloud;
For the whole race of men had turned to clay;
Like logs (**Uribi**) the corpses floated hither and thither.
I opened the window and the light fell upon my face.
I writhed in agony; I sank down; I gave myself up to weeping;
On my face my tears flowed down.
I looked towards the shore,
And to the height of twelve (measures ?) the land rose up before me.
To the land of **Nitsir** (deliverance) I steered (stood) the ship.
The mountains of the land of **Nitsir** held it fast; it could not float.

This is repeated six times for six days; then at dawn on the seventh—

I sent forth a dove; I let it go. The dove went forth and returned.
A resting-place it did not find; it turned back.
I sent forth a swallow; I let it go. The swallow went forth and returned.
A resting-place it did not find; it turned back.
I sent forth a raven; I let it go. The raven went forth and saw the subsiding of the waters.

It ate, it waded about, but did not return.
Then I sent forth to the four winds (all that were on board) (?) I offered sacrifice.
I erected an altar on the summit of the mountains;
I set the sacred vessels in order by sevens :
Underneath them I placed cane, cedar, and cypress (pine?)
The gods smelled the pleasant fragrance,
And like flies gathered round the officiating priest.
Then the great mother at her approach
Lifted up the great splendors (bows?) which **Anu** had made as his **Tsukhu** (?)

This is enough to show that those early days produced some lines of rare poetic beauty; but we omit the consideration of it as a work of art to dwell on its relations to the inspired record of the same event.

The two narratives have many things in common. Each assigns to the Deluge a divine origin. Each affirms that all outside of the ark, or ship, perished. It was characteristic of a maritime people to call it a ship and not a shapeless ark. In each the animals were taken on board by divine direction. Each caulks the vessel inside and out with bitumen, though the quantity in the Chaldean account seems immense—three **shars**; for a shar is sixty shosshes, and a shossh contains sixty smaller measures, so that a shossh is 10,800 measures of some kind. Each affirms that the vessel was built on dry ground, that it had a roof or deck, and that, after the inmates had entered, the door was closed, though in one account man closes it by divine command, and in the other God does it with his own hand—an important difference, in view of the pressure that might have been used at the last moment to keep it open. It was fitting, too, that God himself should shut out those outside as well as shut in those inside—a point specially important now, when men question whether the door will be shut hereafter, and those outside, through their own fault, shall plead in vain, "Lord, Lord, open unto us."

The two narratives also present some marked contrasts. Though they both agree that the race was destroyed, yet the reason given is not the same. The Bible tells us it was because the wickedness of man had become so flagrant that it could no longer be endured—a reason worthy of a holy God, who declares death to be the wages of sin.

Then, though the flood was dreadful, yet it was righteous, yea, even beneficent; for, had the foul orgies and bloody violence then prevailing been allowed to go on, greater suffering would have fallen to the lot of a greater number, as the race went on increasing, or it would have arrested that increase and the race had perished by a lingering process through its own corruption.

It was mercy, then, that sent the flood to arrest this process and prepare the way for better things. On the other hand, the Chaldean account simply says that the gods set their minds on causing a flood, but no reason is given for that determination. Then the gods take sides. Some passionately bring it on. The angry **Bil** demands, "Has any one come out alive? let not a man live from the destruction." Others oppose and bewail it. One god rebukes another for losing his temper, and after that the passing statement that "the sinner has borne his sin" carries with it no moral force. Not so does the word of God recount his righteous judgments.

In Prof. Sayce's "Fresh Light," p. 27, is the following: "It has often been remarked that, though traditions of a universal or a partial deluge are found all over the world, it is only in the Old Testament that the cause assigned for it is a moral one. The Chaldean account of the Deluge offers an exception to the rule. Here, as in Genesis, **Sisuthrus,** the Accadian Noah, is saved from destruction on account of his piety, the rest of mankind being drowned as a punishment for their sins."

It would be very pleasant to be able to speak so strongly, but while the statement quoted in the text implies that the Deluge was the result of the sins of men, I fail to find any positive record of the piety of Khasisadra.

Prof. Sayce, p. 32, translates **"Ruumi aa ibbatiik shuduud aa—"** may the just prince not be cut off; may the faithful not be destroyed. But unless he has a different text from that in D. L., 3d edition, the words simply mean, "Have compassion; let him not be cut off; be kind; let him not —" the rest of the sentence is wanting. Evidently some verb followed equivalent to the "cut off" of the previous clause, but there is nothing whatever concerning the moral character of **Khasisadra,** though we may infer from his being "raised to be like the gods" that he was not unworthy of that honor.

The proportions of the ark in Genesis are those of our best ships, but the extravagant measurements which some have read into the Chaldean accounts are of no authority whatever. Unfortunately the numbers are illegible, as the tablet is injured at that place, and we must wait for the discovery of another copy to fill the blank; but so long as the Turkish Government pursues the "dog-in-the-manger" policy of neither excavating themselves nor suffering others to make excavations, it is to be feared that the day of additions to our present stock of material is far distant.

There is another seeming discrepancy between the two accounts, which is only seeming. Genesis says that the ark rested on the mountains of Ararat, while the Chaldean tradition makes the ship ground on the mountains of **Nitsir,** now Mount Elwend. So also a Moslem tradition designates a third place, Jebel Judi, in Kurdistan. At first the contradiction seems hopeless, but when we remember that a line from southern Babylonia to Mount Elwend if prolonged goes into Armenia, that a line from Mesopotamia drawn through Mount Judi touches the same region, and that the inspired writer does not say Mount Ararat, which is one prominent mountain, but the mountains of Ararat, *i. e.*, of Armenia, for so the Assyrian inscriptions designate that country (**Urardi**), the seeming contradiction is in a fair way to be explained.

In some things, however, the two accounts do not agree; as, for example, the number of those who were on board. Genesis limits it to Noah and his family, including his sons' wives and perhaps their little children. There may possibly have been servants also, to help care for so many animals. Still they are not mentioned, and it is not best to be wise above what is written. The Chaldean account, however, adds not only manservants and maid-servants, but relatives and mechanics, and even sailors also. Now if the ship had cleared for a foreign port, and must be navigated into a specified harbor, sailors might have been essential; but if it is merely to float about till the flood subsides, what need of sailors? Wherever it touches dry land, that will be its destination, unguided by human care.

The accounts differ also in the duration of the flood. According to Moses, the windows of heaven were opened on the 17th day of the second month. Then the waters continued rising for forty days, and prevailed upon the earth 150 days. Then the ark grounded on the 17th day of the seventh month, and the tops of the mountains appeared seventy-three days later. Forty days after that Noah sent out the raven that never came back, and then the dove which returned. A week later he sent it forth again, and it brought back an olive leaf, a pleasant proof that the waters were drying up. Then, on the first day of the new year, Noah removed the covering of the ark and looked out, and lo! the face of the ground was dry. He did not leave the ark, however, till the 27th day of the second month, 375 days after the date when the Lord had shut him in. This long period is required for the rise and slow decrease of so great a mass of water; but the Izdubar story makes it reach its height in seven days, and then disappear in seven more, a manifest incongruity. Even had it reached its height in seven days, then the tempest was of course proportionately severe, and how could the sailors endure it? When **Khasisadra** wants to look out he must open a window, and we do not read that it had been opened before. Were the sailors, then, on deck? But why expose them to such a tempest when they had nothing to do? and if, like the others, they remained under cover, then why were they there at all? If they were outside, were their provisions outside also? or how were they fed?

Both accounts mention the sending forth of the raven and the dove, but in Genesis the raven characteristically does not return. The dove returns twice, and poetry presents no picture more beautiful than its return with the olive leaf in its mouth. Perhaps the Babylonians had some mythological idea connected with the swallow that led to the insertion of that bird in their tradition.

Each account mentions that sacrifices were offered after the flood, but one calls forth the gracious promise that no deluge shall ever again destroy the earth, with the beautiful rainbow for its seal. It is doubtful whether the character translated splendors may not be an error of the scribe for rainbow, since the sign for bow very much resembles it; still there is no mention of the promise of which it is the divinely appointed memorial.

Idolatry is noted for the want of love to its gods, who are served through fear, and not from affection. Even the Moslem, though he maintains the unity of God, does not make heaven consist in the enjoyment of God, but in being ministered to by 80,000 beautiful attendants and the seventy-two houris assigned to him for his special delectation; in the 300 golden dishes that shall be set upon his table, each containing a different food, the last morsel of which shall be as delicious as the first, and eaten with equal relish; in perpetual youth—in fact, in anything and everything but God. We are not surprised that the expectants of such a heaven are like the heaven which they expect.

One hardly needs to contrast the moral influence of the two narratives. We have already seen the lack of that clear exhibition of the demerit of sin in the Chaldean tradition as compared with the inspired record, which tells us that the wickedness of men was so great as to grieve God at his heart and call for a righteous retribution that would prevent the waters of a more destructive deluge.

Two other points may be briefly alluded to. Genesis, subordinating the reputation of a good man to the well-being of the race, impartially and without any attempt at apology tells the sad story of the drunkenness of Noah. The Chaldean epic makes **Khasisadra** lay in wines, to use his own words, "like the waters of the rivers," without one hint of danger, while the sin of the patriarch is passed over in silence.

Again, Holy Scripture in like manner exposes the falsehood of Gehazi, the servant of Elisha, and shows how the leprosy of Naaman was transferred to the untruthful attendant. But this sacred book of Babylonia tells how **Ea** betrayed the purposes of the gods, and then makes him say, "I did not reveal them; I only caused **Khasisadra** to see a vision, and he heard them;" and this pitiful prevarication proceeds from the lips of one of their so-called "great gods." What must have been the

DESTRUCTION BY COMMAND.

1 Sam. 15:18. The Lord sent thee... and said, Go and utterly destroy the sinners, the Amalekites... till they be consumed. v. 19. Wherefore then didst thou not obey the voice of the Lord, but didst fly upon the spoil?

This is the rebuke of Saul by the prophet. The sword of God smites on account of transgression, and not for plunder.

Compare with this the inscription of Asshurbanipal concerning **Madaktu,** one of the leading cities of Elam, R. V. 7. 13, 14. Ass'l. 237, 40, 41: he calls it "**Madaktu** the city which **ina kibit** (by the command of) Asshur and Ishtar I destroyed, laid waste, and carried away its spoil." The contrast is instructive. See also the case of Achan, Josh. 7, though in some cases the ministers of the divine retribution were allowed a reward for their work. It would require a great effort to imagine a king of Assyria forbidding his soldiers to touch the spoils of a city which they had captured.

DETERMINATIVES.

These are a great help in reading Assyrian. They are ideograms, or signs representing classes of objects which are prefixed to objects belonging to that class. Thus, a wedge standing on its point is used to show that what follows is a proper name. The sign **sal** shows that a woman's name follows after it, **mat** indicates that the name of a country or district follows, **alu** denotes that it is the name of a town or city, **ilu** that it is the name of a god, **naru** denotes the name of a river or lake, **arkhu** of a month, **khu,** the ideogram for **itstsuru,** marks out birds, **kakkabu** stars, **aan, ta an** or **kam** numbers, **imiru** animals, **nunu** fishes, **ku** clothing, **amilu** a tribe, or people, or an official, **itsu** a tree, or vessel of wood, or an instrument, **abnu** a stone, whether precious or otherwise.

Of course these signs do not have these meanings always, in other positions, and yet their use as determinatives is a very great help. Generally they precede the words which they define, but some, as **ki,** country, and others, follow after.

DEVILS. שדים

Deut. 32:17. They sacrificed unto demons which were not gods. The Authorized Version reads "devils."

Gesenius renders שדי "idols pp. lords," and adds that the Septuagint rendered it demons because the Jews thought idols were demons who thus caused themselves to be worshipped.

The monuments give a more satisfactory view of the matter. Those who have read the volumes of Layard remember the frontispieces to his first work on Nineveh. Vol. I. showed the lowering of one of the great winged bulls from its place at the principal entrance of the palace in Nimrood, and Vol. II. showed the same *en route* to the Tigris. Another view is given I. 119, though a better head of the animal appears in II. 228. These were called **shidu,** plural, **shidi.** The frontispiece of B. and N. shows the positions they occupied in the palace as it was restored by Mr. Ferguson, and p. 112 gives an Assyrian view of the journey of one of these from the quarry to the royal gate.

These huge idols were the guardian deities of the king's palace, and were believed to defend it from all harm. They were worshipped like other gods, and the sin of Israel consisted in sacrificing to them as to God. Our thoughts revert at once to the worship of the calf at Horeb, and we can appreciate the situation. Their leader has been absent many days. They are strangers in a strange place, unknown trials lie before them, and they feel the need of a guardian who should lead them out of their present perils into safety.

It may be said that they had come out of Egypt, not from Assyria; but the tablets from Tel el Amarna, dating from the reign of Amenophis III., show that a constant intercourse existed between Egypt and Assyria long before the Exodus, and they show also that the golden calf may have full as intimate a relation to the Assyrian **shidu** as to the sacred bull of Egypt. Israel would naturally be more disposed to favor the religious ideas of the Pharaohs that showed kindness to the sons of Jacob than those of the Pharaoh that knew not Joseph, in their alterations of the ritual God had give them.

These **shidi** were also called cherubs. Indeed, the word cherub may have been derived originally from the Babylonian. Does not this description of their office as protectors give new meaning to the expression "covering cherub" applied to Tyre in Ezek. 28 : 14 and 16? True, it may refer to the cherubs covering the mercy-seat with their wings, but the office of the **shidi** as guardians of the palace may show why this form was selected to cover and protect the mercy-seat, as well as a reason why the name is applied to Tyre.

DEVISE EVIL.

To the reader of Scripture this phrase is very familiar; as in Prov. 3 : 29 : "Devise not evil against thy neighbor, seeing he dwelleth securely by thee." Compare also 14 : 22 ; Ezek. 11 : 2 ; Dan. 11 : 25.

It is not less frequent in the monuments. Asshurbanipal says of **Tarquu** (Tirhakah) and other rebellious rulers in Egypt, **ishtiniu amat limuttim**: they devised an evil plot. R. V. I. 128 and A. M. 46. 20. See also R. V. 25, A. M. 48. 6 and Ass'l. 27, 31. Another verb, **ikpuud**, with exactly the same meaning, is also used, R. V. 1. 120. A. M. 46, 11. and Ass'l. 24. 2 ; and the contiguity of the two quotations is an indication how frequently such phrases occur. The latter verb, *e. g.*, occurs also in R. V. 4. 43, A. M. 25, 32 and Ass'l. 162, 100. and in R. V. 4. 68, A. M. 26. 20, and Ass'l. 165, 4. But it is not necessary to go farther.

DIAL.

2 Kings 20 : 11 speaks of the dial of Ahaz. Compare also Isaiah 38 : 8. The Hebrew word is סעלוה, maaloth, which Gesenius renders, "dial, as divided up into degrees;" others, less correctly, understand "the steps of a staircase." It is a peculiarity of the Hebrew, in describing a foreign production, to use some simple term that paints a picture of the object, where the foreign name is not transferred bodily. The Chaldee paraphrase of 2 Kings 20 : 11 is אבן שעיא, hour-stone, and the same expression is used in Isa. 38 ; 8.

Without going into any discussion of the modus of the miracle, for God is never at a loss in such things, our object will be gained if we call attention to the fact that the gnomon or dial originated in Babylonia; and the celebrated one at Delhi, in India, the capital of the Mogul Empire, indicates how they may have existed in connection with the temples, though of course without being necessarily of exactly the same form in all respects. Herodotus says that the Greeks derived the dial from the Babylonians, and Vitruvius says that their knowledge of its most ancient form was obtained from Berossus, the Chaldean. ix. 9. Ahaz seems to have been smitten with the love of new things, as his copying the form of the altar in Damascus shows, 2 Kings 16: 10, and through his acquaintance with Tiglath Pileser III., on the same visit, it may be that he had the dial in question set up in his palace in a position where it could be readily seen from his sick room. Even though he may not have learned about it directly from his Assyrian visitor, yet his tastes in that direction abundantly account for the introduction of the then new and wonderful means for measuring time.

DIVORCE.

Matt. 5: 31, 32. It was said also, Whosoever shall put away his wife, let him give her a writing of divorcement: but I say unto you, that every one who putteth away his wife, saving for the cause of fornication, maketh her an adulteress: and whosoever shall marry her when she is put away committeth adultery.

Our Saviour did nothing to elevate women that wrought with greater efficiency to that end than this stand that he took on the subject of divorce. Man in his tyranny over woman had broken down every safeguard of the sanctities of the home, till woman stood a helpless victim, liable at any moment, on the slightest pretext, to be rudely torn from her throne in that home and cast out to utter misery; not only homeless but separated from those to whom she had given life, and from whom her heart refused to be severed however she might be shut out from their society. Christ stopped this wrong and outrage, and gave her peace; now, so far as society is moulded according to the mind of Christ, woman sits secure from the infliction of such wrong.

Though the testimony of the monuments relieves us from the incubus of that story of Herodotus that every Babylonian woman must perforce sacrifice her virtue once in her lifetime to the gods—and it is a very great relief—yet the following law, that had been handed down from the old Accadian period, shows how absolutely the Babylonian wife lay at the mercy of a rich and unscrupulous husband:

"If a husband say to his wife, Thou art not my wife, half a maneh of silver he weighs out" (by way of fine). R. of P. III. 24.

It is to be hoped that even this paltry sum went to the divorced wife for the supply of her present necessities, though the law contains no hint to that effect. But note the unblushing wickedness of the statute. Not even the shadow of a reason is assigned for the procedure, nor even a hint that the pretence of assigning a reason forms a part of the ceremony. The man may do this because he wants to do it, without any other cause. Then there is no question that she is his wife, for the law is based on the assumption that she is, and as such possessed of all the rights of any wife; but if to his true and lawful wife he simply utters the lie, "Thou art not my wife," that lie *ipso facto* is changed into the truth! While the man might send away the woman on the payment of so much money, unfaithfulness on her part was punished with death. Thus **Nabu ikhi addin,** in the days of Nebuchadrezzar, put into the marriage contract—if such a document may be so called—that in case he divorced his concubine and married another he should pay her six manehs of silver—about $250; but if she committed adultery she should be slain with an iron sword. Prof. Sayce's Social Life among the Assyrians, 46. It is some relief, however, to know that even a concubine must be divorced before a man could take another in her place. Then polygamy could have no place among such a people.

DOGS.

Job speaks, 30:1, of those "whose fathers I disdained to set with the dogs of my flock."

We find a striking illustration of these words in the declaration of Asshurbanipal concerning the Arab chief Vaiteh, son of Hazael, R.V. 8. 10–12 : **Ana kullum tanitti ilu Asshur u ilani rabuti** biliya annu kabtu imidsu ma, itsu shigaru ashkunshuma itti asi kalbi askunsshuma ushaantsir shu abulli qabal alu Nina nirib mashnakti adnaati : In order to show forth the glory of the god Asshur and the great gods my lords, I laid a heavy punishment upon him ; I put him in a cage, with asi (?) and dogs I enclosed him, and caused him to be kept inside the gate of Nineveh called **nirib mashnakti adnaati.**

Again, lines 27-29, he repeats, **Ina kibit ilani rabuti biliya ulli kalbi ashkunshuma ushaantsir shu shigaru :** By the command of the great gods my lords, with the dogs I placed him ; I caused him to be kept in a cage.

See also R. V. 9. 108-111. " With the dogs I placed him at the eastern gate in Nineveh ;" etc., etc.

The Jewish estimate of the dog is forcibly set forth in the question of David, 1 Sam. 24 : 14 : After whom dost thou pursue? after a dead dog, after a flea.

The dog does not appear in the earlier art of Assyria, even in Babylonia, where a valued breed existed. The only image of the animal we find belongs to the Sassanian period. Yet Merodach was said to have owned four divine hounds, named **Ukkumu,** the seizer; **Akkulu,** the devourer; **Ikshuda,** the capturer, and **Iltebu,** the pursuer.

In the fragment of a legend relating to Rammanu, a shepherd is told to rejoice for the message sent him by Ea through Merodach. " Ea has heard thee ; when the great dogs attack thee, then seize them from behind and throw them down, hold them and overcome them ; strike their head, pierce their breast," etc., etc. The dog is here an object of hate ; and a prayer against evil reads, " From the baleful fetter which injures the feet, the dog, the snake, the scorpion, the reptile, and whatever is baleful, may Merodach preserve us." H. L. 287-289.

In the palace of Asshurbanipal terra-cotta statuettes of his best dogs have been found, and bas-reliefs representing their achievements in the chase. P. and C. II. 144-147.

DOUBLED.

In Gen. 4 : 32 we read, both in the old version and the new revision, "and for that the dream was doubled unto Pharaoh twice." But if doubling anything makes two instead of one, doubling twice makes four out of one. Is that the meaning of the Hebrew in this passage? Was the dream repeated to Pharaoh four times? It is not strange that translators in the year 1611 should give such a rendering, for Hebrew grammars and lexicons were then very imperfect, but it is strange that our revisers in the year of grace 1885 should leave the error uncorrected.

The question hinges on the meaning of the Hebrew term *hishanoth* השנות infinite, absolute: niphal, from *shanah* שנה which Robinson's Gesenius renders to do the second time, to repeat, also to be different, to be changed. The niphal conjugation he renders to be repeated, and refers to this passage. In Syriac and Arabic *shanah* becomes *thanah*. Castell renders the Syriac *iteravit, repetiit, renarravit*, and Freytag translates the Arabic *thanah flexit, duplicavit, iteravit, repetivit*. Then the Hebrew might be rendered "for that the dream was repeated unto Pharaoh twice," which is precisely the rendering given of this sentence in the excellent Arabic version of our missionaries in Beirut: *wa ama a'n tikrar el hilim a'l a Phar'oon murretain* (and whereas the dream was repeated unto Pharaoh twice), and it is in accordance with the facts: for the seven years of famine were foretold to him twice—once under the figure of seven lean and ill-favored kine and again as seven blasted ears of grain.

It is interesting to note the mental process by which the verb "to double," came to mean show, or set forth. A narrative was counted as a repetition of the event narrated. The event itself was the original and the account given of it a duplicate of that original; hence such words an *re*late, *re*count, *re*peat, *re*port, *re*iterate, *re*hearse, *re*present, etc. This was the first step. Next the idea of repetition was lost sight of in the simple idea of telling or giving information. Thus, if a servant was sent to count sheep, his report might be taken as a counting over again, or as only making known the result of the count. A painting might be viewed as a second presentation to the eye of the object that had been before it once, and then simply as a representation of it in the sense of picturing it out. So a letter or written character represents a sound not by reproducing it, but simply serving as its symbol. In this case the seven years of famine were first symbolized by the kine, and again by the ears of grain, and the verb denotes the symbolizing of them twice over, and not a doubling of them twice, which would be a fourfold repetition. Again, our revisers render this same verb repeat in Prov. 17:9: "He that repeateth a matter separateth very friends." If *shanah* must always be rendered "doubled" why is it not so rendered here? and if it may be rendered "repeat" in Proverbs, why not in Genesis also? If it would be absurd to say, "He that doubleth a matter separateth friends," is it less absurd to speak of doubling a dream twice when the fact was that it was only set forth in two different ways? Surely the rendering of the Syriac and Arabic forms of the word by "repeated," ought to have suggested and sanctioned the same meaning here.

The Assyrian, however, renders very efficient help to the right rendering of this passage, for in that language the verb is exactly the same as the Hebrew, with the simple exception of the final termination. That according to Assyrian usage is **u : shanu** instead of *shana*. As yet we have no Assyrian lexicon, but the *Worterbuch* in D. L. renders it first *doppelt*, doubled, *zweifach sein*, to be twofold, then *erzahlen*, to tell, and *kundthun*, to make public, and A. M. renders it to be double, to repeat, inform.

If anything more was needed we have it to the full in the use of this verb in the inscriptions. Asshurbanipal the king of Assyria B. C. 668-626 (R. V. 2. 202. and A. M. 22. 17), in telling of a vision seen by Gyges, king of Lydia, adds, he sent by the hand of his messenger, **u ushaanaa yaati,** and repeated or showed it to me. Here the meaning of doubling is wholly out of the question. In R. IV. 50. 18 exactly the same word is used in the sense of "he revealed the decrees of the gods." Again, the same king says that a messenger of Ishtar of Arbela, R. V. 1. 63 and Ass'l. 123. 52, **ushaanaa yaati:** informed me, as before. The goddess of goddesses **shii tushannaka umma:** she repeateth to thee, or telleth thee thus. R. V. 1. 63 Ass'l. 125. 63. See also Ass'l. 103. 42 and 123. 52, and 119. 21 and 23. The last passage reads **ushaanuu:** they repeated the purport of his news. Would any one render it, they doubled the purport of his news? Again, after sending a threatening message to Indabigas, king of Elam, 180:104, he adds, "the messengers **la ushaannushu,** did not inform him, of the fixedness of my purpose." It would hardly do to render it, they did not double him of its fixedness.

In view of this repeated use of the same verb in Assyrian can we hesitate to render the Hebrew in this passage, "The dream was set forth or repeated to Pharaoh twice"? *i. e.*, by two different symbols.

DRAGON.

In Rev. 12:7 and 8 we read: "And there was war in heaven: Michael and his angels going forth to war with the dragon, and the dragon warred, and his angels; and they prevailed not, neither was their place found any more in heaven. And the great dragon was cast down, the old serpent, he that is called the Devil and Satan, the deceiver of the whole world; he was cast down to the earth, and his angels were cast down with him."

It is not proposed to give an exegesis of this prophecy, or to determine its position in chronology. Without undertaking to determine the relation of the two things to each other, or whether they have any connection at all, it is interesting to know that Chaldean mythological legends in connection with creation narrate a battle between **Bil Marduk,** *i. e.*, lord Merodach, the son of **Ea** or **Hea,** and **Tiamat** (Heb. תחום), the champion of the seven evil spirits, the dragon of the abyss (**apsu**). A previous creation seems to have taken place under evil auspices, and this combat was necessary to redeem it from the powers of darkness and bring it into relations with the light. The conflict enlists the deepest interest of the good gods. Bil Marduk is armed with the bow of Anu. He wields thunderbolts, evil winds, and a peculiar weapon, shaped like a sickle, that is usually represented in the bas-reliefs of this battle. In one of them, now in the British Museum, the dragon is represented with horns, wings, and a tail, four feet, and a head like a wild beast; its feet are like birds' feet and armed with claws. See Prof. Sayce's edition of Smith's Genesis, 62. The combat is described pp. 104-114, also in R. of P. 9. 135-140. But a better account of the whole legend appears in the new R. of P. I. 122-146, from the pen of

Prof. Sayce. It contains the best translation that has yet been made.

DREAMS AND VISIONS.

Some may wonder that an apostle should allow a vision of the night to influence his movements as Paul did, Acts 16:9, 10, but before the Bible was completed and in the hands of men dreams and visions played a much more important part in divine revelation than they do to-day. God spake to Abraham through them, Gen. 15:1, to Pharaoh, Gen. 41:1, to Job, 4:12–16, to Daniel, 1:17, 2:26, and to Nebuchadrezzar, Dan. 4:5. It is not strange, then, if they are mentioned frequently on the monuments. Asshurbanipal, R. V. 3. 120 and Ass'l. 123. 50, gives an account of a seer who saw a vision. This had reference to his campaign against Teumman, king of Elam, and is translated in R. of P. VII. 68.

Again, he tells that Asshur his god made Gyges, king of Lydia, to have a dream that led to his submission to Assyria. R. V. 2. 97, A. M. 22. 11, Ass'l. 73. 15. Again, R. V. 5. 98 and Ass'l. 221. 22–24, he says that Ishtar of Arbela, the goddess of war, made his army see a vision of approaching victory over Elam, which doubtless contributed to its own fulfilment. Nabonidus also, R. V. 64. 16, 17 and A. M. 35. 14, claims that Merodach in a vision commanded him to rebuild E Khulkhul, the temple of Sin (the moon god) in Kharran.

In R. IV. 66. 2 is a prayer offered after a bad dream, translated in R. of P. IX. 151 and 152.

Izdubar, like Pharaoh and the king of Babylon, offered a reward for the interpretation of a dream. C. G. 202 seq. 2d. ed.

DRINK-OFFERING.

The drink-offering or libation is appointed and described in Num. 15:5, 7, 10, also 28:7, 14; *viz.*, a quarter of a hin of wine for a lamb, a third of a hin for a ram, and half a hin for a bullock. So the pious Hebrew took the cup of salvation and called on the name of the Lord. At the same time he was forbidden to pour out drink-offerings to other gods. Jer. 7:18; 44:17, 19, 25.

Under the head of "Rites" will be found some account of Assyrian libations. One difference between them and the Jewish drink-offering was the use of beer as well as wine. R. IV. 62. No. 2 obv. 56 and 59 says **shikaru** (Heb. *sheker*) **u karanu iqqi:** offer beer and wine. The sheker is translated strong drink in our English version, and **iqqi** is literally "pour out." R. IV. 64 obv. 5 also says pour out **biris**, which was another kind of beer, but in what the exact difference consisted who knows? The libation was a favorite form of worship, and the use of the verb **naqu** to describe the act of sacrifice would seem to give prominence to the pouring out of the blood. The burning of the sacrifice was not made so prominent as it was in the Hebrew ritual.

DROUGHT, HORRORS OF.

Jer. 14:5. The hind also in the field calveth, and forsaketh her young because there is no grass.

This pitiful picture of animal suffering from excessive drought may be compared with the following from the description of the suffering in Arabia caused by Asshurbanipal taking possession of their wells of water, R. V. 9. 65–67, A. M. 32, 18–20, Ass'l. 276. 49–51: **Baakru sukhiru gutsur, lunum ina ili** VII. **taan mushiniqaati iniquuma shiispu la ushabbuu karasishunu:** The droves of young camels (?), the young buffaloes (?), and the lambs (though) they sucked their dams even seven times could not get enough to satisfy their hunger (stomachs).

One feels a sort of relief to think that those Assyrian soldiers, however callous they had grown in shedding human blood—and God only knows how much they did shed and with what aggravations of cruelty—yet noticed and recorded the sufferings of those dumb beasts as though they pitied them, so strangely inconsistent is man; or did they enter into such details because they enjoyed the suffering—as men now attend cockfights, and editors dilate on the bloody details of pugilistic encounters for the delectation of their readers?

DUST.

Gen. 3:14. Dust shalt thou eat all the days of thy life. Isa. 65:25. Psa. 72:9. And his enemies shall lick the dust. Mic. 7:17. This unusual use of language in the Hebrew, descriptive of the utter humiliation of the serpent, condemned to mingle the dust with the food which it ate from it—if not to eat dust itself—finds a parallel in the Assyrian.

In the account of the descent of Ishtar into Hades, R. I. 31. 8, D. L. 110. 8, A. M. 52. 8, the under world is described as **ashar iprati bubuussunu akalshunu tiittu**: a place of dust—their food, their eating, clay. Perhaps they got the idea from the fact that dust or loam was the food of the earth-worm in its under world.

DUST ON THE HEAD.

Joshua and the elders of Israel fell to the earth and put dust upon their heads before the ark of the Lord when Israel was defeated by the men of Ai, Josh. 7:6. Job's friends sprinkled dust upon their heads when they came to visit him, Job 11:12. Compare Neh. 9:1; 1 Sam. 4:12; 2 Sam. 1:2; Lam. 12:60, and Rev. 18:19.

In R. V. 4. 29, and Ass'l. 161. 88, **Asshurbanipal** says, Tammaritu, king of Elam, kissed the feet of my royalty, and **Qaqqaru ushishir ina ziqnishu**; threw earth (literally caused it to collect) upon his beard.

Joshua with his companions and Tammaritu, could either party have been ushered into the presence of the other during this acting out of their sorrow, would have needed no interpreter to tell how they severally felt, but only to explain the occasion of their trouble.

EAR, HEARING.

Isa. 50:4. He wakeneth my ear to hear, as they that are taught. v. 5. The Lord God hath opened mine ear.

These expressions show how much intelligence in those days was associated with hearing, and not as now with the use of the eye in reading, when almost every one reads and there is so much to be read. The same thing appears, only more fully, in the inscriptions.

Asshurbanipal says, Ass'l. 11. 6, 7: "The great gods in their assembly a prosperous fate have decreed to us, and have given me a broad ear **uznu rapaashtu**, *i. e.*, so as to take in sound better. So much did he pride himself on this that he mentions it in the colophon of works copied by his scribes from the Accadian. For a good illustration of this see R. V. 51. 4. 46, where at the close of the hymn to the sun god he says that Tasmitu (wife of Nebo) had given him broad ears.

EARRINGS AND IDOLS.

It is written in Gen. 35 : 4, "They gave unto Jacob all the strange gods which were in their hands and the rings which were in their ears, and Jacob hid them under the oak which was by Shechem."

This would seem to imply that figures of their idols were also on the earrings, else why were they hidden with the rest?

Is there, then, any trace of earrings discovered in the ruins of Assyria with images of idols traced on their surfaces? Mr. Layard (B. and N. p. 596) gives copies of moulds discovered in Nimrood and **Koyunjik** for casting earrings, and on these are several symbols of their gods, and also one image of a god with what seems to be a dog's head standing in a boat or ark, and holding up an object in each hand. On looking at it we are sure that if Jacob had found such an earring among the family jewelry he would at once have consigned it to the grave he had dug under the oak near Shechem.

P. and C. II. 362 give engravings of two earrings found at Niffer (**Nipur**), Babylonia, now in the British Museum. They represent a child with a very large head and long hair, who may be some mythological personage.

EDEN.

All feel an interest in Paradise, the place where man was created and where he began his eventful history. Many volumes have been written trying to discover where it was, and it has been located all the way from Syria to India. In our own day Prof. Delitzsch has discussed the subject, nor has he been the last writer on the interesting theme.

Of all the localities assigned it, none has so good a claim as Babylon. Here is the land of Shinar. Here rose the heaven-seeking tower of Babel. Here were Accad and Erech, Babylon and Calneh.

Eridu was one of its most ancient seaports. Though its

site is now far up the river, at Suk esh shiookh (the market of the chiefs or sheikhs), originally it was, like Ur, a seaport on the Persian Gulf. Nowhere in the whole earth does the land encroach faster on the sea, and still it encroaches. But when one of the *bourgeoisie* of ancient Eridu spoke of the country back of the town he called it " Eden," *i.e.*, the country, or the plain ; and the garden was planted "eastward in Eden," or back in the interior from the shore. Then its rivers were the Euphrates and Tigris or Hiddekel (Assyrian, **Idiklu**), the Pishon, which is the Babylonian for canal, and the Gihon. Prof. Sayce tells us that **Gukhan** was the name of a river near Babylon (Fresh Light, p. 26). Besides that, the sacred pine-tree, or tree of life, is often mentioned in its literature, and bitumen and bricks are still the building material of the region. We do not read that any houses were builded in Paradise, but in it or out of it the first one constructed was no doubt a brick house, or, as our neighbors in Mexico would call it, an *adobe* house, and the abundance of trees along the river banks there to-day show that God planted his trees in a region admirably adapted for their growth. All things point to the region of the junction of the Tigris and Euphrates as the probable seat of the original Paradise. It may be objected that back from the rivers the garden would need irrigation, but the Creator could provide that also, not by laborious digging of water-courses, as would be necessary on our part, but just as He said " Let there be light," and there was light.

EDUCATION.

Acts 19 : 9. He departed from them and separated the disciples, reasoning daily in the school of Tyrannus.

A nation that had grammars and dictionaries (syllabaries), works on astronomy, geography, and natural history, also public libraries—for the libraries of Sargon I. and of Asshurbanipal, like others, were open to the people—must have also had schools; but while we find ample records of war and conquest as yet nothing has come to hand concerning her institutions of learning. Classical writers tell us that Babylonia had universities, but the monuments leave us to infer that fact from the measure of intelligence that prevailed in the land.

Asshurbanipal, however, leaves this on record (Ass'l. 6. 31–33): "Within the royal palace of my father Esarhaddon I acquired the deep wisdom of Nebo, the whole of the inscribed tablets, even all of the clay tablets—which were their books—their contents I learned." Again he says (11. 7 and 8), speaking of the great gods: "Broad ears they gave me—*i. e.*, fitted to hear well—and to all the inscribed tablets they caused me to give attention." So then in the palace of Nineveh it was not all luxurious self-indulgence or royal magnificence, but there was some good hard work, such as is now done in our higher institutions of learning.

Still, some may think that in the harem at least it was all splendor and gayety. Fortunately we have a glimpse also into the daily life of the king's daughters, showing us that even the education of women also was attended to in those ancient days, however it may have been neglected since. **Serua edherat**, the eldest daughter of **Asshur ebil ili yukin** (620–607 B. C.), writes a letter to her grandmother, the wife (widow?) of Asshurbanipal. B. L. 78, and R. III. 16. 2.

This shows that princesses in those days were educated. They were not only taught to read but to write the difficult and cumbrous cuneiform script, containing hundreds of characters, some of them involved and complicated. Then, doubtless, they had private tutors in the palace, and custom would require that they belong to their own sex—for a eunuch would scarcely be found capable of such work—and this again would involve a degree of education among women in general, for we should hardly expect the royal family to engage in such employment.

Prof. Sayce is very clear in his utterances on this subject. He says (Social Life among the Assyrians, etc., p. 42): "Women as well as men enjoyed the advantages of education. The Babylonian contract-tablets prove this, where women as well as men appear as parties to suits and partners in commercial transactions, signing their own names. Woman was not jealously secluded in ancient Babylonia as she is in the East of to-day, and it is probable that boys and girls studied at the same schools."

It is wonderful how many things are connected with a seemingly trivial statement; so that, in studying one fact, we find ourselves face to face with many others, and each one of the greatest importance.

Young ladies in our colleges could not find a more prolific theme for a composition than this same Miss **Serua edherat.** One wonders what became of her in those last days of the monarchy, and whether she perished in the funeral pyre kindled by the despairing king when he found that all his efforts to beat back the foe from Nineveh were vain.

ELAM.

Gen. 10 : 22. The sons of Shem : Elam and Asshur, etc.

Elam was a very ancient kingdom and occupied an important place in ancient history. It is mentioned repeatedly in the Old Testament, and furnished a part of the audience on the great day of Pentecost. Acts 2 : 9.

Its home was among the mountains to the east of the Tigris, opposite Babylonia. Its capital, Susa, or Shushan (the old city), was situated near the river Choaspes, now the Kerkhah, or rather on the Euloeus (Ulai, Dan. 8 : 2), an artificial connection of the Choaspes and Coprates.

The name Elam is simply the Assyrian word high, **elamu,** and was given to it on account of its great elevation. It was also called Cissia and Susiana by the Greeks, Numma by the Accadians, and Ansan. Prof. Sayce called it Western Ansan in his Ancient Empires of the East, p. 240, and Ansan, or Anzan, simply, in his Fresh Light from the Monuments, 41 and 144, and as the last is the latest work by several years we must take this as his maturer judgment.

The importance of Elam is seen in the subjugation of Babylonia by **Khammuragas,** a Kassite king, about B. C. 2290, and Asshurbanipal records in his annals that **Kudur Nankhundi** (servant of **Nankhundi**), king of Elam, conquered it 1635 years before his own taking of Shushan.

One of the kings of Elam also subdued southern Palestine in the days of Abraham. See "Chedorlaomer."

But the most striking fact about this country is that Cyrus, who till now has been supposed to be a king of Persia, has been proved by the monuments, and especially by his own records, to have been king of Ansan (Elam). See R. V. 35, also A. M. 39–41, and Fresh Light from the Monuments, 135–140. This confirms the words of Isaiah, 21 : 1–10, who does not summon Persia, but Elam and Media, to go up and destroy the city of Babylon.

Prof. Sayce says (Fresh Light, 145), that Ezra 1 : 2 was originally written Cyrus king of Elam, but gives no authority for the statement.

The kingdom of Elam was overthrown by Asshurbanipal, king of Assyria, about B. C. 645.

The country afterwards was included in the Persian Empire, and the most conspicuous ruins in Shushan are those of the palace of Xerxes, where the feast described in Esther I. was held.

ELOHIM.

This name of God is usually written in the plural. Prof. J. G. Murphy says (Genesis, p. 25), " The name is found in the Hebrew Scriptures 57 times in the singular and about 3,000 times in the plural." Various explanations have been given of this. Dr. W. L. Alexander, in his edition of Kitto's Cyclopedia (II. 148, col. 1), inclines to the opinion that "it rests on a principle pervading the language; viz., that words describing objects which combine plurality with unity are used in the plural, and generally with verbs in the singular." Whatever the reason may be, it is interesting to know that in the tablets found at Tel el Amarna several of the correspondents of Amenophis IV. address him as "my sun-god" and also as "my gods," using the name in the plural. This is true of **Su-yardata**, R. of P. new V. 77, lines 2 and 7, of **Malchiel**, 79. 2, 7, 10 and 16, also 80. 2 and 7, of the woman **Urasmu**, 83. 2 and 6, of **Abisharru**, 88. 1, and of **Zimriddi**, 89. 1 and 6. The fact that so many adopted this style goes to show that the *usus loquendi* of Canaan in the fifteenth century B. C. was to employ the plural form of the name of God in the sense of the singular.

EL SHADDAI.

There is no name of God that describes him perfectly. One sets forth this excellence and another that; but even those that hold up to view one attribute of God do not present it just as it exists in his perfect character, but with more or less of imperfection. This is especially true when the attempt is made to illustrate what is in God by familiar objects, so that when one compares God to one object, often, as if conscious of its inability to do justice to the divine subject, he immediately adds another, and goes on adding illustration to illustration, as though in despair of adequately setting forth the divine perfection. We have a striking instance of this in Psalm 18:2: "The Lord is my rock, and my fortress, and my deliverer; my God, my strong rock; in him will I trust; my shield, and the horn of my salvation, and my high tower." It is as though, when the writer said, "The Lord is my rock," he felt that to be indefinite: a rock may be viewed in many aspects which would do injustice to God; so he adds, by way of specifying what he means, "my fortress;" but then a fortress is without life, mere inert matter; and so he goes on, "my deliverer;" and still, as even that only sets forth one side of God, he falls back on "my God," which indeed includes all, though it describes none.

There is one name of God which is seldom brought into the foreground, though, like everything pertaining to him, it will well reward our study. When Abraham was ninety and nine years old the Lord appeared unto him and said, "I am *God Almighty;* walk before me, and be thou perfect." Gen. 17:1. Compare 28:3, 35:11, 43:10, 48:3, 49:25. The Hebrew is אל שדי, and in both King James' version and the new revision is rendered as above. What is the origin of the name? Gesenius makes Shaddai *pluralis excellentiæ* from *shad*, mighty, powerful; but שד does not appear in his Lexicon, though a word of the same form is rendered violence, oppression, desolation, destruction. He also derives Shaddai from *shadad* שדד, to practice violence, to oppress, to destroy, to desolate. If this is the correct derivation, then אל שדי is not the Almighty, but the destroying God, which would hardly do justice to him who is love.

We may conclude, therefore, that the Hebrew can furnish no better derivation, else Gesenius would have discovered it. Let us turn, then, to the Assyrian. There **shadu** is a mountain, and **shaddai** would be the regular adjective form, as **gimirrai**, from

Gimiru, Gomer, or **Mutsrai**, from **Mutsur**, Egypt, Hebrew Mitsraim מצרים; and if it is objected that in **shaddai** שדי the ד is reduplicated, the answer is that in R. III. 14. 42 we have **shaddai martsu** instead of the more familiar **shadu martsu**, a rugged mountain. Prof. Delitzsch proposed this derivation, and Prof. Sayce says of it, H. L. 407, " It is possible that Prof. Delitzsch is right in proposing to see in the Assyrian **shadu** the explanation of the Hebrew title of God, El Shaddai. At all events God is compared to a rock in the Old Testament. Psa. 18:2." But as some Assyriologists are not satisfied with this derivation, let us bear in mind that the statement is not that a mountain is God, or that God is confined to mountains, but that just as the term אל, strong, mighty, has a meaning that renders it fit to represent one view of God, just as the word יהוה is adapted to set forth another view of God, just as the term Word has a peculiar fitness to describe the second person in the Trinity previous to his incarnation, so the word mountain is fitted to suggest some delightful views of God. The Assyrians must have thought so when they called Asshur, the head of their pantheon, **Shadu rabu**, a great mountain. R. V. 8. 5, also A. M. 28. 19, also Senn. 2. 4, and R. I. 37. 10.

The question arises, How did the thought of God become associated in the minds of the Assyrians with a mountain? Of course they had not those Scriptures from which we derive our most precious views of God. Even Abraham, apart from his direct communion with God, had only some of those documents which may have aided Moses in writing the book of Genesis; but, feeling in their hearts that God was great, they could find no better symbol of his greatness than the mountains which towered up in massive greatness towards heaven. "The great mountains" was the expression that rose naturally to their lips. Even the Psalmist sings, "Thy righteousness is like the great mountains," 36:6, just as in the same verse he adds, "Thy judgments are a great deep." So the prophet says, Isa. 2:14, "The day of the Lord shall be upon all the *high* mountains." Why? Because, v. 17, "The Lord alone shall be exalted in that day." Even the high mountains shall no longer serve to show forth the exaltation of one so high above them. How striking, in such a connection, is that word of God, Isa. 57 : 15, " I dwell in the high and holy place, with him also that is of a humble and contrite spirit."

Again, men felt that God was all-powerful, and how could they express this better than by saying (Psa. 65 : 6), " Who by his strength setteth fast the mountains; being girded about with might;" or (Job 28 : 9), " Who overturneth the mountains by the roots;" or (Isa. 40 : 12), " Who weighed the mountains in scales;" or (Nahum 1 : 5), " The mountains quake at him, and the hills melt"? Compare Hab. 3 : 10.

So too men felt that God endured while they themselves passed away, as it is beautifully expressed, Heb. 1 : 11, 12, " They shall perish, but thou continuest; and they all shall wax old as doth a garment ... but thou art the same, and thy years shall not fail:" and how grandly this is set forth by Habakkuk, 3 : 6; " He stood, and measured the earth," he did not need to move from his place in doing it; " he beheld, and drove asunder the nations," a look sufficed for this, " and the eternal mountains were scattered, the everlasting hills did bow; (but) his goings were (*i. e.*, continued) as of old."

So also in times of ancient violence — and it was terrible; we have nothing now to compare with it—God was felt to be often the only refuge, and this most precious view of God was gloriously set forth by the mountains: not only do they enclose the dwellings of his people in their protection, Psa. 125 : 2, but, Isa. 2 : 2, the Lord's house is established in that most inaccessible place the top of the mountains, and while the Psalmist says to his enemies, 11 ; 1, " In the Lord put I my trust. How say ye to my soul, Flee as a bird to your mountain (refuge)?" to God he says, 30 : 7, " Thou, Lord, of thy power hast made my mountain (refuge) to stand strong." One cannot help recalling how often the merciless Asshurnatsirpal records in his standard inscription such passages as these: col. 2. 16, " To the inaccessible mountain they trusted, and the summits of the mountain I attacked and captured. In the midst of the mighty mountain I slew their warriors. Like wool I dyed the mountain with their blood;" col. 2. 40, " The mountain which they occupied as their place of refuge was, to look on, like the blade of a sword. After them I climbed up, and threw their bodies down the cliffs or piled them on the rocks." But not such is the result of trusting in El Shaddai.

It is a delightful addition to these views of God, suggested by this name, that when the good man is cast down by the sight of abounding wickedness, not only in the world, where we expect it, but sometimes also in those from whom we had looked for better things, he can turn to God and say (Psa. 36:6) "*Thy* righteousness is like the great mountain:" vast, firm, and enduring through the ages.

It may be objected that worship on the mountains is condemned in the Old Testament. Certainly. But we are not defending worship in the forbidden high places, we only seek to show how man, under the teaching of Him who is the light of the world, has by means of the mountains climbed up to the knowledge of God; for not only (Rom. 1:20) are "the invisible things of God since the creation of the world clearly seen, being perceived through the things that are made," but those same things also suggest names of God through which we express the ideas thus obtained.

It was on a mountain that God gave his law to Israel, it was on a mountain that Christ was transfigured before a chosen few of his disciples, and it was from a mountain that he stepped up into the glory which he had with the Father before the world was; and though the time will come when neither on Gerizim nor at Jerusalem men shall feel that they must worship God, that does not forbid that the name El Shaddai came into existence in the manner here supposed, nor is such a derivation of it inconsistent with the most spiritual worship on earth or in heaven.

ENTERING OF THE GATE.

The Bible speaks not only of the gate, but of entering of the gate. Josh. 8:29; 20:4; Judg. 9:35, 40, 44; 18:16; 2 Sam. 10:8; 2 Chron. 18:9. Perhaps the entering of the gate means the passage through which one enters into the city, in distinction from the open space outside or inside, or the point where one ceases to be outside the city and is inside the wall.

The Assyrian monuments in like manner speak sometimes

of the opening of the gate, as in R. I. 18. 62. The word is **puut**, construct of **putu**, which Prof. Lyon in A. M. renders opening, entrance, side. Another word is **niribu**, from **iribu**, to enter, which the same writer translates entrance, pass. See R. V. 8. 14 and 9. 100. It is singular that these expressions should occur in both Hebrew and Assyrian when, as it would seem, the simple word gate would answer the purpose equally well. The phrase **atsii abulli alisu**, Senn. 62. 22, which G. Smith renders "the exit of the great gate of the city," Prof. Lyon in A. M. renders (see 70. note on 12. 16) "the one coming out," *i. e.*, of the gate, etc.

R. IV. 31. 5. describes Hades as "the house that has an entrance, but no exit."

ETERNITY.

Matt. 25:46; John 3:15, 4:36, 5:39, 6:54, 10:28, 12:25, 17:2, 3; Rom. 5:21, 6:23; Tius 1:12; 1 John 1:2, 5:11. Isa. 57:15. The holy One that inhabiteth eternity.

We should hardly expect to find the idea of eternity brought out so clearly in the inscriptions as in the Scriptures, and yet it is there.

In R. V. 64. 3. 21, Nabonidus prays to the god Shamash that "the strong weapon which thou hast made my hands to grasp may rule **ana duuri daari**," to eternity, or for ever. So the Arabic expresses the same idea by *ila daher eddahur*. Psa. 45:6.

So Cyrus says (R. V. 35. 32 and A. M. 41. 24) that he restored the gods and caused them to dwell in their everlasting (**duraata,**) habitations.

EVENING AND MORNING.

In Gen. 1:5 we read that the evening and the morning were the first day. In like manner the record of each succeeding day of creation bears witness that the evening precedes the morning. The Hebrew day always commenced after sunset, and it touches the heart to read in the account of the crucifixion that towards its close "the Sabbath drew on," (Luke 23:54): while the Saviour was enduring such agonies the day of rest procured by them was coming to a world of sinners.

Did Babylonians also begin their day at sunset? We should hardly expect a direct statement of the fact, for there are very few occasions that would call forth such a declaration, and yet we have information on this point as clear as it is unlooked for.

Old English printers had a way of putting the first word of the next page at the bottom of the preceding one, so that the reader need not pause in his reading while turning the leaf. And Assyrian scribes had a fashion of putting at the end of a clay tablet that was to be followed by others belonging to the same series the first line of the next tablet; so a tablet containing a hymn to the setting sun, that was to be sung at Babylon in the temple of **E Babara** (house of the oracle or revelation) " at the beginning of the night," ends thus: First line of the next tablet, " O sun, rising in the shining sky ;" showing that among the Babylonians also the evening came first and after it the morning.

This is confirmed by some of the bilingual hymns, for in places where the Sumerian reads " day and night " " female and male "—for they politely put the ladies first--the translator into Assyrian is always careful to put " night and day," " male and female," in accordance with Assyrian ideas. H. L. 430.

EVIL, THE PROBLEM OF.

The prophet is commissioned to say for God, Isa. 45 : 7, " I form the light and create darkness. I make peace and create evil. I am Jehovah that doeth all these things."

This utterance of God shows that there was occasion for it in the thoughts of the people to whom it was addressed, and that need was nowhere more urgent than among the inhabitants of lower Mesopotamia. It is not necessary to settle the disputed date of the birth of Zoroaster in order to appreciate this. The polytheism of Babylonia taught the existence of evil deities as well as good. As Prof. Sayce says (H. L. 347), " Persian dualism was no new thing in Babylonia, the gods of good and the spirits of evil had been struggling there, one against the other, since the remote days of Sargon of Accad." Ever since man had broken away from the knowledge of the one only living and true God revealed in Eden, Rom. 1 : 18–25, he had advanced deeper into this darkness. At first every object was thought to have a **zi,** or spirit, which produced both injurious and beneficent effects; but soon they became sorted into two classes, as those effects were seen to be generally favorable or unfavorable to human welfare. By degrees the spirits rose to the dignity of gods, who occupied two opposite camps, one friendly to man and the other hostile; one erecting and upholding, the other attacking and destroying. To the Accadian even the heavens and the earth were gods waging eternal war with darkness and chaos, and so, in daily life, the tempest, the eclipse, and the pestilence showed that the enemy was getting the advantage; on the other hand, the calm, the sunshine, and returning health indicated the return of the good to power. All alike, however, were controlled by the **Sabba** or fate, and that could be manipulated by the spells and incantations of the conjuror, who could at will either remove or produce disease, and even compel the gods to do his bidding, There were hymns also in which conscience sought to express its sense of guilt, and the heart yearned after some one in whom it could repose its trust, but even these were hopelessly mixed up with the old conjurations. It shows this duality in their gods, that in the account of the deluge while Ea, the god of the sea, and Anu, the god of the sky, were friendly to the human race, Bil or Mullil, the god of the under world, was its bitter enemy. "He stood still and was filled with wrath against the (other) gods and the **igigi** (spirits of heaven). 'What soul has escaped?' he cried. 'Let no one remain alive in the great destruction.'" A.M. 61. 5, 6, also D. L. 106. 162, 163. It is seen also in the combat between Bel Merodach and Tiamat, where, though the former overcame the powers of evil, yet there was no antecedent certainty of his success.

It may be supposed by some that this duality in the character and conduct of their gods would improve in the course of the ages, but the question is, Did it so improve? The inquiry is not one of theory but of fact, and as such must be answered. Neither Babylonian nor Assyrian could ever forget that conduct of Mullil at the Deluge, and how could they ever put their trust in such a god, or in other gods more friendly but not higher than he, and so liable at any moment to have their efforts thwarted more successfully than on that occasion?

Just as there is no physical life that originates itself, just as all such life must proceed either directly from a creator or through a parent, so there is no spiritual life aside from that which is wrought by the Holy Spirit. Nations do not grow up into Christianity, but grace and truth come by Jesus Christ, John 1:17, and his method of imparting that grace is made sufficiently clear in his last command, Mark 16:15, and in Rom. 10:14: "How shall they believe in him of whom they have not heard? or how shall they hear without a preacher?"

It is very true that Christ is the light of man, John 1;4, but only the man that followeth him shall have the light of life, 8:12. If God chose the Jewish nation to be the depositary of his truth, if he not only instructed it through his prophets but led it through manifold and severe discipline, and yet the result of all was that only a remnant was saved, for "they are not all Israel that are of Israel," Rom. 9:6, 27, we may be very sure that no people left to itself will regenerate itself, and, as has been already intimated, the only question is what was the actual result of Babylonian and Assyrian idolatry as seen in the history of these nations? There is no spiritual life apart from the knowledge of the only true God, for as Christ says, John 17:3, "This is life eternal, that they should know thee, *the only true God*, and him whom thou didst send, even Jesus Christ."

EVIL MERODACH.

This evil name is not charged in Scripture with any very evil deed. He is said, 2 Kings 25:27, 30, to have lifted up the head of Jehoiachim, king of Judah, out of prison, to have spoken kindly to him, and set his throne above the throne of the kings that were with him in Babylon; also to have given him a daily allowance all the days of his life. The same thing is repeated Jer. 52:31-34.

The seeming charge of evil-doing wholly disappears in the Assyrian. "The Accadian *m* was either *m* or *v*; so the Assyrians had to use the same character for *m* and *v*." (A. L. and S. 34.) Thus **Amilu** may be also read **Avilu**. That word, however pronounced, meant simply man or servant. So that **Amilu marduk** means "the servant of Merodach," just as in Arabic Abdallah means "the servant of God," and Abedne(b)o, as we have seen, the servant of Nebo; for Abednego is apparently the mistake of a copyist.

He was the son of Nebuchadrezzar, whom he succeeded B. C. 562, and after a reign of only two years was assassinated by conspirators under the lead of his brother, **Nergal shar ezer** (**Nergal sharra utsur**): Nergal defend the king, who in this case woefully belied his name.

EYES.

2 Kings 25:7. And they slew the sons of Zedekiah before his eyes, and put out the eyes of Zedekiah, and bound him in fetters, and carried him away to Babylon.

Mons. Botta found at Khorsabad a bas-relief of Sargon who built his palace there. It represents a prisoner kneeling before the king in a most pitiful attitude, and held by a cord in the left hand of the monarch that passes through the flesh of the lower lip of his victim. Sargon is prodding the eyes of the suppliant with a spear held in his right hand, while two other kneeling prisoners, fettered hand and foot, and held by cords similarly inserted in the lower lip, seem patiently awaiting their time to suffer. See Smith's History of Assyria, p. 169. Also Rawlinson's Anc. Mon. I. 243.

Asshurbanipal inflicted on Vaitch, king of Arabia, similar cruelties. "At the command of Asshur and Beltis with a **khuutni mashiri** (some kind of weapon) I cut in pieces the flesh of his **mitsu,** whatever that was. In the **lakhu** (ball?) of his eye I put **tsiritu** (vitriol?). I put upon him the collar of a dog and at the eastern gate of Nineveh at the entrance of **masnakti adnaati** I shut him up in a cage." R. V. 9. 107-109, also A. M. 33. 18-22 and Ass'l. 280. 86-93.

FACE.

(*a*) To set the face toward. Luke 9:51: He steadfastly set his face to go up to Jerusalem.

A similar expression is used by Sennacherib (**Sin akhi iriba,** Sin has increased brothers), B. C. 705-682. He says **paan niriya utir,** the face of my yoke I turned, towards this place or that. See R. I. 38. 7, and Senn. 47. 7. Also R. I. 39. 49, and Senn. 74. 49. Also R. I. 40. 2, and Senn. 82. 2.

(b) To set the face against. Lev. 20:3, 6; Jer. 44:11; Ezek. 14:8; 28:21; 29:2.

This same phrase is used in R. V. 3. 53, and Ass'l. 113. 108: Against Dimanu the Gambulian, who trusted to Elam, I set my face, **ashkuna paniya.**

(c) To flee from the face of. Rev. 20:11; Gen. 35:1; Ex. 2:15. Asshurnatsirpal (Asshur protects the son), B. C. 883-859, says **Ultu pani kakkiya ipparshidu**: from the face of my weapons (soldiers) they fled. R. I. 22. 82. It is a striking evidence of the small value set on human life that an army was counted only as so many weapons wherewith to destroy men's lives. See "Look upon the face of."

FAITH THE CORRELATE OF GRACE.

Though grace is absolutely free yet it would avail us nothing without some way in which to appropriate its benefits. We appropriate them through faith. God reveals to us his grace in Christ, and we enter on its possession by simply setting to our seal that the revelation is true. Nor can there be any other way of appropriating grace without destroying grace itself; for the moment we put anything else in the place of the great redemption wrought out by Christ we seek to be saved by our works, and not through the free grace of God.

One hardly expects Assyrian tablets to endorse a truth in theology which some who have the Bible in their hands are bold to deny; and yet they do endorse it thoroughly when they make the word **Tukultu** mean both trust in God for help, and the help received in answer to that trust. It is the same thing, only in one case it is viewed from the divine side and in the other from the human side. In the first aspect it is the help which God bestows, in the second it is the faith through which that help is received, and in the point of contact they are one. In many places where the word occurs it may be rendered either hope or trust according as we stand at one point of view or the other. Prof. Lyon translates the word in his Manual, "confidence, reliance, aid," and refers to R. I. 9. 70; 12. 45. Layard 1. 2. In all the passages the reader may render it either trust or help and find both equally appropriate.

FAMINE IN EGYPT.

In Gen. 41 we have an account of seven years of famine in Egypt in the days of Joseph. Is there any record of a like calamity in history outside of the Bible?

Under the 12th dynasty, Ameni, an officer of Usertasen I. left this record in his tomb at Beni Hassan:

"No one was hungry in my days, not even in the years of famine, for I had tilled all the fields of the province of Mah up to the southern and northern frontiers. Thus I prolonged the life of its inhabitants. . . . No one in it was hungry. I distributed equally to widows and to married women. I did not prefer the great to the humble in all that I gave away." (Fresh Light, etc., 51).

It is seldom that the inundation of the Nile is so low that the crops fail for even one year, and it is very seldom that they fail for several years in succession, but the inscriptions in the tomb of a nobleman named Baba at Elkab in southern Egypt tell us "When a famine arose, lasting many years, I distributed corn to the city each year while it lasted." (Fresh Light, etc., 52). Baba lived about the time of Joseph, and probably refers to this very famine.

The last famine in Egypt that continued for seven years was in A. D. 1064–1071 under the Khalif El-mustansir billah. A vivid description of its horrors, in the original Arabic of Abdullatif, may be found in Oberleitner's Arabic Chrestomathy, Viennae, 1823, pp. 162–218.

FAST, PROCLAIMING A.

Many who read of the effect produced by the preaching of Jonah on the people of Nineveh and on their king, as recorded in Jonah 3:5–9, may desire to know whether there is mention of such a spirit on any of the monuments. The prophet Jonah, according to our received chronology, went to Nineveh about B. C. 862, which was towards the close of the reign of Asshurnatsirpal, one of the most cruel and ferocious of her kings. If he was the king at that time, it may be that the consciousness of the extreme cruelties he had practiced on so many, disposed him the more to give heed to the startling announcement of the Hebrew prophet, but there is no special record of the fact. Later on, however, in the days of the last king, Esarhaddon II., and just before the destruction of the city in B. C. 602, we read, H. L. 77, that he prayed to Shamash, the sun god, that he would remove the sin of his people, and ordered the **khal** (prophet) to appoint the legal solemnities (**meshari isinni**) for 100 days and 100 nights from April (Iyyar) 3 to July (Ab) 15. See R. of P. new IV. 9 for a translation. Prof. Sayce says (Anc. Empires of the East, p. 140), "Though Esarhaddon II. proclaimed public fasts and prayers to the gods, Nineveh was besieged, captured, and utterly destroyed."

FEAR.

The prophet Isaiah begins several exceedingly great and precious promises with "Fear not." See chaps. 41 : 10, 13 ; 43 : 1, 5 ; 44 : 2, 8. So also the goddess Ishtar commences her answer to the prayer of Asshurbanipal, saying, Fear not, **la tipallakh.** R. III. 32. 42. Ass'l. 123. 2.

Obadiah says to Elijah, 1 Kings 18 : 12, "I, thy servant, fear the Lord from my youth." And the son of Gyges, king of Lydia, says to Asshurbanipal, I am thy servant that feareth thee: **ardu palikh ka.** R. V. 2. 125. A. M. 23. 11. Ass'l. 68. 42.

FEAST.

Dan. 5 : 2 gives an account of the last feast of Belshazzar, who "commanded to bring the golden and silver vessels which Nebuchadrezzar his father had taken out of the temple which was in Jerusalem, that the king and his lords, his wives and his concubines, might drink therein."

Some have deemed this so contrary to oriental customs that it could not be true, but a bas-relief in the British Museum, brought from the palace of Asshurbanipal at Koyunjik, shows that in Assyria woman was thus accustomed to share in the banquets of the king. It shows us the king and queen together banqueting under their own vine (1 Kings 4 : 25) which is full of large clusters of grapes; birds are singing on the trees, a band of musicians is playing, and attendants hold up, behind both king and queen, those peculiar instruments with which they either fanned those seated at the banquet or brushed away the flies. It gives a sad insight, however, into the Assyrian idea of enjoyment to see a ghastly human head hanging among the branches of the tree behind the queen. P. and C. I. 107, 108, also Rawlinson's Anc. Mon. I. 493. It is possible that some of the trees in the bas-relief were meant for fig-trees, according to the saying of Rabshakeh, 2 Kings 18:31, but the resemblance is not very apparent. Fig-trees, however, are represented very plainly in the bas-relief of Sennacherib on his throne before Lachish. See frontispiece of Smith's Sennacherib.

FEET.

In 2 Kings 4:27 the woman of Shunem caught hold of the feet of Elisha. The kings of Assyria described the submission of kings by saying that they clasped the feet of my royalty : **izbatu shipi sharutiya.** So Asshurbanipal speaks of Ummanaldus, king of Elam, R. V. 7, 57, and Ass'l. 241, 75. And in R. V. 2. 103–106, also A. M. 22. 103–107, he says that from the very day that Gyges, king of Lydia, embraced the feet of my royalty he captured the **Gimirraai** (Gomerians) who had not done so. He uses the same language concerning the people of various cities. R. I. 20. 10 ; 21. 46, 78, and R. I. 22. 90.

In Isa. 58:13 we are bidden to turn away our foot from the Sabbath. Asshurbanipal complains that **Vaiteh,** king of Arabia, " hindered his feet from seeking my peace," **ana sha'al shulmiya shipishu ipruus ma.** There may be a difference in the use of the foot, but it is a striking similarity that the foot is made to be the instrument used in both cases.

The command in Josh. 10:4, " put your feet on the necks of these kings," is illustrated in line 4, of the standard inscription of Asshurnatsirpal (R. I. 17. 15, and A. M. 5. 10), who styles himself **mukabbiis kishad a'abishu:** he who treads on the necks of them that hate him.

FILIAL DUTY.

In a tablet of ancient Accadian laws copied and translated by the scribes of Asshurbanipal it is written, " His father and his mother (a man) shall not deny." A decision of the courts reads as follows: "(If) a son says to his father, 'Thou art not my father,'' and confirms it by (his) nail mark (on the wet clay tablet) he binds himself in a recognizance, and silver he gives him." Another decision reads thus: "If a son says to his mother, 'Thou art not my mother,' his hair is cut off, (in) the city, they deny him earth (and) water, and expel him." In the Accadian it reads, "and in the house imprison him." R. of P. III. 23 and 24.

There is one pleasant side to these old laws, and that is their appreciation of a mother's love, shown in the severer penalty visited on the guilty despiser of it.

In the Old Testament we are confronted three times with the stern requirement, " He that curseth his father or his mother shall surely be put to death " (Exod. 21 : 17 ; Lev. 20 : 9, Prov. 10 : 20) ; and from the last book (30 : 11) goes up the wailing cry, "There is a generation that curseth their father, and doth not bless their mother." It is as though the writer could not bear to admit that any child could be so far lost to all that was good as to curse its mother.

It is humiliating to find such a record in Holy Scripture, but we must not forget that Scripture is not the cause of such wickedness, it is the consequence of the depravity that is not confined to this nation or that, but is co-extensive with the race ; as it is written, "For all have sinned, and fall short of the glory of God." Rom. 3 : 23, 5 : 12.

It does not follow that because filial impiety was visited with more condign punishment by the divine law, therefore it abounded more under the law. The mere statement of the penalty may have sufficed to deter men from incurring it, while the lighter retribution of another land may have encouraged evil-doers in their wickedness.

Nor can we base any argument on the comparative guilt of cursing and disowning parents. The cursing may have been a hasty outbreak of temper followed by bitter repentance, and the disowning may have been the final outcome of a life of wickedness that found in that its climax.

There are many things that need to be taken into account

before we are prepared to decide on the comparative guiltiness of different lands. They cannot be all enumerated here; it is enough to assert squarely that the severer penalty does not necessarily involve the greater prevalence of the crime condemned, and to remind men that sinning against greater light always induces a greater boldness on the part of those whose hearts are fully set in them to do evil.

Notwithstanding the severity of the divine law so much complained of, we are firmly convinced that there was a far greater measure of domestic enjoyment and a far higher standard of family character in Israel than in the nations round about them; and now that Christ has come with his more glorious manifestation of love, and of character formed under the influence of love, we expect as the result to see the will of God done on earth as it is done in heaven, and so all cavilling shall be hushed for ever, according to Matt. 5 : 16.

FIRE.

Nehemiah (2 :3) told the king, "The city, the place of my fathers' sepulchres, lieth waste, and the gates thereof are consumed with fire." This was the work of the king of Babylon, and there is a phrase in the annals of the kings of Assyria so frequently recurring that a tyro learns to recognize it before everything else. Tiglath Pileser I., who reigned B. C. 1120–1000, had it "**Ina ishati ashruup abbul aqqur,**" with fire I burned, I destroyed, I devastated. Centuries passed on with this refrain occurring continually, the only change being in the words, not in the ruin that was wrought. Sennacherib, B. C. 705–682, wrote it, "**Abbul aqqur ina ishati aqmu,**" but the destruction was the same, only the order was reversed : "I destroyed, I devastated, with fire I burned." References are hardly needed, but a few are given. Tiglath Pileser I., R. I. 9. 94 to 10. 1, A. M. 2. 1, R. I. 13. 3, and A. M. 3. 26. Sennacherib, R. III. 14. 51, A. M. 18. 9, Senn. 134. 51, etc. Asshurbanipal, Ass'l. 85. 52, 91. 39, 92. 50; and the cruel Asshurnatsirpal repeats it eighteen times in his inscription, R. I. 17–26. He narrates very coolly that he burned the cities of Qurkhi with fire, R. I. 20. 21 ; that he burned 3,000 captives from Kinabu (col. 1. 108) and 200 from Mariru (col. 1. 111). Concerning no less than seven cities he leaves the following record: "Their young men and maidens I burned as a holocaust." How he did it, whether in the furnace or saturating their clothing with bitumen, he does not say, but passes it over as something not worth describing.

The Hebrews burned Jericho, Josh. 6:24, Hazor, 11:11, and Laish, Judg. 18:27. The Amalekites burned Ziklag, 1 Sam. 30:1, and Pharoah burned Gezer, 1 Kings 9:16. The Philistines threaten to burn a woman and her father's house, Judg. 14:15, as though it was an ordinary occurrence, and 15:16 tells how they kept their word.

FIRSTBORN, THE.

The Lord Jesus Christ is called "the image of the invisible God, the firstborn of all creation," Col. 1:15, and the reason of this title is, v. 16, "for in (or by) him were all things created." Some ask, How can the Creator be the firstborn of creation?

The Babylonians and Assyrians had no difficulty on that score, for their gods were created, and so Nebuchadrezzar says, "The firstborn, the glorious, the firstborn of the gods (*i. e.*, Merodach) heard my prayer and accepted my petition." H. L. 97. Farther down on the same page we read, "O Merodach, my lord, firstborn of the gods, the mighty prince, thou didst create me, and hast entrusted to me the sovereignty over multitudes of men. As my own dear life do I love the exaltation of thy house," etc. While he was addressing this prayer to a created god he did not know that the only living and true God had said, Jer. 27:8, "The nation and the kingdom which will not serve the same Nebuchadrezzar the king of Babylon, and that will not put their neck under the yoke of the king of Babylon, that nation will I punish, saith the Lord, with the sword and with the famine and with the pestilence till I have consumed them by his hand." But having originated such a title of God under a mistaken apprehension of his nature, the title remains as an expression descriptive of his greatness and glory, even though we know that he is self-existent and had no beginning.

H. L. 128 gives a hymn to the god Asshur that contains

these titles of that god: "The Father who has created the gods, the supreme firstborn of heaven and earth."

FLAY.

Amos, 3:2, speaks of some of the princes of Israel as hating the good and showing that hatred in the horrid way of plucking off their skin; we might have hoped that this was only done metaphorically, but in the next verse he describes it very plainly: "Who flay their skins from off them."

It is a horrible way of inflicting human suffering: for the surface of the body under the skin is more sensitive to pain than it is deeper down. But the monuments leave no room for metaphor, since they picture the revolting process right before our eyes on the inner walls of the palace of Sennacherib at Koyunjik (Nineveh). See B. and N. 457. The victim is fastened on the ground by pegs, with feet and hands stretched wide apart, while, knife in hand, the executioner kneels to his task. More than one Assyrian king glories in this his shame, blazoning it on his palace walls. What a public sentiment must that have been that made such representations to be looked on as royal ornamentation. Asshurnatsirpal, R. I. 19. 110, says, "**Khula,** the ruler of their city **Kinabu,** I flayed alive, his skin I spread upon the wall of **Damdamusa.** See also R. I. 19. 90. More than six examples of this cruelty are commemorated in his inscriptions.

Asshurbanipal says, R. V. 10. 5 and A. M. 34. 6, "I flayed Aamu, the brother of Abiyati, in Nineveh." See also Ass'l. 283. 112. He also slew the inhabitants of three cities in Egypt, not leaving one man alive. Their dead bodies they hung on stakes, the sharp point of the stake being inserted in their breasts, and with their skins they clothed the city walls. R. V. 2. 3 and 4. A. M. 49. 6. Let us hope the flaying in these cases was not done till after death.

FLESH OF MEN.

The Psalmist complains, Psa. 79:2, "The dead bodies of thy servants have they given to be meat unto the fowls of the heavens, the flesh of thy saints unto the beasts of the earth;" and Goliath said to David, 1 Sam. 17:44, "Come to me, and I will

CAPTIVES IMPALED BEFORE THE WALLS OF NIMROOD.

give thy flesh unto the fowls of the air, and to the beasts of the field," and David replies, vs. 45-47, "Thou comest to me with sword and spear and shield, but I come to thee in the name of the Lord of hosts, the God of the armies of Israel whom thou hast defied. This day will the Lord deliver thee into my hand and I will smite thee, and take thy head from thee, and I will give the dead bodies of the hosts of the Philistines this day unto the fowls of the air, and to the wild beasts of the earth, that all the earth may know that there is a God in Israel."

The Philistine thinks of nothing but what he is going to do to the unarmed stripling before him. David on the other hand is full of what God is about to do for him and for his people.

The coarse cruel spirit of heathenism is seen even more clearly in the monuments, which gloat over the details and find delight in specifying the beasts as follows: "As to the rest of the men who were with **Shamash shum ukin** (the rebel brother of Asshurbanipal), their flesh cut into pieces I fed to dogs, **shaki** (bears?), wolves, vultures, fowls of heaven, and fishes of the sea." R. V. 4. 74 and A. M. 26. 24. Ass'l. 166. 10, 11. It is not necessary to pursue the unpleasant theme any farther.

FOOT MARKING.

Job 13:27. "Thou settest a print upon the soles of my feet." This is such an out-of-the-way statement that we hardly expect to find any illustration of it. Yet Prof. Sayce (Social Life among the Assyrians, etc., p. 42) gives the following from an old Accadian Folk-story: A foundling has been taken from among the dogs of the street to be adopted into the family of a king. First the child is brought to the **aship** (wizard), who marks the soles of his feet with his seal, and then hands him over to the nurse, to whom the boy's food and clothing are guaranteed for three years.

The marking may have been a mere *opus operatum* before witnesses, leaving no trace on the foot, or some corrosive poison may have been put on the seal that left its marks in the flesh, or tattooing along the lines of the seal may have made a permanent record of the act. Be that as it may, this is certainly a wonderful and unexpected corroboration of the words of Job, such as we might look for in vain elsewhere.

FOOTSTOOL.

The throne of Solomon had a footstool of gold. 2 Chron. 9:18. Psa. 110:1 speaks of enemies being made a footstool.

We have a beautiful illustration of a footstool in connection with a throne in the sculpture that represents Sennacherib at Lachish. (See under "Feast," and B. and N. 150.) It is very artistic in form, the feet ending in lion's paws. It was cased in embossed metal, and was just high enough for the feet of the king to rest on it while seated on the throne. A Persian footstool in front of a throne may be seen in Kitto's Cycl. Bibl. Lit. III. 476, also in Rawlinson's Anc. Mon. III. 203.

As for making enemies a footstool, see Josh. 10:4 and A. M. 5. 10, where Asshurnatsirpal is called "**Mukabiis kishad aabishu,**" he who treads on the necks of them that hate him. A human footstool may be seen in Rawlinson's Anc. Mon. III. 7, though it may be that the foot is planted on the breast of the prostrate man as a preparation for the blow with the mace that is to break his skull, and the victims held by a bridle in the hands of an attendant are waiting their turn to undergo the same dreadful fate. See "Bridle."

FOREORDINATION.

Deut. 7:6, 8: Jehovah thy God hath chosen thee to be a peculiar people unto himself, etc.

One would hardly look for such a doctrine in the Assyrian, and yet even the Old Testament has nothing stronger than the following from Asshurbanipal, R. V. 1. 3-7: A. M. 19. 18-25, and Ass'l. 4. 3-7:

Sha Ashshur u Sin bil agi ultu umi ruquti nibit shumshu izkuru ana sharruti u ina libbi ummishu ibnuu ana riuut mat Ashshur. Shamash Ramman u Ishtar ina purussishunu kiini iqbuu ipish sharrutiya. Ashshurakhiiddina shar mat Ashshur abu banuua amat Ashshur u Bilit ilani tiikliishu itta'i'id sha iqbuushu ipish sharrutiya. Whose name Asshur and Sin, lord of crowns, made mention of from remote days for the kingdom, and in the womb of his mother created him for lordship over Assyria. Shamash,

Rammanu and Ishtar by their firm decrees commanded the formation of my royalty (or kingdom). Esarhaddon, king of Assyria, my father and creator, honored the commands of the gods, Asshur and Beltis, in whom he trusted, who ordered him to establish my kingdom. See also R. V. 10. 7, and Ass'l. 300. 114.

So Asshurnatsirpal says: "I am the powerful king, the king of Assyria, named of Sin (the moon god), the favorite of Anu (god of the sky), the beloved of Rammanu (the air god), the mightiest of the gods, a weapon which spares not, but brings slaughter to the land of his enemies—the destroyer of cities and mountains, the king of the four regions, who enslaves all his foes, the king who subdues the rebellious, who has conquered the whole race. This is the destiny which from the mouth of the great gods has issued forth for me, and they have established it firmly." R. I. 17. 33, seq. and R. of P. new II. 137. 33. seq.

Nebuchadrezzar says: "Merodach, the great lord, lifted up the head of my majesty, and invested me with lordship over all the peoples." R. I. 59. 40-42 and R. of P. new III. 105. 40-42.

Nabonidus says: "I am Nabonidus, the great king, the mighty king, the king of all, the king of Babylon, the king of the four zones, the nourisher of **E Saggila** and **E Zida,** whom **Sin** and **Nergal** in the womb of (his) mother have destined to the destiny of sovereignty."

There can be no question that Babylonians and Assyrians believed in "a divinity that shapes our ends."

FORGIVING TRANSGRESSION.

Ex. 34:7. Forgiving iniquity and transgression and sin.

In R. V. 4. 38, A. M. 25. 28 and Ass'l. 162. 95, we read:

Anaku Ashshurbaniapl libbu rapshu, la katsir, ikkimu, pasisu khitaati, I am Asshurbanipal, large of heart, not contracted, wise, forgiving sins or rebellions.

Another expression equivalent to this is very common: **riimu arsishu,** favor I granted him. See R. V. 2. 62, A. M. 21. 10, Ass'l. 60. 97. Also R. V. 4. 39, A. M. 25. 29, and Ass'l. 162. 96, 97. For Asshurbanipal at least, among the kings of Assyria, sometimes showed a good deal of forbearance. The same could not be said of all of them.

A penitential psalm (R. IV. 29. No. 5, and H. L. 521) contains these lines:

" I thy servant ask thee for rest ; to the heart of him who has sinned thou speakest words of blessing.
Thou lookest on the man and the man lives, O ruler of the world,
Lady of mankind, O compassionate one whose forgiveness is ready, who acceptest prayer.
   Above thee, O God, have I no director.
   Ever look upon me and accept my prayer. . . .
   When, O my goddess, shall thy face incline to me in pardon ?
   Like a dove * I mourn. On sighs do I feast.

FORSAKEN OF GOD.

There are two meanings to the expression "forsaken of God." One is the sense of being forsaken by him, such as Christ felt upon the cross when he cried out, " My God, my God, why hast thou forsaken me ?" (Mark 15 : 34). This involves some desire after God, if not actual communion with him. There may have been some of this in Babylonia. Yet even the cry for forgiveness may proceed from a selfish desire of good, rather than from grief at having done that which is displeasing to God.

Another is in the sense of being a reprobate, without God, and so even manifestly and offensively ungodly. This sense of the phrase is used more in speaking of others than of one's self. Men are not apt to count themselves reprobates, but they are often strongly tempted to pronounce harsh judgment on others, and of this we find examples in the monuments. Esarhaddon, (R. I. 43. 1. 38) pronounces **Sanduari**, king of **Kundi** and **Sizuu**, as one whom the gods had forsaken, *i. e.*, given over to destruction. And Asshurbanipal gives very broad hints that his rebel brother **Shamash shum ukin** was no better, as he says, Ass'l. 160. 81 and 82, " For these things which he boasted of Asshur and Ishtar turned from him," and again, 162. 100, 101, " Those who devised evil with him famine seized them. For food they ate the flesh of their sons and daughters."

* Compare Isa. 59 : 11.

FOUNTAINS, A LAND OF.

Deut. 8:7 describes the promised land as a "land of brooks of water, of fountains and depths springing forth in valleys and hills." It is a lovely Arcadian picture, but he who would appreciate it to the full must travel in Bible lands, and after suffering the extremity of thirst all day come at evening to such a region. Then he will understand the beauty of the description.

Asshurbanipal speaks of nine cities in the mountains of **Khuukkurunu**, and calls it **ashar kuppi nambai sha mi**, a region of fountains and springs of water, and then adds that over them all he set guards, and so cut off the water of the life of their souls and made water for drinking very costly to their mouths; *i. e.*, to be obtained only at the hazard of their lives, so that they died of thirst and hunger. R. V. 9. 27-35 and A. M. 31. 21-26.

He had previously told that in Laribda, a fortified city built of sheet stone, whatever that might be, "I pitched my tent among cisterns of water." This also is pleasant, but the next sentence is, "My army destroyed the water for drinking so that the enemy might have no supply." Of course the same result followed here also.

FUNERALS.

Luke 8:2. Now when he drew near to the gate of the city, behold there was carried out one that was dead.

It is evident that the burial took place outside of the gate. So in Babylonia the cemetery was outside of the city walls and the mourners carried the dead there on a bier, as at Nain. The body was laid on the ground wrapped in reed mats covered with bitumen. It wore the dress and ornaments it had worn in life. The woman wore her earrings and other ornaments, and her distaff was placed in her hand. The man had his seal and weapons, also some of the tools of his trade, and the child still wore his necklace of shells. Above all was laid a layer of clay, strewn often with branches of palm and other trees, and the whole was burned to ashes. In later times oven-like chambers were built of brick, and the cremation was not so complete but that the skeleton often remained fairly preserved. Offerings such as dates, calves and sheep, birds and fish, were buried with the body. The result of the cremation if complete enough was placed in an urn inside of a brick tomb, or a tomb was erected over the remains that had been only partially consumed by the fire. The cemetery rose higher as the roofs of the tombs of one age became the floors for those of the next, like the stories of a building. The tombs of the rich consisted of several chambers, and sometimes they were adorned by monuments commemorating their names and virtues, or by statues in a sitting posture perpetuating their features.

Only kings and their families could be buried inside the city walls. They were interred in their own palaces, or gardens. See 2 Kings 21 : 26 and 2 Chron. 33 : 20; and one king is said to have been burned or buried in the palace of Sargon. Prof. Sayce's Social life among the Assyrians, etc., 54–57.

Does not the above also illustrate 2 Chron. 16 : 14: "And they made a very great burning for him" (Asa), also 21 : 19 and Jer. 34 : 5?

FURNACE OF FIRE.

Dan. 3 : 6. Cast into the midst of a burning fiery furnace. Compare verses 11, 15, 17, and 19–27.

In the monuments we have the destruction of life by fire, yet there is some question as to the mode. The word **miqit** is used, the construct form of **miqtu**, from the verb **maqatu**, to fall. That may possibly have been the ordinary term used for furnace, as that into which the doomed men fell down or were thrown down, Dan. 6 : 23, or that which caused them to fall, *i. e.*, destroyed them.

In R. V. 4. 51, 52 and A. M. 26. 6, 7, Ass'l. 163. 108, 109, Asshurbanipal says of his rebel brother **Shamash shum ukin** "They cast him into a **miqit** of consuming (literally cursed) fire and destroyed his life."

The many other accounts of the destruction of life by fire (see under the word "Fire") may have been by means of a furnace, but we have no record of the mode of applying the fire, or of the form and construction of the furnace.

It would seem, however, to have been such as could be got up readily and speedily when wanted. They do not seem to have thought it necessary to say how it was done. They did not anticipate that a day would ever come when the readers of their annals would feel interest enough in the immense destruction of human life there set forth to inquire how it had been brought about.

GASHMU.

The name Gashmu occurs in Neh. 6:6 as one of the talking enemies of the Jews. To the readers of the English version it is a name, nothing more, and many never think of it as having any significance; but to the man of Assyria it brought up the image of an old Accadian goddess whose name denoted "The wise one." She is identified with the goddess **Zarpanitu,** or as is sometimes written **Zirbanitu** (creator of seed), the wife of **Bil Marduk,** the god of Babylon.

It is one of the pleasant testimonies to the accuracy of Holy Scripture even in little things, when what might have seemed a mere meaningless name is thus linked in with the mythological traditions of a neighboring people, and represents one of the dwellers in their Olympus.

Aside from this, is there not a stroke of quiet humor conveyed by the statement, "'The wise one' saith it,"? as if for that reason the malicious slander must certainly be true.

GATE (CITY).

Great prominence is given to the gate of the city in Scripture. It was there that judicial transactions took place. Ruth 4:1-11, Amos 5;15, Zech. 8:16. The king sometimes sat there, Jer. 38:7, and princes, Jer. 39:3. Mordecai sat there, Esth. 2:19, 21, and Daniel, Dan. 2:49. So we find in the Assyrian monuments (R. I. 19. 99) that Asshurnatsirpal set up inscriptions celebrating his illustrious majesty in the gate of **Khiindanna,** and Asshurbanipal, after mutilating and torturing **Vaiteh,** king of Arabia, exposed him in a cage at the eastern gate of Nineveh (R. V. 8. 12, 13, and A. M. 28. 23; 33. 20; R. V. 9. 109, 110); and when Sennacherib would describe the straitness of the siege of Jerusalem he says (R. I. 39, 22, and A. M. 12. 16), "Him who came out of the gate I turned back." He also tells how the sons of Babylon, wicked devils, barred the gates and set about making war. R. I. 41. 5, 6, and A. M. 14. 6, 7.) See under "Entering of the Gate."

GENESIS 10.

This chapter is the one reliable ethnological chart of ancient history. Appreciated to some extent in the past, its value shines out as never before in the light of modern discoveries. Of course its statements have been challenged, as all truth is, sooner or later, but the more thorough the investigation the higher has this scripture risen in the estimation of investigators. A suggestion of Prof. Sayce corrects a misconception of some of its assailants. He says (Fresh Light, etc., 36), "The nations are here grouped according to geographical position, not according to ethnologic relations; *e. g.*, non-Semitic Elamites are classed with their neighbors, the Semitic Assyrians, and Phœnicians with Egyptians. Keeping this in mind, the chapter is in perfect harmony with the latest results of modern research."

Japhet is the Assyrian **ippat** (the white race), Ham is **khammu** (the burned black race), and Shem is **shumu** (the intermediate, or, as Prof. Sayce has it, olive-colored race). Gomer is the **Gimirrai** of the monuments, defeated by Esarhaddon, B. C. 570; Javan (Ionian) is the Hebrew name of Cyprus (Assyrian **Yavnan**), visited by Sargon of Accad B. C. 3750; Tubal and Meshech (**Tibareni** and **Moschi**) are yoked together in Assyrian as in Hebrew. Both dwelt in Cappadocia. Ashkenaz (Assyrian **Asguza**) lay between Ekbatana and the **Minni.** Cush lay south of the first cataract of the Nile, now Nubia. Mitsraim was the two *matsors* (walls), *i. e.*, forts built to defend Egypt from the Bedawin. The Pathrusim were the dwellers in *Peto res* (the south land). Phut is *Puut* on the Somali coast. The Lehabim were the Libyans. The Caphtorim were the men of **Keft ur** (greater Phœnicia), on the delta of the Nile, and so on.

GLADNESS AND REJOICING.

No one familiar with the Old Testament can have failed to notice how gladness is set forth by an accumulation of terms expressing the sense of enjoyment. One word is not sufficient to express the delight that fills the heart, and so duplication and iteration are employed to describe what otherwise had been unutterable. Examples will readily occur to all. Ps. 45:15 says, "With gladness and rejoicing shall they be brought;" *i. e.*, the bridesmaids of the queen. Ps. 51:8 prays, "Make me to hear joy and gladness." Perhaps the two Hebrew words employed most frequently to denote this superabundance of joy are ששון and שמחה. These occur together in Isa. 22:13, 35:10 and 51:3, 11. One of these passages furnishes another similar combination, "songs and everlasting joy," 35:10, still carrying out the iteration.

The Assyrian furnishes numerous examples of the same overflow of joyful emotion : **ina khidaati u rishaati** will at once occur to every tyro in that language. They may be rendered " with joy and rejoicing." Nabonidus uses them to describe his joy at finding the corner-stone of a temple of Shamash laid by Asshurbanipal (R. V. 64. 2. 2, and A. M. 36. 15), and also his delight when the gods **Sin, Ningal, Nusku** and **Sadur nunna,** p. 66, brought him into Babylon (R. V. 64. 20, and A. M. 36. 33), and yet again when **Shamash** and **Rammanu** revealed to him in a vision the corner-stone laid by **Naram Sin,** the son of Sargon of Agade. R. V. 64. 63, and A. M. 38. 5. Compare R. V. 64. 3. 6, and A. M. 38. 12.

So also Asshurbanipal entered with joy and rejoicing into **Bit riduti,** the palace of his father Esarhaddon. R. V. 2. 23, and A. M. 20. 6.

GLORIFY GOD.

Rev. 15:4. Who shall not fear thee, O Lord, and glorify thy name? for thou only art holy. 1 Pet. 4:11 : That God in all things may be glorified. 1 Cor. 10:31 : Whether therefore ye eat, or drink, or whatever ye do, do all to the glory of God. It surely is a token for good when we find the heathen moved by the desire to glorify the idols, who in their minds take the place of God.

The priest in the temple of **Bil Marduk** at Babylon, at the feast **Zagmuku,** on the night of the new year, sang a hymn of which these lines form a part. The Assyrian copy in R. IV. 47 is badly mutilated. Prof. Sayce's translation in H. L. 81 seems to have been made from a more perfect copy :

O Bil (lord) of the world, light of the spirits of heaven, utterer of blessings,
What mouth does not murmur of thy righteousness?
Or speaks not of thine exaltation, and celebrates not thy glory?

In R. V. 9. 112, A. M. 33. 22, and Ass'l. 281. 94, Asshurbanipal, after placing **Vaiteh,** king of Arabia, in a cage at the eastern gate of Nineveh, adds: "To show forth the glory of **Asshur, Ishtar** and the great gods my lords, I showed him mercy and spared his life." When just before this (R.V. 8. 12) he had said that he "shut him up with his dogs to show forth the glory of Asshur and the great gods," it seemed in keeping with the general current of Assyrian affairs, but one is surprised to find the declaration that the exercise of mercy glorifies the one who is supposed to have inspired it; yet in implanting such ideas in the mind of the king of Nineveh God has not left himself without witness that Jesus Christ is the light of the world. John 8:12.

GO BEFORE, OR, GO FORTH WITH.

Exodus 13, 21, 22. And the Lord went before them by day in a pillar of cloud, to lead them the way, and by night in a pillar of fire, to give them light, etc. Psa. 108:11. Thou goest not forth, O God, with our hosts.

In R. I. 20. 25, 26, Asshurnatsirpal says: The great god Marduk went before me (**alik pania**) with the mighty weapons of Asshur, the lord of night.

Also in R. V. 9. 88, 89, and A. M. 33. 4, and Ass'l. 279. 72–74, Asshurbanipal says: "The god **Nusku,** the exalted messenger, the author of government, who by the command of Asshur and Beltis, the mighty goddess of war, went forth with my armies (**idiaa illik ma**) and preserved my royalty; in front of my army he held (his place) (**itsbat ma**) and destroyed my enemies."

Also, in R. V. 1. 82: **Asshur, Bil, Nabu,** the great gods my lords, marching by my side (**alikut ittiya**) in the broad field of battle, I accomplished his overthrow—*i. e.*, of Tirhakah.

GOD OF GODS.

Deut. 10:17. For Jehovah your God is God of gods and Lord of lords.

This is a clear and explicit declaration of the superiority of the true God above all that is called god, a declaration needed in some quarters to-day as much as it was ever needed in the past. Compare 1 Tim. 6:16; Rev. 19:16.

One of the lines of the hymn sung to **Bil Marduk** in his great temple at Babylon was, "Thou art the god of gods." H. L. 99.

Asshurbanipal tells us, Ass'l. 73. 16, that the god **Asshur** caused Gyges, king of Lydia, to see a vision in which he was told to submit himself to the yoke of the king of Assyria, "the beloved of **Asshur** king of the gods and lord of all."

While Merodach was only "*primus inter pares*" among the Babylonian gods, and that simply because Babylon bore rule over the other cities, Asshur was the king of the Assyrian pantheon to all his worshippers.

GODS, ANIMAL.

The question must often occur to those that think, How could rational men worship irrational brute beasts? When Israel bowed down to the golden calf they said, "These are thy gods, O Israel, which have brought thee up out of the land of Egypt." Exod. 32:8.

It is easy to say that animals are symbols of qualities, any one can see that, but it affords not the least justification of beast worship. We do not worship symbols but the living God, as it is written, from the lips of Jesus, "Thou shalt worship the Lord thy God, and him only shalt thou serve." Matt. 4:4.

Though we may not be able to explain it save as the Bible ascribes it to the working of ungodliness and unbelief, yet the monuments furnish abundant corroboration of the fact that they were guilty of this folly. It is well known that the Egyptians represented their gods under the forms of animals. And the sacred bull of Egypt must have given shape to that idolatry of Israel in Horeb.

The oldest forms of idolatry in Babylonia also point in the same direction. **Ea,** the god of ancient Eridu, was known as "the antelope of the deep," "the antelope the prince," "the antelope the creator." **Merodach,** the god of Babylon, was "the

ONE OF THE SHIDI. (see p. 98.)

bull of light." He had also two other bulls attached to him, one named "the god of the field of Eden," and the other, "the god of the house of Eden." Another name of Ea was "the princely gazelle," "the gazelle who bestows the earth," and his son **Asshur ilim** was known as "the mighty one of the gazelle god." H. L. 280-284. The gods of the ancient Babylonians seem to have corresponded to the Totems of our own Indians. The winged bulls also at the gates of the Assyrian palace were its divine guardians. The body of the animal denoted strength, and the human head rational intelligence, and so its worshipper might claim that it did not belong to the brute creation.

GODS MANY AND LORDS MANY.

The reader of 1 Cor. 8:5 in our English version asks, What is the difference between the two expressions? The Assyrian gives a very clear answer to the inquiry in the very familiar expression "such and such a god my lord;" *e.g.*, Asshurbanipal (R. V. 2.107) says, **ina tukulti Asshur u Ishtar ilani biliya**: by the help (or in the service) of the gods Asshur and Ishtar my lords," *i. e.*, these two deities to whom I owe allegiance and in whom I trust. The word god denotes one who is regarded as a deity by some nations somewhere, but the word lord denotes the chosen object of personal worship and obedience. So he speaks of **ilani rabuti biliya**: the great gods my lords. R. V. 4. 60, 8. 30, 9. 91. Nabonidus also, R. V. 64. 18, speaks of **ilu Sin ilu Ningal ilu Nusku u ilu Sadarnunna biliya**, the gods Sin, Ningal, Nusku, and Sadarnunna, my lords. It is precisely the distinction that was in the mind of Thomas when he cried, "My Lord and my God," John 20:28; only in the fervor of his love he puts the particular before the general and personally appropriates both.

GOETH.

The centurion said to Christ, Matt. 8:9, "I also am a man under authority, having under myself soldiers, and I say to this one 'go' and he goeth, and to another 'come' and he cometh."

It is in curious correspondence with this that we find the Assyrian verb "**saparu**," to send, used also in the sense of "to govern." Sargon, in the 45th line of his cylinder inscription, speaks of the 350 kings who before him **iltanaparu baulat Bil** (the 1.3.* form of the verb), meaning literally "were sending the subjects of Bil," but he used it in the sense "were governing" or ruling them. See also Layard 33. 5, **ultashpiru baulat Bil**. (the III.2 * form of the verb with the same meaning.)

This last text contains another illustration of this in the word **mu'aru** in the sense of ruler. The verb **maaru** means also to send, but the derived word **numairu** likewise means ruler or general, precisely corresponding to the statement of the centurion. The word occurs in an inscription of Sennacherib, R. I.

---

* This is a technical designation of one of the several forms of the verb.

41.70, and also in one of Shalmanezer II., 858-824 B. C. Layard 87. 8.

The words of the centurion have a striking illustration in the records of Tiglath Pileser I. (R. I. 12.52): **Ilu Asshur bil umai'ranni ma allik.** "Lord Asshur sent me and I went."

GOINGS OUT.

The reader of the Old Testament meets now and then with this somewhat strange expression, and wonders what it means. See Num. 33:2; Deut. 33:18; Num. 34:5, 8, 9, and 12; Josh. 15:4, 7, and 11; 16:3, 8, etc.

The Hebrew is מוֹצָא, a noun formed from a verb meaning to go forth. And the Assyrian uses the same word, **muutsa,** from the same verb, and having precisely the same meaning. R. V. 3. 132 and A. M. 24. 26. Asshurbanipal says of Sippar (Sepharvaim), Babil, Barsip (Borsippa), and Kutu, "I seized their outgoings" **muutsashun,** and he says the same of Miimpi (Memphis) (R. V. 2.26 and A. M. 48.27).

Both in Hebrew and Assyrian the country was pictured as going out from the centre until it reached the boundary of a neighboring State, and there came to an end.

So the **mutsa** of waters was a fountain, and the goods exported from a country were also its **mutsa.**

GOLD.

It is amazing how much of this precious metal was used in and about the temple. The mercy-seat was of pure gold. Ex. 25:17. The ark was overlaid with pure gold (verse 11) both within and without. The candlestick was of pure gold (verse 31), so were the dishes and spoons (verse 29), and even the snuff-dishes—snuffers (verse 38). The porch in front, 20 cubits long and 120 cubits high, was overlaid with pure gold. 2 Chron. 3:4. And Solomon garnished the house with precious stones for beauty (verse 6). House-beams, thresholds, walls, and doors were overlaid with gold (verse 7). The Holy of Holies was overlaid with 600 talents' (55,950 lbs.) weight of gold, and the weight of the nails was 50 shekels (verses 8, 9).

So in the description of the ark (**papakhu**) of Merodach. R. II.

25. 10. Its serpent-like oar had a golden handle, and its mast was pointed with turquoise. H. L. 67 and 527. The cedar work of the great temple of Bel Merodach in Babylon was over laid by Nebuchadrezzar with gold and silver, and its furniture, also like that of the temple at Jerusalem, was made of massive gold.

The following selections from the India House inscription show this: "Silver, gold, brightness of precious stones—what thing soever is precious in large abundance—into his presence I brought. **E kua**, the Adytum of Merodach, the lord of the gods, I made its walls to shine like suns with abundant gold. The chapel of the lordship of Merodach, the open-eyed ruler of the gods, I overlaid with glistening gold, and the vessels of the temple with large gold. The barque of Merodach I made bright as the stars of heaven with **Zariru** stones. The huge cedar beams for the roof of **E kua** I overlaid with shining gold, the panels underneath I made bright with gold and precious stones. The cedar of the roof of the Adyta of Nebo I overlaid with gold The cedar of the roof of the gate of **Nana** I overlaid with shining silver. The throne in the chapel was made of silver," etc., etc. See R. of P. new III. 102–123.

GOURD. קִיקָיוֹן.

Jonah 4: 5, 6. Then Jonah went out of the city and sat on the east side of the city, and there made him a booth and sat under it in the shadow till he might see what would become of the city. And the Lord God prepared a gourd and made it to come up over Jonah, that it might be a shadow over his head, to deliver him from his evil case.

Jerome rendered קִיקָיוֹן in the vulgate by the Latin word *hedera*. The Septuagint and Syriac versions translate it *gourd*. And both Augustine and Luther follow their example. Some think it is the *Ricinus Palma Christi*, or castor oil plant. This last is not unknown in the neighborhood of ancient Nineveh to-day, for the natives burn castor oil in their lamps it is so common, but Niebuhr, with his accustomed accuracy, says that both Jews and Christians there understand by it the gourd, *el kerra*. Dr. Henry Lobdell, one of our missionaries there from 1852 till his death in 1855, though at first inclined to the *Ricinus* theory, was constrained as he became better acquainted with the facts to take a stand in favor of the gourd, and the writer never heard any other idea advanced in all that region; and yet Smith's Dict. of Bible, after stating the testimony of Niebuhr and Dr. Lobdell, adds (p. 961), " There can, we think, be no reasonable doubt that the **kikayon** which afforded shade to the prophet is the castor-oil plant."

So far is that from being true, that the Scripture narrative seems to forbid it, no less than the unanimous native tradition in which Jews and Christians are agreed, without exception, however they may differ in other things; for the prophet himself tells us that he erected a booth for shelter from the sun, and the Lord made the gourd to come up over him—of course while under his booth, to make the protection more complete, or to supplement the withering of the leaves wherewith he had covered it by something more sufficient; and who ever heard of a castor-oil plant being trained over a booth? Well does Dr. Lobdell say (Memoir, p. 258), " The castor-oil plant is never trained, like the *kera* or pumpkin-squash, to run over structures of mud and brush to form booths in which gardeners may protect themselves from the terrible heat of the sun in this region. I have seen at one glance dozens of these 'lodges in a garden of cucumbers' (Isa. 1:8) around the old walls of Nineveh, covered with kera vines, of which there are numerous species, with fruit varying from one to fifty pounds' weight." See also Bibliotheca Sacra, April, 1855.

GRAMMATICAL FORM.

An interesting illustration of the accuracy of Holy Scripture and its conformity to the circumstances in which it was written occurs in the use of an unusual grammatical form in Dan. 2:20 and 3:18. The form להוא is found in both these passages, and Prof. Gesenius says of them in his Lexicon (Boston, 1844, p. 252. col. 2. note), " In the formation of the future of this verb there occurs this singularity, that in the third person singular and plural is found the prefix ל (l) where we should expect the preformative י (y) and this with the regular and usual signification of the future or subjunctive." He adds, " Forms of this kind are found in the Targums. From all this it appears that the forms are not infinitives, as is sometimes supposed, but that in such examples, either the ל is put for the **nun** of the Syrians, or else these forms have arisen out of the Hebrew usage which began to put לקטל *liqtol* instead of יקטל *yiqtol*."

Thus does that learned Hebraist voice his perplexity; but had he lived to read Assyrian he would have found a far better explanation of this unusual form. The Assyrian has what is called a precative form of the verb, denoting a wish that the action may take place. It is formed by prefixing **lu** or **li** to any form of the aorist. Prof. Sayce's Elem. Ass. Gram. 66, and A. M. 38. 2.

In his A. L. and S. Prof. Sayce says, p. 91: "The precative is generally used only in the third person; occasionally it is found in the first, and once or twice in the second person." The third person singular precative of the regular verb **shakanu** is **liishkun,** and in this passage from Daniel we have the Assyrian precative form applied to a Hebrew verb, as would be likely to be done by those accustomed to converse in Assyrian when they wrote in Hebrew. Daniel said, "Let the name of God be blessed from eternity to eternity;" and his three associates said, "Let it be known unto thee, O king!" etc.

Though this is a technicality in Assyrian grammar it is a beautiful illustration of the help afforded by the Assyrian language to the right understanding of the Hebrew Scriptures.

GREAVES.

1 Sam. 17:6. And he had greaves of brass upon his legs.

The greaves worn by the Greek soldier were of metal and intended to protect the leg, but we find nothing of the kind in the bas-reliefs. There we have a kind of laced boot, as pictured in L. N. II. 261. 268. and B. and N. 458. It may be made of cloth or of leather—it evidently is one of the two. Still it is not the "hosen" of Dan. 3:21, for that is a mistranslation, and should be rendered "tunics," *i. e.,* the inner garment or shirt. The only word that can describe them is סאון, Isa. 9:5, which Gesenius renders "shoe," translating that passage "every shoe of the shod," *i. e.,* of the soldier, who specially seems to have been privileged to wear them. Our version renders wildly "every battle of the warrior," and the revised version "all the armor of the armed man."

In the bas-reliefs it certainly seems to be a very comfortable covering for the foot, protecting it from injury from the roughness of the road, and enabling the wearer to travel far without discomfort.

HADADRIMMON.

Zech. 12 : 11. In that day shall there be a great mourning in Jerusalem, as the mourning of Hadadrimmon in the valley of Megiddon.

Rimmon was the supreme god of the Syrians of Damascus. When Benhadad was king of Syria, Naaman the captain of his host was healed of his leprosy by Elisha, and in leaving he said to the prophet (2 Kings 5 : 18) : When my master goeth into the house (temple) of Rimmon to worship, leaning on my hand, and I bow myself with him, the Lord pardon thy servant in this thing. Hadad was the sun god of Northern Syria, and he was called Rimmon as corresponding to Rammanu, the god of the air in Assyria, and was worshipped as far south as Megiddon. The special worship and mourning referred to by Zechariah was the annual mourning for Tammuz. (See under "Tammuz)."

Prof. Sayce affirms that the Assyrian inscriptions prove the identity of Rimmon and Hadad, and in the records of Shalmanezer II. Benhadad appears as **Dada idri** or Hadadezer. See inscriptions of Shalmanezer II. in R. of P. new IV. 71. 98 and 76. 2.

HAMATH.

2 Kings 14 : 28 speaks of Hamath as belonging to Judah, but that city is so far off that it cannot be said to belong to the territory of that tribe, and we have no record of its having been captured in war and so made a dependence of that kingdom. Even David at the time of his greatest prosperity did not subdue Hamath. For its king only sent a friendly message and presents by his son Joram because David had conquered Hadadezer, with whom he was at war. 2 Sam. 8 : 9, 10. The careful reader, however, will notice that the verb "belonged" is not in the Hebrew. It is supplied by the translators, and the monuments

tell us that the city was on friendly terms with Judah, and Jeroboam detached it from Judah and drew it over to the side of Israel.

Sargon speaks of a **Yahubidi** of Hamath, whose name implies that he was a worshipper of Jehovah, and so most likely from Judah, which was noted for loyalty to the true God. He was also known as **Ilubidi** (worshipper of God.) Prof. Lyon's Sargon. Cyl. 25.

HANAMEEL AND JEREMIAH.

The monuments shed a fresh light on the legal transaction recorded in Jer. 32 : 6-15.

The prophet, forewarned of the coming of his nephew to ask him as the nearest of kin to redeem a piece of land in Anathoth, complies with the request, and makes the bargain for 17 shekels of silver. Then, precisely as would have been done in Babylon or Nineveh, he weighs out that amount in bars of that metal. The deed is written on a tablet of soft clay. The prophet subscribes it and affixes his seal, the witnesses do the same, and the silver is formally reweighed in their presence, it may be, also, in their balances, or in those of the man who received the money. The tablet is then encased in an envelope of clay, as we put our letters in one of paper, only the clay fits more snugly, so that both become practically one, though the outside one can be peeled off and leave the enclosure intact. A summary of the deed inside is then inscribed on the envelope to distinguish it from other documents that may be laid away with it. Jeremiah delivers both the wrapper and its enclosure to Baruch in the presence of Hanameel and his witnesses, with directions to put them in an earthen vessel for preservation. Deeds and similar documents written on clay, that have been discovered, were found in earthen jars buried in the earth precisely as the prophet directed Baruch to dispose of this. Prof. Sayce adds, "Who can say whether we shall not yet recover the deed of sale signed by Jeremiah, and the jar to which it was entrusted, as we have already recovered similar deeds signed by his contemporaries in Babylonia?" Social life of Assyrians, pp. 32 and 73.

HANNAH AND SAMUEL.

1 Sam. 1. This story is too familiar to need repetition here, and though we may hardly have looked for such a thing yet the monuments furnish a case somewhat similar, though by no means so striking. Nor does it touch the heart like the narrative of the devout Hebrew mother and her boy.

The following is the substance of a tablet published by Dr. Strassmayer and reprinted in R. of P. new IV. 109-113.

Ummudhabat (the mother is good), wife of **Shamash Yuballidh** (the sun god gave life), brought a tablet to the priest of the god **Shamash**, and also **Shamash edhir, Nidditu** and **Aradkin**, her three sons, and said, " They have not yet entered the house of the males (**Bit zikaru.**) With my sons I have grown old till they are counted among the men." She then made written application for their admission, as she desired to devote them to the service of the sun god. Here follow the names of the witnesses.

" The house of the males " was a sort of monastic institution attached to one of the temples. Its superintendent received monthly supplies of provision for himself and associates, who lived together and aided in the daily services of the temple. The institution resembled that in which Daniel and his three friends were placed by Nebuchadrezzar, only, while that was for the service of the state, this was for the temple exclusively.

HARAN—KHARRAN.

Terah emigrated from Ur to this city (Gen. 11 : 31) and died there, (v. 32,) and Abraham was 75 years old when he departed out of it (12 : 4) for Canaan. The name is spelled in various ways: Haran, Harran, and Kharran. The last is the Assyrian form, and is an old Accadian word meaning " road." This name was given to it probably because it was on the road to the Mediterranean Sea from Babylonia—a sort of half-way house. Then, like Ur, it was sacred to Sin, the moon god, whose temple in Kharran rivaled that of Ur. The name Kharran occurs in early texts, and Nabonidus records his restoration of the temple of the moon god there, which he says had stood from time immemorial. R. V. 64. 8 and 23-29. A. M. 35. 7 and 37. 1-7. Sargon, also, whose palace has been brought to light in Khorsabad, records that he had ex-

HARPS.

tended his protection over Kharran and by the command of Anu and Dagan had written (again) its laws. S. 13. 10 and 40. 10. The famous temple called **E Khulkhul**, house of rejoicing, which was restored by Nabonidus about B. C. 550, had previously been repaired by Shalmaneser III., B. C. 783-773, and by Asshurbanipal, B. C. 668-626. Showing how frequently such structures needed renovation.

HARPS.

The subject of music will be presented under that head, but some readers may look for an allusion to that touching passage in the Psalms (138: 1, 2): "By the rivers of Babylon there we sat down, yea, we wept when we remembered Zion. Upon the willows in the midst thereof we hanged up our harps," and so that instrument is here spoken of separately.

This passage is as distinct as a photograph. We can see the weeping willows along the banks of the sluggish canals, where the exiles retired to be alone in their sorrow and indulge in thoughts of their distant home. They hang up their harps on the branches, for they are too sad to find comfort in them, and they may also have wanted them safe from the injury that might befall them if left within reach of the children, who had gone out with them, and who—more easily comforted than those who remembered Zion—might be tempted to indulge in uncongenial music.

The bas-relief under "Music" gives a very good idea of the Babylonish harp. If one has good eyes he may count as many as fifteen strings on some of them, and also note openings in the hollow frames of two of them to make them more resonant. The artist has left out the fastening that must have held the instrument in place so as to leave both hands free for playing, and we see at once how unsuited were the quick measured step and clapping of the hands to the state of mind of these Jewish exiles. One can readily picture the sharp antagonism of such a procession to the grief of the Jews, and the taunting sarcasm which as their haughty conquerors swept by would sneeringly call for one of the songs of Zion from the heartbroken captives.

HEAD.

1 Sam. 31:9. And they cut off his head. 1 Chron. 10:10. And fastened his head in the house of Dagon.

These passages relate the treatment which the corpse of Saul received from the Philistines. A similar record is made by Asshurbanipal concerning the king of Elam. R. V. 3. 36 he says, "I cut off the head of Teumman, their king." So in Ass'l. 129. 100, "The head of Teumman king of Elam by command of Asshur and Merodach, the great gods my lords, before the assembly of his army I cut off;" and 137. 57, "The decapitated head of Teumman in front of the great gate in Nineveh I set up as a votive offering."

G. S. translates **Umakhkhira makhkhuris** "I raised on high;" but **makharu** means to be in front of, hence to pray, or offer sacrifice, and **makhuru** is prayer, or offering, with the adverbial termination meaning like, or, in the style of.

HEAD, CARRYING OFF.

1 Sam. 17:54 tells us that David took the head of Goliath, which he had cut off, and brought it to Jerusalem. This does not accord with the practices of modern war, but it was perfectly in accord with the customs of his time. Mr. Layard gives a copy of a bas-relief (L. N. II. 147) representing warriors bringing the heads of their slaughtered foes to be counted by the scribes of the army, and in R. I. 45. 47-51 and A. M. 19. 13-15 we have the following record: "Because of the power of Asshur my lord, to men were exhibited the heads of **Saanduarri** and **Abdimiilkuuti** suspended from the necks of their great men;" and a copy of a bas-relief in B. and N. 457 shows a man with such a ghastly burden under the leading of a warrior.

HEART STIRRED HIM UP.

Ex. 35:22. And they came, every one whose heart stirred him up and every one whom his spirit made willing, and brought the Lord's offering.

The object of a translation is to express in another language the idea before us just as it stands, adding nothing to and taking nothing away from the original statement. Now

HEART STIRRED HIM UP. 153

in the Hebrew there is no hint of "stirring" up. That implies excitement and commotion; but instead of that is the calm, steady movement of "lifting" up. They came, every one whose heart "lifted him up" to a higher level of beneficence. Nor is this a distinction without a difference. The heart may be stirred up by social excitements, by dancing, by games of chance, by the prospect of a lucky ticket in a lottery, and all these things have been resorted to in order to "stir up" people to build a house of worship; but none of these is the Lord's way. His way is so to move the heart by his Spirit that it shall be raised to a higher spirit of consecration and so lift up the whole man, and make him disposed, not through the working of ungodly excitement, but through the indwelling of the Spirit of God, to bring the Lord's offering.

In this matter it will do professed disciples of Christ no harm to learn a lesson from one whom they may have looked down on as a heathen king.

Nebuchadrezzar, king of Babylon, in the India House inscription (III. 18, 19), tells us, "To build **E Saggilla** my heart lifted me up;" the identical verb used by Moses in the Hebrew, נשא, occurring here in the Babylonian.

It may be objected, however, that in using that word the king of Babylon only gave another expression of his pride and self-sufficiency, such as we find in Daniel 4: 30: "Is not this great Babylon, which I have built for the royal dwelling-place by the might of my power, and for the glory of my majesty?" but, if such is the impression any one receives from lines 18 and 19, let him read lines 33-35 in the same column: "For the building of E Sagilla daily I besought the king of the gods, the lord of lords" (Bel Merodach). When the heart of a disciple of Christ lifts him up to build a house for the service of his Master, and he daily feels constrained to go to God in prayer and implore his blessing on the undertaking, we do not feel called on to say much of his pride and self-sufficiency. I repeat it, then: it will do professed disciples no harm to learn a lesson from this heathen king.

See further under "Nebuchadrezzar."

HEAVEN.

Several things are called by this name in the Holy Scripture:

a. The air which is above the earth; so birds are called the "fowl of the air," Gen. 2:19, and also "the fowls of the heaven," Psa. 104:12.

b. The sky or firmament, Gen. 1:17, 22:17; Deut. 1:10.

c. "The heaven of heavens," Psa. 168:4; called also "the third heaven," 2 Cor. 12:2. There is the throne of God, Psa. 103:19, 123:1, and there also is our home "not made with hands," 2 Cor. 5:1.

This threefold meaning of the word appears also in the Assyrian:

a. The air; **itstsuri shamii,** birds of heaven, R. V. 4. 76, and A. M. 26. 25. also 10. 10.

b. The sky or firmament. Shamash the sun god is called **dan shamii u irtsiti,** the judge of heaven and earth, in the inscription of Shalmanezer II. A. M. 7. 5. Sennacherib speaks of the dust raised by the march of an army covering like heavy clouds the face of the broad heaven, **paan shamii rapshuti.** R. I. 41. 46 and A. M. 15. 13. The deluge tablet speaks of a black cloud rising from the horizon, **isid shamii** (foundation of the heaven), A. M. 58. 11. The same tablet speaks of destructions raining from heaven. A. M. 58. 1.

c. Though we cannot look for such views of heaven in the monuments as are set before us in the New Testament, yet the same tablet last quoted refers to something higher than the visible firmament when, describing the distress and consternation produced among the gods by the deluge, it says that they **itelu ana shamii sha ilu Anu**: ascended to the heaven of the god Anu. A. M. 59. 1. At any rate, it was the serene abode of a deity, undisturbed by the storms of this lower world.

HEBRON AND HITTITES.

That is a beautiful picture of oriental life in Gen. 23 where Abraham rises up from before his dead and purchases a place wherein to bury the body of his beloved Sarah. We cannot see such a scene in the East to-day any more than we can see the beauty of a stream in the prairie after an army has broken down its banks and churned them into mud by the crossing of its wagons and artillery. That which was sincere kindness and sympathy on the part of Ephron the Hittite, the son of Zohar, is now a mere form, not empty indeed, but full of shameless greed and undisguised duplicity.

The Rev. T. K. Cheyne, however, has advanced an objection to the narrative such as hardly ever occurred to others. He says (Encyc. Brit., under "Hittites"): "The undoubted authentic inscriptions of Egypt and Assyria represent the Hittites in far different guise—as preëminently a warlike, conquering race." Can it be that he means to contrast with the "undoubted authentic" nature of the inscriptions a doubtful, unreliable nature of Holy Scripture? He must be not only a bold but a reckless man who could make such a charge in the light of the confirmations of Scripture history that are coming to light on every side, and it would seem to be unfair even to think that he could make such an insinuation. But we are not left to any inference from his words. In another sentence he tells us that this Scripture narrative "cannot be taken as of equal authority with Egyptian and Assyrian inscriptions." We turn to those inscriptions, as described under the head "Hittites" on another page, and are amazed that any man in his right mind should think of comparing the rhodomontade of Pentaur with the simplicity of Moses. Are we told that Pentaur was not only a poet, but poet of the royal court? We reply, Rameses himself did not fall behind him in the exaggerations he stereotyped in the granite of the Ramesseum, and this can be paralleled in Assyria without long searching, while such facts as the destruction of 188,000 men, 2 Kings 19:35, are wholly ignored. More than one disastrous defeat has been set down in the inscriptions as a splendid victory, and yet Holy Scripture, according to the Rev. T. K. Cheyne, cannot be taken as of equal authority! No, for it is as much more truthful as the heavens are higher than the earth.

But let us return to the reason for the condemnation. It is simply this: The Hittites are "preëminently a warlike race;" and because a nation is warlike is it without arts of peace? Does the bloody deck at Trafalgar involve no skilled artisans to build it, no scientific learning to plan it, and no prosperous homes to provide the funds needed to construct and fit out the fleet? Does not the frightful carnage at Waterloo involve like things— many happy homes and also fair ladies' bowers filled with mourning and sorrow? Could the Hittites have carried on the wars they did, and for such a length of time, without a corresponding prosperity at home to sustain them? and do not the gold ornaments found by Schliemann at Hassarlik, with Hittite emblems, no less than the hard basalt wrought in high relief at other places, bear witness to that prosperity and refinement?

Let no one, however, be tempted by this blunder of one man to look with alarm on the most thorough investigation into the reliablity and value of Scripture history. The rock of revelation can let all the floods dash over it, and come out of them not only unharmed but more trusted than before.

As for evidence from outside the Bible that a colony of Hittites lived for a time at Hebron, we should expect that a people so noted for energy and enterprise would send out colonies. They always do. If they are found in Mysia in one direction, why not at Hebron in another? Then the stone in the Louvre from Egypt, belonging to Amenemhat, of the XIIth dynasty, records the overthrow of Hittite palaces in that region, and if they had palaces in the field of Zoan why not possessions also in Hebron? And why did the mention of Hebron in Num. 13:22 call forth the statement, "now Hebron was built seven years before Zoan in Egypt," if there was not such an association of ideas between the Hittite builders of the two that the mention of the one recalled the other? Brugsch Bey, referring to this stone of Amenemhat, says: "The mention of Kheta at this time is remarkable, for it appears to prove that at this time they were *close to Egypt;*" and then Mariette Bey holds that one of the Hyksos dynasties was Hittite, and Dr. Isaac Taylor says: "To the south, at a time prior to the Exodus, their dominion extended as far as Hebron," and Prof. Sayce says (Anc. Emp. of East, 214): "A Hittite tribe even succeeded in settling in the south of Palestine."

HIGHWAYS.

Let us thank God even for the blunder that directs our attention to such confirmations of Scripture history.

HELMETS.

Sam. 17:5: He (Goliath) had a helmet of brass upon his head.

Among a people so warlike as the Assyrians we expect to find armor of all sorts, nor are we disappointed. Their helmets exhibit a great variety of form. There is the round form, like an inverted bowl, the conical and crested forms; no two of them exactly alike. These may be seen in Anc. Mon. I. 441, 442; L. N. II. 236. Herodotus attributes the crested helmet to the Carians, but it seems rather to have originated in Assyria, along with many other things that in time past have been credited to the Greeks.

Ezekiel 27:10 speaks of hanging up the shield and helmet. Do those disks resembling shields on the sides of a ship illustrate this passage? See Anc. Mon. I. 550, and L. N. II. 297.

HIGHWAYS.

Sometimes a whole history is wrapped up in a single term. Many read the name highway and think only of a principal road, larger and more travelled than ordinary ways; but it is more than that. No one who has travelled in Bible lands but must have been impressed by the old Roman roads, with their huge cubical blocks of stone raised above the surface of the soil. And even before the advent of the Roman the prophet cried, Isa. 57:14, "Cast ye up, cast ye up, prepare the way;" *i. e.*, raise it in a convex form above the surface on either side, so as to afford a dry road in the rainy season, like the roads now cast up on our western prairies. If one should describe our railroads by a single epithet he would call them excavated roads, for the hills dug through make a stronger impression, except in rare cases, than the valleys filled up, especially as the railroad seeks the lowest levels. But the Hebrew called the king's road a מסלה *mesillah*, a raised way, or highway, from *salal*, to lift up. Judg. 20:31, 32. And the Assyrian called it **urkhu itlutu** with precisely the same signification. See the inscription of Tiglath Pileser in R. I. 12. 56: **arkhi itluti, durgi la pituti ushetiiq**: raised ways, roads unopened I made passable.

HITTITES, THE.

Josh. 1:4. From the wilderness and this Lebanon even unto the great river, the river Euphrates, all the land of the Hittites.

This people for centuries have been among the lost tribes, but of late years have attracted much attention. Prof. Sayce in several of his works, especially in his Anc. Emp. of East, Rev. W. Wright of Damascus in Trans. S. B. A., and Emp. of the Hittites, London, 1884-1885, and Prof. J. Campbell of Montreal, The Hittites, their Inscriptions and their History, 2 vols, have done much to make us acquainted with them.

The Hebrews called them החתים, the Egyptians *kheta*, and the Assyrians **Khatti.** Ethnographically they were the sons of Heth. Gen. 10:15-18. And Caanan begat Zidon his first-born, and Heth, and the Jebusite, and the Amorite, and the Girgashite, and the Hivite, and the Arkite, and the Sinite, and the Arvadite, and the Zamarite, and the Hamathite.

Their inscriptions have been found at Hamath, Aleppo, Marash, Ibreez, Jerablis (Carchemish), Tyana, and other places. Their monuments at Boghaz Keuy (Pterium) in Angora, and south of that at Eyuk to the west of Cæsarea, at Ninfi (Nymphœum) between Smyrna and Sardis, at Ibreez near the Cilician gates, at the Karabel pass, Giaour Kalessi, and elsewhere.

The inscriptions have not been deciphered sufficiently to determine the language with certainty, but the prevailing impression of scholars is that it is not Semitic. The hieroglyphics are very different from the Egyptian, and many arbitrary signs are found among them.

We have as yet few Hittite inscriptions, and are not able to read even these well enough to learn much of their ancient history. We do not know when the children of Heth left the primitive home of the race, or when they found their way up into Kappadokia. They may have sauntered in oriental style along the road, or even settled down once or twice before they reached the region where they remained so long, but their energy and enterprise, that made them "leaders and commanders" among their neighbors, seem traits produced by a residence for many generations in pure mountain air, corroborating the testimony to the same fact that has been found in the turned up toes of their boots. They seem to have been more intimately connected with Lydia than with any other kingdom. Still they were not confined to any one locality, but as Prof. Sayce says, Anc. Emp. of East, 217, "It is with the Hittite period that Lydian history begins." Ephesus, Smyrna, Kyme, Myrina, Priene, Pitane, were all of them founded by Hittites. Cyprus also was of Hittite origin. Their priestesses, the Amazons clad in the national costume and armed with the double-headed axe, performing their sacred dances with shield and bow in honor of Atargatis or Derketo, the goddess of war and love, gave rise to the myth of a nation of women warriors. (Do. 223.) The Thermodon, on the banks of which the poets placed them, was near Eyuk and Boghaz Keuy, and at Komana in Cappadocia 6,000 ministers served the goddess. She took the place of the Chaldean Nana, and Atys represented the sun god Shamash. They had also gods named Sutekh and Sandon. In Ephesus Atargatis or Ma was named Artemis, and also Kybele and Amma, and her worship as the goddess of reproduction was marked by the same immoralities as in Syria and Babylonia.

Perhaps we should not think of them only as one homogeneous people, but while in some places that was true, in others they may have intermarried more or less with the tribes around them, and were thus enabled to enlist in their wars many more than their own numbers could furnish.

Brugsch Bey (Egypt under the Pharaohs, II. 405, quoted in the Emp. of Hittites, 14) says that on an Egyptian monument in the Louvre, dating from the first king of the XIIth dynasty, is a record of Hittite towns and palaces destroyed on the borders of Egypt. That would be at least 2380 B. C., and Mariette Bey holds that one of the early dynasties was Hittite. About the middle of the 17th century B. C. Thothmes I. began a war against the Hittites which was carried on by his successors for nearly 500 years. (Brugsch Egypt, etc., I. 336, in Wright's Empire of H., 14.) Thothmes III., 1600 B. C., who was victorious

Central Africa to the border of India, prosecuted this war
great energy. On the 25th anniversary of his coronation
ight the battle of Megiddo with the Hittite king of Kadesh,
ad under him all the kings from Egypt to the Euphrates;
he Phœnicians and the army of Cyprus—119 tribes and
. Thothmes was victorious, and took 924 chariots, and the
ot plated with gold used by the Hittite king. He then at-
d Carchemish and Kadesh, the two Hittite capitals. Seven
later he destroyed Kadesh, and drove the Hittites north-
In his ninth campaign—his seventh was in the thirty-
year of his reign—he again stormed Kadesh, and yet after
eath, 1566 B. C., the Hittites became formidable as before,
is successors carried on the war with varying fortunes
as Brugsch Bey says (Egypt, etc., I. 379, in Wright's Em-
etc., 18), "Even Egyptian inscriptions honor the kings of
heta and speak of their gods with reverence." Seti I., who
to the throne 200 years after the death of Thothmes III.,
ied Phœnicia and stormed Kadesh. Under his successor,
reat Rameses II., the oppressor of Israel, war again broke
tween Egypt and the Kheta. The king of the latter ral-
is forces from all parts of his empire. His allies came
Mesopotamia and from Mysia, from Arvad and Kappado-
he Dardanians from the Troad, the men of Aleppo, and
ardy warriors of Gauzanitis. The battle was fought with
carnage. At one time Rameses seems to have been alone
 midst of his foes, but fought his way out. Yet the Egyp-
ccount of it is even ridiculous in its exaggerations. He is
sented as contending alone with 2,500 chariots, manned by
men. The 5,000 horses are dashed in pieces. The hearts
e enemy fail them; their limbs give way; they cannot
t a spear. No one resisted, and none escaped. With his
hand Rameses had slain hundreds of thousands, and yet,
gely, the "vile, miserable" king of the Kheta who entered the
 comes out of it the "great" king. Then there is no record
nder taken to Egypt, as is customary in other campaigns.
 becomes very popular towards the end of the battle, and
he king of the Kheta who dictates the terms of the treaty
alls it an alliance between Kheta and Kemi. The Hittite

is put before the Egyptian (Emp. of Hittites, 109, note), and the great king of Egypt married the daughter of his late adversary in the 34th year of his reign. This treaty was kept to the end of the long reign of Rameses, and through that of his son, Mineptah II., the Pharaoh of the Exodus. More than a century later Rameses III. inscribes among the names of the conquered on the temple of Medinet Abou, " The miserable king of the Hittites." Do. 35.

In "The Observations of Bel," an astronomical work originally written in the time of Sargon of Accad, we read: "The king of the Hittites . . . on the throne seizes," and Prof. Sayce learns from an inscription of Nabonidus that Sargon lived 3750 B. C.; so we might find mention of the Hittites in the Assyrian inscriptions as early as that date did not the professor suggest that Kheta was substituted for **akhitu** (foreign) by the translators or copyists of Asshurbanipal.

Prof. Sayce says of the wars of Tiglath Pileser I., 1120-1110 B. C., that they "weakened the power of the Hittites in the north, and allowed the small states of Syria to make head against them. For more than a century the latter had no powerful neighbors to fear" (R. of P. new I. 88), and Esarhaddon speaks of twenty-two kings of the Hittites, twelve belonging to the shore of Syria and ten to the island of Cyprus. (R. of P. III. 107, 108.)

After the time of Sennacherib Syria was known as the land of the Hittites, though they had been forced back to the northward before the days of Solomon. Asshurnatsirpal, 883-859 B. C., carried the arms of Assyria to Tyre and Sidon, and levied tribute on the Hittites. His son, Shalmanezer II., 858-824 B. C., took Carchemish and carried off many horses and chariots. From Hamah he took 700 war chariots. The Black Obelisk tells that he received the tribute of all the kings of the Hittites, and carried off their chariots. At one time he says, "I captured countless cities," and at another, " 89 cities I took." Shalmanezer died in 823 B. C., and war continued till the time of Sargon, who destroyed Carchemish and slew its king, Pisiri, in 717 B. C.

That must have been a strong nation that, standing between two such powers as Egypt and Assyria, bore the brunt of both of them for more than sixteen and a half centuries. The wonder is not that it succumbed at last, but that it stood so long.

Prof. Sayce supposes that the Hittite occupation of northern Syria took place about the sixteenth century before Christ, and that from 1300 B. C. to 1100 B. C. was the time of their greatest enlargement. Emp. of Hittites, 228.

Hittite art and culture, based on those of Babylonia—for Assyria was then just emerging into notice—date from the time of the founding of their Syrian capitals. Their monuments in Asia Minor were many of them near some silver mine which they had wrought, and some of their records were inscribed on plates of that metal. Their copy of the treaty with Rameses II. was written on silver, and accompanied by a silver plate bearing a likeness of their god Sutekh with an inscription round it, and this probably suggested the idea of silver coins, which were said to be invented by the Lydians; most likely by Hittites in Lydia, for silver plates were a common material for writing among them (Anc. Emp. of the East 229. 231). They had a syllabary of their own, used in Asia Minor before the simpler Phœnician alphabet, and it was still used in Cyprus in 400 B. C. Besides silver, gold and emery were dug out of their mountains. They constructed two highroads for trade, one by Giaoor Kalessi and Ancyra to Boghaz Keuy, used by Krœsos when he marched against Kyros, and the other through Lykaonia and Thonion, by the Kilikian gates, to Antioch and Scanderoon. This trade was so flourishing that the *mina* of Carchemish was the standard all through Western Asia for weighing silver.

The Egyptian monuments speak of **Khilip Sira** (King Khilip) as the writer of the books of the vile Kheta, and Kirjath-sepher (Book-town) was the name of one of their towns. Judg. 1:11.

Their mountain boots have already been described. On the head they wore sometimes a close cap, and again a tiara or a Phrygian cap. They wore an outer tunic with an embroidered edge so arranged as to leave the right arm free. The inner tunic reached only to the knees. They shaved the entire face, and also a place above the ear.

HITTITE CHARIOTS.

2 Kings 7:6. The Lord had made the host of the Syrians to hear a noise of chariots and a noise of horses, even the noise of a great host, and they said one to another, Lo, the king of Israel hath hired against us the kings of the Hittites, and the kings of the Egyptians, to come upon us.

Prof. F. W. Newman says of this, "The unhistorical tone is too manifest to allow of our easy belief in it," and again, "The particular ground of alarm attributed to them does not exhibit the writer's acquaintance with the times in a very favorable light." Once more: "No Hittite kings can have compared in power with the king of Judah, the real and near ally who is not named at all, nor is there a single mark of acquaintance with the contemporaneous history." History of the Hebrew Monarchy, 178, 179.

It seems as though the Almighty allowed such a supercilious attack to be made on his word in order to call attention to the facts in the case.

What have the monuments to say to all this? Prof. Sayce tells us that the empire of Aram Naharaim had been followed by that of the Hittites as far back as the time of the XIXth dynasty (B. C. 1600?), and in the days of Tiglath Pileser I. (B. C. 1130) the Hittites were still paramount from the Euphrates to the Lebanon. (Trans. S. B. A. V. 28.) Asshurnatsirpal (B. C. 883-858) says (R. of P. new II. 168. 57) "To the city of Carchemish, in the country of the Hittites, I took the road. To the country of Bit Bakhiani I approached," and then he tells how he received tribute of chariots, teams, horses, etc., "and chariots, riding horses, and grooms, I took away with me;" and repeats precisely the same things of the country of Azalli. Then in line 65 he says, "The tribute of Sangara, king of the Hittites, twenty talents of silver, beads of gold, a chain of gold, etc., the multitudinous furniture of his palace, of which the like was never received, couches and thrones, dishes, etc., of ivory, two hundred slave girls, variegated cloths, linen vestments, etc., **sirnuma** stones, elephant tusks, and small images of gold in quantities I received." The palace that contained such things belonged to no insignificant monarch or rude savage. "The chariots, riding horses and grooms of Carchemish I carried off."

Then from Kunulua, another Hittite city, he received twenty talents of silver, one talent of gold, one thousand oxen, ten thousand sheep, and rich furniture again in great variety: and their chariots, horses, and grooms he carried off. From all which it appears that the Hittites were noted for their chariots and horses, and that, instead of the sacred writer being "unacquainted with contemporaneous history," it is Prof. Newman who must plead guilty to his own indictment.

And if anything is needed to aggravate his condemnation let the Theban poet Pentaur furnish the evidence. He says that the king of the Hittites had brought with him all the peoples from the uttermost ends of the sea, the peoples of Naharaim Arathu, the Dardani, the Masu, the Pidasa, the Malunna, the Karkish, the Leka, Qazuadana, Carchemish, Akerith, and the whole people of Anaugas Kadesh and Mushanath. He left no people on his road; their number was endless. They covered the mountains and plains like the locusts; and afterwards he describes Rameses II. as engaged in fight single-handed with twenty-five hundred chariots drawn by five thousand horses, and manned by seventy-five hundred men.

True, that belonged to a previous generation, but the memory of it had not passed away when Samaria was besieged. Nor had the empire of the Hittites then passed away. See Rev. W. Wright's Emp. of Hittites, 106, 113–120.

HONOR.

Thoughtful readers of Holy Scripture must have admired the wise selection of the verb in the fifth commandment, Exod. 20:12. "Obey thy father and mother" might have been met by a mere formal and perfunctory obedience in which the heart had no part; "love thy parents" might have been put off with a gush of feeling that yielded no fruit of obedience; but "honor" them carries with it both the love and the obedience. The child who does not obey his parents cannot render to them the honor that is their due, and as little can he honor his parents who does not love them. Think of returning a mother's love by anything that was not pervaded through and through with the warmest affection. In such a case the lack of love would be an insult, but love honors father and mother in obeying them.

The Assyrian also uses the verb honor in the sense of obey. Asshurbanipal says of Esarhaddon, his father, that he honored (**itta'iid**, literally, exalted) the command of Asshur and Beltis, the gods whom he served. R. V. 1. 9. A. M. 19. 23. He lifted up their command to a position of honor by obeying it. So, two lines after, he speaks of it as the **pii muttalli**, the honored or exalted command; muttalli being the causative form from the verb **ilu**, to be high, as **itta'iid** is from **naadu** with the same meaning.

The same thing occurs in the Chaldean tradition of the flood. See D. L. 102. 28 and 29, where after Khasisadra is ordered to build a ship he says, **att'iid anaku**, I honor (thee, or thy command); I do (it), or, as we say, I will do it.

HORSE.

When the king asked Haman, "What shall be done unto the man whom the king delighteth to honor?" Esther 6:6, Haman answered, vs. 8, 9: "Let royal apparel be brought which the king useth to wear, and the horse that the king rideth upon, and on the head of which a royal crown is set, and let the apparel and the horse be delivered to the hand of one of the king's most noble princes, that they may array the man withal whom the king delighteth to honor, and cause him to ride on horseback through the street of the city, and proclaim before him, Thus shall it be done to the man whom the king delighteth to honor."

The Assyrians were accustomed to ride in chariots, and the Persians in their rugged mountains chose the saddle. Bearing this one difference in mind some of the bas-reliefs from Assyria enable us to form a very vivid picture of this royal parade in the streets of Shushan. Take for example that picture of some great man riding in a chariot, sumptuously adorned, with servants leading the horses and an officer of the court striding on before (L. N. II. 273). If we only transfer the rider to a saddle we have a striking illustration of that pageant described in the book of Esther.

HOSTS, LORD OF.

The Assyrians believed in 300 spirits of heaven or angels (**igigi**) and 600 spirits of earth or demons (**annunaki**). Asshurnatsirpal speaks of 65,000 great gods of heaven and earth, and if every city, town and hamlet had its own gods, that number might not be far out of the way, even making allowance for duplicates.

Even so large a number might be easily offset by the 10,000 times 10,000 of Rev. 5 : 11 ; but the multitude of the hosts is not the principal thing. There is another contrast of much more importance.

Those 65,000 great gods of Assyria might not even have heard of each other. They had nothing in common but the one fact of their being gods. For the sake of argument, then, let us for the moment suppose that they actually existed ; so shall we be better able to enter into the feelings of their worshippers and see how things appeared to them.

How could they know that they were not thoroughly opposed to each other? They actually held that many of them were as much set against each other as Satan is set against God. Then, as they made out only 300 angels, and over against these were 600 demons, just twice the number, how could they know that their power was not in the ratio of their number? and how could they tell that any effort of their own gods to help them would not be at once and forever thwarted? In such circumstances what peace could they have in the present, or what hope for the future? What comfort could they find in prayer? and would not each flash of the lightning and blast of the storm fill them with dismay?

As we think of these things we are prepared to appreciate the revelation of one God and Father of all—one Saviour, whose is all power in heaven and on earth, and all the hosts of heaven not his slaves, doing his will through force and fear, but all rendering the glad service of love; for are we not taught to pray that the will of our Father may be done on earth as it is done in heaven? and are they not all ministering spirits sent forth to do service for them that shall inherit salvation? How it lifts up the heart to look out on that great cloud of witnesses all working together for good to them that love God; and not they only, but also all things and all events joining to promote the same end, and, what is best of all, the whole working under the constant and immediate superintendence of the one living and true God!

Heathenism cannot open up a view like that, or give occasion for such joy in God.

HOURS.

Our Saviour asks, John 11:9, "Are there not twelve hours in the day?" It is an interesting question, where and when did this division of the day into hours originate? The Jews divided the night into three watches: the first from 6 P. M. till 10, the second from 10 P. M., till 2 A. M., and the third from 2 A. M. till 6. The Babylonians had the same three watches, though the Romans had four: 6 to 9 P. M., 9 to midnight, midnight to 3 A. M., and 3 to 6, or sunrise.

But besides this division of the night into three watches, the Babylonians, and after them the Assyrians, divided the entire day into twelve **kasbu**, or periods of two hours each, and these were each divided into sixty minutes, and each minute again into sixty seconds. We recognize the relations of duration and area by using the same word to denote both time and space. Thus Acts 5:7, "It was about the *space* of three hours after," and Rev. 14:20 (old version), "by the *space* of a thousand and six hundred furlongs." So also the Babylonians used the same word, **kasbu,** as a measure of distance. Thus Asshurbanipal (R. V. 8. 91, and Ass'l. 268. 77, and A. M, 30. 12) says, **"100 kasbu-qaqqaru ultu Nina,"** one hundred kasbu of ground from Nineveh, etc., etc. It is the old Persian *parasang*, and, curiously enough, it is the modern "hour's distance" all over the East, showing what may have been the original idea, as it is to-day: "the space travelled over in an hour." At that rate the Assyrian kasbu ought to have been twice as long as the modern hour's journey, for their kasbu was two hours in duration. A. M. 72; note on 16. 25.

The gnomon or dial was a Babylonian invention, as some of their temples show, and so was the clepsydra, at a later period.

The number twelve seems to have had an astronomical origin in connection with the twelve divisions of the equator, twelve signs of the zodiac, twelve months of the year, etc. It is worthy of note in this connection that the first mention of an hour is in the book of Daniel, who dwelt at Babylon, and the word is used by him as many as five times: 3 : 6, 15 ; 4 : 19, 33, and 5 : 5.

HOUSE OF THEIR FATHERS.

This is a phrase of frequent occurrence in the Hebrew. See Num. 1 : 2, 4, 18, 20, 22, 24, 44, 45 ; 1 Sam. 22 : 16; 24 : 21 ; 2 Sam. 3 : 29, and often. The Jewish tribes (*Shibatim*) were divided first into families (*Mishpakhoth*), and these again into Fathers' houses (*Beith Ha Aboth*).

Precisely the same phrase occurs in the Assyrian. In R. I. 60, found also in A. M. 11. 10, 11, Sennacherib says that Tsidqa, king of Isqaaluna (Ascalon), who did not submit to my yoke, the gods of the house of his fathers (**ilani bit abishu**), himself, his wife, his sons, his daughters, his brother, the seed of the house of his father (**zir bit abishu**) I carried off by force and brought to Assyria.

The same expression occurs frequently in the inscriptions of Asshurbanipal. See Ass'l. 160. 83, 162. 97, 176. 56, 177. 83. Found also in R. V. 4. 23. 40, and in A. M. 25. 17. 29.

IMMORTALITY.

Job. 20 : 25–27. But I know that my Redeemer liveth, and that he shall stand up at the last upon the earth, and after my skin had been thus destroyed, yet from my flesh shall I see God, whom I shall see for myself, and mine eyes shall behold, and not another.

In view of this wonderful utterance of the man of Uz we cannot help asking, What were the views of the Babylonians as to the life to come? This question, however, is much easier to ask than to answer, for besides the difference between those who think profoundly and the ignorant multitude, different cities had diverse creeds. The men of Eridu held to a Hades "beyond the mouths of the rivers" in connection with their god Ea, whose home was in the sea, but the men of northern Babylonia placed their heaven on or above the high mountain of **Kharsag karkara,** mountain of the world. They also spoke of a **Kharsag Kalama,** mountain of mankind. See "Mount of the Congregation." Their ideas concerning the future life varied at different periods; they grew dim or became more clear as ages passed by, for the period under review extended across many centuries. Sargon of Accad lived 3750 B. C. and Nineveh was destroyed 606 B. C., leaving a space between of more than 3,000 years. There is no nation on earth that has not experienced very great changes of opinion during so long a period.

We should expect to find some traces of the primitive faith in immortality among their early traditions, and so we find Ea, the god of primitive Eridu, is known as "the god who raises the dead to life;" and though, as Prof. Sayce suggests, this may have become a mere thought of bringing the dead back again to the life that now is, yet it must have had some connection with Edenic tradition, although the clearness of that had become dim. Nor would this be strange, for if man did not like to retain God in his thoughts neither would he like to retain a belief in future retribution. Even Christians need exhortation to set the mind on things which are above. Col. 3:2. Still this title seems to reveal a glimpse of more than a return to this life, and even granting that this is not incontrovertible, yet it would be difficult to hinder thinking men from passing through that door into the idea of a life beyond.

Moreover some things bring out this belief in a future life more plainly. Izdubar finds the Chaldean Noah, who had been long dead, dwelling among the gods. And if one man may be so favored why not others also? H. L. 359.

More than this. A list of the gods of the cities of Assyria contains a prayer that the writer may see "the land of the silver sky," which can be nothing else than a name for heaven. H. L. 356. R. III. 66. 6, seq.

The spirit of **Ea bani,** also, in the epic of **Izdubar** is represented as rising like a cloud of dust to heaven, where he lives among the gods (H. L. 365), reclines on a couch, and drinks pure water. The Hades of Babylonia resembles that of Greece.

And yet even so, belief in a hereafter was so dim and was confined to so few that it still remains true that Christ "brought life and incorruption to light through the gospel," 2 Tim. 1:10; for he alone revealed it clearly, and gave assurance of it unto all men in that he hath risen from the dead. Acts 17:31 compared with John 10:18.

INCANTATION.

Ex. 7:11. And they also, the magicians of Egypt, did in like manner with their enchantments.

Deut. 18:10–12. There shall not be found with thee any one . . . that useth divination, one that practiceth augury, or an enchanter, or a sorcerer, or a charmer, or that consulteth with a familiar spirit, or a wizard, or a necromancer, for whosoever doeth these things is an abomination to the Lord.

Do the monuments throw any light on this subject? The early Accadians were Shamanistic in their opinions. They saw evil in the world, but they did not enter into its moral significance. The looked on it as the work of demons, or a decree of fate, rather than the result of sin, and to be removed by the spell of the magician rather than in any other way. The same fire which cooked their food also destroyed life, and they sought to enjoy the benefit and avoid the injury by means of their sorcerers. The following are specimens of their magical texts:

> Incantation. Seven are they. Seven are they.
> In the hollow of the deep they are seven.
> In the brightness of the sky they are seven.
> From the hollow of the deep, from a palace came they forth.
> Male they are not, female they are not.
> They are dust-storm ghosts, travelers are they.
> Wife they possess not, child they beget not.
> Compassion and kindness they know not.
> Prayer or supplication they will not hear.
> Horses bred in the mountains are they.
> Of the god Ea they are enemies.
> The throne-bearers of the gods are they.
> To injure the canal in the street are they set.
> Evil are they, evil are they.
> Seven are they, seven are they, twice seven are they.
> O spirit of heaven, conjure, O spirit of earth, conjure. H. L. 207. 457.

The idea was that the repetition of these words as they were written in the Accadian language would effectually protect a man from the mischief of these seven demons.

From 38 pages of similar incantations we select these:

Incantation. The evil curse like a demon has fallen on the man.
The voice as a scourge has fallen on him.
The voice ill-boding has fallen on him, the evil curse, the ban, the madnesss, the evil curse has slaughtered this man like a sheep.
His god has gone far from his body.
His goddess, the giver of counsel, has stationed herself outside.
The smiting voice like a garment has covered and bewitched him.
Merodach regards him, he goes down into the house, to his father Ea, and says,
"My father, the evil curse like a demon has fallen on the man."
Twice did he say, "What this man should do I know not; what will give him rest?"
Ea to his son Merodach made answer:
"My son, what dost thou not know? what shall I tell thee more?
Merodach, what dost thou not know? what shall I add to thy knowledge?
What I know thou also knowest. Go, my son Merodach,
Take the man to the house of pure sprinkling, remove his ban, expel his bane, the evil that troubles his body, whether it be the curse of his father, or the curse of his mother, or the curse of his elder brother, or the destructive curse of a man whom he knows not.
May the ban, by the spell of Ea, like garlic be peeled off, like a date be cut off, like a branch be torn off.
The ban, O spirit of heaven, conjure, O spirit of earth, conjure.

Then follows, as a part of the same spell,

Incantation. Like this garlic, which is peeled off and cast into the fire, the burning flame shall consume it; in the garden it shall not be planted, in pool or canal it shall not be placed, its root shall not seize the earth, its stem shall not grow and shall not see the sun, for the food of God and king it shall not be used.
So may the guardian priest cause the ban to leave him, and loose the bond of the torturing disease, the sin, the backsliding, the wickedness, the sinning, the disease which exists in my body, my flesh and my muscle.
Like this garlic may it be peeled off, and this day may the burning flame consume it.
May the ban depart that I may see the light. H. L. 471-73.

Similar incantations follow this last one concerning a date and branch, wool, goats' hair, dyed thread, and a pea; but enough has been quoted to give the reader an idea of these sorceries.

INSCRIPTIONS, THE.

I. Their quantity. One is surprised at the amount accumulated in so short a time. The five large folios of "The

Inscriptions of Western Asia" contain only a part of them. The more numerous and well-filled pages of Strassmeyer contain more, and there are many not yet copied from the originals. There are far more of them than there are of Holy Scriptures, which though bound in one volume form a library rather than a book.

II. Their dates. As the Bible is made up of books written from near the close of the fifteenth century B. C. down to near the end of the first century A. D., so the inscriptions date from an uncertain period previous to Sargon of Agade, who lived 3750 B. C., down to the Achæmenian rulers of Persia centuries after Cyrus, who lived in the last half of the sixteenth century B. C.

III. Their languages. Our Scriptures were writen first in Hebrew, then partially in Chaldee, and last of all in Greek. The inscriptions began in Sumerian or Accadian, then used the Babylonian or Assyrian, for they were practically one, and belonged to the Shemitic family of languages, as the Accadian did to that of the Finns and Turks. They also were written in Elamitic, in Persian, and in the language of Cappadocia, besides others which were necessary to make subject nations acquainted with the laws.

IV. Their material. We have none of them on paper, or similar perishable material, but we know that such materials were used, for the clay seals, and the fastenings that attached them to the documents that have perished, bear silent testimony to what had been. Only in the dry air of Egypt could rolls of papyrus survive the ages.

Sargon of Dur Sargina inscribed one of his records on tin, another on silver, and a third on gold; and we have precious stones, such as agate, jasper, cornelian and chalcedony, bearing inscriptions as well as figures of men, and animals, and other objects.

The marble walls and floors of the royal palace were also utilized as material for inscriptions. The writer well remembers the inscriptions on the floor of the principal entrance of the palace at Khorsabad, where the engraved parts of the characters had been filled with lead to prevent too rapid wear by the feet that walked over them. Also the long strips of inscription, many lines in depth, that began on the wall at one side of the door of a royal hall, passed under the bodies of the **lamassi** (bull colossi) and across the bas-reliefs of gods and cities all round the apartment, till it ended on the other side of the door. The engraving in all these cases was large and distinct, so as to be read with ease.

The favorite material, however, was baked clay. This bore many forms. Cylinders round and many-sided, pentagonal, hexagonal, octagonal. Tablets, cushion form, in the shape of a cake of soap, and as varied in size as our modern books.

The cylinders, of which a specimen is here given, were often deposited in the cornerstones of the temples and palaces to immortalize the builder, and, so used, they were called the **timmin** of the structure. When tablets were used as books, instead of making them so large as to be unwieldy a series was used, and so numbered that the reader knew the order in which to read them. Sometimes the characters used were very fine, so that it must have been very trying to the eyes of the reader.

INSCRIBED CYLINDER.

ISAIAH 10.

This chapter has been the stumbling-block of the commentators. Some, like Cowles and Fausset, never seem to dream that it can apply to anything else than the campaign of Sennacherib and the destruction of his army, and they make desperate efforts to make it apply. Ewald supposes the description drawn from actual occurrences, but applying to an event still future. Gesenius and Hendewerk look on it as an ideal picture of the invasion, and not a narrative of what actually occurred. Dr. Edward Robinson takes the same ground on account of the impracticability of the route described, and J. D. Michaelis even supposes the invasion to be that of Nebuchadrezzar. But the prophet expressly mentions the Assyrian and not the Babylonian. Then Sennacherib came up from the southwest, not from the north as here described, and of him Isaiah said by the word of the Lord (37 : 33), " He shall not come into this city, nor shoot an arrow there, neither shall he come before it with shield, nor cast up a mount against it." But the Assyrian here set forth is to take the spoil, and to take the prey, and to tread them down like the mire of the streets (verse 6). Only a remnant was to escape destruction (verse 20) and that remnant was to return again (vs. 21 and 22), *i. e.*, from captivity in Assyria.

The monuments come here to our help and make all plain. It was not Sennacherib, but his father Sargon, who took Carchemish B. C. 717, Samaria B. C. 722, and Hamath B. C. 720. Damascus had been taken by Tiglath Pileser II. B. C. 732, and Arpad a few years before. Now Sargon tells us that he captured Jerusalem B. C. 711, and it was his swift, sudden, and irresistible approach to the doomed city that is so vividly described by the prophet. Sargon halted at Nob, only one hour from Jerusalem, on the very day that this prophecy was spoken.

So clearly and satisfactorily do the monuments confirm the words of the inspired penman, pointing the way out of a labyrinth from which commentators otherwise could find no means of escape.

ISRAEL.

Israel in Scripture is the name both of a person and of a country. It is the new name given to Jacob, Gen. 35 : 10, it is also the name of the northern kingdom as distinguished from

JEHOVAH.

the southern. The land of Israel and the land of Judah or Judea, Ezek. 27, 17.

In the inscriptions the house of Israel is usually called the house of Omri, **mat Bit Khuumria.** Sargon. Cyl. 19 and 20. It is also in one place called **mat Sirelaa.** R. III. 8. 92. This occurs in the inscription of Shalmaneser II. found at Kurkh, who mentions Akhaabbu (Ahab) as its king. Such things show how intimately connected are the monuments and Holy Scripture, for, as Shalmaneser II. reigned 858–824 B. C., the occurrence of the names of Israel and Ahab in his annals may shed some light on the chronological questions raised in this connection.

IVORY PALACES.

Psa. 45:8. Out of ivory palaces stringed instruments have made thee glad.

Some were called palaces of cedar because that was the principal wood used in their construction, and so of other woods. There could have been none built of ivory. But the cornices and other portions were often adorned with bronze or with alabaster. In some cases ivory was used for the same purpose, and hence the appropriateness of the expression "ivory palaces," a term used also in the monuments. Or, the furniture of a palace may have been adorned with that material, and the name given for that reason. See, *e. g.*, the ivory throne of Solomon, 1 Kings 10:18. Sargon says, Cylinder 63, A palace of ivory, **ushu** wood, box wood, cedar, cypress, etc., I built by the high command of the gods for the abode of my royalty.

JEHOVAH.

Exod. 6:3. I appeared unto Abraham, unto Isaac and unto Jacob as God Almighty (שדי) but by my name Jehovah (יהוה) I was not known unto them.

There has been much dispute about the proper pronunciation of this last name, and it is certain that it should not be pronounced Jehovah, as in our authorized version, for the first letter is y and not j. The Hebrew alphabet was used to express consonants only, the vowels were supplied by the reader. This was all very well so long as Hebrew was a spoken language, but afterwards the knowledge of the correct pronunciation depended on tradition, and this tradition was fixed by the Masoretes of Tiberias, *circa* A. D. 570. Unfortunately this proper name of the God of Israel was held to be too sacred for utterance. In the Septuagint it was rendered by the Greek word κυριος, and so wherever it occurred the Masoretes gave to יהוה the vowel points of אדני (Adonai), the usual equivalent of κυριος, thus indicating that that word was to be pronounced by the reader. The prevailing opinion now seems to be that Yahveh is the true pronunciation.

In the Assyrian monuments the word when occurring in proper names is rendered **Yahu,** or **Yahua.** Thus Hezekiah is **Khazakiyahu** (Senn. 58. 71), and Jehu is **Yahua** (R. III. 5. 6. 64). Fresh Light 61. 64.

Unfortunately we are a little in the dark as to the Assyrian pronunciation, for that is also a dead language, and there may have been an obscure sound of v along with u, as **Yahuv** and **Yahuva.** See A. L. and S. 45.

JERUSALEM.

There has been much dispute concerning the origin of this name. Some have derived it from ירוש and שלים, meaning the possession of peace, and others from ירו, foundation, with the same ending, making it "the foundation of peace." Here also the Assyrian helps us to a better derivation. The ordinary name for city in Assyrian is **alu.** A bilingual tablet, however (R. II. 2. 393), gives the Accadian equivalent of this as **uru.**

The first part of the name, then, means city; but according to Ebed Tob, the priestly king of the place, whose despatches to Amenophis IV., king of Egypt a century before the exodus of Israel to Canaan, have been recovered in Tel el Amarna, here was the temple and oracle of the god Salim, *i. e.*, god of peace, and so we have the name city of Salim, corroborating the title of Melchizedek as "king of Salem, which is king of peace" (Heb. 7 : 2). It may be objected to this that in Hebrew Salem begins with ש while the Assyrian has ס. It is sufficient answer to this that while the Hebrew spells Ashqelon with ש the Assyrian has ס. The same is true of Shimron and **Usimuruna** (Samaria) and Lakish and **Lakisu** (Lachish), Ashdod and **Asduda;** and with such an array of examples there need be no difficulty concerning ירושלים and **Urusalim.** See R. of P. new V. 61.

JUDGE.

The usual term for ruler is king, but the rulers of Israel between Joshua and Saul are known as judges, and that period is known as "the days when the judges ruled." Ruth 1:1. The idea at the root of the word is authority, especially in dispensing justice and punishing evil-doers. So the men of Sodom said of Lot, Gen. 19:9, "This one fellow came in to sojourn, and he will needs be a judge," and the Hebrew who wronged his brother demanded of Moses, Exod. 2:14, "Who made thee a prince and judge over us?" So Deborah judged Israel, Judg. 4:4, 5, for the children of Israel came to her for the adjudication of their strifes about property and rights.

So also the usual term for ruler in Assyrian is **sharru,** king, but in saying that one espouses the cause of another they used the expression, "he does his judgment." R. V. 4. 32 and A. M. 25. 24, where it is joined with "coming to his help."

Shalmanezer II., 858–824 B. C., calls the god Shamash the judge of heaven and earth, the ruler over all. Layard 87. 8 and A. M. 7. 5. So also does Nabonidus, R. V. 64. 2. 47, and A. M. 37. 24, and Asshurbanipal calls him **danu rabu ilani,** the great judge of the gods, as having authority over them. R. V. 62. 19 and A. M. 24. 7.

JUDGMENT, RIGHTEOUS.

John 7:24. Judge not according to appearance, but judge righteous judgment.

Take an Assyrian illustration. Asshurbanipal, while carrying on the war with Ummanaldas king of Elam, thus addressed the goddess Ishtar: "Give to me life, length of days, and joy of heart as I tread the way to thy temple, **Bit masmas,** till my feet grow old." Ass'l. 305. 8 and 9. This seems to indicate greater joy in his favorite goddess than some Christians find in the living God, but that impression disappears when we find that her priests had told him in her name, "O Asshurbanipal, thou king whom my hands have made, I march before thy army." Ass'l. 221.

24 and 25. Before that she had sent word, "Feast, drink wine, make music—I will grant to thee the desire of thy heart." Ass'l. 125. 65-68. This sets his words in another light. It is one thing to love a god who engages to give success to our own undertakings, it is another thing to love Him who commands us to make his will ours, and pray "Thy will be done on earth as it is in heaven."

In this matter of human desert and divine retribution some deal in universal, or at least general statements. They may not go so far as to say that Christian nations are saved and all others lost, for they know that the best Christian nations contain many of "them that are without," whose guilt is measured by their greater knowledge; but they are so impressed by the unspeakable wickedness of heathendom as to lose sight of the fact that "in every nation he that feareth God and worketh righteousness is acceptable to him" (Acts 10: 35), and though they know that Judas was one of the twelve, and Ananias a Pentecostal convert, yet they seem to count all church members as true disciples. But God does not judge men by their position but by their character, nor does he decide the eternal doom of any without taking into account every element that enters into that character. God forms no mistaken judgments. He is not imposed on by a mere show of piety, and he waits patiently for the penitence that may justify forgiveness; and when he finds it he rejoices with exceeding joy.

He does not doom men by classes, but inspires his apostle to say, "As many as have sinned without law shall also perish without law: and as many as have sinned under law shall be judged by law." Rom. 2: 11, 12. This means that every one who outside the written law deliberately and persistently practices what he knows is wrong shall not be excused. "For the wrath of God is revealed from heaven against all ungodliness and unrighteousness of men who hinder the truth in unrighteousness, because that which may be known of God is manifest in them, for God manifested it unto them—so that they may be without excuse." Rom. 1: 18–20. They are not overlooked, then, because they had no written law, but perish because they wilfully went contrary to the knowledge which God gave them. Each one, however, is judged by himself and each item of his record enters into the formation of the perfect judgment of God.

Those who judge men by classes, when they find a fact that seems to contravene their judgments, are tempted to go to the opposite extreme and contradict their previous decision. But the true way is to judge each case by itself and, if after a careful examination of all sides of it we are still unable to form a decision, leave the matter to the Lord, assured that whatever his decision may be it will be the most merciful that can be made consistent with truth and right, and command the approval of the universal conscience; even as when on earth his bitterest enemies could not help approving each one of his replies to their ensnaring questions.

JUSTICE.

Prov. 29:14. The king that faithfully judgeth the poor, his throne shall be established for ever. 2 Sam. 23:3 and 4. The God of Israel said, the Rock of Israel spake to me, One that ruleth over men righteously, that ruleth in the fear of God, he shall be as the light of the morning when the sun riseth, a morning without clouds, when the tender grass springeth out of the earth through clear shining after rain.

The name Sargon, **Sharrukenu,** the father of Sennacherib, who reigned B. C. 722–705, meant either the rightful or the righteous king; it was, literally, the true king, which might be understood either as the legitimate or the just. He says in his cylinder inscription, lines 50–52, In accordance with my name, which is for the promotion of right and justice, and which the great gods gave me to protect the helpless and preserve the weak from harm, the price of the fields on which I built the city of **Dur sargina** (fortress of Sargon) I paid to the owners thereof in silver and copper, according to the estimates recorded in the enduring tablets, and that no wrong might be done to any, even in the case of a piece of land that for any reason was not wanted, I gave field for field wherever the owner chose to select it.

Of course this is his own account of the matter, but he would hardly dare to insert in an inscription anything which every reader would know was not true. At all events it shows that he had very clear ideas of what was right and just, and if in anything he did not live up to the requirements of duty, it was not for the want of knowledge as to what that duty was.

So these words of Sargon furnish a striking illustration of the truth that "when Gentiles who have no (written) law do by nature the things of the law, these, having no law, are a law unto themselves; in that they show the work of the law written in their hearts, their conscience bearing witness therewith, and their thoughts one with another accusing or else excusing them." Rom. 2: 14, 15.

KING OF KINGS.

The victorious Redeemer is represented in Rev. 19: 16 as having on his garment and on his thigh a name written, "King of kings, and Lord of lords;" and even before his victory, while the war still raged between his enemies and his kingdom, he is called "Lord of lords, and King of kings." 17. 14. Perhaps no special lesson is intended to be conveyed in this reverse order of these titles. Do they occur anywhere in the monuments?

In the beginning of his great inscription, Asshurnatsirpal, 883–859 B. C. (R. I. 17. 5), calls the god Uras, known also as Adar and Ninip, among other things, **Bil bili**, lord of lords, showing that this epithet was used concerning a god even at that early day.

Asshurbanipal assumes the title **Shar sharrani,** king of kings, in his account of his temple restorations. R. V. 62. 2 and A. M. 23 : 14.

Asshurnatsirpal makes a title for himself out of the two names, **Shar bili** (R. I. 17. 19), and in the next line calls himself **Shar kali malki,** king of all the princes. It is fitting that the God-man should have a title compounded of one used concerning God and another used concerning men, and his people look forward with joyful hope to the day when earth and heaven shall unite in calling him King of kings, and Lord of lords.

KINGDOM AGAINST KINGDOM.

In Isa. 19: 2 we read, "I will stir up the Egyptians against the Egyptians, and they shall fight every one against his brother, and every one against his neighbor, city against city, and kingdom against kingdom."

There is a noteworthy parallel to this in a quotation Prof. Sayce makes from an old inscription (H. L. p. 312): "And the warrior Nerra spake thus, Sealand against Sealand, Sumasti against Sumasti, the Assyrian against the Assyrian, the Elamite against the Elamite, the Kossæan against the Kossæan, the Kurd against the Kurd, the Lullubite against the Lullubite, country against country, house against house, man against man, brother against brother, let them destroy one another, and afterwards let the Accadian come and destroy them all and fall upon their breasts."

KIRJATH SEPHER.

The American edition of Smith's Dict. of Bible, p. 1568, says "Kirjath Sepher is generally assumed to mean 'city of books' (from the Hebrew word *Sepher*, book), and it has been made the foundation for theories of the amount of literary culture possessed by the Canaanites. Keil, *Josua* 10, 39. Ewald: I. 324. But such theories are, to say the least, premature during the extreme uncertainty as to the meaning of these very ancient names."

Of course we cannot point to the results of the exploration of Kirjath Sepher, for it has not yet been explored, but the tablets found at Tel el Amarna in Egypt (see p. 184) make the above remarks of Dr. Smith entirely uncalled for, and prove that the literary culture of the Canaanites existed not in theory only, but in fact. Egypt, however, is not alone in her testimony on this point; Canaan is a second witness by whom the fact is established. After the brilliant discoveries of Dr. Flinders-Petrie at Tel el Hesy (Lachish), in 1890, Mr. Bliss from Beirut continued the exploration there. Among the Tel el Amarna tablets was one from Zimrida, the Egyptian governor of Lachish, to Amenophis IV.; and now from the ruins of that Amorite city Mr. Bliss unearths a tablet from Amenophis to Zimrida. Well may Prof. Sayce say (R. of P. new VI. xiii), "Nothing more extraordinary ever happened in the annals of archæology. The discovery had hardly been made that a governor of Lachish named Zimrida wrote letters in the Babylonian language and script to his suzerain the Pharaoh of Egypt, when the site of Lachish was identified by Dr. Petrie and a letter found by Mr. Bliss in which the name Zimrida occurs twice. For more than 4,000 years the broken halves of a correspondence that had been carried on before the Exodus had been lying under the soil—the one half on the banks of the Nile, the other half in Canaan—and the recovery of one was followed almost immediately by the appearance of the other."

Prof. Sayce thinks that Mr. Bliss has reached the door of the archive chamber of the old Amorite city of Lachish, and that ere long we may have in our hands a Canaanitish library that was in existence before the Exodus from Eygpt. He gives a transliteration and translation of this old letter. R. of P. new VI. 14 and 15.

KISS.

The reader of the Bible must be struck with the frequent recurrence of this word. Isaac asked his son Jacob to come near and kiss him, Gen. 27:26; Jacob kisses Rachel, 29:11; and Laban and Esau kiss Jacob, 29:13; 33:4. Laban kisses his sons and his daughters, 31:55, and Joseph kisses all his brothers, 45:15, and his father, 50:1. Aaron kisses Moses, Exod. 4:27, and Moses kisses Jethro, 18:7. Naomi kisses her daughter-in-law, Ruth, 1:9, Samuel kisses Saul, 1 Sam. 10:1, and Jonathan and David kiss each other, 20:41. David kissed Absalom, 2 Sam. 14:33, and Absalom kissed all that came near, 15:5. David kissed Barzillai, 19:39, and Joab took Amasa by the beard to kiss him, 20:9. Christ complains that Simon his host gave him no kiss, Luke 7:45, and Judas betrayed him with a kiss, 22:47 and 48, showing that he was accustomed to kiss and be kissed by his disciples. The elders from Ephesus kissed Paul, Acts 20:37, and Christians are exhorted four times to give each other a holy kiss: Rom. 16:16; 1 Cor. 16:20; 2 Cor. 13:12, and 1 Thess. 5:26, to which may be added 1 Pet. 5:14.

The inscriptions are no less free in using the word. The common phrase used by the kings of Assyria to denote submission to them is that kings kissed their feet. Sennacherib says of Menahem of Samaria, Tubal of Sidon, Abdiliti of Arvad, Urumilki of Jebail, Mitinti of Ashdod, Puduil of Bit Ammon.

Kamusunatbi of the Moabites and Malikrammu of the Edomites, "They kissed my feet." Compare Luke 7 : 45. R. I. 38. 47-57. So Asshurbanipal tells us, R. V. 2. 67, 72 and 81-87, that Mugallu of Tabal and Yakinlu of Arvad, with his sons Azibaal, Abibaal, Adunibaal, Sapatibaal, Pudibaal, Baalyashubu, Baalhanunu, Baal Maluku, Abimilki, and Akhimilki, did the same. The kings and governors of Egypt did likewise. R. V. 2. 32. 33. Cyrus uses the same expression in describing the submission of Babylon, R. V. 35. 18. Asshurbanipal speaks of Immanigas king of Elam kissing the ground before his ambassador. R. V. 3. 18 and 19. Compare Rev. 3. 9.

The custom is much more prevalent in Oriental lands than with us. The writer was surprised on going on board the steamer at Smyrna for Constantinople, on his first arrival in Turkey, to see men kissing men on both cheeks as they bade each other good-bye. It is there the ordinary mode of salutation, and he would be counted churlish who did not heartily enter into the spirit of the act.

KNEES.

Every reader of Scripture must have noticed how these members of the body are mentioned in connections where we would not think of them. Thus Job 4 : 4, "Thou hast strengthened the feeble knees." Psa. 109 : 24, "My knees are weak through fasting," Compare Isa. 35 : 3. Ezek. 7 : 17, " All knees shall be weak as water," also 21 : 7 and Heb. 12 : 12. Dan. 5 : 6, The knees of Belshazzar "smote one against another." Compare Nahum 2 : 10.

The Assyrian, however, gives equal prominence to the knees. We read of strong oxen **sha la innahhuushunu birka shunu,** whose knees do not grow weary. R. V. 65. 34. 6.

It is said of Shuzub, king of Babylon, **sha la i shuu birki,** who has no knees, *i. e.*, is feeble. R. I. 41. 9.

Sennacherib calls his eldest son, **Asshur nadin shun, tarbit birkiya,** the offspring of my knees. R. I. 39. 64.

The same monarch tells that, when climbing the mountains on foot after his enemies, his knees found a resting-place upon the stones. R. I. 39. 78.

KNEW NOT JOSEPH.

Exod. 2 : 8 states that "There arose a new king over Egypt that knew not Joseph." We should naturally look to the hieroglyphics of that country for illustrations of this, but we are indebted to the most complicated forms of the cuneiform inscriptions for a very satisfactory explanation.

Amenophis IV., known also as Khu en Aten, reigned about B. C. 1430, and was the son of Amenophis III. by the Mesopotamian princess Tadukhepa, daughter of Duisratti, king of Naharaina, the Aram Naharaim of Judg. 3 : 8. He surrounded himself with Semitic courtiers, as his father had done before him, and, like his mother, worshipped the winged solar disk named Aten in Egyptian. This was so distasteful to the priesthood of Thebes that he had to build a new capital at Tel el Amarna, half-way from Minieh to Siout, on the eastern side of the Nile, and among the ruins of his palace there the royal correspondence between him and the rulers of the provinces has been discovered in the form of clay tablets written in Babylonian. They are governmental despatches from Babylonia, Assyria, and even as far off as Kappadokia. Now Amenophis IV. was nearly the last king of the 18th dynasty, and the 19th came in with Ramses I., who restored the national religion and removed the capital back to Thebes. Such a king would not "know Joseph" in the sense of regarding either him or his people with favor, and the Pharaoh of whom this was said by Moses is now identified as Ramses II., who is familiarly spoken of as the Pharoah of the Oppression, and we now, thanks to the cuneiform tablets of Tel el Amarna, see very clearly how it came to pass that he knew not Joseph. The exodus is supposed to have occurred about B. C. 1320, under Menephtah II.

KNOWLEDGE OF THE FATHERS.

There is one way of honoring parents that is not popular with Young America, and that is honoring their knowledge. The tendency among the youth of to-day is to feel that none have ever known so much as they, and that previous generations are to be pitied for their ignorance. In some lines of truth there is no question that the knowledge of this generation exceeds that of its predecessors. This is true of inventions and discoveries. No previous age had such a knowledge of applied electricity, or of the means of rapid transit, and yet only yesterday I read of the rediscovery of the lost art of hardening copper: for in ancient times that metal was made to be as hard as steel.

Far different was the estimate put on the knowledge of previous ages in ancient times. Then men honored their fathers as the great sources of knowledge. They may have felt that those who had lived hundreds of years to their scores must have accumulated richer stores of knowledge than they as yet had gathered. At any rate the knowledge possessed by their fathers was to them the perfection of attainment, and to say that anything was unknown to them was equivalent to pronouncing it unknowable. Thus Moses threatens a plague of locusts such as "neither thy fathers nor thy fathers' fathers have seen since the day they were upon the earth unto this day." Exod. 10:6. So God threatens to bring Israel "unto a nation which thou hast not known, thou nor thy fathers." Deut. 28:6.

This same style of speaking occurs in the Assyrian monuments. Asshurbanipal (R. V. 2.96 and A. M. 22:10) calls Lydia a far-off region, "the mention of the name of which the kings my fathers had never heard."

Tiglath Pileser I., B. C. 1106, says (R. I. 15.17-27), "The cedar (and other trees) which among the kings my fathers who were before me none had planted, I planted," etc. For translation see R. of P. new I. 115. 17-27.

So Asshurnatsirpal, B. C. 883-858, in R. I. 18. 50 and 62, speaks of "mountains which none of the kings my fathers had penetrated." It may be objected that these last quotations speak of achievement rather than knowledge, and yet they show the same spirit of highly esteeming the attainments of the fathers.

KOYUNJIK.

The mound of Koyunjik, literally "sheep pasture," is a very conspicuous object to one looking from Mosul east across the Tigris. It is not its absolute height that makes it so conspicuous, for it is only some thirty-five or forty feet high, but that it rises so abruptly and stands by itself with the lofty mountains for a background. One can easily ride up the sheep tracks to the top on horseback, though there are places so washed away by the winter rains that it would be hard to climb them on foot without making quite a detour.

The mound is an irregular pentagon over a mile and a half in circumference. At the southwestern angle nearest Mosul the palace of Sennacherib (705-681 B. C.) has been explored, forming a rectangle of 600 by 330 feet. One hall of 176 by 40 feet and another of 124 by 30 have been found, and the names of Jehu, Hezekiah, and other kings of Israel and Judah. Nearly at the opposite extreme is the palace of Asshurbanipal (668-626 B.C.) in one of the chambers of which was found his famous library of clay tablets, which have found their way to the British Museum, the Louvre, and many a less noted library on both sides of the Atlantic. Nor is it at all certain that there remains no more to be recovered from its unknown interior of both sculptures and inscriptions, besides additional tablets.

The mound of Neby Yoonas is reserved in the providence of God for the future, when it may be more needed than now, or when the Turk shall not stand in the way of its thorough and scientific examination. The French have left nothing more to be expected from Khorsabad, so exhaustive have been their researches there. In spring Koyunjik is one mass of green, but later on it is an arid heap—bare and unattractive.

LACHISH, לכיש, LAKISU.

The name of this city may be translated either "the smitten" or "the impregnable." It occurs twenty-two times in the Old Testament. We mention only two : 2 Kings 18: 14 and 17.

A bas-relief in the palace of Sennacherib at **Koyunjik** shows the king elaborately dressed, sitting on a portable throne ; his feet rest on a footstool highly ornamented. Two attendants stand behind, each holding a fan or fly-flapper over the head of the king with one hand, and an embroidered napkin in the other. The royal tent stands behind them, and the king's war chariot below that. The artist seems to have got everything into the picture that would gratify the monarch. The Rabshakeh, or general, poses before Sennacherib in apparel almost as splendid as that of the king, and is receiving the royal decision as to the fate of the captives, who occupy various positions of abject submission or impassioned yet seemingly hopeless entreaty. Further off some whose fate has been already decided are being tortured, and others butchered by the soldiers, while palm-trees, vines and fig-trees fill in the background. It forms the large frontispiece of Smith's History of Sennacherib, covering both pages, and is described in B. and N. 149-153. See also p. 69.

The following inscription is engraved in the bas-relief:

"King Sennacherib, king of all, king of Assyria, sat on a stationary throne and the captives taken in Lachish came before him." **Nimidu,** here rendered stationary, is from **imidu,** to set, to place. Both Smith and Layard mistake the meaning of the closing sentence. Layard renders it " I give permission for its slaughter," and Smith says, " The spoil of Lachish came before me." But Prof. Delitzsch renders **shalaat,** which is the construct of **shallatu,** "*Beute, kriegs gefangene,*" and the latter is plainly the meaning in this passage.

LANDMARKS.

Deut. 19:14. Thou shalt not remove thy neighbor's landmark. Comp. 27. 17 and Prov. 22:28.

Fortunately we have a good specimen of these landmarks, of which there are many, in what is known as the *Caillou Michaux*, now in the French National Library. It was brought to France in the year 1800, is of hard black marble, 19¾ inches high, and weighs about seventy pounds. Nearly two-thirds of it is occupied by a deed of the land, which is accurately described and bounded and the names of adjoining owners given. The upper third is pictorial, giving the emblems of gods who are invoked to curse whoever may in any way invade the rights of the owner or assail his title to the land. These figures are given in R. III. 45. and IV. 43, also in P. and C. II. 200, 201.

The curses are very acrid, involving the extirpation of the wrong-doer and of his family, clothing him with leprosy, casting him to the wild beasts, infiltering poison into his bowels so that he shall be cursed with irrevocable malediction. They must have been a great terror to believers in the power of the ban.

THE CAILLOU MICHAUX.

The stone was found near the Tigris, not far from Ctesiphon. A translation is given in R. of P. IX. 94-96, and a similar stone is described and translated pp. 96-103.

LANGUAGES.

In Esther 1:22, 3:12 and 8:9, the king of Persia commands letters to be written "to every province according to the writing thereof, and to every people after their language;" and this was needful because more than one language was spoken by the inhabitants of Persia.

The inscriptions furnish one illustration of this in the

bilingual hymns to the gods, and other tablets, written both in Accadian and Assyrian, but a perfect and enduring illustration of this fact relating to Xerxes is the great triumphal tablet of Darius Hystaspis, containing nearly one thousand lines of inscription, on the face of a precipitous rock four hundred feet above the plain at Behistun (place of the god), near Kermanshah, in Persia. It is in three languages, Aryan, Shemitic, and Scythic, and we are indebted to Sir Henry Rawlinson both for a copy of the inscription itself and for its translation. He was engaged on the work at intervals from 1837 to 1843, and published it first in the Journal of the Royal Asiatic Society in 1846, also in 1850 and 1852. A translation of it be may found in R. of P. I. 109–132.

LEARNING OF THE CHALDEANS.

King Nebuchadrezzar commanded that promising young men among the Jewish captives, skilful in all wisdom, and cunning in knowledge, and understanding science, and such as had ability to stand in the king's palace, should be taught the learning and tongue of the Chaldeans (Dan. 1:4.), and after a three years' course of study the king seems to have conducted their examination in person (verses 19 and 20); showing that he himself was not ignorant of letters.

It is in complete accordance with this that Asshurbanipal says in the account he gives of his early life (R. V. I. 31, 31, also A. M. 10. 11–14): In the palace **Bit riduti** (harem) I acquired the deep knowledge of **Nabu** (the god of intelligence) and I inspected all the tablets of all the sciences, as many as there were." So that there seems to have been a royal training school, and Daniel and his three companions were either admitted into such an institution, or, to use a modern phrase, into a university extension, where they received lessons from the regular professors.

As to the extent and variety of Chaldean learning, see under "Deluge" and "Hannah and Samuel."

LIFE, WATER OF.

Besides the tree of life Scripture speaks also of the water of life. Rev. 22:1. And he showed me a river of water of life bright as crystal proceeding out of the throne of God and of the Lamb in the midst of the street thereof."

So also, in the Assyrian account of the descent of Ishtar into Hades, Allat says to Namtar, the keeper of the gates, "Over Ishtar pour the waters of life, and bring her before me." It was these waters that Ishtar had come to obtain for her husband, Tammuz, that by means of them he might be restored to life, for whoever drank of them became immortal. See the whole legend translated in H. L. 221–227.

It is evident that the Babylonians believed in a future life, for they filled vases of clay in their tombs with dates and grain, wine and oil, and the rich were careful to conduct rills of living water through the chambers of their dead, not only for their use, but as a symbol of these waters of life in Hades, and an expression of their belief in the life represented by them. Many a bereaved one among them must have found great consolation in leading these living streams through the tombs of their departed friends, and thinking of the immortality they brought to mind.

No doubt in later times the traditions were so altered that they were made to represent in one region the revival of vegetable life in spring-time, after the desolation of winter, and in another a like revival of verdure in autumn after the summer drought had burned up every trace of life in the fields; but the question is, Why even then did they not describe literally these annual changes in the face of nature, but spoke of a life beyond after this one had passed away? and the only satisfactory answer is, The original tradition of a life to come had been handed down from Eden—a name that still survives in their ancient literature, and a locality recognized to this day among their oldest traditions.

Is it not also an additional confirmation of that word concerning Christ: "In him was life, and the life was the light of men"? John 1:4. Not a self-moved seeking after life on the part of man but a personal work wrought by Christ in human hearts according to his own declaration, "I am the light of the world." John 8:12.

This Babylonian tradition was an unconscious prophecy of

Him who said to the woman of Samaria, "Whosoever drinketh of the water that I shall give him shall never thirst, but the water that I shall give him shall become in him a well of water springing up unto eternal life." John 4:14.

LIFTING UP OF THE HANDS.

That is a beautiful synonym of prayer, Psa. 141. 2: "Let my prayer be set forth as incense before thee—the lifting up of my hands as the evening sacrifice," and it was a beautiful illustration of it also—during the battle with Amalek—that when Moses held up his hand Israel prevailed, and when he let down his hand Amalek prevailed. But Moses' hands were heavy; so they seated him on a stone, and Aaron and Hur stayed up his hands till the going down of the sun, and Israel triumphed. Ex. 17:11. So in the monuments (R. V. 2. 121, also A. M. 23. 7, also R. of P. I. 71. 37) Asshurbanipal speaks of "that evil work which, at the lifting up of my hands, the gods my protectors had destroyed." Again (R. V. 9 103, also A. M. 33. 16), he makes mention of "the lifting up of my hands which I prayed for the capture of my enemies;" we would say, "the prayer which I offered for," etc. In like manner Nebuchadrezzar (India House inscription, col. 9. 60, and R. of P. new III. 122. 60 and H. L. 97) in his approach to Merodach says, "Accept the lifting up of my hands. Hear my prayer." It would be easy to furnish other examples.

LIFT UP THE HEAD.

The Psalmist (3:4) calls God the lifter up of his head. See Psa. 110:7 and 27:6; Luke 21:28; Judg. 8:28; Gen. 40:13. Just as sadness depresses the heart and makes a man bow down, so joy elates and makes him march with head erect. That was a beautiful name given to the temple of Bil at Babylon which dated from B. C. 2250, E Saggilla or E Sagilu, "The house of the raising of the head." For that is the *beau ideal* of a house of worship. The house that comforts and strengthens and enables men to go with the head lifted up, and not bowing down like a bulrush. See H. L. 94, and for a description of the temple see pp. 437-440.

LIGHT.

The beloved disciple says of his Lord, "In him was life, and the life was the light of men," John 1:4; and Christ himself says, "I am the light of the world," John 8:12. He was this light not only while he was a man among men, but in all lands and in all the ages he has been the giver of that measure of spiritual knowledge which men have possessed, and the source of all those aspirations after better things which sometimes flash on us out of the midst of darkness.

We may detect the yearning of men after Christ in some of the titles which they give to their gods.

In R. I. 32. 11, Shamash, the sun god, is styled "the light of the gods." In R. IV. 9. 19. Sin, the moon-god, is styled "the god who creates the light from the horizon to the zenith, opening wide the doors of the sky and establishing light. The illuminator of living creatures." The whole hymn is given, H. L. 160–162. This last title, "The Illuminator," is repeated in it many times. Another hymn to Shamash (H. L. 100) says:

> "O Lord, the illuminator of darkness, thou that openest the face of the sick,
> Unto thy light look the great gods.
> The spirits of earth look upon thy face,
> Yea, thou art their light in the far-off sky;
> In the broad earth thou art their illumination.
> Men far and wide behold thee and rejoice."

LILITH.

Isa. 34:14 reads, in the old version, "The screech-owl shall rest there." The new revision reads, "The night-monster shall settle there." The Hebrew word is לילית, and the Assyrian helps us to understand its meaning. The old Accadian word **lilu** signified originally a cloud of dust, and as ghosts were believed to assume that form it came to mean a disembodied spirit. The Shemitic Babylonian added the feminine, **Lilatu,** and in the course of time this came to mean a night-monster, a vampire or evil spirit that ate the bodies of the dead and sucked the blood of the living. When Ishtar descended to Hades she threatened if her requests were not granted to let loose all the dead, thus to destroy the living. The Rabbins held Lilith to be a beautiful

LITANY.

woman who had been the first wife of Adam, but fed on the blood of children whom she killed at night. The Arabs give us Lilith under the name of Ghoul, and any one may find them described in the Arabian Nights' Entertainments. Such evil spirits were thought to frequent desolate ruins as their fitting abode, and the prophet threatens that Idumea shall become an appropriate home for these night-monsters.

LION.

1 Sam. 17 : 34, 35. And David said unto Saul, Thy servant kept his father's sheep, and when there came a lion or a bear, and took a lamb out of the flock, I went out after him and smote him, and delivered it out of his mouth, and when he arose against me I caught him by his beard, and smote him, and slew him.

This is paralleled by several encounters of Asshurbanipal with lions, represented in bas-reliefs and described by inscriptions. One reads as follows: "I am Asshurbanipal, king of all, king of Assyria, the manly one. My majesty (being) on foot a strong lion (appeared), whose back (body) I seized by his ears. By the help of Asshur and Ishtar, the goddess of war, with the spear which was in my hands I transfixed his body."

Dan. 7 : 4 sees a lion with eagle's wings in one of his visions, and we could not form a more vivid picture of such an object than we have in L. N. I. 76.

LITANY.

The reader who has heard of Assyrian litanies may like to see a specimen. They were written in Accadian previous to the days of Sargon of Accad, and were generally attached to a penitential psalm. The following is taken from H. L. 522. See also 336:

"Mother goddess, destroyer of evil, whose hand no god attacks, exalted lady whose command is mighty,
A prayer let me utter, and let her do unto me as seemeth her good.
My lady, from the day when I was small much am I yoked unto evil.
Food have I not eaten, weeping has been my veil,
Water I have not drank, tears have been my drink.

My liver has not been enlightened, like a hero I have not walked, bitterly I mourn.

My transgressions are many, my liver is full of anguish.

O my lady, tell me what I have done, establish for me a place of rest.

Absolve my sin, lift up my countenance.

* O my god, the lord of prayer, let my prayer address thee.

O my goddess, the lady of supplication, let my supplication address thee.

O **Matu**, lord of the mountain, let my prayer address thee.

O **Gubarra** (flame of fire), lady of Eden, let my supplication address thee.

O **Ea**, ruler of heaven and earth, ruler of Eridu, let my prayer address thee.

O **Damkina**, mother of the house supreme, let my supplication address thee.

O **Marduk**, lord of Babylon, let my prayer address thee.

O spouse of his, the royal bond of heaven and earth, let my supplication address thee.

O messenger of life, the god whose good name is pronounced, let my prayer address thee.

O bride, first-born of **Ira**, let my supplication address thee.

O lady of him who binds the mouth of the dog, let my prayer address thee.

O **Gula**, exalted one, my lady, even the goddess **Nana**, let my supplication address thee.

May it say to thee, Regard me with favor. Turn to me thy face. Let thy liver be quieted.

Let thy heart, as the heart of a mother who has borne children, return to its place.

As a mother who has borne children, as a father who has begotten them, let it return to its place.

For additional litanies see H. L. 532-40.

LIVER THE SEAT OF EMOTION, THE.

In all languages feeling is associated with the viscera of the human body. The heart is the symbol of feeling. We speak of a large heart, or a tender heart, and where we speak of a hard heart the Assyrian, true to his warrior instincts, spoke of a strong heart. So Gyges is said to have made his heart strong when he rebelled against Assyria, R. V. 2. 113 and A. M. 22. 28. Merodach is described as large hearted, **libbi riitpashu**, R. V. 35. 23, and A. M. 41. 2.

In Arabic we have *rahmet*, mercy, and *rahman* and *rahim*, merciful, from the word *rahim* or *rihm*, the womb. In Assyrian is the verb **ramu**, to pity, the noun **naramu**, love, **rimu**, beloved, but I do not know if they have the same association as in Hebrew and Arabic. Then there is a peculiar idiom in all these lan-

* The litany proper begins here.

LONG LIFE.

guages that associates emotion with the liver. Mr. Layard quotes a letter from a Turkish cadi to a friend of his whom he addresses as "the joy of my liver." That is good Arabic. B. and N. 663. In Hebrew we have נשפך לאָרץ כבדי, *nishpak 'laaretz kibaedee*, Lam. 2:2, my liver is poured out upon the ground. Comp. Job 16:13 and in Assyrian, R. V. 1. 64. and A. M. 42. 13: **libbi igugma itstsarruuh kabitti**: my heart was enraged and my liver was angry. See p. 196, ll. 1, 2 and 19.

LIVING CREATURES.

Rev. 4:17. And the first creature was like a lion, and the second creature like a calf, and the third creature had the face of a man, and the fourth creature was like a flying eagle. Compare with this Ezek. 1:5–11, especially verse 10. They had the face of a man, and they four had the face of a lion on the right side, and they four had the face of an ox on the left side, they four had also the face of an eagle.

One cannot read such scriptures without recalling the fact that these four faces are found in all the rediscovered palaces of Nineveh. Only one more is to be added, the face of a fish: though this appears in the form of a cloak thrown over the head of an image rather than the head belonging to the wearer himself. See C. G. 325.

Ezekiel doubtless looked on these mythological images of Assyria and Babylonia with his own eyes, and the beloved disciple based his imagery on that of the prophet who preceded him. Verily these monuments of old Assyria have a real connection with Holy Scripture; one worthy to be sought out and recognized, to our better understanding of the word of God.

LONG LIFE.

Prov. 3:16. Length of days is in her right hand.

Dan. 6:6. Then these presidents and satraps assembled together to the king, and said thus unto him, King Darius, live for ever.

Cyrus writes (R. V. 35. 34 and 35) "Let all the gods whom I restored to (caused to enter into) their cities daily speak before **Bil** and **Nabu** in behalf of the length of my days." Nabonidus (R. V. 64. 3. 11-21) thus prays to the sun god: " O **Shammas**, great lord of heaven and earth, light of the gods, their father! Offspring of **Sin** and **Ningal** (the great lady), in thy entrance and abode in **E Babara**, the home of thy delight, thy enduring sanctuary, to **Nabuna'id** the king of Babylon, the noble, thy adorner, gladdener of thy heart, maker of thine abode, joyfully regard with favor my great good work, daily in ascension and declension, in heaven and earth, be gracious to my work; let my sighing be an acceptable offering; favor my prayer. May the sceptre and true sword which thou hast caused my hands to hold rule for ever." A slightly different translation may be found in R. of P. new V. 174. 11 seq.

He prays to Sin (the moon god) R. of P. new V. 172. 35 seq.: "May he lengthen my days, may he extend my years, may he firmly establish my reign." Nebuchadrezzar prays (India House inscription, 10. 2), "O merciful Merodach, may the temple I have built endure while Babylon exists, and with its fulness may I be satisfied. Within it may I reach to hoary age."

In an address of Ishtar of Arbela to Esarhaddon, imperfectly copied R. IV. 68, and translated R. of P. XI. 59-72. also in H. L. 274. She says, "Length of days and everlasting years will I give to Esarhaddon, my king."

LOOK EACH OTHER IN THE FACE.

A very unusual form of speech occurs in 2 Kings 14:8, 11. where the phrase to look each other in the face is used to denote engaging in battle, but, unusual as it is, an equally strange expression is used by Sargon (Cylinder 27) where he says, **Itlu qardu sha ina rebit Durilu itti Khumbanigash Shar Elamti innamru ma ishkunu takhtashu**: The high, the mighty one, or the strong hero who in the suburbs of Durilu with Khumbanigas king of Elam *was seen; i. e.,* fought; he effected his overthrow.

In both the Hebrew and the Assyrian the idea seems to be that they confronted each other in the battle. As Sir Walter Scott puts it :

> ' Then, hand and foot and eye opposed,
> In dubious strife they darkly closed."

At any rate in those good old times men seem to have thought that two kings could not get a sight of one another without at once coming to blows. So **tamkharu**, battle, is from **makharu**, to be in front of; as though two men could not meet without fighting, or would not come together except for fighting.

LOOKING-GLASSES.

Ex. 38:8. And he made the laver of brass, and the base thereof of brass, of the mirrors of the serving women who served at the door of the tent of meeting.

Serving women here does not mean domestics, gathered there to be hired out to service, but women who rendered some kind of service in connection with the tabernacle. The old version reads "looking-glasses" instead of mirrors, and many a thoughtful reader has wondered how looking-glasses could furnish brass enough to make so large a casting as the brazen laver. They may have thought of brass frames round the mirrors, but ancient mirrors were not made of glass at all, but always of metal, often largely of copper, with a highly polished surface.

It is strange that we have no accounts of similar mirrors in Babylonia or Assyria, for intercourse between these countries and Egypt was so frequent, even Mesopotamian princesses being installed as queens in Egyptian palaces, *e. g.*, Tadukhepa, daughter of Duisratta, king of Mitanna (Naharaim) and wife of Amenophis III. (R. of P. new III. 55); and Nahum, speaking against Nineveh, declares that "there is none end of the store, the glory of all pleasant furniture" (2. 9). But the contributions from Assyria are not all in yet; when they are we may have a different invoice to present.

LOOK UPON THE FACE OF.

Psa. 84:9. Look upon the face of thine Anointed. This phrase does not at all accord with our modern style of speech, but it is in perfect accord with Assyrian usage.

There is an Assyrian verb generally rendered to trust, though sometimes to protect or help. The verb is **Dagalu** or **Tagalu**. The literal meaning is to see, or look upon, but as one looks up to the one in whom he trusts, and looks after, as we say, those whom he protects or helps, so the verb passed out of the primary into the secondary meanings. It is used as a synonym for **amaru**, to see. R. III. 15. 1. 10 and 11. The goddess Ishtar of Arbela, corresponding to the Bellona of the Romans, said to Esarhaddon, **Mutukh enika ana aishi dugulanni :** Direct thine eyes to me. Look to me. Delitzsch renders נרגל Psa. 20:6, We will keep our eyes fixed upon the name of our god. So also the דגול of Cant. 5: 10 is, the cynosure among ten thousand, or he who attracts all eyes to himself among the ten thousand. See Prof. D. G. Lyon in Bib. Sacra. 1884. p. 379.

Sennacherib says (R. I. 37. 63), In my second campaign, Asshur my lord **utaggil panima,** looked upon my face, *i. e.*, protected and prospered me; the identical expression used in the Hebrew. It is also of frequent occurrence elsewhere.

Asshurbanipal (R. V. 1. 70 and 76) speaks of kings as **ardani dagil paniya,** servants subject to me; literally, looking upon my face. So Shuzub king of Babylon is said contemptuously to be a **dagil paan**, a looker on the face, of the satrap of Lahiri. R. I. 41. 9. Compare Psa. 123:2, "As the eyes of servants look unto the hand of their master, and as the eyes of a maiden unto the hand of her mistress," etc. See "Faith the correlate of grace," and "Dagal.""

LORD OF ALL.

When Peter mentioned the name of Jesus Christ in the house of Cornelius the Centurion, he added, "He is Lord of all," Acts 10: 36; and the sight of the title suggests at once the wellknown hymn that bids us "crown him Lord of all." This title, which so fitly belongs to him who is "King of kings and Lord of lords," Rev. 19:16, is in substance assigned to Sin, the moon god, in a hymn addressed to him as the supreme god of the city of Ur, which must often have fallen on the ears of Abraham as it was sung by the priests in the stillness of the night from the lofty sanctuary of the temple.

R. IV. 9. 21, 23, 24, 33, and H. L. 161, 162 :

21. Lord, the ordainer of the laws of heaven and earth, whose command may not be broken.
23. In heaven who is supreme? Thou alone; thou art supreme.
24. On earth who is supreme? Thou alone; thou art supreme.
33. O lord, in heaven is thy lordship, on the earth is thy sovereignty. Among the gods thy brethren a rival thou hast not.

So did the spirit of man, under the influence of the spirit of God, struggle up towards the true idea of God in spite of the darkness of polytheism, that sought to put out the light.

It also deserves notice here that the kings of Assyria had for one of their titles **Shar kishat** (king of all).

MAJESTY.

King Ahasuerus "showed the riches of his glorious kingdom, and the honor of his excellent majesty many days," Esther 1:4, and Nebuchadrezzar said, Dan. 4:30, "Is not this great Babylon, which I have built for the royal dwelling-place by the might of my power, and for the glory of my majesty?" From these glimpses of oriental life in Scripture we should expect in the records of oriental monarchs a style of speech not only self-asserting but self-laudatory also, and we are not disappointed. The king is not only the great king, but he is the king of hosts, the unrivalled king, the king of all the four regions of the world, the sungod of men, who has no rival, fears no opposition, who subdues the rebellious, who treads on the necks of his enemies, who tramples them down, the king of kings, the hero of the great gods, and the conqueror of the world.

Nor do they hesitate to put it in the first person singular: I am king, I am sovereign, I am exalted, I am strong, I am glorious, I am the first born, I am the champion, I am a lion, or even, I am the mighty monster (**usumgal**). Then they speak not so much of "me" as of "my lordship,' or "my majesty," or "my royalty," or "my sovereignty," and these expressions are so common that any specific references are superfluous. Go where we will, and read what we will, the same grandiloquence meets us at every turn. Such expressions as these lie before me in consecutive sentences: At that time an image of my majesty grandly I made. My power and exaltation I inscribed on it. In the midst of the palace of the conquered king I set it up. I erected my *stelæ*. The record of the exaltation of my strength I inscribed upon them. R. I. 22. 98, 99.; also R. of P. new 144. 98, 99.

The impression is constantly made upon the reader that in these ancient monarchs we see the supreme exercise of autocratic human power, free from the opposition that to-day would confront it at every turn, and along with that is the deep conviction that the enjoyment found in the perfection of such power is not worth mention in comparison with the joy which the very humblest may find in loving their fellow-men and doing them good.

MANASSEH.

2 Chron. 33:11. Wherefore the Lord brought upon them the captains of the host of the king of Assyria, who took Manasseh among the thorns, and bound him with fetters, and carried him to Babylon.

It has been objected to this that the empire was now Assyrian: how then would he be carried to Babylon? The answer is very simple, and as satisfactory as simple. Esarhaddon had succeeded to the throne in B. C. 681, and was noted for his mildness and moderation. Unlike his father, Sennacherib, who had destroyed Babylon in B. C. 691, so that the Euphrates was choked with its ruins, Esarhaddon rebuilt that city, and conciliated the Babylonians by making it his capital for six months of the year; so that it depended wholly on the season of the year whether a political prisoner would be taken to Nineveh or to Babylon. Fresh Light, etc., 122.

MEAT AND DRINK.

Ezra 3:7. And meat and drink and oil to them of Sidon. Compare 7. 22. A hundred measures of wheat, a hundred baths of wine, and a hundred baths of oil. It is evident that the drink of chap. 3. is the same as the wine of chap. 7. Compare Dan. 1:10, also Rom. 14:17 and Col. 2:16.

The mention of oil in connection with meat and drink is illustrated by the 41st line of the cylinder inscription of Sargon, which speaks of oil as **balti amiluti**, the life of men, which heals sores. As for the food and drink, Sennacherib (R. I. 38. 38-42) speaks of **Tsiduunu** (Sidon), **Bitzitti, Tsariiptu** (Sarepta), **Muhalliba, Usu, Akzib** and **Akkuu** (Accho) as strong fortified cities, "places of food and drink," *i. e.*, store cities. Prof's. Delitzsch and Lyon thus translate **riti u masqiti.** Prof. Sayce, H. L. 161. 27 and note 3, renders the words "the stall and the fold;" but **ritu** means literally pasture, hence the food which the pasture furnishes, and **masqitu** is a noun from the verb **saqu**, to drink.

MELCHIZEDEK.

There is an air of mystery about Melchizedek that makes him very interesting. He flashes on us out of the darkness, and then with equal suddenness disappears. Who has not longed for a better acquaintance with this unique personality?

He is introduced in the epistle to the Hebrews, 7:1, as "king of Salem," and at the same time "priest of the Most High God." The offices seem to us inconsistent, but they constitute what Peter calls "a royal priesthood," 1 Pet. 2:9, reminding us that "priests of God and of Christ shall reign with him a thousand years." Rev. 20:6.

Inconsistent as these offices may appear, some facts in Scripture make their combination at least familiar. Samuel judged, *i. e.*, ruled, Israel, and also blessed the sacrifice. 1 Sam. 9:13. The king of Moab offered up his eldest son for a burnt-offering. 2 Kings 3:27. And we may add with reverence our great High-Priest is also King of kings.

The monuments of Assyria also set forth this strange union. There the palace often contained the temple. In Khorsabad (Dur Sargina) a bas-relief represents Sargon worshipping before the sacred tree. P. and C. II. 98. Asshurbanipal also offers a libation over a wild bull which he had slain. P. and C. II. 40, 204. Asshurrishilim, B. C. 1150-1120, is called the priest, **shangu**, of Asshur. R. III. 3. 12. Asshurnatsirpal, B. C. 885-860, claims the same title, and gives it to his father, Tiglath Adar, B. C. 891-885, and to his grandfather, Ramman Nirari, B. C. 913-891. R. III. 3. 39. And Nebuchadrezzar, king of Babylon B. C. 605-562, styles himself the supreme high priest (**patesi**), the beloved of Nebo. India House Inscription, col. 1. 5, 6; R. of P. new III. 104.

The same truth is seen in the different meanings given by different scholars to the same Assyrian word. Thus some render **patesi** viceroy, and Prof. Delitzsch, D. L. 9, renders **Nisakku** *Priester? Furst?* as unable to decide between them. Prof. Sayce, H. L. 59, says the records of Assyria go back to a time when there were as yet no kings, but only high-priests (**patesi**) of Asshur, and quotes an inscription "palace of **Nebo shum eshir,** the son of Dakur the high priest (**patesi**) of Merodach." So while Prof. Lyon translates **Shakkanaku** in his A. M., governor, and also in S. 79. No. 2. 2, Prof. Sayce says of it, H. L. 109, note: "It is sometimes identical with the king and sometimes distinguished from him." R. I. 64. 9. 64. Thus Esarhaddon calls himself **shakkanaku** of Babylon, but king of Sumir and Akkad. R. I. 48. No. 6. Like **shangu** it denoted servitude to God." G. Smith, Senn. 57. 69 and 60. 1, translates it priests, and Schrader (K. A. T. 588) gives *Herr, Oberherr*. See also 301. 23 and 302. 4. and notes, where he renders *der hochster*, or *oberste beamter* the highest civil official. Prof. Delitzsch, D. L. 29, renders it *machthaber*, ruler.

Amenophis IV., Khu en Aten, the heretical king of the XVIIIth dynasty in Egypt, had for his maternal grandfather Duisratta, king of Mesopotamia, and forsook the national religion to worship the winged solar disc (**aten**). This caused a rupture with the priesthood in Thebes, so that he built a new capital at a place now known as Tel el Amarna, east of the Nile, and half way between Minyeh and Es Siout. Here, in A. D. 1887, a number of cuneiform tablets were discovered, being the despatches received from various officers of the government in all parts of the empire, especially from Palestine. Communications from Burna Buriyas of Babylonia, B. C. 1425–10, and from Asshur Muballidh of Assyria, B. C. 1400–1370, fix the date at about a century before the exodus of Israel from Egypt.

Among these correspondents was Ebed Tob, who was king of the city of Salim by virtue of his priesthood to its god, Salim, whose temple and oracle stood on Mount Moriah. This beautifully lights up the fact that Melchizedek was (Heb. 7. 1.) "king of Salem and priest of the Most High God." In Accadian **uru** represents the Assyrian **alu** (city), so **Urusalim,** the Assyrian name of Jerusalem, is "The city of the god of peace." We are further told (Heb. 7:3), that Melchizedek was "without father, without mother, and without genealogy," and Ebed Tob writes to the king of Egypt, R. of P. new V. 66. 9-13, "Behold, neither my father nor my mother has exalted me to this position, but the prophecy of the mighty king has caused me to enter the house of my father." In other words, he did not inherit his position, but he was appointed to it by the oracle of the god whom he served; and so important does he consider this fact that he repeats it in another letter, 68. 13, etc. How well this suits the argument of the Epistle to the Hebrews it is not necessary to show.

A skeptical Assyriologist might smile at the thought of that language testifying for Melchizedek when it contains no form of the Hebrew word for righteousness (צדק) that constitutes a part of his name, but uses the term ישר instead: **isharu**; yet just as Arabic in Mosul contains words from the Kûrdish, and Turkish in Smyrna has words from the Greek, so in old Salem Assyrian had words from the Phœnician, and among them Ebed Tob gives us, letter 6. line 32, **tsaduq** (righteous). This is the more striking as the only two kings of ancient Salem that we have any record of are Melchizedek, Gen. 14:18, and Adonizedek, Josh. 10:1. In ways so unexpected, and at the same time beyond all contradiction, does ancient history corroborate the truth of God.

Prof. Sayce also calls attention to the fact that "these letters of Ebed Tob show us why Melchizedek went forth to bless Abram after the defeat of the confederate kings. His god was Salim, the god of peace, and that victory over the invaders had assured peace to the country for a long time to come. Then, too, as the sacred character of the priest-king of Salim was acknowledged in all the region, the victorious Abram felt that it was fitting that he should offer to him the customary tithes."

MENE, TEKEL, UPHARSIN.

These were the fateful words written by a divine hand on the plaster of the wall of the palace of Babylon, Dan. 5:25, and we should expect some light would be shed on them by the inscriptions. Still some may expect too much, for they were not written in the language of Babylonia but in the kindred dialect of the Aramaic. **Mene** and **Tekel** are past participles in the singular number, and **Peres** the same; but in the form **Pharsin** it was plural, the **u** preceding that word being the conjunction "and" both in Assyrian and Aramaic. The whole was in that terse epigrammatic style that fixes attention on the warning and will not let it rest on smaller things.

Mene is identical with the Assyrian. We find it in R. V. 1. 122, where Egyptian rulers plotting against Assyria say **attuni ashabani mini**: as for us (the days of) our dwelling (here are) numbered; and a very frequent description of spoil is **ina la mini**: without number. The word is repeated to call attention to it, like the "verily, verily" of Christ.

Tekel in Assyrian would begin with *sh* instead of *t*, as the numeral two begins with sh instead of t, as in Aramaic.

Peres is the Hebrew or Aramaic form for the Assyrian **Parsu** or **Parsua**; **parasu** is the Assyrian verb that means to divide.

We do not expect to find any mention of this event on the monuments, for they never record unfavorable events, but only those that promote the glory of the king or the prosperity of the kingdom. See under "Plaster."

MERATHAIM.

Jeremiah writes (50:21) "Go up against the land of Merathaim." This was a district in southern Babylonia adjoining the Persian Gulf, and noted for its great salt marshes. So it was known in Babylonia as **marratu** (salt marsh). The climate was very hot, and the heat was rendered yet more insupportable by the great humidity of the atmosphere.

In this district was **Bit Yagina**, the city of Merodach-Baladan, to whose ambassadors king Hezekiah so unwisely displayed his treasures. Isa. 39:1 and 2. It was also the native land of the Chaldeans (**Kaldu**).

MERODACH-BALADAN.

Isa. 39:1. At that time Merodach-baladan, the son of Baladan, king of Babylon, sent letters and a present to Hezekiah, for he heard he had been sick and was recovered.

METHUSELAH.

This name shows the greater accuracy of the original inscription over the oft-copied volume. Baladan means "gave a son," and to complete the sense needs the name of some god who is said to have given it. The monuments say Merodach-baladan, son of Yagina. Some careless scribe has looked up to his copy and caught the wrong name.

After the death of Tiglath Pileser II. Babylon threw off the yoke of Assyria and remained free five years. Then, in B. C. 722, Merodach-baladan, the chief of the tribe of the Kaldai, who dwelt in the marshes near the mouth of the Euphrates, seized the vacant throne and so the Chaldeans became prominent in Babylonia. For twelve years he reigned in peace, but seeing that Sargon was preparing to attack him he sought to strike the first blow, and sent ambassadors to enlist Elam in the east, and Palestine with the adjoining countries in the west, against Assyria. This was the real object of his embassy to Hezekiah, and Sargon, who understood that well, at once marched against the Jewish king. The Tartan (general-in-chief) was sent against Ashdod, and Sargon himself seized Jerusalem.

Ashdod was destroyed and its people carried into captivity in B. C. 711, Edom and Moab were also punished, and next year the whole force of Assyria was hurled against Babylon. The king was driven back to his marshes, Elam was smitten, and a year later Sargon drove him to **Bit Yagina,** his ancestral home.

After the death of Sargon Merodach-baladan reoccupied Babylon for six months, when Sennacherib again drove him out, and four years later he left **Bit Yagina** to found a new colony on the western shore of Elam ; but there also Sennacherib followed him in Phœnician ships and destroyed the town, and we hear no more of him. He was a man of great energy and indomitable perseverance, and deserved a better fate.

METHUSELAH.

In H. L., 185. note, Prof. Sayce suggests that "the two varying forms of Methuselakh and Methusael should be **mutu sha ilati :** the husband of the goddess, *i. e.,* the sun god Tammuz, the husband of Ishtar." As he offers it only as a suggestion, and not as a positive statement, it hardly needs an apology for declining to accept it. If it does, he furnishes an ample one in his A. L. and S. 2, where he says: "The teacher and the pupil must both alike be learners—there is no authoritative standard to refer to."

Recent writers, while admitting a resemblance in names between some of the descendants of Cain and Sheth, Gen. 4 and 5, yet deny the identity of the two lines of descent.* Yet this suggestion would make one name from one line and a different one from the other refer to the same person. Then Methuselakh cannot represent a goddess, for it ends in Hheth, not in He, an ending never used to denote the feminine, while the ending of Methusàel is masculine only.

Mutu sha ilati refers to Tammuz in Assyrian, but can that be a ground for transferring that meaning to the Hebrew Methusael? Is it said that the goddess Ishtar is sometimes spoken of as masculine? The professor furnishes a reply to this when he tells us (H. L. 253-4) that Ishtar in Accadian is without gender, so that in using it the Shemites were in doubt whether to treat it as masculine or feminine. Indeed one tablet, speaking of the planet Venus, then called Ishtar, says that it is "a female at sunset and a male at sunrise." But what has that to do with the Hebrew name for God? Is it good logic to say, Assyrians in doubt about the sex of an idol spoke of it now as male and now as female, therefore there is the same uncertainty about the Old Testament name of God?

Were this only a question about names it would not call for notice, but it is more than that; for if in the days of Mehujael, the father of Methusael, so soon after the creation, men believed in goddesses, why not from the beginning? In that case polytheism dates from Paradise, and man has been ever since slowly climbing to monotheism; but Scripture teaches us that the one only true God revealed himself to Adam, and walked with Enoch and with Noah. And when men had gone over to idolatry because, though God had revealed himself to them, they refused to have him in their knowledge, God chose Abraham

---

* See J. H. Kurtz, D. D., Hist. of Old Covenant, I. 88-95, and commentaries of E. Harold Brown, D. D., Prof. C. F. Keil, F. Delitzsch, J. P. Lange and J. G. Murphy.

and his seed to bring back the race to the knowledge of God in Christ. And such truths are too fundamental to be overlooked even for a moment. See " Names Compounded."

MILK OF SHEEP.

Deut. 32:14. Butter of kine and milk of sheep.

Moses is here describing the goodly inheritance God had provided for his people, and the thoughtful reader will notice that, while the best butter is here said to be made from the milk of cows, the milk that is esteemed most highly is that of the sheep, a fact familiar to dwellers in Bible lands.

The writer was once travelling across the high lands of Asia Minor, and one night nothing could be had but ewes' milk. Knowing the strong aversion of his companion to that beverage, though she had never tasted it, he put the abhorred article on the table and said nothing. After supper came the inquiry, " Where did you get such good milk to-night? It was unusually rich and sweet."

In one of the magical texts occur the following lines:

> On the butter which is brought from a pure byre,
> The milk which is brought from a pure sheepcote,
> On the pure butter of the pure stall, lay a spell.

H. L. 462. 16–18. We also read in a hymn (R. IV. 28. 3, and H. L. 285):

> The milk of a light-colored goat, which in a pure feeding place the shepherd of Tammuz has reared.
> The milk of the goat let the shepherd give thee with his pure hands, etc.

MOABITE STONE, THE.

In 1869, Dr. Klein, a German missionary, discovered in Dhiban (Dibon of Moab) a stone of black basalt, rounded at the top, 2 feet broad and nearly 4 feet high. On it was an inscription of 34 lines in Phœnician letters. He copied a part, and after the negotiation of a year with the Arabs and Turks he bought it for £80 in behalf of the Berlin Museum. Then Mons. Clermont Ganneau, of the French Consulate at Jerusalem, offered £375 for it. Of course both Arabs and Turks were greatly excited, and the former, to prevent the talisman leaving the country, put fire under it, poured water over it, and sent the pieces of it as charms throughout the tribe. M. Ganneau, however, bought most of the pieces, and they are put together in the Louvre at Paris.

2 Kings 3 narrates the campaign of Israel, Judah and Edom against Moab. They evidently retreated without completing its subjugation.

Mesha, king of Moab, takes up the entire story in this *stela*, and narrates it as follows: "I, Mesha, am the son of Chemosh Gad, king of Moab, the Dibonite. My father reigned over Moab 30 years, and I reigned after my father, and I erected this stone to Chemosh at Kirkha, a stone of salvation (1 Sam 7:12), for he saved me from all despoilers (Psa. 18:39 and 44:7) and made me see my desire upon all my enemies (Psa. 54:7 and 92:11), even upon Omri, king of Israel (1 Kings 16:16). Now they afflicted Moab many days (Isa. 32:10: Dan. 11:33), for Chemosh was angry with his land (2 Kings 17:18, Num. 32:14 . His son (Ahab) succeeded him, and he also said, I will afflict Moab. In my days (Chemosh) said, Let us go, and I will see my desire upon his house, and I will destroy Israel with an everlasting destruction (2 Thess. 1:9.). Now Omri took the land of Medeba and occupied it in his days, and in the days of his son, 40 years. And Chemosh had mercy on it in my days, and I fortified Baalmeon (Ezek. 25:9), and made therein the tank, and I fortified Kiriathaim (Jer. 48:1, 23). For the men of Gad dwelt in the land of Ataroth from of old (Num. 32:34), and the king of Israel fortified for himself Ataroth. And I assaulted the wall and captured it, and killed all the warriors of the wall for the well pleasing of Chemosh and Moab, and I removed from it all the spoil and offered it before Chemosh in Kirjath, and I placed therein the men of Siran and the men of Mochrath. And Chemosh said to me, Go, take Nebo against Israel (1 Sam. 23:2). (And I) went in the night and fought against it from the break of dawn until noon, and I took it, and slew in all 7,000 (men, but I did not kill) the women (and) maidens, for (I) devoted them to Ashtar Chemosh. And I took from it the vessels of **Yahveh** (Jehovah) and offered them before Chemosh (Jer. 48:13). And the king of Israel fortified Jahaz (Num. 21:23), and occupied it when he made war against me, and Chemosh drove him out before (me) (Num. 21 : 32) (and) I took from Moab 200 men, all its poor, and placed them in Jahaz, and took it to annex it to Dibon (Num. 21 : 30 and 32 : 34). I built Kirkha, the wall of the forest and the wall of the city, and I built the gates thereof, and I built the towers thereof, and I built the palace, and I made the prisons for the criminals within the walls. And there was no cistern in (side) the wall at Kirkha, and I said to all the people, Make for yourselves, every man, a cistern in his house. And I dug the ditch for Kirkha by means of the (captive) men of Israel. I built Aroer (Num. 32 : 34), and I made the road across the Arnon (Nu. 21 : 14). I built Beth-Bamoth (Josh. 13 : 17), for it was destroyed; I built Bezer (Josh. 20:8), for it was cut down by the armed

THE MOABITE STONE.

men of Dibon, for all Dibon was now loyal, and I reigned from Bikran, which I added to my land. And I built Beth-gamul (Jer. 48:23) and Beth-diblathaim (Jer. 48:22) and Beth Baal-meon (Josh. 13 : 17), and I placed there the poor of the land (2 Kings 25:12). And as to Horonaim (Isa. 15 : 5), (the men of Edom) dwelt therein (from of old), and Chemosh said to me, Go down, make war against Horonaim and take (it. And I assaulted it and took it and) Chemosh restored it in my days."

The rest is illegible. I have given references to passages in Scripture which illustrate the text, mentioning the same places, or using the same phrases. Prof. Sayce says that the language differs less from Hebrew than do some English dialects from each other. See Fresh Light, etc. 73-78.

MOLLIFIED WITH OIL.

Isa. 1:6 speaks of "wounds, bruises and festering sores (that) have not been closed, neither bound up, neither mollified with oil." One hardly looks for an illustration of this in the monuments, nor would such a find be helpful in the way of confirming any Bible doctrine. Nevertheless, it is interesting in such a connection to find Sargon, 722-705 B. C., the king of Assyria mentioned in Isa. 20:1, who also built Khorsabad (Dur Sargina), mention among other blessings attending his reign that "the oils, the life of mankind, serving also to soothe or mollify sores, were not expensive in my territory. **Simsim** (sesame) was of the same price as ordinary grain." Cylinder Inscription, line 41. S. 7.

MONOTHEISM.

Rom. 1:21-23. Because that, knowing God, they glorified him not as God, neither gave thanks, but became vain in their reasonings, and their foolish heart was darkened. Professing themselves to be wise, they became fools, and changed the glory of the incorruptible God for the likeness of an image of corruptible man, and of birds, and four-footed beasts, and creeping things.

It is not necessary to quote many Scriptures to prove that they teach that men originally knew the one living God, and that when they refused to have God in their knowledge he gave them up to believe the lie of polytheism, with all its bitter fruits. The passage quoted above tells us that men knew the one God, and when they did not glorify him as God they became polytheists and idolators; and the word of God is our only rule of faith.

What have the monuments to say on this subject? No explicit Assyrian record of the original monotheistic period has come down to us. All the monuments date after the change to polytheism had already taken place, so that they mention directly only polytheism; and yet even among these records are many hints and traces of the primeval faith in one God.

There is first the fact that **Ilu,** the Assyrian word for God, is identical with **Anu,** the name of one of the earliest gods. So it would seem that there was a time when no other god existed to dispute the title; and it confirms this view that when, during the deluge, the gods are said to have ascended to heaven, it is called the heaven of **Anu.** Fresh Light, etc., 30. A. M. 59. 1.

Then sometimes we meet with the generic statement that God did thus and so, as though there was but one being to whom it could refer. This also can be nothing less than a relic of ancient monotheism, working its way through the mass of polytheism to the light. Some of the hymns to the gods even speak of "the one god" (H. L. 191), and such a palpable contradiction speaks eloquently for the truth.

There are also many expressions that point unmistakably to monotheism. One is "the father of the gods," "the father who has created the gods" (II. L. 128), showing the concept of a God before and above all gods. Indeed, in the same line we read, "the supreme first-born of heaven and earth." Then there is the title "king of the gods," implying authority over all other gods, who must needs be inferior and subordinate to him.

It may be objected that some of these epithets apply to more than one god. Yes, because each one was eager to claim the priority and superiority belonging to the supreme God for his own deity, and it is interesting to see how in this matter

" Truth crushed to earth shall rise again;
The eternal years of God are hers."

MONTHS.

The influence of a people may be measured by the extent to which their language affects the nomenclature of surrounding nations. Thus the influence of the Roman empire is revealed in the manner in which their names of the months were used by neighboring nations. Not Italy alone, but France and Germany, Austria and Switzerland, England and Holland, Denmark and Scandinavia, Spain and Portugal, to say nothing of peoples farther east or of the New World, adopted to a greater or less extent their names of the months. How far was the influence of Assyria felt along the same line?

Previous to the Captivity the Jews generally referred to their months by their numbers. They spoke of the first, the seventh or tenth month, though they had other names for several of them. Thus the first month was also known as Abib (ear of corn). Exod. 13:4, *et al.* The second month was also called Zif (beauty, or flowers). 1 Kings 6:1, 37. In the next verse the eighth month is also called Bul'(rain) the name given to it also in the Phœnician inscription of Ashmanezer king of Sidon. The Land and the Book II. 644. N. Y., 1882. The seventh month was also known as Ethanim (gifts?). 1 Kings 8:2.

In the later years of the kingdom of Judah this was all changed. The Assyrian names of the months were adopted, as is seen in the books of Nehemiah, Esther, Zechariah and Ezekiel. This was the result of the political supremacy of Assyria, though the literature of the empire was Babylonian; but Assyria carried with it the literary influence of Babylonia as Rome carried with her the literary supremacy of Greece. Indeed the Assyrian names of the months gave place to their Babylonian nomenclature as well as the Hebrew names.

These Babylonish names were written ideogrammatically with an Accadian basis. Each month consisted of thirty days, with a month intercalated once in six years to conform to the solar year. Their names are given in R. IV. 33, 1, also in Vol. V. 29. 1, and more fully on p. 43 of this last volume. See also Ass'l. 325 and 326. This last list was compiled from unpublished tablets in the British Museum. A good list is found in D. L. 92 and 93. See also R. of P. I. 166, 167, also VII. 169, 170, also new I. and III.

Though only seven of the Assyrian names of the months are mentioned in Scripture they were probably all in use; the others are mentioned in the Talmud. The seven names are *Nisan*, Esther 3:7, Neh. 2:1; *Sivan*, Esth. 8:9; *Elul*, Neh. 6:15; *Kisleu*,

MONTHS.

ENGLISH.	ASSYRIAN.	HEBREW.	ARAMAIC.	ARABIC.	SACRED TO
April	Nisannu	ניסן	Nisan	Nisan	Anu and Bil.
May	Airu or Aaru	אייר	Iyyar	Iyyar	Ea (god of waters).
June	Simanu or Sivanu	סיון	Khaziran	Khaziran	Sin (moon god).
July	Duzu	תמוז	Tammuz	Tammuz	Adar (Ninip).
August	Abu	אב	Ab	Ab	Allat (Queen of Hades).
September	Ululu	אלול	Ailula	Ailul	Ishtar (Aphrodite).
October	Tashritu	תשרי	Teshri Qadmaya	Teshrin el Awal	Shamash (sun god).
November	Arakh Samnu	מרחשון	Teshri Akhraya	Teshrin et taneh	Marduk (Merodach).
December	Kisilimu or Kislivn	כסלו	Kanun Qadmaya	Kanun el Awal	Nergal (King of Hades).
January	Tabitu or Tebetu	טבת	Kanun Akhraya	Kanun et taneh	Papsukul (messenger).
February	Shabatu	שבט	Shibat	Shebat	Rammanu (air god).
March	Addaru	אדר	Adar	Adar	
Intercalary	Arkhu Makhru or Ve Addaru	ואדר			

Prof. Delitzsch explains the meaning of these months as follows:

  Nisannu, the beginning.   **Duzu**, the only-begotten.
  Addaru, the cloudy.   **Tebetu**, the showery.
  Shebat, the destroying or devastating.   Bib. Sacra 1884. 384.

Neh. 1:1, Zech. 7:1 ; *Tebet*, Esth. 2:16; *Shebet*, Zech. 1:7, and *Adar*, Ezra 6:15, Esther 3:7. *Tammuz* appears in Ezek. 8:14, as the name of a person only.

The Assyrian months overlap ours; *e. g.*, Nisan extends a little into May, and so all round the year.

The accompanying table shows at a glance how the Babylonian gave form to the Hebrew, Aramaic, and Arabic. The Moslems have never been able to displace the Assyrian calendar, which holds its own in Turkey to this day. Mohammedan months are lunar, and revolve all round the year once in thirty-three years and a half. They are Mokharram, Sufar, Rabeea el Owwal, Rabeea et taneh, Joomad el owwal, Joomad et taneh, Rejeb, Shaaban, Ramadan, Showwal, Zoo el qadeh, Zoo el khejjeh.

MONUMENT.

1 Sam. 15 : 12. Saul came to Carmel, and behold he set him up a monument (יד). Gen. 35 : 14. Jacob set up a pillar (מצבה) at Bethel, and another (v. 20) over the grave of Rachel. Absalom also set up one in memory of himself. 2 Sam. 18 : 18.

From the shores of the Mediterranean as far east as Persia, and from the Black Sea to the Persian Gulf, we find to-day the *stelæ* of the kings of Assyria. Besides the one at the top of the pass at Keli shin (Green Pillar) Dr. A. Grant found another half an hour east from the village of Sidek (Dr. Grant and the Mtn. Nestorians, 225) on his way to Oroomiah from Ravendûs.

Asshurnatsirpal (B. C. 883–858) set up one in the land of **Eqi** at the head of the river (Tigris?) (R. I. 18. 68. R. of P. new II. 141), another at the gate of the city of **Suri** (R. I. 19. 98 and R. of P. new II. 144), another at the head of the **Supnat,** now the Sebbeneh soo, which flows into the Tigris above Diarbekir (R. I. 19 104, 105 and R. of P. new II. 145), another at the city of **Tuskha,** between Mt. Masius and the Tigris, south of Diarbekir (R. I. 20. 5 and R. of P. new II. 147), another at the city of **Mattiyati** (R. I. 22. 91 and R. of P. new II. 157), and another in the city of **Suru** (R. I. 24. 25 and R. of P. new II. 165).

Shalmaneser II. (**Shalmanu asharidu,** Shalman is leader), B. C. 860–824, set up very many. In his obelisk found at Koyunjik, copied in Layard's Inscriptions 87–98 and translated in R. of P.

new IV. 38-54, he speaks of a *stela* set upon Mt. Lallar, R. of P. IV. 39, one at the sources of the Tigris, 42, another at the caverns near the source of the eastern Tigris, 43. Also Miss. Herald, 1870, 128, 129.

Then in his monolith at **Kurkh,** copied in R. III. 7 and 8 and translated in Hebraica Vol. III., 1887, also in R. of P. new IV. 53-71, he speaks of a *stela* erected on an eminence overlooking lake Van, R. of P. new IV. 58, also 67, another at the source of the river Saluara near the foot of Mt. Amanus, 60, another on the shore of the Mediterranean, 61, also 75, and on Mt. Atalur, near one set up previously by **Asshur irbi (Asshur rab buri?)** 61 and 75, another in the city of Saluria at the foot of **Qireqi** which is near the Moorad soo above Paloo, 65, and still another on the mountains of Eritia, 66.

Tiglath Pileser II., **Tugulti pal esira,** B. C. 745-727, erected one at **Turuspa** on Lake Van (G. Smith's Hist. of Assyria, 85), and Sargon, B. C. 722-605, set up one in the island of Cyprus which is now in the British Museum.

Sennacherib, B. C. 705-681, erected one among the mountains between Sulimanieh and Kermanshah, Smith's Assyria, 117. R. of P. I. 27 and 28, in the country of the **Kasshii** and **Yasubigallaa.** It is needless, however, to pursue the subject further.

MOON, WORSHIP OF THE.

Among other protestations of his integrity Job says (31 : 26-28): "If I beheld the sun when it shined, or the moon walking in brightness, and my heart hath been secretly enticed, and my mouth hath kissed my hand, this also were an iniquity to be punished by the judges, for I should have lied to God who is above." These words indicate a strong pressure constraining to sin in that direction, as well as a declaration of uniform loyalty to the true God throughout his whole life, notwithstanding such influences. Is there anything that explains this special temptation of that good man?

The land of Ūz lay between Palestine, or rather Mt. Seir, on the west and Chaldea on the east, and Chaldea was the stronghold of Sabianism, or the worship of the heavenly bodies. **Urukh,** the earliest king of that land of whom we have any

THE GREAT TEMPLE AT MUGHEIR.

knowledge, built a temple to the sun god at **Larsa,** now Senkereh, which was the centre of that worship until its fame was eclipsed by another temple to the same god at **Sippara,** called Sepharvaim in Scripture. Isa. 36:19. The early Accadians, however, thought much more of the moon than of the sun, the exact opposite of the better knowledge of to-day. With them the moon was masculine and the sun was feminine. Indeed, they made **Sin,** the moon god, father of **Shamash,** the sun god, and while the temple at **Larsa** differed little, if at all, from other temples, that built by **Urukh** at **Ur** for the moon god was noted for its magnificence; so that while other temples in Chaldea have been buried out of sight, this one alone, though erected in the grey dawn of history, about B. C. 3000 or 2500, still towers aloft to the height of 70 feet, which is only a part, however, of the original elevation. Not many structures of our times will remain equally prominent 4,000 years hence.

As the splendor of this structure represents the power of that influence which Job resisted so successfully, let us look on it as set before us in the pages of Loftus' Chaldea and Susiana (128-134). Here we have by far the best picture of the ruins as they now appear, though other engravings have been reduced from this.

First of all a spacious solid platform of sun-dried bricks was built up to the height of 20 feet above the plain. The centre of this is now buried deep under the talus of debris that has fallen from above. The first story, 198x133 feet, rose 27 feet above above this, with pilasters 8 feet wide and 13 inches in depth buttressing the walls on the north and west sides. These were formed of red fire-burned brick to the depth of 10 feet; inside of that a solid mass of sun-burned brick left only a passage from the door on the middle of the east side to the platform above. Like all Chaldean structures, the angles, not the sides, faced the four cardinal points, and the walls gradually sloped inwards at an angle of 9°. Another evidence of the science of those early days is found in the narrow openings into the interior of the mass, through which the hot dry air of summer is brought in contact with every part. P. and C. I. 157. Their arrangements for drainage also evinced no little skill; vertical drains with very narrow openings at the top received the rain water from the upper surface. These soon enlarged into the form of an inverted cup, perforated with holes so as to receive the excess of moisture, and extended to the bottom of the mass in the form of a hollow column composed of drums of terra cotta 2 feet long and 18 inches in diameter, one above the other, with their sides made slightly concave in order to secure greater strength, and these perpendicular drains were filled and surrounded with broken pottery, which added to their strength while it did not interfere with the drainage. P. and C. I. 159.

On the top of this first story, or, more likely, on a second story removed by Nabonidas when he built another in its place, stood the sanctuary of the god. Abraham must often have looked on it, even though he did not enter as a worshipper, and must often have heard the chants of the priests borne on the still night air, though, like Job, he maintained his loyalty to God.

MORDECAI.

Esther 2:5. There was a certain Jew in Shushan the palace whose name was Mordecai.

This name is in Assyrian **Mardukaa, or Mardukai,** and means a worshipper of the god **Marduk** (Merodach); and the question at once arises, How could a pious Hebrew, who believed in the one true God, be called by such a name? It seems like a bold transgression of the first commandment.

Mr. T. G. Pinches gives the very satisfactory explanation of the matter (R. of P. new IV. 108), that the word **marduk** often meant simply god, and quotes a tablet that speaks of **Nergal** as the **marduk** of **gablu**, fight, combat; **Zagagu** as the **marduk** of **takhazu**, battle, war; **Bil**, the **marduk** of dominion. **Sin is marduk** the illuminator, etc. This would make Mordecai to mean the godly man, or worshipper of God. The tablet was found by Mr. Hormuzd Rassam about 1881 in the vicinity of Babylon and **Sippara** (Sepharvaim).

MORNING STAR, THE.

The Lord Jesus promises this star as a gift to his faithful servants. Rev. 2:28. Later on, 22:16, he affirms, "I am the bright and morning star." This is true in a higher sense than had ever been true before, and that makes it all the more important to know the sense in which it had been used.

The Babylonians were devoted to the study of the stars, and their mythology was strangely mingled with their astronomy. In it Shamash was the sun god, Sin the moon god, and Ishtar was represented by the planet Venus. In the time of Sargon of Agane (Akkad), which H. L. 21 puts as early as 3750 B. C., they knew that the same planet was both morning and evening star. So in an old Accadian hymn Ishtar says (H. L. 269):

> Ishtar, deity of the evening sky, am I.
> Ishtar, deity of the dawn, am I.

Now the name of this planet was **Dilbat** (Announcer), which it could be only as in the morning it heralded the dawn. Now, just as it heralded the sunrise, Jesus Christ heralds the coming glory of that day when the benefits of his redemption shall dawn on an admiring universe, and all the glory of that day shall proceed from that redemption and for ever and ever shall it show forth his praise; for the whole of it is only the shining out of the glory that is in him as our Redeemer.

MOSES AMONG THE BULRUSHES.

The story of Moses laid by his mother in a little ark of bulrushes and committed to the Nile is too familiar to need repetition. See Ex. 2: 1-10. A very nearly similar account is given of Sargon of Agane (Accad) in R. III. 4. No. 7; a translation is given in H. L. 26 and 27 note:

Sargon (the true king) the mighty king, the king of Accad, am I.
My mother was a princess, my father I know not, the brother of my father dwells in the mountain,
In the city of **Azupiranu**, which is situated on the bank of the Euphrates,
My mother the princess conceived me, in a secret place she brought me forth.
She placed me in a basket of reeds, with bitumen the door she closed.
She committed me to the river, which did not drown me.
The river bore me along, to **Akki** the water-carrier it brought me.
Akki the water-carrier in his goodness of heart took me up.
Akki the water-carrier reared me as his own son.

The characters of this tablet are of the latest style, such as were used in the days of Asshurbanipal, and as Sargon was a ruler and patron of learning it may be possible that some literary admirer, centuries after his death, conceived the idea of ascribing to him such an experience in infancy as report had brought to Babylonia concerning the great Hebrew lawgiver and writer.

MOUNTAINS.

Ezek. 32:5. I will lay thy flesh upon the mountains, and fill the valleys with thy height. Gesenius renders, instead of height, heap of corpses, worms. Also 35:8. I will fill the mountains with thy slain, in thy hills, and in thy valleys, and in all thy water courses, shall they fall that are slain with the sword.

No modern battle is described in this way; but they so resemble some of the descriptions of Assyrian warfare contained in the monuments that it seems as though Ezekiel must have read through the long annals of Asshurnatsirpal at Calah (Nimrood). This is quite possible, for that king died B. C. 860 and the prophet was at the river of Chebar about 260 years afterwards. He may then have visited Calah before the fall of Nineveh. Asshurnatsirpal says, **damishunu kima napasi shadi lu atsruub,** and Prof. Sayce translates it "with their blood the mountains I dyed like wool," though there is some doubt about the word he renders "wool." The king then goes on, "hollows and water-courses devoured the rest of them." This description is repeated in several places: R. I. 18. 53; 20. 17 and 18; 22. 114. In this last he says: "1,000 of their warriors I slew in the rugged mountain; with their blood I made the mountain to flow, with their bodies the ravines and water-courses I filled." These passages are translated in the new R. of P. II. 139. 148, 159.

MOUNT OF THE CONGREGATION.

Isa. 14:13 makes the king of Babylon to say: "I will ascend into heaven. I will exalt my throne above the stars of God, and I will sit upon the mount of the congregation in the uttermost parts of the north;" *i. e.*, I will sit among the gods in the high mountain to the north where they make their home. For before the Greeks had their Olympus the Babylonians and Assyrians

MOUNT OF THE CONGREGATION. 221

had their **kharsag kalama,** or mountain of the universe. Prof. Sayce says, H. L. 360, " Here the gods were imagined to have been born, and to have their seats. Its summit was hidden by the clouds and the starry firmament seemed to rest upon it. It is possible that it was identified with the mountain of **Nizir,** the modern Rowandiz."

This last statement is somewhat confusing. The modern mount Elwend or Elvend is generally identified as the ancient **Nizir,** and I have not heard of any prominent mountain named Rowandiz, and yet Prof. Sayce says, " Rowandiz towers high above its fellows in the Kurdish range." May it not be that more than one mountain had this honor—for the idea seems to call for a summit visible from afar—and that, while the southern Babylonians made Elwend the dwelling-place of their gods, they of Assyria chose one farther north as the home of Asshur and his associates? The *Toora 'd Jelu* towers high above all else that is visible from Assyria, and if any mountain was to be selected as the scene of their Valhalla, that would, before all others, be the successful candidate. The writer has often looked up at its unbroken covering of snow, from the hot banks of the Tigris in early summer, and when he opened his eyes, from his bed on the flat roof in the dawn of the morning, the first object to meet his gaze was that white, glittering cone that dominated all the peaks of Kurdistan.

Mr. Layard says, B. and N. 430, " Before reaching the rocky ridge of the *Sappa Durek* we had to cross a broad tract of deep snow, over which we painfully dragged our heavily loaded mules. On the crest of the pass we found ourselves surrounded on all sides by rugged peaks, among which the highest was *Toora'd Jelu,* of which we had scarcely lost sight since leaving Mosul. It is probably the highest peak in Central Kurdistan, and cannot be under 15,000 feet in height. On its precipitous sides the snow cannot rest, but around it are eternal glaciers. Some Nestorians assured me they had followed the wild goat even to its summit, whence they looked down on a view of vast extent and grandeur—the desert stretching away like a vast sea beneath, and Mosul distinctly visible in the distance." Those bragging Nestorians may never have reached the summit, but we give our ballot for the mountain of Jelu. No other in all the region is so worthy to represent the mountain of the Assyrian Olympus in the uttermost parts of the north.

MOUTH.

There is one meaning of the Hebrew word פה that does not appear in our English Bible. In Gen. 24:57 Laban is said to inquire "at the mouth" of Rebekah. Gesenius makes him simply "ask counsel" of her, and he gives the same rendering to the word in Josh. 9:14, "asked not counsel of the Lord." See also Isa. 30:2.

The Assyrian endorses this rendering of Gesenius in the following manner: In R. V. 8. 48, see also A. M. 29. **17**, Asshurbanipal says that Abiyati, king of Arabia, **piishu ishkimma,** literally "set his mouth," with the Nabateans. Obviously he so took counsel with them that their hearts had the same purpose, and their mouths spoke the same things. Thus the old Assyrian records endorse the rendering reached independently by modern Hebrew scholars.

The Hebrew פה is also used in the sense of command: Gen. 45:21; Ex. 17:1; Eccles. 8:2. So also is the Assyrian **pu.** A striking instance of this occurs in R. V. I. 13, and A. M. 19. 26: **pii muttalli,** exalted command. See under "Honor."

MUSIC.

The ancient Hebrews had a great fondness for music, which they used abundantly in their religious services, in their pilgrimages to Jerusalem, their civic and bridal processions, their public and private banquets, and even at their funerals. The notices of music in Scripture indicate several things concerning it. First, something of variety in musical instruments. Daniel 3:7, 10 and 15 speaks of cornet, flute, harp, sackbut, psaltery and dulcimer. Psa. 33:2 speaks of the psaltery of ten strings, Psa. 81:3 of trumpets, and Psa. 150:5 of two kinds of cymbals. One rather wonders at the omission of the drum, which is so common in the Orient, but it must have been known then under some other name, as timbrel, Exod. 15:20; at any rate, the word drum is not found in our English version. Second, musical performers were of both sexes, Ex. 15:20, 1 Sam. 18:6, 7, Judg. 11:34. Third, the music was processional, to borrow a phrase from modern usage. Miriam, the daughter of Jephthah, and the women from all the cities of Israel, when Goliath was slain, marched as they sang.

Precisely the same state of things obtained among the Assyrians. On page 455 of Layard's B. and N. we have a musical procession of twenty-three persons— four men, eleven women and eight children. Of the men, two have a harp of even more than ten strings. One is an *auletes*, playing on double pipes, and one has a flat instrument, perhaps a dulcimer, which he strikes with a short stick. Four of the women have harps of the same form and size as the men: one is an *auletes*, and one strikes with her hands a small drum or timbrel like a modern *tubl*. Two of the remaining five have one hand raised as if beating time, one has her hand raised to the throat like oriental women when they make the shrill *zughareet*, or cry of joy, and the rest are clapping their hands in concert with the children. I should have noticed that two of the men have one foot raised as though dancing, or at least beating time. Thus this one bas-relief illustrates all three of the Scripture statements concern-

MUSICAL PROCESSION (KOYUNJIK).

ing music. When the women came singing and dancing to meet Saul with timbrels, with joy and with instruments of music, and sang responsively, "Saul hath slain his thousands and David his myriads," they must have presented just such a sight as we have on the preceding page.

The inscriptions endorse its testimony. Esarhaddon (**Assur akh iddina,** Asshur has given a brother), who reigned B. C. 681–668, had conquered the two cities of **Kundi** and **Siznu,** and also the king of Sidon, who had gone to their help. After the return of the victors to the capital there was a great triumph, and the heads of the slaughtered kings were borne aloft in the procession, and the record adds, " with musical performers, male and female, in the broad square of Nineveh I marched triumphant." This also covers all the three points alluded to. R. I. 45. 52, 53.

After the subjugation of Elam and the sack of Gambuli, King Assurbanipal says, " with musicians making a great jubilation I entered into Nineveh with great rejoicings." Ass'l. 134. 46, 47.

NAME OF GOD, THE.

Holy Scripture gives special prominence to the *name* of God. It occurs often when we would speak of God himself. Thus God says to Pharaoh, Exod. 9:16, " I have raised thee up ... that my name may be declared throughout the earth," *i. e.*, that I may be known everywhere. So God speaks of "places where I record my name," Exod. 20:24. He also says, 1 Sam. 7:13, " He (Solomon) shall build a house for my name." God speaks of his name being blasphemed, Isa. 52:5, of its being great among the Gentiles, Mal. 1:11, of giving glory to his name, Mal. 2:2, and of "you that fear my name," Mal. 4:2. The third commandment forbids to take the name of God in vain, Exod. 20:7. Christ teaches us to pray, not " Be thou glorified; but, " Hallowed be thy name," Matt. 6:9. And the glorified Redeemer commends one church because, to use his own words, "thou hast not denied my name," Rev. 3:8, and another, " for thou holdest fast my name." This is a very marked *usus loquendi*. We cannot fail to be impressed by it. Has the Assyrian any light to throw on this peculiar form of speech?

As the old realistic philosophy held that words denoting genera and species not only represented an idea but an actual entity, so the old Babylonians held that names were things; real equivalents of the things they represented. "The name in fact was the personality." Thus an account of the creation, reads, line 1, "When the heavens above had not yet announced, nor the earth beneath recorded a name," D. L. 13, and A. M. 62. The writer means to say, when as yet nothing had been created, but he speaks as though announcing a name was equivalent to creating the object named. So lines 7–9 of the same tablet: "When the gods had not yet any of them come into existence—were mentioned as yet by no name—then the great gods were created." Here his meaning cannot be mistaken; he clearly affirms that creating and mentioning a name are identical.

Their magical formulæ also confounded persons and names. Many of these have been found, and it only needed a name to be inserted in reading the spell for the owner of the name to suffer the evils it invoked or the healing which it was designed to effect, for whatever was spoken concerning the names took effect on the person who bore it. The idea also that such formulæ could injure by means of pictures, locks of hair, parings of nails, or even shreds of clothing, seems to have originated in Babylonia (R. II. 17, 1. 30, also H. L. 330 and 442), but the use of the name was more common because it was deemed more efficacious. They believed that the result was effected by spirits who had their abode in every thing that existed, and had power to confer good and, especially, to inflict evil, and though all things were under the control of the great gods yet both gods and spirits were subject to fate, and the sorcerer could control this fate by his spells. So great was the power inherent in the use of a name.

This identification of a name with its owner made the name an object of supreme regard. The adoption of a time-honored name lifted a *novus homo* into the line of succession and established his throne, *e. g.*, Sargon of Dur Sargina. This is seen also in the dreadful curses invoked by Assyrian kings on whoever erased their names from their inscriptions.

Tiglath Pileser I. (**Tugulti pal esira,** my confidence, *i. e.*, the god in whom I put my trust, let him guide the son). B. C. 1120–1110, writes thus: "In future days when the temple of the great gods my lords Anu and Rammanu and these lofty towers (**ziggurat**) shall decay, let whoever fills the throne repair the falling structure, anointed with oil let him restore my memorial tablets to their places and offer sacrifices. Let him also inscribe his own name along with mine on the renovated structure, and the great gods Anu and Rammanu will keep him in gladness of heart and in the enjoyment of victory, as they have kept me. But whoever shall break my records in pieces, cover them up or burn them with fire, whoever shall bury them in a grave (literally, in the house of the pure god—Ia, the Chaldean Pluto) or put them in a place out of sight, and where no man goeth, whoever shall erase the name that is written or put his own name in its place, and consign my memorial to a dark oblivion (literally an epoch of night), let the great gods my lords Anu and Rammanu inflict on him terrible destruction, and curse him with a dreadful curse. Let them overthrow his kingdom, remove the foundation of his throne, and swallow up the royal armies. Besides this destruction of his soldiers let them break his weapons, and make him to bow down always before his enemies. (Compare Rom. 11 : 10.) Let Rammanu smite his land with destructive lightning, fill it with famine, and strew it with dead bodies. Against his lordship let him utter his most terrible curses, and cause his name and his posterity to perish from the earth." R. I. 16. 50–88. Also Prof. Sayce's Elem. Gram. 111–113. Compare Psa. 109 : 17, 18, new revision.

Asshurbanipal (Asshur creates a son), B. C. 668–626, writes in a gentler mood (R. V. 62. 23–29, also A. M. 24. 14–22.): "In the last days (compare Gen. 49 : 1 ; Micah 4 : 1 ; Acts. 2 : 17 ; Heb. 1 : 2 ; 2 Pet. 3 : 3,) let the ruler in whose reign this structure shall decay build up again its ruins. Let him write my name along with his own; my inscription let him look on; let him anoint with oil (on this rendering see A. M. 75, top), sacrifices let him offer, and with his own inscription let him set it up, and Shamash (the sun god) will hear his prayer; but he who shall treacherously destroy my name and the name of my beloved brother, he who will not inscribe my name along with his own, and with his inscription does not set it up also, let Shamash, who is lord of all above and below, destroy him in anger, and let his name and posterity perish from the earth." Compare Psa. 41:5; 109:13.

He also closes an account of his rebuilding the palace in which he was born in these words: "When this Harem (**Bit riduti**) becomes old and ruinous, let that name among the kings my descendants whom Asshur and Ishtar shall then have proclaimed ruler of the land and the people repair its ruins. Let that remote descendant see the written name of myself, my father, and my father's father. Let him anoint with oil and offer sacrifices, then place it along with the written record of his own name, and let all the great gods named in this inscription confirm to him the power and glory which they have given me. But whoever shall destroy my written name, and that of my father and father's father, and with his own name does not set them up, let Asshur, Sin, Shamash, Rammanu, Bil, Nabu, Ishtar, of Nineveh, the divine queen of Kidmuri, Ishtar of Arbela, Ninip, Nergal and Nusku judge him with a judgment worthy of the naming of my name." Could language set forth with greater clearness the importance attached to a name?

The risen Redeemer saith to the church at Pergamos, "To him that overcometh, to him will I give of the hidden manna, and I will give him a white stone, and upon the stone a new name written." Rev. 2:17. Asshurbanipal thus writes of Pharaoh Necho (R. V. 2. 8–13, A. M. 48. 8–14. and Ass'l. 27. 34–28. 40): "I clothed him with (**birmi**) embroidered (?) garments, and a chain of gold, the insignia of royalty, I gave him (compare Joseph, Gen. 41:42, and Daniel 5. 6); rings of gold I bound upon his hands (Luke, 15:22), on a steel girdle-dagger (such as Kurds and Arabs wear to-day) with a golden hilt I wrote the naming of my name and gave to him." Doubless that dagger was looked on by both giver and receiver as the most precious item in the gift, because it bore the name of the royal giver. Do not these extracts from the records of a kindred race throw light on the way in which the Scriptures teach us to look upon the name of God?

NAMES COMPOUNDED WITH THE NAME OF GOD.

Few studies are more fascinating than the meaning of names. The Blacks and Browns, Smiths and Taylors, Hunters and Fishers are plain enough, but to learn that Leonard is "the lion hearted," Westcott "the occupant of the west cottage," Sheldon "the resident by the fountain on the hill," that Forsythe is "the honest man," Luther "the celebrated man," and Morgan "the one born at sea," is continuous delight. It is like looking into a revolving kaleidoscope, when each moment surprises with a new joy.

Originally each name had its meaning. It might point to some peculiarity of character or some physical singularity. It might denote an occupation. The writer knew a resident in old Assyria named **Nakkar**, millwright; but when he turned his hand from mill stones to watches his name became **Saati,** watchmaker. Or it might have to do with the location of his home; thus Woodworth is "the occupant of the farm in the wood," and Northrop "the man in the north hamlet."

We see this very clearly in Bible names, where the manner of their origin is often mentioned with the name. Adam was the man formed from "red earth" and Cain the man "obtained" from the Lord. Saul is the one "sought for," and David the "beloved." Dido in the language of Phœnicia had the same meaning. Ruth is the "lady friend." Susan or Susanna is "lily." Even the Hebrew term for "name" was given as a name to one son of Noah. Ham is the "hot" one, and Japhet the "wide spreading."

In Bible names we are struck with the large number of which the name of God forms a part. To us this may seem irreverent, but in the simplicity of the early ages this grew out of a feeling of genuine reverence for God. The Hebrew has several names for Deity. One of these is the generic term El (pronounced Ail). It means "the mighty one," and it is noticeable that both in Hebrew and Assyrian all other attributes are subordinate, and supreme power is the one thing suggested by the name of God. The Assyrian vocabulary abounds in synonyms for strength, power and force, and they seem to be exhausted in the description of their gods.

When this name of God is used to form a human name it is placed either at the beginning or the end, as Eliezer or Eleazar, God is his help; Elizur, God is his rock; Eliphalet, God is his deliverance; Eliakim, whom God appointed; Elnathan, whom God gave; and Elisha, God is his salvation. So also Samuel, heard of God, and Ishmael, whom God hears, Raphael, whom God healeth, Gabriel, the strong man of God, Daniel, made judge by God, and Abdiel, servant of God—Arabic, Abdullah.

Another name of God which enters into many human names is Jehovah, or more correctly Yahveh. This was not merely the name of the national god of the Hebrews, as though there was another god called Baal and still another named Moloch or Asshur, but it was the proper name of the true God, besides whom there is no god. We see its meaning in that appeal of Elijah on Carmel, "How long halt ye between two opinions? If Jehovah is God, follow him, but if Baal (is God) follow him," 1 Kings 18 : 21, and in the repeated confession of the prostrate people, "Jehovah, he is the God;" and so the first commandment was, "Thou shalt have none other gods before me." Among the human names of which this most sacred name forms a part are Jonadab, whom Jehovah impels; Jonathan, whom Jehovah gave; Jehoram, whom Jehovah created; Joshua, whom Jehovah saves; Jehoshaphat, whom Jehovah judgeth, *i. e.*, protects from wrong. So also Hezekiah, whom Jehovah strengthens; Benaiah, whom Jehovah created; Adonijah, Jehovah is my Lord; and Malchiah, made king by Jehovah.

A like desire to be associated with idols appears in the inscriptions. Thus **Asshurbanipal** is Asshur created a son. Esarhaddon (**Asshur akh iddina**) is Asshur gave a brother: Shalmanezer (**Shalman utsur**) is **Shalman** protected. **Shalman** is the god of peace. See Rom. 16 : 20. This name was borne by four kings. In most of these cases the king selected his own name. **Rammanu nirari,** Rammanu (the god of the atmosphere) is my helper, was the name of two kings. **Asshur dan** (Asshur vindicates) was a name borne by three occupants of the throne, and **Tugulti Ninip** (Ninip is my trust) was the name of two others.

So in Babylon we have Belshazzar (**Bil shar utsur**), Bil (in this case Merodach) preserved the king. Nebuchadrezzar (**Nabu ku-**

duri, or **kudurri, utsur)** Nebo preserved the crown, or the land, and **Bil Marduk,** Merodach is the lord, may serve as specimens of many more.

The question arises, Who set the example in this style of names, the Hebrews or the Babylonians? Certainly not the Assyrians, for **Ismi Dagan** (Dagon heard), who reigned B. C. 1850–20, was the earliest of their kings. The earliest among the Babylonians was **Naram Sin,** the favorite of the moon god, son of the celebrated Sargon of Agane (Accad), who Nabonidus, the last king of Babylon (B. C. 556), tells us lived 3,200 years before, or *circa* B. C. 3750. This according to our chronology would place him 1402 years before the deluge, which occurred, in our reckoning, B. C. 2348, but according to the Babylonians Naram Sin lived long after the deluge, how long is not yet ascertained. Then, however the two chronologies may be harmonized, Narum Sin was no antediluvian. But Scripture speaks of men incorporating the name of God into their names long before the flood; two at least in the line of Cain—Methusael, man of God, and his father, Mehujael, smitten of God—and one in the line of Sheth, Mahalaleel, praise of God, who according to our reckoning was born B. C. 3069; 1260 years before the flood.

The earliest mention of this kind of name is in Scripture, and it is in connection with the name of the true God, and not in connection with that of any idol, whether Babylonian or belonging to other nations.

For some notice of a suggestion of Prof. Sayce on the names Methusael and Methuselakh, see " Methuselah."

NEBUCHADREZZAR.

This name is commonly written Nebuchadnezzar, but the correct reading is Nebuchadrezzar. The original is **Nabu kudurri utsur,** Nebo protect the crown, or frontier, or servant? He reigned B. C. 605–562, and was by far the greatest of the kings of Babylon. We may add that he is also the most lovable; no one can read some parts of his great Inscription and not find his heart going out in love towards the writer. True, Daniel 4:30 introduces him as saying, " Is not this great Babylon which I have built for the royal dwelling place, by the might of my power and for the glory of my majesty?" but one who had built so well may be pardoned if he knew it, and we honor the man who tells so honestly the way in which God humbled his pride, and then adds (v. 37), "Now, I, Nebuchadrezzar, praise and extol and honor the King of heaven, for all his works are truth, and his ways judgment: and those that walk in pride he is able to abase." We can scarcely expect a record of this in his inscriptions, but it was something to have written it at all, and his public records deepen the good impression made on us by this confession of the greatness and power of God. The following expressions occur in what is known as the India House Inscription, R. I. 53–58, especially col. 1. 55 to the end. See also H. L. 97 and R. of P. new III. 106. 55 to the end. I have placed in the margin various scriptures the spirit of which seems to have been expressed by these words of a heathen monarch. The address is to Bil Marduk, his god:

O prince who art from eternity. Psa. 90:2; John 1:1; Gen. 1:1; Heb. 1:10.
Lord of all that exists. Psa. 103:19; John 17:2; Rom. 9:5; Acts 10:36.
For the king whom thou lovest. John 11:3; Rev. 1:5.
Whom thou callest by name. Isa. 43:1; Jer. 14:9; Dan. 9:18 and 19.
As it seemeth good unto thee. Matt. 11:26; Luke 10:21.
I, the prince who obeyeth thee, am the work of thy hands. Psa. 138:8.
Thou hast created me. Psa. 119:73; Job 10:8; Isa. 64:8.
* And hast entrusted to me sovereignty over multitudes of men. Jer. 27:8 and
    28:14; Ezek. 29:19; Dan. 5:18.
According to thy goodness, O lord, wherewith thou crownest all of them. Psa.
    145:9.
Let me love thy supreme lordship. Matt. 22:37 and 38.
Let the fear of thy godhead dwell within my heart. Eccl. 12:13.
And give what seemeth good to thee, since thou maintainest my life. Acts. 17:28.

One is amazed to read (col. 3. 33), "For the construction of E Saggilla (the temple of Merodach) daily I besought the king of the gods, the lord of lords;" and again, (col. 7, 26–35;) "From the time that Merodach created me for sovereignty, from the time that Nebo his true son entrusted his people to my care, as my own dear life do I love the exaltation of thy house (Psa. 26:8). Among all mankind have I not seen a city fairer than thy city of Babylon, which I love." It seems almost

* See also line 42 in col. I.

as though we were reading from the Psalms of David rather than from the records of a king of Babylon.

NIMROD.

Gen. 10:10. And the beginning of his kingdom was Babel, and Erech, and Accad, and Calneh, in the land of Shinar.

One would naturally expect that the monuments would pour a flood of light on one who filled a position of such prominence, and some seek to identify him with the hero Izdubar or Gisdubar. They may be correct, but the names are totally unlike, and we have no evidence that that name is to be read ideographically in any way that resembles the name Nimrod. Future discoveries may furnish the required identification, but, as at present informed, we must hold ourselves in readiness either to accept this identification on sufficient warrant, or any other that may be presented with more satisfactory endorsement.

If we could only get at the records now hidden in the ancient mounds of Babylonia this and many other questions would at once receive ready solution, but so long as the Turkish Government pursues its dog-in-the-manger policy, we must watch and wait. God, whose hand is in all these things, may be holding back those records for a time when their discovery shall tell with greater efficiency for the advancement of his kingdom.

NIMROOD.

No one who has read Mr. Layard's fascinating volumes, or visited the British Museum, or the Assyrian rooms of some of our American colleges, fails to feel an interest in Nimrood.

The river Tigris flows almost straight south from Mosul, and on the left bank of the river, about six leagues from the city, the tower, or rather the ruins of it, is the most conspicuous object in the landscape, rising to the height of 140 feet. Mr. Layard thinks that originally it was 200 feet high. Extending south from this, and gullied by the rains of centuries, is a mound 1,300 yards by 750. Here stood the ancient city of Calah; not the first Assyrian capital, but the earliest centre after the kingdom became an empire. Its rulers delighted to expend their treasures in its embellishment. The city of Shalmanezer I. (1300-1271 B. C.) indeed soon disappeared, but Asshurnatsirpal (885-860 B. C.) rebuilt it, and erected the northwest palace, between the tower and the southwest corner of the mound. His son Shalmanezer II. succeeded him in 860 B. C., and built the central and part at least of the southeast palace. Vul (Rimmon) Nirari III. (812-783 B. C.) built the temple of Nebo and the upper part of the southeast palace, and Tiglath Pileser II. (745-727 B. C.) rebuilt the centre palace, which by this time was in ruins. Sargon (722-705 B. C.), besides his splendid erections at Dur Sargina (Khorsabad), restored the northwest palace, and his grandson Esarhaddon (681-668 B. C.) built, apparently in great haste, the southwest palace, and it was never really finished, though he did not hesitate to appropriate freely valuable material from the structures erected by his predecessors; and **Asshur etil ilani,** one of the last kings of Assyria, rebuilt the temple of Nebo. Thus there was hardly an Assyrian monarch of any note who did not leave his mark upon Calah, and yet it was the oldest of all that furnished the best sculptures that Mr. Layard sent home, and as the American missionaries were at that time in Mosul, they also were able to procure some for a few of our own institutions of learning.

NINEVEH.

Jonah 3 : 3. Now Nineveh was an exceeding great city of three days' journey.

This is a very indefinite description of the size of the city. Does the three days' journey measure the circumference of the city? or the distance to be traversed in proclaiming the message of the prophet so that it should be generally known to the inhabitants? Perhaps the time has not yet come for the final answer to these questions. New discoveries may furnish data that are now lacking. Several points, however, are already known, and these may help us to form some idea of the problem.

1. The name **Nina** was used to denote the city directly opposite Mosul, whose dimensions are accurately marked out by the existing earthen mounds, between 40 and 50 feet in height, that enclose a space 13,200 yards, or 7 English miles and 4 furlongs, in circumference. This is proved by the Bavian inscrip-

tion of Sennacherib, who in connection with a group of 17 cities says, "Sixteen channels I excavated; to the midst of the river **Khusur** I fixed their course: from the boundary of the city **Kisiri** to Nineveh I dug a channel for their waters." Senn. 158. 10-12 and R. of P. IX. 24. 10-12. Other similar passages occur in the same inscription, and the river Khausser still flows from the vicinity of Khorsabad and empties into the Tigris below the mound of Koyunjik.

2. These mounds may have enclosed the centre of the city, while the houses of the common people extended out on all sides—except the west, where the Tigris flowed—far into the fertile plain of Assyria.

3. Just as there was an original London which swallowed up Southwark, Westminster, Lambeth, Whitechapel, and many other suburbs, the name sometimes denoting the original nucleus and sometimes including the whole territory annexed to it, so the name Nineveh, though strictly belonging only to the enclosure opposite Mosul, may also have been applied to the whole of the dense population occupying the plain of Assyria as far south as Nimrood, and as far north as Khorsabad, and from Shereef khan on the west to Karamles on the east.

4. The fact that the same king built palaces in cities as far apart as Asshur (**Kalah Shergat**) and Nineveh favored this looking on them all as forming one body politic, and giving to it the name of the most important city. Thus Shalmanezer I., B. C. 1300, enlarged the palace at Asshur and built two others, one at Calah (Nimrood), and the other at Nineveh (Koyunjik). Passing on nearly 400 years, Asshurnatsirpal, B. C. 885-860, transferred his capital from Asshur to Calah, where he built more than one palace, besides a temple to Nebo. He also built a palace and rebuilt the temple of Ishtar at Nineveh. Shalmanezer II., B. C. 860-825, lived at Nineveh for 12 years, where he enlarged the palace of his father and adorned the temple of Ishtar. Then he removed to Calah, completed that city, built a ziggurat (tower) that is still 140 feet in height, and also a new palace. Rimmon Nirari III., B. C. 812-783, besides building one palace at Calah, erected another at Nineveh (**Nebby Yunus**), and a new temple to Nebo and Merodach at Koyunjik, besides a

temple to Nebo at Calah containing two colossal statues of that god. It is not necessary to carry these details further, for sufficient has been said to show the substantial unity of these several cities where the same monarch occupied his own palace now in one of them and now in another, and though the exact era of Jonah is unknown yet he must have lived some time during or between these reigns.

5. It is not strange, then, if a prophet of Israel, who had heard of these things before his arrival in the country, should speak of all the inhabitants of that plain, then so populous, as belonging to one city, and that that city should be Nineveh, the capital of the king, who resided now here and now there, according to the exigences of the hour and his own desire.

NISROCH.

Isa. 37:38. And it came to pass as he (Sennacherib) was worshipping in the house of Nisroch his god, that Adramelech (Adar is king) and Sharezer (he protected the king) smote him with the sword, and they escaped into the land of Ararat, *i. e.*, Armenia.

This item of history is confirmed by the monuments in everything except the name of Nisroch. There was no god known in Assyria by that name. It may be that some copyist, not being familiar with either name, wrote Nisroch instead of **Nusku**, the associate of Nebo, the god of literature, or, having seen the eagle-headed figures in Assyrian palaces, he may have given that name from the Hebrew *nasr* (eagle).

NOUNS.

In Assyrian, nouns have stems either simple or doubled, or with the addition of other elements, and these last may be prefixed, affixed, or inserted in the middle. There is no neuter gender, only masculine and feminine. The dual number seldom occurs save in objects which exist in pairs, as hands, eyes, and ears. The plural ending is **u, i, ani** and **uti**, and f. pl. in **ati** or **iti**.

The Arabic forms named *madhmoom, maksoor,* and *meftookh, i. e.*, Nom., Gen., and Accus., are found also in Assyrian and are distinguished by the same vowels, *i. e.*, **u, i,** and **a.** Mimmation also occurs in Assyrian as well as in Hebrew and Arabic. So also does what is called the construct state, where the first noun loses its final vowel, and the second is used in the genitive. In *segholates* the noun becomes disyllabic, as **uzun** from **uznu,** ear, **napshat** from **napishtu**, soul, life. The construct state is very common before suffixes, as **matshu**, his country, **qatshu,** his hand.

Nouns, as in other languages, exist both as substantives and adjectives. Many nouns in Assyrian correspond with the Hebrew both in form and meaning; others agree in form but differ in meaning, as in Hebrew מלך is a king, but in Assyrian **malku,** is a prince or ruler, while **sharru** denotes a king.

NUMBER OF A NAME.

Rev. 13:18. It is the number of a man, and his number is 666.

Without going at all into the exegesis of this, I simply throw out the inquiry whether line 65 of the cylinder inscription of Sargon (S. 10) throws any light on this Scripture. It reads thus: "Four shars, three ners, one shoss, three reeds, two cubits (Prof. Lyon adds them up 16,280 cubits), so much my name signifies.... The mass of the wall I built, and on stone from the high mountains I made strong its foundations." The correspondence is certainly suggestive, but I cannot find formal proof that the Assyrians, like the Greeks and Latins, and indeed the Hebrews also, used letters to represent numerals. The fact that Hebrews did so affords a presumption, however, that Assyrians did the same.

OMENS.

Ezek. 21:21 and 22. For the king of Babylon stood at the parting of the way, at the head of the two ways, to use divination: he shook the arrows to and fro, he consulted the teraphim, he looked in the liver. In his right hand was the divination for Jerusalem, to set battering rams, to open the mouth in the slaughter, etc.

An omen is an augury or prognostication, something supposed to portend a future event, and in Babylonia the connection of omens with their fancied results rose to the dignity of a science. There were tables of omens from dreams, see R. III. 56. 2; from the moon and its appearance, R. III. 51. 2, 3, 4, also 6, 7, 8, 9; also 54. There were auguries from the earth and the heavens, R. III. 52. 3; omens for each month, R. III. 55. 4; also from the inspection of the hand, palmistry, from the inspection of the entrails of animals, as afterwards among the Romans; and even from the objects a traveller meets on a journey, as in some countries to-day a man turns back if on setting out he meets an unlucky object. Even the movements of dogs were counted ominous. If a dog entered a palace and lay down on a bed they held that that palace could never be captured by an enemy, but if he lay down on the throne that was a token that the palace would be burned. So if a white or black dog entered a temple that was a sign that the temple would go to ruin, but if a blue or yellow dog entered, its offerings would abound, while the entrance of a spotted dog betokened the favor of the gods. R. of P. V. 169.

There are some curious birth portents, R. III. 65, translated in R. of P. V. 171–176. When the right ear of a babe is small the father's house will be destroyed, when it is wanting the ruler will live long, and if both ears are wanting an enemy is in the land and it will not prosper. When the upper lip of a babe overhangs the lower, or if it has a stiff knee, the people will prosper. When a child has six toes on each foot the result will be that children do not go to school, but six toes on the right foot foretokens an increase of the population—and so on.

As for the divination by arrows, one can hardly see how the rendering of the old version, "he made his arrows bright," could furnish any omen, but "he shook them to and fro" makes it more intelligible, for any stir or agitation that left one of two arrows pointing this way and the other that might indicate whether to turn to the right hand or the left, according to a prearranged interpretation.

We hear much of the superior intelligence of our age and of pity for the superstitions of the past, but so long as men assure themselves of good fortune because they find a bit of old iron in the road, or fasten up old horse-shoes on the walls or over the door for the sake of luck, it may be that, after all, our age is not so far in advance of the old Chaldeans as we thought it was.

PADAN ARAM.

Gen. 25:20, 31:18. Gesenius in his Lexicon, Robinson's Ed., explains this as the plain of Syria, deriving it from the Syriac word **pidana**, which Erpenius renders *campus, desertum*. Gesenius describes it as "Mesopotamia, with the desert west of the Euphrates, as distinguished from the mountainous region along the Mediterranean." The Assyrian suggests a different derivation. **Padanu** in that language means a way. Asshurbanipal, R. V. I. 74, says that he caused certain kings to take **urkhu padanu**, the way, the road, with his army. Tiglath Pileser I. (R. 10. 4) says that the rest of **Kummakhu** (Commagene) fled to **Shiriishi**, by the roads (**padani**) on the other side of the Tigris. Padan Aram, according to this, is the way Aram, *i. e.*, the Aram that lay on the way between Babylonia or Chaldea and the Mediterranean; for then as now the Bedawin made the direct road unsafe, and travel had to go round *via* Oorfa and Kharran. And it is a confirmation of this view that Kharran also in Assyrian means the way, *i. e.*, the city on the way to Palestine and the Mediterranean; as we would say, the half-way city.

PARTICLES.

These are composed of adverbs, prepositions, and conjunctions, and for convenience of reference some of the more important ones are given in the order of the Hebrew alphabet.

Aa, ai, not, negation, like **la** or **ul.**
Adi, and, up to, until, as far as, together with.
Adi mati (R. IV. 29. 54), how long. (Heb. עד תמי.)
Agannu, (Behistun 12), **aganna** (Ass'l. 125. 63), here.
Akkai, akka, how, as, like. (D. L. IX.)
Ana, to, unto, against.
Ana libbi, within.
Ana mukhi, upon, literally on the head.
Ana mini, written **ammini,** why. (A. M. 63. 7. 10. 13. 16. 19. 22.)

PARTICLES.

Ana shu, written **ashshu,** in order to, because. (A. M, 18. 14. 22. 26).

Arka, arki, after, afterwards, also **arkanu.** (A. M. 14. 6, 20. 4).

Balu, without, (A. M. 40. 18) in the sense of not having.

Birit, ina biri, or **birti,** between. (D. L. IX.)

Gadu, together with, also.

Ili, over, above, upon, at.

Ilish, above.

Illamu, before, in front of,

Ina, in, with, by, during, when.

Ina ili, at, over, above, upon, more than.

Ina kirib, or **qirib,** into, in the midst of.

Ina libbi, into, in the inside of.

Ina mahar, before, in front, in the presence of.

Ina muhhi, upon, over, above.

Ina pan, pani, before.

Ina tartsi, opposite, in the time of.

Ininna, now.

Inuma, at the time when.

Ishtu, like **ultu,** from, out of, etc.

Ki, as, like.

Kiam, thus.

Killalan, round, around, about.

Kima, like, similar to.

Kum, instead of.

La, not, negation, same as **ul** or **aa.**

Lapan, before, in front of.

Lu, verily, truly, adverb of affirmation.

Mahar, before, in front of.

Matima, ever. **La matima,** never.

Pana, panama, before.

Shaplish, below.

Timali, yesterday.

Ul, not, negation.

Ulla, of old, formerly.

Ultu, same as **ishtu,** from, after, from the time when.

Ultu kirib, or **qirib,** out of, outside, from out.

Umma, thus, introducing a quotation.

Any noun or adjective, singular or plural, may form an adverb by adding **ish**; thus **damqu**, favor, **damqish**, favorably, graciously. Those thus formed are generally adverbs of manner.

PEACE, GOD OF.

This is a frequent name of God in the epistles of Paul. See Rom. 15:33 and 16:20; 2 Cor. 13;11; Phil. 4:9, and 1 Thess. 5:23, also Heb. 13:20.

In Assyria there was a god named Shalmanu, a name, it will be seen, identical with our Solomon. It may seem as though we should hardly expect to find a deity having such a name among so warlike a people. Yet Shalmanu does not mean peaceful in contrast with warlike, but rather perfect as opposed to imperfect, complete in distinction from unfinished; prosperous, successful, safe, unharmed. Four kings of Assyria bore the name of Shalmaneser, and the aggregate of their reigns amounted to 79 years. The name means Shalman guides, makes straight or correct. See H. L. 57. 58.

PETHOR.

Numb. 22:5 states that Balak "sent messengers to Balaam the son of Beor to Pethor, which is by the river of the land of the children of his people," but Pethor has been so thoroughly lost sight of by Biblical scholars that even the large American edition of Smith's "Dictionary of the Bible" says "its position is wholly unknown." The Assyrian monuments, however, enable us to locate it very satisfactorily. Shalmanezer II. (in Assyrian, **Shalmanu asharidu**, Shalman is leader) was the son of Asshurnatsirpal, and reigned B. C. 858–823. He set up a monolith at Kurkh, on the upper Euphrates, to commemorate the victories of the first four years of his reign. A copy of the inscription is given in R. III. 7 and 8, and it was translated first by Prof. Sayce in R. of P. III. 81–100, and again by Rev. V. Scheil in R. of P. new IV. 53–79. The 36th line reads, "The city of **Ana Asshur utir atsbat** (to Asshur I restored, I have taken), which the Hittites call **Piitru** (Pethor), which is upon the river **Sagura** on the farther side of the Euphrates," and on modern maps we find the river Sajoor flowing from near Aintab (where the American Board has a large flourishing mission, where also is the college of Central Turkey) down to the Euphrates. On the banks of that river stood Pethor, the home of Balaam. It is to be hoped that the pick of the explorer shall make us acquainted with its ruins, and that they shall be found neither barren nor unfruitful in contributions to our knowledge of those ancient days.

PITCH.

Gen. 6:14. Thou shalt pitch (כפרת) it within and without with pitch. כפר.

Pitch here is asphaltum, or mineral pitch, which is found in many parts of the world. The root כפר means to cover, hence *kopher* means a village, as that which covers or shelters the inhabitants, and *kopher* also means pitch, as that wherewith anything is covered, as here the ark. The word is **kuupru** in the Assyrian, and Shamash Napishti tells us (R. IV. 50. 2. 10, 11. D. L. 103. 62, 63):

    III sharí kuupri attabak ana kiiri,
    III shari iddu uddua? ana libbi.

"Three shars of bitumen I poured upon the outside, three shars of asphaltum I smeared upon the inside;" statements which record an explicit carrying out of the directions given to Noah in Genesis, only the quantity is specified in the Assyrian and not in the Hebrew, though the question may be raised whether so large an amount was used.

PLASTER OF THE WALL.

Daniel records (5:5) that the fingers of a man's hand wrote over against the candlestick upon the plaster of the wall of the king's palace. It is strange that Mr. Layard makes no mention of candelabra among the articles discovered by him in the old Assyrian palaces. They must have had them to light up the darkness of those halls that even in the brightest days of summer were so secluded from the light, and in the dark days of winter were so much more in need of artificial illumination. The tall lamp-stands of that region to-day point back to more costly ones in ancient times of which they are the humble imitators, but, in our ignorance of their peculiar form, may they not have been really discovered, but their nature and use misunderstood, so that they failed to be recognized? On pp. 178 and 179 B. and N. he gives copies of what he calls "tripods or stands for supporting vessels and bowls." May they not in fact be stands for supporting the bowls of magnificent lamps for the illumination of those royal halls? The writer, riding one day where the present road is cut through the ancient walls of Nineveh, picked up a segment of a circular piece of basalt which he has always regarded as a piece of the base of a lamp-stand. But, however we may be in doubt about the candlestick, there is no doubt about the plaster. Some very fine specimens of Grecian and Roman structures may have been without any plaster on the inner walls, but it was not so with the structures of Babylonia and Assyria. Perrot and Chipiez, in their magnificent work on the Art of those countries (I. 271), say, "Explorers are unanimous in the opinion that neither burnt nor sun-dried brick was ever left uncovered; it was always covered with a coat of stucco. At Nineveh this was formed by a mixture of burnt chalk with plaster, which adhered very tightly to the clay wall; its thickness was never more than one or two millimetres, and yet it was so cohesive that it afforded efficient protection. It has often been found upon the walls of both courtyards and chambers, and on the under side of vaulted ceilings," and in a note they refer to Dan. 5:5. W. K. Loftus, in describing the ruin called **Wuswas** at Warka (Chaldea and Susiana 176) says, "The whole front has been undoubtedly coated with white plaster from two to four inches thick." This obviously refers to an outer wall, but on p. 180 he adds a description of some chambers which he explored: "The largest measured 57 feet by 30, and the smallest 9 by 30. A shaft was dug in the former, and the rubbish cleared out of the latter to the depth of twenty-three feet and a half. The walls were rudely plastered, but showed no trace of color." Of course these were interior walls, for they were uncovered by clearing out the chamber.

So minute is the testimony of the antiquities of Chaldea and Assyria to the accuracy of the statements of Holy Scripture.

POLYTHEISM.

It is difficult for a believer in the Bible to appreciate the views and feelings of a polytheist. One Scripture incident, however, helps us very much in this direction. Good King Hezekiah had carried out the divine requirement that sacrifices should be offered to God only in the place which He had chosen for his worship (see Deut. 12). The Rabshakeh of Sennacherib heard of it, and this is the way in which the obedience of the king presented itself to his mind: "But if thou sayest to me, 'We trust in Jehovah our God,' is it not he whose high places and whose altars Hezekiah hath taken away, and said to Judah and to Jerusalem, Ye shall worship before this altar?" Isa. 36:7. We are amazed at this misunderstanding, and yet it was no intentional deception. The Rabshakeh honestly believed what he said, and thought of course that the Jews understood the matter just as he did, for to his mind each city had its own god, who could be worshipped with acceptance nowhere else. Of course, then, to prohibit his worship in that place was to interdict it altogether. A follower of Zoroaster would understand the action of Hezekiah just as it was, for he also believed in one God, but every Babylonian would misunderstand it just as the Rabshakeh did.

This whole subject finds a good illustration in the case of Nabonidus, king of Babylon. He undertook to substitute a national for the local worship that had prevailed so long in Babylonia, and to this end gathered together the gods of the various cities in Babylon, the capital, but he thereby made enemies of the whole country. The other cities resented this robbery of their gods, and Babylon was angry because he had brought in other gods to be rivals of their great Merodach, and in this way he lost the crown; for Cyrus came as the servant of Merodach and the other gods, whom he restored each to his own city, and so entered Babylon without a battle, and ascended the throne with the universal approval of the people. According to his own inscriptions, Cyrus was no Zoroastrian, but a worshipper of the gods of Babylonia.

POOR IN SPIRIT.

Our Saviour said, "Blessed are the poor in spirit: for theirs is the kingdom of heaven." Matt. 5:3. That was the key-note of the beatitudes, and was followed by like benediction on the meek, the merciful, and the peacemakers.

We do not find an echo of such sentiments in Assyrian monuments, but rather a marked contrast to such teaching, and the direct opposite of such a spirit. Take for an example Asshurnatsirpal, who begins his inscription with an invocation to Ninip, whom he addresses as "the strong, the almighty... the powerful warrior... whose onset in battle has no equal; (1) the crusher of opposition, (2) who treads down the broad earth," and so on, and then introduces himself as "the powerful king, the monarch of all, the king without an equal" (9 and 10). "The warrior hero who marched forward in the service of Asshur his lord, and among the kings of all lands has no equal. The ruler (shepherd) who fears no opposition... who subdues the rebellious, who has overcome the race. The mighty hero who tramples on the necks of his enemies, treading down all opposers, breaking in pieces the forces of the mighty, who through the help of the great gods his lords, has marched on and conquered all lands and even the rough mountains to their remotest bounds" (12-16). "Then Asshur the lord proclaimed my name, and enlarged my kingdom, he committed his weapon that spares not to the hand of my lordship (even to me),.. the mighty monster (**usumgal,** vampire)... the consumer of the violent, who is crowned with terror, who fears no opposition, the valiant one, the supreme judge that spares not, but conquers resistance" (17-20). And after a repetition of similar phrases, among them, "who has fixed the bodies of his enemies on sharp stakes" (29), he breaks out,." I am king, I am lord, I am exalted, I am strong, I am glorious, I am powerful, I am the firstborn, I am mighty, I am the warrior, I am the lion, I am the hero... a weapon that spares not, which brings slaughter to the land of his enemies, am I" (32-34), with more of the same tenor which it were too tedious to quote.

If any wish to read more they will find the original in R. I. 17 seq., and a good translation in R. of P. new II. 134 seq.

PORCH.

2 Chron. 3:4. And the porch that was before the house, the length of it according to the breadth of the house was twenty cubits and the height one hundred and twenty, and he overlaid it within with pure gold.

This verse has been a trouble to the commentators, many of whom have had recourse to that last resort of perplexity, the suggestion of an error in the reading; but we may find such help in the monuments as relieves us from the need of that violent method of relief.

The earliest known inhabitants of Babylonia were the Accadians (compare Accad, Gen. 10:10), whose original home was among the high mountains of southwestern Persia, east of the lower Tigris. In that elevated region their temples occupied the high places, which they deemed to be nearest the gods. Lev. 26:30; Num. 22:41 and 33:52; 1 Kings 3:2 and 13:2. So when they migrated to the low plains of Chaldea they built their temples on artificial mounds elevated above the surrounding plain. Still even this did not satisfy them. Besides this, they made a ziggurat, or tower, seven or eight stories high, and generally solid.

In 1 Kings 12:31 and 13:32, also 2 Kings 17:29, we read of "houses of the high places." These Babylonian temples were literally such. Indeed their Accadian name was **E kur,** house of the mountain, which in Assyrian became **Bit shadu.** Does not this name illustrate Isa. 2:1 and 3, repeated in Micah 4:1 and 2? "And it shall come to pass in the latter days that the mountain of the Lord's house shall be established in the top of the mountains, and shall be exalted above the hills, and all nations shall flow unto it, and many people shall go and say, Come ye, and let us go to the mountain of the Lord, to the house of the God of Jacob."

The temple at Jerusalem was built on the top of Mt. Moriah, which had been enlarged by substructures to accommodate conveniently its buildings and its courts. This was 2,438 feet above the Mediterranean, and though the northern part of Zion was higher (2,540 feet), and some parts along the present northern

CHALDEAN TEMPLE.

city wall even higher still (2,680 feet), still the site of the temple showed to the best advantage in contrast with the deep valley of Jehoshaphat directly beneath.

Are not the 120 cubits (180 feet) of 2 Chron. 3:4 like the ziggurat of the Babylonian temple? only the Jews utilized the space by having halls within, that could be overlaid with gold. Mr. Layard gives the present height of the ruined ziggurat at Nimrood as 140 feet, and supposes it was originally 200 feet, which is only twenty feet higher than the porch of the temple. The grandest of Babylonian temples, that of Bil Marduk at Babylon, had a ziggurat 300 feet in height.

The following are its dimensions as given in a Babylonian text translated by G. Smith in H. L. 439:

The first stage was 300 feet square and 110 in height. The second 260 feet square and 60 in height. The third, fourth and fifth were each 20 feet high. In lateral dimensions the third was 200, the fourth 170, and the fifth 140 feet square. The dimensions of the sixth stage are not given, probably it was 110 feet square and 20 feet in height, and upon this rested the sanctuary of Merodach, 80 feet in length, 70 feet broad, and 50 feet high.

Does not this ziggurat of the Babylonian temple furnish the original not only of the porch of the temple at Jerusalem, but also of the towers and spires of our own churches? It has set the fashion for all the centuries. Only Greece and Rome did not follow it in their classic constructions, and the spirit that has forbidden so-called dissenting churches in Great Britain to be marked by tower or spire has forbidden the distinctive mark of a building set apart for worship. If any would appreciate the grandeur of these structures as they appeared in ancient days, let them turn to the artistic pages of P. and C. I. 370. 374. 378 and 380, one of which is here given, and then picture the lofty sanctuary glowing with the sheen of polished gold under the brightness of a Babylonian sun.

POTIPHAR, WIFE OF.

It is not necessary to go over the story in Genesis 39. It finds an illustration in the Egyptian tale of the two brothers, written in B. C. 1300. **Anepu** sends his younger brother **Bata** from the field to the house for corn, who finds his sister-in-law braiding her hair and asks for the corn. When he is ready to return to the field the tale says that her heart knew him . . . (some details are here omitted). She laid hold of him and said "Come and enjoy an hour's rest with me." He replies, "Thou hast been to me like a mother; why hast thou proposed this great sin? Never repeat such words again and I will never betray thee." So he returned to his brother and finished their day's work. Meanwhile the woman took means to give her person the appearance of one who had suffered violence. Her husband found her lying prostrate; she gave him no water for his hands, and the house was dark, for she had not lit the lamp. When he spoke to her she accused his brother of having tempted her to evil, and when she refused him, of having resorted to force, adding, "If you let him live I will kill myself." Anepu then took a knife and went out to seek his brother. The cows, however, warned Bata of his danger, and the sun god placed a river full of crocodiles between the brothers. Then when Anepu at length learned the truth in the case he hurried back and put his wife to death.

One cannot help contrasting the reticence of the sacred narrative as to vile details with the freeness of the other. Then how different the childish miracles of the tale from the love that went with Joseph into prison and devised that wonderful deliverance from a dungeon and exaltation to a palace. The tale also ends with its infliction of a human vengeance, while Scripture quietly leaves the wrong-doer to be dealt with by the Lord.

POTTER'S VESSEL.

Psa. 2:9. Thou shalt dash them in pieces like a potter's vessel. Compare Isa. 45:9 and 30:14; also Jer. 19:11; and Rev. 2:27.

This very impressive figure is repeated in the inscription on the cylinder of Sargon, line 9, discovered by Mons. Botta at Khorsabad. It reads, **matati kulishina kima khatsbati udaqqi-quma.** I dashed in pieces all their lands like potsherds.

PRAYER.

If we could find an Assyrian prayer offered to one of their gods in circumstances similar to those in which a prayer was offered that is recorded in Holy Scripture, a comparison of the two might be very profitable.

The Rabshakeh (general) of Sennacherib had written to Hezekiah, "Let not thy God in whom thou trustest deceive thee, saying, Jerusalem shall not be delivered into the hand of the king of Assyria. Behold, thou hast heard what the kings of Assyria have done to all lands, by destroying them utterly: and shalt thou be delivered? Have the gods of the nations delivered them which my fathers have destroyed, Gozan and Haran and Rezeph, and the children of Eden which were in Telassar? Where is the king of Hamath, and the king of Arpad, and the king of the city of Sepharvaim, of Hena, and Ivah?" And Hezekiah received the letter . . . and went up into the house of the Lord and spread it before the Lord. And Hezekiah prayed before the Lord and said: "O Lord, the God of Israel, that sittest upon the cherubim, thou art the God, even thou alone, of all the kingdoms of the earth; thou hast made heaven and earth. Incline thine ear, O Lord, and hear; open thine eyes, and see; and hear the words of Sennacherib, wherewith he hath sent him to reproach the living God. Of a truth, Lord, the kings of Assyria have laid waste the nations and their lands, and have cast their gods into the fire; for they were no gods, but the work of men's hands, wood and stone; therefore they have destroyed them. Now, therefore, O Lord our God, save thou us, I beseech thee, out of his hand, that all the kingdoms of the earth may know that thou art the Lord God, even thou only." 2 Kings 19: 10-19. This is a beautiful example of worshipping God in spirit and in truth (John 4: 24) for even before the coming of Christ the Spirit helped the infirmity of good men in prayer. There is in this prayer no trace of either fear or revenge. It contains no request for injury to the Rabshakeh or his master. It does not even ask for personal blessing to be bestowed on Hezekiah. Self is lost sight of, and the interests of the kingdom of God fill the whole range of thought. If only God's name may be hallowed, his kingdom come, and his will be done on earth as in heaven, the good king asks for nothing more. So thoroughly does the spirit of the Lord's Prayer pervade this supplication.

Alongside of this intercession of the good Hezekiah let Asshurbanipal, the grandson of Sennacherib, describe one of his prayers, which he offered to Ishtar of Arbela, the Assyrian goddess of war. See Ass'l. 117. col. 5, translated in H. L. 275 and 276:

"When Teumman strengthened himself in Elam, I looked to Ishtar, who looks on me. I obeyed not the order of his rebellious mouth. I surrendered not the fugitives. Teumman devised evil, and the moon god devised evil for him. In the month Tammuz an eclipse during the morning watch obscured the lord of light, and the sun was darkened, and as he rested, so did I rest for three days, that the years of the king of Elam might be ended. In the month Ab (July, August), the month of the appearance of the star of the bow, the festival of the glorious queen, the daughter of Bil, to worship her, the great goddess, I remained in Arbela, the chosen city of her heart. Of the invasion of the Elamite, who marched impiously, they informed me as follows. 'Teumman says . . . that he will not depart till he has fought with Asshurbanipal.' Because of this threat of Teumman I prayed to the exalted Ishtar, I wept before her, I bowed beneath her, I did honor to her deity, and she came to me with favor.

"O lady of Arbela, I am Asshurbanipal, the creation of thy hands (and the creation of Asshur), the father who created thee, that I might restore the shrines of Assyria and complete the strongholds of Akkad. I seek thy courts to worship thy deity, and he, the king of Elam, who regards not the gods, comes to make war. Thou art the lady of ladies, the terror of battle, the lady of war, the queen of the gods, who in the presence of Asshur thy father dost utter blessings. As for Teumman, who has rebelled against Asshur the king of the gods, the father that created thee, and against Merodach thy brother, and against me, Asshurbanipal, who is to give rest to the heart of Asshur and (Merodach), he has gathered his army and urges his soldiers to march to Assyria; do thou, who art the archer of the gods, strike him down like lead (a weight) in the battle, and smite him like a tornado."

In reading this prayer we are conscious of breathing another air. It is no longer one who loses sight of his own interest in the greater interest of the kingdom of God, but one who magnifies himself to the utmost, and instead of seeking what is for the highest good of all, bends his whole power to secure personal revenge in the destruction of his rival. He whines and weeps, reminds Ishtar of his good deeds and devotion to the gods her relations. He flatters the goddess, he magnifies the evil in his adversary, and concludes by invoking on him a summary and terrible vengeance. By their fruits we know them. Can a man gather grapes of thorns, or figs of thistles? If we want good fruit we must first of all make the tree good. Only so, according to the highest authority, shall we succeed. Matt. 7:17, 18, and 12:33.

PRESENTS.

1 Kings 4:21. They brought presents and served Solomon all the days of his life. Compare 1 Kings 15:19, 2 Kings 8:8, 16:8, and 17:3, 4. also Psa. 68:29.

We should expect to find these Scriptures abundantly illustrated in the monuments, and we are not disappointed. R. V. 7. 90, A. M. 27. 23 and Ass'l. 257. 104 record that Vaiteh, king of Arabia, **iklaa tamarti mandaatashu kabittu**: ceased or stopped his presents and his abundant tribute; a kind of statement which is very common, and illustrating 1 Sam. 10:27: "They despised him (Saul), and brought him no presents."

Gyges, king of Lydia, also saw a vision in which the god Asshur advised him to submit to Asshurbanipal and so overcome his enemies. Accordingly, **itti tamartishu kabitti ushibila adi makhriya**: he sent (a messenger) with his great gifts to my presence. R. V. 2. 110, and A. M. 22. 24, Ass'l. 66. 22, 23. **Nudunni** takes the place of **tamarti** in R. V. 2. 78, A. M. 21. 23, and Ass'l. 60. 102 with the same meaning. R. V. 2. 86, A. M. 22. 1 and Ass'l. 63. 123 read, **itti tamartishunu kabitti illiku nimma unaashshiqu shipiya**: came with their great presents and kissed my feet. And so in many other places.

2 Chron. 9:24. And they brought every man his present (**minkhatho**, מנחתו), vessels of silver and vessels of gold, and raiment, armor and spices, horses and mules, a rate year by year. This was what the kings of the earth brought to Solomon.

The idea of bringing presents year by year of a specified character and value was so identical in Assyria with tribute that the same word is used for both. So Sennacherib, king of Assyria, B. C. 707-682, says of **Tuba'alu**: In the throne of the kingdom I seated him; tribute, the gift of my lordship, every year unceasingly I appointed to him. R. I. 38. 44-46.

As a specimen of such gifts we have those of Hezekiah, R. I. 39. 34-41: "With 30 talents of gold, 800 talents of silver, precious **gukhli, daggassi**, large **angugmi** stones, ivory bedsteads, stationary thrones of ivory, elephant hides, ivory, **usu** and **urkarini** wood, everything very precious, whatever its name; also his daughters, the females of his palace, male and female musicians, into Nineveh, the city of my lordship, after me he sent (caused to bring); for the giving of a present and the rendering of homage he sent his ambassador."

The reader will notice that while Sennacherib claims to have received 800 talents, 2 Kings 18:14 says only 300. There are two explanations of this. One, that all the silver found in the house of the Lord and in the king's treasury was added to this (v. 15), and the other that there were two standards of value, and 300 talents of the one equalled 800 of the other.

In view of both these explanations, we need not be much disturbed by the discrepancy.

PRICES.

2 Kings 7:16. So a measure of fine flour was sold for a shekel, and two measures of barley for a shekel, according to the word of the Lord. See v. 1.

Nothing brings us more *en rapport* with the every-day life of a people than a knowledge of the price of daily commodities, and this is furnished to us by the Assyrian monuments. We know the market prices of grain and other things in the days of Nebuchadrezzar, Nabonidus, Darius, and Cambyses. Thus, *e. g.*,

200 sheep sold for 15 **manehs** of silver (£135 sterling) in the days of Darius, 18 under Nabonidus for 35 shekels, or nearly 6 shillings each, and 8 fine ones for 58 shekels (£8. 14s.) in the reign of Cambyses. This, however, included a bakshish to their Arab shepherd. One ox cost 13 shekels (£2) under Darius and 10 shekels (£1. 10s.) under Cambyses.

In the same reign "a mouse-colored ass, seven years old" was sold for 50 shekels (£7 10s.), though a less valuable one went for 13 shekels (£2, nearly). At that time two **artabs** (100 qts.) of grain cost 6 1-2 shekels, about 2 1-3 d. per quart. So that a poor Babylonian might find himself for 3 d. a day. Under Nebuchadrezzer a quart of sesame cost a little over a penny, and under Nabonidus a little less than 1 1-2 d. In the seventh year of Nebuchadrezzar dates cost 1-2 d. a quart, and in his 38th year 1-25 d. for the same quantity.

Wages were very cheap: a granary porter received only 1-2 shekel per month; but he must have had his food besides. A seal cutter received one **maneh**, 7 shekels, (£10), showing that skilled labor, then as now, commanded a high price.

A large house and field brought 4 1-2 **manehs** (£40 10s). Under Cambyses one house rented for 16 shekels per annum, and another for only 5. See Social Life, etc., chap. V.

But while grain and fruit were so cheap the regular rate of interest was 20 per cent.; so while the farmer got a low price for his produce the rich man could live luxuriously on the income of his money. The same influences controlled prices then as now. Social Life, etc., p. 67.

Speaking of prices, we have the following resemblance between Ahab and Sargon:

1 Kings 21 : 2. And Ahab spake unto Naboth, saying, Give me thy vineyard, that I may have it for a garden of herbs, because it is near unto my house: and I will give thee for it a better vineyard than it; or, if it seem good to thee, I will give thee the worth of it in money.

Sargon, the builder of Khorsabad, in giving an account of his arrangements for its construction, says (S. 8. 50–52):

"According to the meaning of my name, which the great gods gave to me for the guarding of right and justice, the protection of the defenceless, and doing no wrong to the weak, I paid to their owners the price of the fields of that city in silver and copper according to the recorded valuation of the deeds; and in order to prevent all injustice, when one did not wish to take the price of his field, I gave him field for field in any place which he preferred."

PRIESTHOOD.

The time has not yet come for a full setting forth of the relations of the religion of Babylonia to that of Judea, since the materials for the comparison are not yet provided; but a beginning may be made, noting facts as they come to light, and so paving the way for the more complete investigations that are sure to follow. These brief notes on the Priesthood and Rites (see " Rites ") of the two countries are offered as a slight contribution towards an intelligent apprehension of the subject, in the hope that others may go further and shed greater light on a matter so full of interest.

No class has yet been found corresponding to the Levites among the Jews. It is not known that any family was set apart for religious service as they were, though the priesthood may have descended regularly from father to son.

The Hebrew כהן, *cohen*, is represented by the Babylonian **shangu**, priest (**shanguti**, priesthood). The term denotes one devoted or bound to a god or to his sanctuary; and it is significant in this connection that **shangu** also means a chain. R. II. 375. Kings gloried in calling themselves the **shangu** of this or that god. Asshurnatsirpal styles himself the **shangu** of Asshur; the son of Tiglath Adar, the **shangu** of Asshur; the son of Rimmon Nirari, the **shangu** of Asshur, R. III. 3. 39.

Over the Jewish priesthood was the high-priest, הכהן הגדול and here we are plunged at once into deep waters. Seldom do we find such a decided contradiction as in the rendering of **shakkanakku** and kindred terms by different Assyriologists. See "Melchizedek." Prof. Delitzsch in D. L. 27 interprets it *machthaber*, potentate. Prof. D. G. Lyon, S. 79. note 2, explains it as composed of **shangu**, high, and **kunaku**, door, *i. e.*, "he who is over the city gate, or over the going out and coming in, im-

SARGON BEFORE THE SACRED TREE. (IN THE LOUVRE.)

plying supreme control of the city." Compare the Sublime Porte of to-day.

On the other hand, G. Smith renders it priest, Senn. 5. 69, and 60. 1, and Prof. Sayce says high-priest, H. L. 109, note; and adds, "Sometimes he was identical with the king, and again he was distinguished from him; and the **shakkanakku** of Babylon was a special title. Thus Esarhaddon calls himself **shakkanakku** of Babylon, but king of Shumir and Accad. Like **shangu**, the term denoted servitude to the god."

Another ideogram, **nuab,** is read **nisakku**, and is synonymous with **patesi**. See "Melchizedek." Prof. Sayce renders it supreme high-priest, H. L. 59, and adds, "In the far off pre-Semitic age there were kings of Telloh as well as high-priests of Telloh, and the kings did not take the title of high-priest nor the high-priests the title of king. The records of Assyria go back to a period when as yet there were no kings, but only high-priests of Asshur (R. I. 15. 62 and 63): and on a weight of green basalt brought from Babylonia by Dr. W. Hayes Ward we read, 'The palace of **Nebo shum esir,** the son of **Dakur,** the high-priest of Merodach.' A distinction is drawn between the king and high-priest in R. IV. 12. 36, 37. The old rendering of **patesi** by viceroy rested on a mistake; the word always has reference to the worship of a god." H. L. 59 and 60.

The fact that Melchizedek was both king of Salem and priest of El Elyon (Gen. 14:18; Heb. 7:1) may furnish the key to the reconciliation of these conflicting opinions.

In Assyria the temple and the palace were parts of the same structure. At Khorsabad Sargon is represented on the palace walls as worshipping before the sacred tree. P. and C. II. 98. Asshurbanipal also offers a libation over a wild bull which he had slain. Do. 40 and 104. See "Melchizedek."

PRONOUNS.

These resemble pronouns in other Semitic languages, and are as follows:

PERSONAL.

	Singular.	Plural.	As object.	Plural.
1	**Anaku**	anini	yatu, yati, yashi, aashi	
2m.	**Atta**	attunu	katu, kati, kasha	kashunu
f.	**Atti**	attina	kati or kashi	
3m.	**Shu**	shunu	shashu	shashunu
f.	**Shi**	shina	shashi	

PSALMS.

With nouns.		SUFFIX.	With verbs.	
Singular.	Plural.	Singular.		Plural.
-i-ya-a	-ni	-ni		-nashi
-ka	-kun(u)	-ka		-kunushi
-ki	-kina	-ki		
-shu-sh	-shun(u)	-shu-sh		-shunuti
-sha-sh	-shin(a)	-shi-sh		-shinati

DEMONSTRATIVE.

This, **Annu,** pl. **Annuti,** f. **Anniti.**
That, **Ullu,** **Ulluti.**

Sing.	Pl.	Sig.	Pl.
m. **Shuatu,** **Shuati,**	**Shuatunu,**	f. **Shiati.**	**Shuatina.**

The first **u** in these is sometimes omitted.
The relative pronoun for all persons, genders and numbers is **sha.**
Interrogative, **mannu,** who; **minu,** what; **mannan,** whoever.
Reflexive, **ramanu,** one's self. See A. M. 29–32 and D. L. 9.

PSALMS.

Every one is familiar with the Psalms of David. There is no need to quote from their sacred pages. There were also psalms in Assyria and Babylonia. As good a specimen as has yet been discovered is a psalm to **Sin,** the moon god, in Ur, that must often have been heard by Abraham as it rang out from the lofty sanctuary on the still night air among the palm-trees. In the Orient to-day, when the city is hushed in silence, whether at noon or night, the voice of the muezzin call to prayer from the minaret sounds impressive in the stillness. Mohammed may never have heard of Urukh and his great temple in Ur, but the chant of the priests of **Sin** arose in the calmness of the night when silence brooded over land and sea, when the cries of the sailors were hushed along the shore and not even a bird-note broke the stillness. Thus this psalm to **Sin** may have formed the historic basis for the Moslem call to prayer that has usurped its place. The times of Mohammed seem far off to us as we look back through the vista of more than 1,200 years, but they are modern compared with this antiquity of more than 3,000 years beyond. It is as follows (R. IV. 9, and H. L. 160, 162):

1. O Lord, ruler of the gods, who in heaven and earth alone is great,
2. Father, illuminator, lord of the firmament, the exalted among the gods.
3. Father, illuminator, lord of heaven, the exalted among the gods.

4. Father, illuminator, lord of the moon, the exalted among the gods.

5. Father, illuminator, lord of Ur, the exalted among the gods.

6. Father, illuminator, lord of the temple of the great Shamash, the exalted among the gods.

7. Father, illuminator, The lord who maketh the crown (moon) to rise, the exalted among the gods.

8. Father, illuminator, who maketh the crown complete (full moon), the exalted among the gods.

9. Father, illuminator, who strideth along with great slaughter, the exalted among the gods.

12. Merciful one, father of the universe, who among living creatures makes his illustrious home.

13. Father, compassionate and full of forgiveness, whose hand upholdeth the life of all lands.

14. Lord, thy deity like the far-off heavens fills the wide sea with fear.

15. Placing temples on the earth he proclaims their names.

16. Father, producer of gods and men, causing the dwelling to be inhabited, establishing the sacrificial offerings.

17. Who proclaimeth dominion, who bestows the sceptre, who fixes destiny even to days remote.

18. First born, mighty, whose heart is vastness, and no one can know it.

19. Whose limbs are firm, his knees rest not, he opens the paths of the gods his brethren.

20. He is the god who maketh it light from the horizon to the zenith, and opens the doors of heaven.

21. Father, creator of the universe, illuminator of human beings....sending....,

22. Lord, who ordaineth the decrees of heaven and earth, whose command may not be broken.

23. Thou holdest the rain and the lightning for all living creatures, no god hath discovered thy fulness.

24. In heaven who is supreme. Thou alone, thou art supreme.

25. On earth who is supreme. Thou alone, thou art supreme.

26. As for thee, thy will is made known in heaven, and the angels bow their faces.

27. As for thee, thy word is made known on earth and the **Annunaki** (spirits of earth) kiss the ground.

28. As for thee, when thy word is on high like the wind, with skill food and drink are renewed.

29. As for thee, when thy word is given on the earth the grass is created.

30. As for thee, when thy word is perceived in the cattle-pen and sheepfold it increaseth living creatures.

31. As for thee, thy word hath created law and justice; to men it uttered laws.

32. As for thee, thy word is the remote heaven and hidden earth which no one knoweth.

33. As for thee, thy word, who has learned it? who can contend with it?

34. O lord, in heaven is thy lordship, on earth thy supremacy. Among thy brother gods rival thou hast not.

35. King of kings, of whose . . . no man is judge, whose deity no god resembleth.

The colophon at the close reads thus: "Like its ancient copy copied and published. Tablet of **Ishtar shum eshesh,** chief scribe of Asshurbanipal, king of all, king of Assyria, and son of **Nabu zir eser,** chief of the penmen."

In this psalm is a strange mingling of good and evil, just such as we would look for from a people who had not yet forgotten Noah, and through him retained still some memories of the revelations made in Eden, but who yet had gone so far in idolatry as to show the trail of the serpent in their holiest things. How else can we account for the degradation manifest in such an address to a god as we have had to omit in lines 10 and 11?

On the other hand, the name of father is given to the god worshipped in this psalm no less than twelve times. See lines 2-9, 12, 13, 16 and 21. No one can read that beautiful recognition of a father's love in line 13 and then say that name was never applied to a god until Christ taught us to say "Our Father." We can explain the occurrence of the name here only by the memories of that Father who planted a garden eastward in Eden for his children, and afterwards clothed them with skins (Gen. 3:21); nor that only, but came down to walk with his children in the cool of the day (3:8). Even after man had fallen, one who had returned to his father was permitted to walk with him (5:24) as a loving child walks with his father.

Another fact which almost startles us is that in this psalm we find the same term applied to God which the Evangelist gives to Christ before his incarnation (John 1:1 and 14). As Prof. Sayce has rendered the term "will," in his translation (H. L. 161. 25—162. 32), it will be needful to justify my rendering. The Assyrian term is "**Amatu,**" and Prof. Delitzsch in his *Lesestucke* renders it "*Wort, befehl, sache, angelegenheit,*" but does not even mention the name of "will." Prof. Lyon in his Manual renders it precisely in the same way: "Word, command, affair, thing," and here too "will" is not mentioned as one of the meanings; and so I feel authorized to call attention to this wonderful corroboration of the use of the term "word," as applied to a divine being no less than eight times in lines 26-33. Some lines, *e. g.*, 24 and 25, seem to favor monotheism; but it is to be feared that the writer only seeks to exalt **Sin** above his "brother gods" in the pantheon, for the same language is used by the worshippers of other Chaldean gods in behalf of their favorites. In lines 11, 13, 22-25, 29-31, are expressions worthy to be used of the true God. Others, as from 2 to 9, are polytheistic. The first clause in 34 and 35 savors of monotheism, and the second clause of polytheism.

As sure as a living man is better than a material sun, the tendency of such idolatry is toward the spirit that led Nebuchadrezzar to ask, Dan. 4:30, "Is not this great Babylon which I have built for the royal dwelling-place, by the might of my power, and for the glory of my majesty?" But the worship of the true God prompts David to give expression to the opposite feelings as recorded in 1 Chron. 20:10-16, and Solomon to say in like manner, 2 Chron. 6:18, "Will God in very deed dwell with men on the earth? Behold heaven and the heaven of heavens cannot contain thee; how much less this house which I have builded!"

PSALMS, PENITENTIAL.

After the incantation came the litany, and subsequent to that the penitential psalm. To this last the litany was frequently joined so as to form a part of it. Zimmern has published a collection of them, *Babylonische Busspsalmen;* also Prof. Haupt, *Akkadische und Sumerische Keilschrifttexte.* See also H. L. 521-531.

The following, taken from H. L. 349-52, is the best specimen I have been able to find:

The heart of my lord is wroth; may it be appeased.
May the god whom I know not* be appeased.
May the goddess whom I know not be appeased.
May the god I know, and (the god) I know not be appeased.
May the goddess I know, and (the goddess) I know not be appeased.
May the heart of my god be appeased.
May the heart of my goddess be appeased.
May the god and the goddess whom I know and know not be appeased.
May the god who has been violent against me be appeased.

* "I know" or "know not," in this case and in those that follow, means "whose name I know" or "know not."

May the goddess who has been violent against me be appeased.
The sin that I committed I knew not.
A name of blessing may my God pronounce upon me.
A name of blessing may the god whom I know and know not record for me.
Pure food I have not eaten ; clear water I have not drank.
The cursed thing of my god unknowingly I did eat.
The cursed thing of my goddess unknowingly I did trample on.
O lord, my sins are many, my transgressions are great.
O my god, my sins are many, my transgressions are great.
O my goddess, my sins are many, my transgressions are great.
O god whom I know and whom I know not, my sins are many, my transgressions are great.
O goddess whom I know and whom I know not, my sins are many, my transgressions are great.
The sin that I sinned I knew not.
The transgression I committed I knew not.
The cursed thing that I ate I knew not.
The cursed thing that I trampled on I knew not.
The lord has regarded me in the wrath of his heart.
God has revealed himself to me in the fierceness of his heart.
The goddess has been violent against me, and has put me to grief.
The god whom I know and whom I know not has distressed me.
The goddess whom I know and whom I know not has inflicted trouble (upon me).
I sought for help, and none took my hand.
I wept, and none stood at my side.
I cried aloud, and there was none to hear me.
I am in trouble and darkness ; I dare not look up.
To my god, the merciful one, I turn ; I utter my prayer.
The feet of my goddess I kiss and water with tears.
To the god whom I know and whom I know not I utter my prayer.
O lord, look upon me ; receive my prayer.
O goddess, look upon me, accept my prayer.
O god, whom I know and whom I know not, accept my prayer.
O goddess, whom I know and whom I know not, accept my prayer.
How long, O god, shall I suffer?
How long, O goddess, shall thy face be averted from me?
How long, O god, whom I know and know not, shall the fierceness of thy heart continue?
How long, O goddess whom I know and whom I know not, shall thy hostile heart be unappeased?
Mankind is made to err, and there is none that knoweth.
Mankind, as many as pronounce a name, what do they know?
Whether he shall have good or ill, there is none that knoweth.
O lord, destroy not thy servant.
When cast into the water of the sea, take his hand.
The sins I have sinned turn to a blessing.
The transgressions I have committed may the wind carry away.
Strip off my manifold wickednesses like a garment.

O my god, seven times seven are my transgressions; forgive my sins.
O my goddess, seven times seven are my transgressions; forgive my sins.
O god, whom I know and whom I know not, seven times seven are my transgressions; forgive my sins.
O goddess, whom I know and whom I know not, seven times seven are my transgressions; forgive my sins.
Forgive my sins; may thy ban be removed.
May thy heart be appeased as the heart of a mother who has borne children.
As a mother who has borne children, as a father who has begotten them, may it be appeased.

Colophon: Psalm of 65 lines, a tablet for every god. Its repetition ensures my peace.

Thus far Accadian; then in Assyrian: Like its original, copied and published: palace of Asshurbanipal, king of all, king of Assyria.

This psalm was surely written out of the depths. The reader will observe that no one god of the pantheon is mentioned, but simply god. (See "Monotheism.") Even that frequent mention of the "god whom I know and the god whom I do not know" seems forced from him by the stress of his trouble. So one has no heart to dwell on its repetitions. But if the reader desires to measure the extent of our obligations to Holy Scripture, let him compare Psalm 51 with this product of Assyria.

PUL.

The name of **Pul**, king of Assyria, occurs in 2 Kings 15:19, and has occasioned no little perplexity, for it was not found in the Assyrian lists. The Eponym canon from B. C. 900 to 666 did not contain it. Some thought the name might be a variation of **Vul lush,** and when that theory was not found tenable others thought that he might be a king who, though he made some conquests in Syria, never succeeded in securing the throne at Nineveh.

Now, however, conjectures are made unnecessary by the discovery of the name in the second dynastic tablet from Babylon, col. 4, line 8. See R. of P. new I. 18, where it occurs as **Pulu,** with the usual Assyrian ending. Prof. Sayce, in a list of the kings of Assyria (R. of P. new II. 205-207), identifies him with Tiglath Pileser III., who reigned B. C. 745-727, and so endorses the conclusions which others, among them E. Schrader,

BAS-RELIEF REPRESENTING PUL. (NIMROUD.)

had already reached in another way; for, proceeding on the basis that in ancient times many had two names, *e. g.*, Gideon and Jerubbaal, Asshurbanipal and Sardanapalus and possibly Asnapper, Ezra 4: 10, they found that Tiglath Pileser reigned at the time referred to in 2 Kings 15: 19; he styled himself king of Chaldea. Pul was king of Babylon B. C. 731, but in that year Tiglath Pileser subdued Merodach Baladan, and **Chinzer** of **Amukkan** and styled himself king of Babylon (K. A. 7. 238, 239). Then the canon of Ptolemy gives **Chinzirus** and **Porus** (another form of Pul) as kings of Babylon from B. C. 731 to 726; but Tiglath Pileser conquered **Chinzirus** about B. C. 731, and succeeded to the throne of Babylon, and Babylonian records give **Chinzirus** as king in 731, and **Tugulti pal e sharra** in 729, so that perplexity about Pul, king of Assyria, is now happily at an end, through the testimony of the monuments agreeing as they do with these other authorities.

A bas-relief of this monarch is given on p. 263. It also gives a good idea of an Assyrian chariot.

QUEENS.

1 Kings 10:1. When the queen of Sheba heard of the fame of Solomon, etc. In Esther 1:9 we read, Vashti the queen made a feast for the women in the royal house, etc. Dan. 5:10. Now the queen came into the banquet-house, etc. Acts 8:27. A eunuch of great authority under Candace, queen of the Ethiopians. Psa. 45:9. At thy right hand doth stand the queen in gold of Ophir.

These and other passages lead us to suppose that queens existed quite generally in ancient times; and if the monuments should make no mention of them we might question the accuracy of the Holy Scriptures. How is it?

The Assyrian monuments show the prominence given to queens on earth when they place the queen of **Kidmuri** among the gods, and queen **Allat**, or **Ninkigal**, as she is sometimes called, on the throne of Hades. Smith's list of Babylonian kings, prefixed to his History of Babylonia, mentions **Bilat Sunat** as queen of Erech, and still later **Ellat Gulu**, queen of Agane who was conquered by **Khammuragas**, king of Babylon, who reigned 2290–2235 B. C. Asshurbanipal also makes mention of **Adiya**, queen of Arabia, in giving an account of his wars with her husband, and we must not forget that Sheba was in Arabia, and Ethiopia not far off. We have a fuller record of queens in the Egyptian monuments, and Egypt was near both to Arabia and Ethiopia.

Look first at a list of queens who reigned conjointly with

their husbands. The monuments give the names of **Khnum nefer het Mentu hetep I.** of the XIth dynasty and **Aah hetep** of the XVIIth, and of the XVIIIth, **Nefertari Aahmes, Aahmes Meri Amen, Hashepsu Maka Ra, Mutemua, Teie, Nefri Thi, Meri Aten, Ankhnes Amen,** and **Thi.** In the XIXth, **Tua, Tauser.**

Then of queens who reigned alone the monuments mention **Nitaker** (Nitocris) of the VIth dynasty, **Aah** of the XIth, **Sebek Nefru Ra** of the XIIth, who reigned nearly four years. **Manetho,** according to Julius Africanus, mentions another in this dynasty, **Skemiofris.** In the XVIIIth the mother of Amenophis I. was for a while regent, and **Khnum Amen Hashepsu Maku Ra** reigned sixteen years. R. of P. new VI. 132-152.

The reader may wonder why no notice is taken of the renowned queen Semiramis, well known to every reader of Rollin's Ancient History. The reason is given by Prof. Sayce, who tells us that the Persian Annals translated for Ktesias consisted, like those of Firdusi, for the most part of legends and myths. So that we have in them not history but mythology, in which Queen Semiramis played the part of the goddess Ishtar, Ninos represented the city of Nineveh, and Ninyas was the sun god. Indeed Zames—a name sometimes given to this last—was only a mispronunciation of Shamash (see Anc. Em. of East, 99. and H. L. 271).

In order to get a correct idea of the position of woman in the far-off past we must give all the facts the most careful consideration.

Queen on the throne. Neh. 2 : 6. The king said unto me, the queen also sitting by him. Comp. Rev. 18 : 7 and Isa. 47 : 1.

This idea of a special throne for the queen is beautifully illustrated in the bas-relief of Asshurbanipal and his queen banqueting under a large vine laden with ripe clusters. See under "Feast," also P. and C. I. 107. 108.

Queen of heaven. Man craves the sympathy of a being higher than himself. The incarnation of the Word (John 1 : 1, 14) fully meets this want. But where that is unknown man devises for himself a queen of heaven. Jer. 44 : 17, 25 tells how the Jews were led away to burn incense to her. Among Buddhists she is known as *Kwan shi yin* or *Kwan yin*, the goddess of mercy.

Among Roman-catholics this name is given to Mary, the mother of our Lord.

In the monuments several queens of heaven are recognized. First of all is **Ishtar.** Whether under that name or the older name of **Nana,** she is called mistress of heaven and earth and queen of all the gods. In an ancient hymn she is called lady of heaven, etc. A. D. 392, 393, and R. of P. V. 158 and 159.

Beltis is also called the mother of the gods and queen of the earth.

Ninkigal (the lady of the great land) is also called queen. D. L. 110. R. IV. 31. 24. A. M. 52. 24.

Sarratu (queen) is the Assyrian form of the name Sarah.

RAB MAG.

Gesenius says that **mag** is the name for priests or wise men among the Medes, Persians and Babylonians—*magus,* pl. *magi*—and that **Rab mag** is the great magus, or chief of the magi.

There are two Babylonian words that may be referred to: one is **makhkhu,** the great one, from the Accadian **makh;** and Prof. Delitzsch prefers this derivation. Gesenius also seems to have this in view, as he defines *mag* great, powerful. See a quotation from Haupt's *Nimrod epos* in H. L. 62. 63. The other is **imqu,** wise, from the verb **imiqu,** to be wise, whence also comes **nimiqu,** deep or profound wisdom. In that case **Rab Mag** would be chief of the wise men. In the Hebrew it is עמק and in Arabic, *a'muk.* Nabonidus says (R. V. 64. 6 and A. M. 35. 5), the son of **Nabu balat su iqbi,** the great wise man, **rubu imqu,** worshipper of the great gods, am I.

As in Assyrian the adjective always follows after the substantive (Prof. Sayce's Elem. Gram. 49,) **rab** and **mag** must both be substantives, or two nouns in apposition : the chief and the great one, or, more probably, the man of deep insight.

RABSHAKEH.

The Hebrew word רבשקה occurs in 2 Kings 18 and 19, also in Isa. 36 and 37. It is not a proper name, as Gesenius renders it (Robinson's edition, 1844), for in R. III. 42. 1. 11 we have a proper name, **Merodach utsur,** and this person is described as **shaq sharri,** *i. e.,* **shaqu** of the king. **Shaqu** is equated with **rishu,** head, so that it must mean a man who is set over others. Smith's Bible Dictionary takes it in the Hebrew sense of cupbearer. But there are two verbs in Assyrian of the same form, **shaqu,** one meaning to drink, to water, and the other to be high, and the title in question is derived from the latter. A common form of this is **shupar shaqi,** or as it may be read, **shuud shaqi,** commonly rendered general, chief officer of the army. In Ass'l. 9. 6 the king says, **amilu shupar shaqi upaquu zikar shaptiya;** the generals obeyed the commands of my lips; again (43. 43) he says, **amilu shupar shaqiya ama'ti annaati ishmu ma :** my generals heard of these things. The generals were in Egypt, and the things heard were the plots of Tirhaka, Necho, Sharludari and others against Asshurbanipal. Again (81. 11) he says, My generals I sent as governors (**pikhati**) over them. A still clearer case is (101. 27) **Merodach zikir ibni shupar shaqi** (of) **Urak,** king of Elam, where the proper name is given first, and then the official title.

Rab shaqu is of rarer occurrence. **Rab** or **rabu** means chief. Jer. 39: 11, **Rab tabbakhim,** captain of the guard — literally, of the slaughterers; Dan. 4:9, **Rab khartummim,** chief of magicians. **Rab shaqeh** occurs (Ass'l. 40. 25), **Rab shaq, pikhati, sharri:** the Rabshakeh, the governors or satraps, the kings. Prof. Sayce renders the first the "prime minister" or "grand vizier" (A. L. and S. 156), and Prof. Delitzsch "commander in the army" (Hebrew in the Light of Assyrian Research, 13), and the person named seems to have been in command of an army. Sargon (Khors. 120) sent seven **shupar shaqi** to the help of a tributary king. That they sometimes acted as governors is shown by Esarhaddon, who says (R. I. 45. 1. 34, also A. M. 19, 5), "My general I set over them as governor," as Asshurbanipal did afterward. Tiglath Pileser (**Tugulti apal isharra,** R. II. 67. 66) says, My **shupar shaqi** I sent to the city of Tyre as **Rab shaqi.** But what the difference between these two titles is cannot as yet be determined. Perhaps the day will come when general and major-general shall be titles as puzzling to future scholars as these are to us. It would appear, however, to be a civil rather than a military position that he sent him to fill in a city so far away, for there is no mention of troops having been sent with him.

The **Rabshakeh** of Sennacherib affords a good illustration of the linguistic attainments of an educated Assyrian. Of course he knew Assyrian, for it was his mother tongue. Then, as one who worshipped at the temples and transacted business at the courts, he was as proficient in Accadian as European scholars used to be in Latin. The men of Hezekiah took it for granted that he would speak in Aramaic, the language of the merchants of Western Asia, and we have seen that he could address Hebrews in Hebrew. Thus he was master of at least four languages, three of them resembling each other and one wholly unlike the other three.

RAIN FIRE, ETC.

Gen. 19:24. Then the Lord rained upon Sodom and Gomorrah brimstone and fire from the Lord out of heaven. Compare Gen. 7:4 and Luke 17:29.

There is a sentence in the Chaldean account of the deluge that reads, "The voice said, In the nights I will cause destruction to rain down from heaven," **ushaaznana shamutan.** R. IV. 50. 2. 31, and D. L. 103. 86. and A. M. 58. 1.

A better illustration is as follows: "Ishtar, who dwells in Arbela, clothed in fire and raised aloft in brightness, rained destruction (**izaannuu nabli**) upon the land of Arabia." R. V. 9. 81, and A. M. 32. 31, and Ass'l. 278. 63.

Still better, however, is a sentence taken from a cuneiform fragment in the British Museum, numbered k. 5001, and quoted in Prof. Sayce, H. L. 4. The speaker is addressing one of the gods: "Thou who rainest stones and fire upon the foe, may thy heart be exalted!" Brimstone is brend-stone, or burnt stone, from the old English verb brennen, to burn.

RAVEN.

Gen. 9:6. And it came to pass at the end of forty days that Noah opened the window of the Ark which he had made, and he sent forth a raven, and it went forth to and fro, until the waters were dried up from off the earth.

In the Chaldean account of the deluge **Shamash Napishti**

says (R. IV. 50. 3. 42-44, and D. L. 105. 144-146, and A. M. 60. 12-14):

> Ushitsima aribi umashir,
> Illik aribi ma qarura sha mi imurma,
> Ikkal ishakhkhi itarri ul issakhra.

I sent forth a raven. I let it go.
The raven went forth and saw the decrease of the waters.
It eats, swims, turns about, and does not return.

The two records are here in perfect agreement, only the Chaldean says also of a swallow precisely what both had said of a dove (see "Dove"), perhaps because of some religious associations with the swallow. Either because it was a Chaldean addition to the truth, or because it was not deemed essential to the narrative, there is no mention of a swallow in the Hebrew.

REDEMPTION.

Redemption is the grand theme of Scripture. They who lived before Christ looked for a redemption to come. Luke 11:38. The good since Christ are they who are justified through the redemption which he wrought out, Rom. 3:24; "in whom we have redemption through his blood," Eph. 1:7; and "in whom we were sealed until the day of redemption," Eph. 4:30; that is, the day when all the as yet hidden glory of that work shall be unfolded to the admiring gaze of heaven and earth.

We should hardly expect to find anything relating to this in the Assyrian monuments, and yet in Prof. Sayce's H. L. 140, occurs this sentence from an ancient hymn: "For their redemption did he create mankind, even he, the merciful one, with whom is life;" a most remarkable statement to come from such a source. R. IV. 61. 40. is rendered in H. L. 527. 22: Accept his gift, receive his ransom (**pitiitu**), Heb. פדה, Arabic, *Fida*, which Freytag renders, *res qua aliquis redimitur et liberatur*.

The idea of vicarious atonement could not be set forth more clearly than in a text which says of the sacrifice of a child (k. 5139 and Prof. Sayce's Elem. Gram. p. 123), "The child for his life he gave. The head of the child for the head of the man he gave. The neck of the child for the neck of the man he gave. The breast of the child for the breast of the man he gave."

Indeed we are startled by such words, not merely because they bear such testimony to the existence of the idea of vicarious atonement in ancient Babylonia, but because they so fully endorse the Scripture account of the sacrifice of children to Moloch. Alas that this should be so true a record!

REPETITIONS IN PRAYER.

Matt. 6:7, Christ says, "And in praying use not vain repetitions, as the gentiles do." Few have any clear idea of what those repetitions are. The following, called by Prof. Sayce a litany to the gods (H. L. 532), may show what they are:

What have I done that I should bear the sin?
To the light I have uttered the spell, and yet I bear the sin.
To Nusku, the supreme messenger of Ekur, I have uttered the spell, and yet I bear the sin.
To the moon god I have uttered the spell, and yet I bear the sin.

To Rimmon	"	"	"	"	"	"	"
To Ea	"	"	"	"	"	"	"
To Merodach	"	"	"	"	"	"	"
To Nebo	"	"	"	"	"	"	"
To the great god and the great goddess	"	"	"	"			
To my god	"	"	"	"	"	"	"
To my goddess	"	"	"	"	"	"	"
To the god of my city	"	"	"	"	"	"	
To the goddess of my city	"	"	"	"	"	"	
To the four streets	"	"	"	"	"	"	
To Suqamunna	"	"	"	"	"	"	"
To Sumaliya	"	"	"	"	"	"	"
To the seven gods and the twin gods	"	"	"	"			
To the god whom I know not	"	"	"	"	"		

To ... khuya I have uttered the spell. May my sins be forgiven.

Since, then, as the apostle says, 1 Cor. 8:4, "We know that no idol is anything in the world, and that there is no God but one," how dreary must be the hopes of those who go through such a round of repetitions and find themselves as unblest at the close as when they began.

REST.

It is delightful to note in how great a variety of ways the Bible speaks of rest. In the beginning God instituted a Sabbath of rest, knowing how much man would need it, and so the Sabbath was made for man, who enjoys rest in proportion as he keeps it holy.

When Israel went forth from Egypt into the great and terrible wilderness, God said, "My presence shall go with thee, and I will give thee rest." Exod. 33:14. Well might they enjoy rest who had the presence of God with them continually. When Naomi set out on her sorrowful return to Bethlehem she said to her widowed daughters-in-law, "Go, return each of you to her mother's house. The Lord deal kindly with you, as ye have dealt with the dead and with me. The Lord grant you that ye may find rest, each in the house of her husband." Ruth 1:8, 9. What a vista of peace that Scripture opens up before troubled souls that speaks of God as giving rest from the days of adversity! When we look forward to such a prospect we may well say, "Return unto thy rest, O my soul, for the Lord hath dealt bountifully with thee." Psa. 116:7.

Some cuneiform inscriptions seem as if designed to illustrate Scripture utterances concerning rest. David, the king, "had it in his heart to build a house of rest for the ark of the covenant of the Lord," 1 Chron. 28:2; and the Psalmist sings, "Arise, O Lord, into thy resting place, thou and the ark of thy strength." Psa. 132:8. A hymn to the god Adar reads thus: "O lord, in thy city which thou lovest may thy heart be at rest. O lord Adar, in thy house which thou lovest may thy heart be at rest. In the temple of Nipur, thy city which thou lovest, may thy heart be at rest." Fragment R. 117. H. L. 483.

Some readers of the gospels wonder that Jesus spoke of rest rather than of pardon or deliverance from sin when he said, "Come unto me, all ye that labor and are heavy laden, and I will give you rest." Matt. 11:28. But his choice of that word shows how well he knew what was in man; he appreciated his utter unrest, and the longing that cannot be satisfied until he finds rest in God.

This unsatisfied longing is manifested very clearly in the Assyrian inscriptions. In a hymn to Nusku, the sun god of Nipur, who had a chapel in the celebrated temple of Merodach at Babylon by the side of its lofty ziggurat (tower), he is addressed as **Mushtalum**, a causative form of the verb **shalamu**: "He who satisfies, or causes to rest." See Heb., *shalom*, and Arabic, *salaam*. The Accadian version reads "giver of rest to the heart," and this title is repeated four times in as many lines. R. IV. 26. No. 3. 30-34. Not that Nusku really gave this rest to his worshippers, save as for a time they might suppose that they had received it—only to suffer a greater disappointment; but this title which they gave him revealed the intense craving of their hearts for rest.

A hymn to Merodach reads, "Look upon (or regard with favor) thy house. Look upon thy city, O lord of rest. Look upon **Babilu** (Babylon) and E. Saggilla (his temple), O lord of rest. May the gods of heaven and earth say to thee, O lord, rest, (or call thee lord of rest)." R. IV. 18. 2 reverse, 25, 27 and 31.

It bears witness to the unrest of his worshippers, that they invoke the gods of the whole pantheon to impart rest to their chosen deity; and that even the gods stood in need of rest, in their estimation, is abundantly manifest from another part of the same hymn:

> May thy city speak rest to thee (it is) thy house.
> May Babilu speak rest to thee (it is) thy house.
> May the great Anu, the father of the gods, say to thee, When wilt thou rest?
> May the great mountain, the father of Mullil, say to thee, When wilt thou rest?

and so on through four lines more. R. IV. 18. 2 obverse, 5-20.

Well might Christ say, "Come unto me and I will give you rest," when men not only despair of finding it themselves but look on their gods also as in need of it from one another. At the feet of Jesus, even here and now, the weary are at rest. Much more, then, there remaineth a rest for the people of God, when they shall see him as he is, and, once entered on that rest, they shall go no more out for ever.

RETURN OF THE YEAR.

2 Sam. 11 : 1. "And it came to pass at the return of the year, at the time when kings go forth"—the translators and revisers add, "to battle;" better "to war," for they do not go forth to fight one battle, but on a prolonged campaign that may involve many battles with different peoples. The kings of Assy-

RETURN OF THE YEAR. 273

ria, as might be expected, furnish no end of illustration in this matter. Asshurnatsirpal, who reigned B. C. 885-860, is very full on this subject. At the end of his tenth year he wrote the large inscription that fills ten folio pages (R. I. 17-26), describing the campaign of each year. The date of departure on the first year is not mentioned. For some reason he was unusually late in the second; not till Ab (July-August) 24, did he leave Nineveh, in the very hottest of the season. He must have moved his army in the night, for at that season the mercury rises as high as 115§ in the shade during the day (col. 1. 69.) In the third year he does not give the date of leaving (121-104). In the fourth year he left Sivan (May) 1 (col. 2. 51). On the same date next year he crossed the Tigris (86, 87). The following year he set out from Calah, Sivan 22 (col. 3. 1). The seventh year he left the same city Sivan 18 (28). Next year his departure was only two days later, Sivan 20 (50). The ninth year saw him on the way from Calah, Iyyar (April) 8 (56), and in B. C. 867 he left Calah, Iyyar 20. With the exception of the second year these campaigns began after the heavy rains of winter and before the severe heat of summer. He was just as regular in going every year to plunder and desolate neighboring nations as our well-to-do citizens are now in taking their annual outing. That was his way of spending vacation. For the translation of this inscription of Asshurnatsirpal see R. of P. new II. 128-177.

Shalmanezer II. also (R. III. 7. 29 and col. 2. 13; for translation see R. of P. III. 86. 29 and 90. 13) left Nineveh, Iyyar 13, to go against **Lakhlakhti,** and again on the same date against **Tulbarsip.** At other times he set out when the river was in flood (Layard 87. 27 and 57 and A. M. 7. 24 and 83). So also did Asshurbanipal (R. V. 8. 79 and A. M. 30. 5; see also G. Smith's History of Assyria 46-61). Now the Tigris begins to rise in the middle of March and attains its height about the middle of May, so that this agrees with the dates of Asshurnatsirpal.

As to the frequency of these campaigns, Sargon says in his annals that for fifteen years he made not one only each year, but often more. See R. of P. VII. 27-52.

On the black obelisk of Shalmanezer II., now in the British Museum, it is recorded that he made annual raids for eight

274   ASSYRIAN ECHOES OF THE WORD.

years; then instead of the ninth year comes the ninth campaign; then, after mentioning those of his tenth and eleventh years, it speaks of his twelfth campaign, and returns to years again till number nineteen once more becomes campaign. After that twenty is a year with its campaign, and twenty-first simply campaign, and after alternating to the twenty-sixth year they remain years from that time till the thirty-first.

RETURN NOT.

One of the things relating to death that impresses itself most deeply on all men, whether rude or refined, is that the dead never come back. So Job says, 7:9, 10, "he that goeth down to Sheol shall come up no more; he shall return no more to his house, neither shall his place know him any more." Compare 10:21; 2 Sam. 12:23.

In the descent of **Ishtar** into Sheol (R. IV. 31. 1, Prof. Sayce's Elem. Gram. 119. 1, A. M. 52. 1, and D. L. 110. 1. third ed.), it is called the land of no return; **mat nugaa; nu** (not) and **gaa** equated with **taru,** to return. This Accadian name was rendered into Assyrian, **mat la nakiri,** the unchanging land. Line 5 describes it as "the house whose entrance has no exit," and line 6 as "the road whose going has no returning." Thus the monuments endorse this Bible characteristic of the other world.

RIGHTEOUSNESS, THY.

Psa. 71:15, 16. My mouth shall tell of thy righteousness, and of thy salvation all the day; for I know not the numbers thereof. I will come with the mighty acts of the Lord God. I will make mention of thy righteousness, even of thine only.

In Rev. 15:4 it is written, "Who shall not fear, O Lord, and glorify thy name? for thou only art holy: for all the nations shall come and worship before thee; for thy righteous acts have been made manifest."

Some may think, Certainly nothing can be found in the monuments to correspond to that, for idolators care nothing for righteousness. And yet an ancient hymn to **Bil Marduk,** the god of Babylon, says (H. L. 81):

"Cause them to behold the light that they may tell of thy

righteousness, O lord of the world, light of the spirits of heaven, utterer of blessings. Who is there whose mouth makes not mention of thy righteousness, speaks not of thine exaltation, and celebrates not thy glory?"

All such utterances, instead of proving that the heathen do not need the gospel, only reveal Him who saith, "I am the light of the world," John 8:12, shining in the darkness. John 1:5.

RIMMON.

2 Kings 5:18 speaks of the house of Rimmon, and we find the word forming a part of proper names, as Hadadrimmon, Zech. 12:11, and Tabrimmon, 1 Kings 15:18.

Before the Assyrian inscriptions were deciphered our knowledge of this deity was very indefinite. Even the latest edition of Smith's Dictionary says that the signification of the name is doubtful. The Jews wrote Rimmon as though it had some connection with the pomegranate, and many have supposed that it had reference to the productive power of nature, as the pomegranate is so full of seeds; but the Assyrian is **Ramanu**, the exalted one—written sometimes **Rammanu**, as though from **Ramamu**, to thunder. So in the account of the deluge, A. M. 58. 10, D. L. 104. 94, and R. IV. 50. 2. 42, **ilu Ramanu ina libisha irtammaamma**: the god Ramanu in it (the cloud) thundered. In the Manual 20. 24. R. V. 1. 45 he is said to give rain: **zunnishu umashshiru**; literally, his rain he let loose. He was the god of the air, as Anu was of the sky, and represented the Accadian god Meri, the exalted one, known also as Mer Mer, the very exalted. In Syria he was called Hadad, and in Arabia, Dadda or Dada, and regarded as the sun god.

RING.

Gen. 41:42. And Pharaoh took off his signet ring (טבעת) from his hand, and put it upon Joseph's hand, and arrayed him in vesture of fine linen, and put a gold chain about his neck.

Esther 3:10. And the king took his ring from his hand and gave it unto Haman the son of Hammedatha the Agagite, the Jews' enemy; v. 12, and it was sealed with the king's ring.

Luke 15:22. And put a ring on his hand.

In like manner Asshurbanipal, speaking of several persons in the island of Arvad, says, "I clothed them in garments of **birmi**, rings (**shimir**) of gold I bound on their hands." R. V. 2. 93, 94, and A. M. 22. 7, 8. The text in Ass'l. 64. 3 and 4 is imperfect.

He says also of Pharaoh Necho, king of Egypt, "I clothed him in **birmi**, and a chain of gold, insignia of his royalty, I made for him; rings of gold I bound upon his hands." R. V. 2. 11, 12, and A. M. 48. 12, and Ass'l. 45. 57.

In the descent of Ishtar into Sheol, when she entered the sixth gate **Namtar** took away the rings of her hands and feet. R. IV. 31. 57, and A. M. 63. 21.

The question arises, Were these rings for the finger, or bracelets? In favor of the former is the noun δακτυλιον from δακτυλος a finger, and also the Hebrew טבעת, *tabaath*, that which is used to make an impression. The verb טבע, *tabaa*, is used to denote printing in both Hebrew and Arabic.

To this it may be replied, that though δακτυλιον is derived from δακτυλος yet it is not confined to the meaning of finger-ring. Liddell and Scott's Lexicon adds, "felloe of a wheel," something much larger than a bracelet; and as to the signet-ring (טבעת), P. and C. tell us, II. 256: "In Chaldea the fashion at one time seems to have been to fasten them to the wrist. In tombs at Warka and Mugheir cylinders were found on the floors close to the wrist bones of the skeletons, and the tombs had never been disturbed."

Then for positive argument in favor of a bracelet, Pharaoh took it not from his finger, but from his hand, and put it not on Joseph's finger, but on his hand. The same is true of king Ahasuerus, and the command in the parable is, "put a ring on his *hand*." Luke 15:22.

Then in the bas-reliefs on the monuments we never see finger-rings worn, but bracelets are very conspicuous on the statue of the king (L. N. II. 13 and 110), on the large statue of Nebo from Nimrood (P. and C. I. 81), on Sargon and nine of his suite from Khorsabad (97), on those who feast with Asshurbanipal, eight in all (107 and 108), on three persons making an offering to a god (109), on a winged genius (II. 87), on the *stela* of **Marduk idin akhi** (95), on Sargon before the sacred tree (99), on the statue of Asshurnatsirpal (123), *stela* of Shamash Vul II. (211), on a bas-relief from Khorsabad (221).

But it is not necessary to go further; enough has been adduced to show that the command to put a ring on the *hand* of the younger son was full as likely to be an order to adorn him with a bracelet as with a finger-ring.

RITES.

The same uncertainty that attends the study of the priesthood follows us in the investigation of the Babylonian ritual, though in some things we recognize the faces of old acquaintances.

The Hebrew קרבנ *qorban*, oblation (Ezek. 20 : 28 ; Mark 7 : 11), appears in Assyrian as **qirbanu**. D. L. 145. The Hebrew daily or continual sacrifice has its counterpart in the Babylonian **sattuku**. Nabonidus, king of Babylon B. C. 555–538, says (R. V. 64. 3. 37. and A. M. 39. 8), **sattuku u nindabii ili sha makhri ushatiir ma ukin makhar shu** : the daily sacrifice (is **nindabu** the Heb. נרבה?) and free will(?) offering I restored even beyond what they had been before. And Asshurbanipal, speaking of Babylon, says (R. V. 62. 7, and A. M. 23. 21), Within its temples I set up their sacred objects and reëstablished the **sattuku** that had been interrupted. The most common name for a sacrifice is **niqu**, from **naqu**, to pour out, and one very common mode of offering was as a libation. When Asshurbanipal had killed three lions he " set up over them the mighty bow of Ishtar, the lady of war, presented offerings over them, and made a libation of wine over them." P. and C. II. 41 gives a bas-relief of Asshurbanipal making a libation over a wild ox which he had slain, p. 205 also shows him making a libation. See also R. I. 7. No. 9. and Prof. Sayce's Grammar, 126. So, just as the pious Hebrew took the cup of salvation and called on the name of the Lord, the Assyrian took his cup of wine and called on his gods. **Zibu**, Heb. זבח, makes prominent the slaughter of the victim. **Makhkhuru** puts the emphasis on its presentation before the god. **Mukhibiltu**, from **khibiltu**, injury, damage, Prof. Sayce (H. L. 69 note 3) renders sin offering. See " Drink Offering " and " Priesthood."

Taklimu, from **kalamu,** to see or show, may be something that resembled the show-bread of the Jews, as Prof. Sayce says, H. L. 73, note 1; but the Hebrew word is מערכה, the row or array of loaves. So **nikasu** may be the stated offering, for **nakasu** means to cut off, and so regular intervals of offering may be implied.

The animals offered in sacrifice in Assyria were oxen, fat sheep, gazelles, goats, and different kinds of birds.

There seems to have been a distinction between clean and unclean animals, we read so often of a pure lamb, a white lamb, a pure gazelle, clean herbs, pure water, etc. In Shemitic texts swine are never mentioned, and reptiles were counted unclean. So also were dogs, as appears in the following prayer against evil: " May Merodach preserve us from the baleful fetter, the fetter which injures the feet . . . the dog, the snake, the scorpion, the reptile, and whatever is baleful." H. L. 287.

Among the Jews were meal offerings (rendered meat offerings in the old version); but among the Assyrians were not only grains of wheat and flour and corn, but dates and pine-cones—whose kernels are still eaten in Syria—honey and butter, oil and fruits, green herbs, clean herbs, pieces of pure food, etc.

I do not recall any sculpture either in Assyria or Babylonia that represents a sacrifice consumed by fire. Nor do the verbs **sharapu, qamu, qalu,** meaning to burn, usually occur in connection with sacrifices of any kind. Many of their altars, too, seem unsuited for the burning of a sacrifice, yet some part of the animal must have been consumed by fire. Prof. Sayce says (H. L. 78) that in the great work on astronomy, called " The observations of Bel," we are told that " on the high places the son is burnt."

This raises the question whether human sacrifice was known in Chaldea, and after reading (2 Kings 3:27) that the king of Moab offered his eldest son for a burnt offering upon the wall we are not suprised to find a tablet (k. 5139, Prof. Sayce's Elem. Gram. 123) declaring that the father "must give his child for his own life, the child's head for his head, the child's neck for his neck, and the child's breast for his own." This shows that they had the idea of a vicarious atonement, and it is to be feared that it was sometimes more than an idea, and practised in a manner the atrocity of which was equalled only by its utter insufficiency. Compare Lev. 20: 1-5 and Jer. 32: 35.

Not only was the burning of sacrifices placed in the background, and attention concentrated on the shedding of the blood, but other things were introduced which we do not find in connection with the sacrifices of the Old Testament. After the deluge **Khasisadra** erected an altar on the summit of the mountain, set the sacred vessels **(adagur)** in order by sevens, and underneath them placed cedar, cane and cypress (?) **riggir** (A. M. 60. 17 and 18, D. L. 105. 149, 150). So also the directions given for a religious ceremony (R. IV. 62. No. 2, obv. 154 seq.) speak of "a green branch and a layer of reeds ... cedar wood, sherbin wood, scented reed, prickly grass, the **pal** grass and saffron." H. L. 539, 540.

Another arrangement requires "a green branch which has grown in a distant place before Merodach . . . a vessel holding one-third of an ephah, **qarbi** (?), and corn, green herbs arranged by twos, in front of the garden, among . . . trees, cedars and palm-trees, **im par,** incense (?), wood of the tall tree, thorn wood, **sisi** and **siman,**" etc., etc. R. IV. 64. obv. 2, and H. L. 536, 537.

Various special dresses were worn during their rites. One is somewhat doubtfully rendered "the mountain dress," "the gossamer cloth," "the white cloth," and "the fillet," "a **barsik** (?) dress," and "the robe of a herald." Priests and Levites might have found some articles among them corresponding to a portion of their own dress, though others might have seemed as strange to them as to us. Ablutions in pure water were strongly insisted on.

The great crowning difference, however, between the rites of Chaldea and Judæa was that, while the last constantly sought as their end conformity in character to a God who was perfect in holiness, the first never aimed higher than the attainment of some temporal benefit, or relief from some present suffering. The great end God has in view in his dealings with men was something wholly beyond their sphere of vision, and redemption from sin never entered into their thoughts. They had no knowledge of happiness beyond the pitiful measure that could consist with the most unbridled selfishness, cruelty and lust.

RIVER OF EGYPT.

In the Hebrew are several words thus rendered in our authorized version: 1. נהר מצרים, Gen. 15:18. This denotes the Nile, on which Egypt depends for its fertility. 2. נחל מצרים, Josh. 15:4 and 47. This is the Wady el 'Arish, on the border between Egypt and Palestine, and is rendered "the brook of Egypt" in the new revision. 3. יאר or יאר מצרים, Jer. 46:7, Amos 8:8, is the Egyptian name of the Nile transliterated in Hebrew, and appears also in the Assyrian, for Asshurbanipal calls the Nile **Yaruhu** (Ass'l. 41. 32). Number 2 is also mentioned by Sargon, who says (S. 2. 13), "The whole of the land of **Mas** (see Massa, Gen. 25:14, and 1 Chron. 1:30), even to **Nakhal Muutsri** (Wady el 'Arish), the spacious country of **Akharri** (Canaan, literally the west land), the land of **Khati** (the Hittites), over the whole of them I reigned." It is very pleasant to note this accuracy of statement in both the Hebrew and Assyrian, an accuracy that it is to be feared has not always been appreciated by the readers of our English version.

RIVERS.

Isa. 41:18, I will open rivers on the bare heights.

This must mean artificial rivers, *i. e.* canals, for the word נהר has that meaning, according to Gesenius, in 2 Kings 5:12, rivers of Damascus, and Zeph. 3:10, rivers of Ethiopia. Asshurbanipal calls himself **pitu naqbi,** opener of canals, R. I 17. 3, and the God Ea is called the opener of canals, **upattira naqbi,** in R. V. I. 45 and A. M. 20. 24. **Patru** is a dagger, and the verb derived from it means to cut open, as one cuts open flesh with that instrument.

ROCKS OF ASSYRIA.

Dr. W. M. Thomson has brought out the wonderful connection existing between The Land and the Book, and much might be written on the relations of Palestine to Assyria. For the present we confine ourselves to one or two features of the rocks of the two countries. The prevailing rock in Assyria and Palestine is limestone of various kinds and degrees of hardness. In the alluvial soil of Babylonia rock was wanting; a westerner would call it a prairie country. The constant disintegration of the limestone made both Syria and Assyria lands flowing with milk and honey. The plains of the land of the Philistines after the continuous culture of millenniums still yield large crops of grain without the use of manure, and the same is true of the plain of Assyria.

The limestone in both countries gives them another common inheritance, referred to in Isa. 2 : 19: "And men shall go into the caves of the rocks, and into the holes of the earth from before the terror of the Lord." Also Rev. 5 : 15: "And the kings of the earth and the princes, etc., hid themselves in the caves and rocks of the mountains."

Abraham bought the cave of Machpelah for a burying-place, Gen. 23; and Lazarus was raised out of a cave, John 11 : 38; David found caves very convenient hiding-places, and Obadiah hid a hundred of the prophets of the Lord by fifties in a cave, 1 Kings 18 : 4. Caves abound in Lebanon.

So also they are frequent in Assyria. I remember one with a spring in it just outside the walls of Nineveh, beyond the village of Nebi Yoonas. C. J. Rich calls it Thisbe's Well. The people of Mosul visit in summer a cave on the mountain above the convent of Sheikh Mattai. In the center of the rocky floor is a crystal pool fed by drops falling continuously from the roof.* Some of the churches of the Mountain Nestorians are part caves and part structures erected in front of them.† One of their villages is called Le Gippa (cave), and the inhabitants of Ashitha and Lezan in 1843 were butchered by the Kûrds in a cave high up the mountain side, whither they had fled for refuge (L. N. I. 164-166).

ROPES ON THE HEAD.

1 Kings 20 : 32. So they girded sackcloth on their loins and put ropes on their heads.

Bähr, in Lange, G. Rawlinson, Dr. Jamieson and Kitto all speak of the ropes as put about their necks ready to hang them with if Benhadad were so disposed, just as Eustace de St. Pierre

---

* Dr. Grant and the Mountain Nestorians, 123.
† The Nestorians or Lost Tribes, 68.

and six of the leading citizens of Calais, France, delivered themselves up to king Edward III. of England, and were spared only through the intercession of Queen Philippa.

An early Chaldean monument shows the king trampling on a prostrate prisoner preparatory to despatching him with the heavy mace he holds in his right hand, while his vizier leads two others by the bridle inserted in the lips, elsewhere referred to, to meet the same fate, and a wretched coffle of six, fastened to each other by ropes round their necks and with their hands tied behind them, advance to receive in their turn the dreaded stroke of the heavy mace in the hands of the king. Anc. Mon. III. 7.

ROYAL HOUSE.

Esther 1 : 9. The royal house, בית המלכות.

Asshurbanipal calls the palace of Nineveh **mushab sharutiya**: the abode of my royalty; an exact translation of the Hebrew in the above Scripture, for to the mind of the old Hebrews and Assyrians the kingdom was not something that existed independent of the king, but formed a part, as it were, of his personal glory. Thus wine of the kingdom, (Esther 1 : 7, יין מלכות) was not wine produced in the kingdom, but wine for the use of the kings. So Esther 5. 1, לבוש מלכות is royal apparel. The use of **sharutiya** and **bilutiya** in this strictly personal sense is very common in Assyrian. The king there speaks of the robes, throne, palace, etc., of my royalty; *i. e.* of my royal person.

SABBATH.

Some regard the Sabbath as merely a Jewish institution, that did not exist before the giving of the law at Sinai, and that ceased to be obligatory with what is generally called the ceremonial law. But the Sabbath did not belong to the Jews, it belonged to God. Four times in the law he claims it as "my Sabbath:" Exod. 31 : 13, Lev. 19 : 3, 30 and 26 : 2 ; and this divine ownership of the Sabbath is asserted many times in the prophets: Isa. 56 : 4 ; Ezek. 20 : 12, 13, 16, 24 ; 22 : 8 and 26 ; 23 : 38 ; 44 : 24. The Jew did not institute the day any more than he originated the prohibition of murder or adultery. It was only entrusted to his care along with other things because God had chosen him to be the depositary of the truth. He had no right to modify or alter the day: it was his to preserve it precisely as it was entrusted to his keeping. God alone, as the Lord of the Sabbath, had any power to change anything that belonged to it. And they who denounce the Sabbath as either Jewish or Puritan betray a sad ignorance as to its real ownership. We have to do neither with a Puritan nor a king Charles the Second's Sabbath, a New England nor a Continental Sabbath, but the Lord's. That is a wonderful statement which God made about his holy day both in the law (Exod. 31 : 13) and in the prophets (Ezek. 20 : 12): "For it is a sign between me and you throughout your generations that ye may know that I am the Lord that doth sanctify you;" a statement as true under the gospel as it was under the law.

So far from its being a Jewish institution we have the authority of the Lord of the Sabbath for saying that "the Sabbath was made for man;" and this word of our Lord is most fully corroborated by the Assyrian monuments, for they testify that long before Moses, and even before Abraham, the day was known to the Babylonians. That cannot be Jewish, then, that was known even in a heathen land before a Jew existed on the earth.

The name occurs in a bilingual tablet (R. II. 32. 16) as **Shabattu**. The sign read "**ba**" was misprinted there, and so has been called a textual emendation by the Ency. Brit., but Prof. Sayce testifies that "**ba**" is the reading of the original tablet (H. L. 76 note), and in a parallel column of the tablet the definition is given as **um nukh libbi**, "a day of rest for the heart," which is an excellent definition of the Sabbath to come from a heathen scribe of Asshurbanipal. "He evidently regarded the word as derived from the Accadian **Sa bat,** heart-resting."

The most important document on this subject, however, is a "Hemerology for the intercalary month Elul." R. IV. 32 and 33. This is written in Assyrian, but is full of Accadian terms. The copy that we have was written by a scribe of Asshurbanipal, but that was copied from a much older one brought from Babylonia, and as different kings used different titles we can learn the date of the original copy from the title it gives the king. Thus Asshurbanipal on cylinder B. (Ass'l 10. 1–5) calls himself **sharru rabu, sharru dannu, shar kisshati, shar Asshur,** shar kibrat arba'i: the great king, the mighty king, the king of all, the king of Assyria, the king of the four regions; offspring of Asshur akh iddina Shakkanakku Babil, shar shumiri u Akkadi. Esarhaddon appears as the high priest of Babylon and king of Shumir (Shinar) and Accad, grandson of Sin, akhi iriba shar kishati shar Asshur: Sennacherib is king of all, king of Assyria. Asshurnatsirpal calls himself (R. III. 3. 39) the appointed (governor) of Bil, the priest of Asshur, and gives the same titles to his father Tiglath Adar, and his grandfather Rimmon Nirari; and Asshur rish ilim is the appointed (governor) of the divine father (Bil), the priest of Asshur. R. III. 3. 12. Now the title of the king used in this tablet is rium nishi rabaati: shepherd of great nations; and Prof. Sayce says (H. L. 70. note 1), "This title refers us to the age of Khammuragas as the period when the work was composed." He was the Kossean conqueror who subdued Naram Sin, the son of Sargon of Accad, and the founder of the city of Babylon. He reigned 55 years, from B. C. 2290 to 2235. Prof. Sayce says (H. L. 23, note), "This agrees with the date arrived at by Von Gutschmidt for the beginning of the Babylonian era. The astronomical observations sent by Kallisthenes from Babylon to Aristotle, B. C. 331, reached back 1093 years, to B. C. 2234. Berossos, according to Pliny (N. H. VII. 57), stated that they began to be made 490 years before the Greek era of Phoroneus, B. C. 1753 or B. C. 2243. Babylon, according to Stephanos of Byzantium, was built 1002 years before the siege of Troy, B. C. 1229, which would bring us to B. C. 2231, while Ktesias made the reign of Belos (Bel Merodach) of Babylon to extend from B. C. 2286 to B. C. 2231, almost identical with the reign of Khammuragas."

This tablet, dating from that reign, says of the seventh day of Elul: "A fast day dedicated to Merodach and Zarpanit, a lucky day, a day of rest (Shabattu). The shepherd of great nations must not eat flesh cooked in the fire (or) in the smoke. He must not change his clothes. He must not put on white garments. He must not offer sacrifice. The king must not drive a chariot. He must not issue royal decrees. The augur must not mutter in a secret place. Medicine for sickness he must not use. For making a curse it is not proper. During the night the king makes his free-will offering before Merodach and Ishtar. He offers sacrifice. The lifting up of his hand finds favor with the god."

The fourteenth day is precisely the same, only Beltis and Nergal are the objects of worship. The same is true of the twenty-first, only it is devoted to Sin and Shamash, and the twenty-eighth day is the same, only it is sacred to Ea.

The nineteenth day is also a **Shabattu,** and as Prof. Sayce says concerning it, "Why it should have been so I cannot pretend to say" (H. L. 77), the writer may be excused if he also does not attempt to explain it. The reason for this extra Sabbath will doubtless appear in due time, when we have more inscriptions to study. Meanwhile the existence of one day in seven sacred to God outside of the Jewish nation, and dating back almost to the deluge, points to a Sabbath made for man in Paradise as well as affirmed to be "made for man" by the Lord of the Sabbath while he was here upon the earth.

If any still insist that the day was instituted by Moses, can it be possible that the heathen preserved the traditions of Paradise so much better than the nation chosen by God to be the depositary of his truth? Or do heathen inscriptions record that truth more accurately than the holy men who of old were inspired of God on purpose for that work?

SAKKUT AND CHIUN.

Amos 5:26. Yea, ye have borne Siccuth your king, and Chiun your images, the star of your god, which ye made to yourselves.

As some reader of this volume may look for a word concerning this Scripture an explanation is here attempted. E. Schrader (Cuneiform Inscriptions and the Old Testament, 442) translates, "As ye have sought after Shakkut your king, and Kiwan your star-god, your images which ye have made for yourselves," etc.

Shakkut is another name for that god of many names, Ninip, Adar, Uras, etc., as is shown in R. II. 57. 40, and so "your king" in this passage agrees perfectly with the meaning of Adrammelech (Adar is king). See "Adrammelech."

Chiun is **Kaaivanu** or **Kaaimanu**, the sign can be read either way (R. II. 32. 25), the name of the planet Saturn. The Peshito version reads here *Kimo*, so Castell.* Schrader says, *Kaivono*.

The reading Remphan or, more correctly, Raiphan, in Acts 7:43, arose from the writers of the Septuagint, which Stephen quotes, taking the Hebrew ב for ר. The name would then read Raivan, which was softened into Raiphan.

SALT, SOWN WITH.

Judg. 9:45. He (Abimelech) sowed the city with salt. 2 Kings 3:25. On every good piece of land they cast every man his stone, and filled it.

We find something to match this barbarous mode of warfare in R. I. 14, 15 and A. M. 4. 25, where Tiglath Pileser says that the whole of the city of **Khunusu** he laid waste; he reduced it to heaps of rubbish and sowed stones of **tsipa,** whatever that may be—perhaps stones of a certain size, as we say paving stones—over its surface. It sounds like the Aramaic word for stone.

SAMARIA PEOPLED FROM ASSYRIA.

2 Kings 17:24. And the king of Assyria brought men from Babylon, and from Cuthah, and from Avva and from Hamath and Sepharvaim, and placed them in the cities of Samaria instead of the children of Israel.

In the annals of Sargon, the builder of the palace at Khorsabad discovered in 1843 by Mons. Botta (Cylinder Inscription, line 20), he is called the conqueror of the people of Tamudi, of Ibadidi, of Marsimani, of Khayapa, the rest of whom trouble befel, and he made them to dwell in **Bit Khumri** (the house of Omri, Samaria); but this only speaks of the deportation of some Arab tribes to Samaria.

An inscription better fitted to illustrate the above scripture is found in Hall II. tablet 3, as numbered by Mons. Botta, where Sargon says, "I took the city of Bit Khumri (Samaria) and led into captivity 27,280 persons. . . . I carried them to Assyria

---

* The explanation may be that the references in Castell's Lexicon refer to another Syriac version of the Old Testament.

and in place of them I caused men to dwell whom my hand had conquered. I set over them my **shuparshaki** (generals) as **pikhati** (governors), and laid on them the same tribute as on the men of Assyria."

1 Kings 17:28 tells us that a priest whom they had carried away from Samaria came and dwelt in Bethel and taught them how they should fear the Lord ; and we are almost startled to read (Sargon, Cylinder, 74) " Sons of Assyria, of intelligent insight in all things, wise and learned in books, I commanded to take good care and teach them to fear God and the king."

According to Isa. 20:1, the Tartan (general) of Sargon captured Ashdod, and his Cylinder Inscription, line 18, records the fact that he carried the king of Ashdod into captivity.

It is not many years since the veracity of Isaiah was called in question because he alone mentioned a Sargon, king of Assyria, and no secular historian made any mention of such a name; but the splendid palace at Dur Sargina, with its voluminous records, has triumphantly vindicated the prophet.

SANCTIFIED FROM THE WOMB.

It is written of John the Baptist (Luke 1:15), " he shall be filled with the Holy Spirit, even from his mother's womb ;" and of Jeremiah the prophet (1:5), " before thou camest forth out of the womb I sanctified thee." These words find a very unlooked-for illustration in the India House Inscription of Nebuchadrezzar, col. 1. 23-29. See R. of P. new III. 105.

" After that the lord my god had created me . . . that Merodach had framed the creature in the mother, when I was born . . . when I was created, even I, the holy places of the god I regarded, the way of the god I walked in."

So also Asshurbanipal says (Ass'l. 3, and R. of P. I. 59) : " I am Asshurbanipal, the creature of Asshur and Beltis, son of the great king of **Bit riduti** (north palace on Koyunjik), whose name Asshur and Sin the lord of crowns from remote days have mentioned for the kingship, and created in the womb of his mother to rule over Assyria;" literally, for the shepherd-hood of Assyria.

Nabonidus says (R. V. 64. 4. 5 and A. M. 35 3 and 4) that

Sin and Ningal in the womb of his mother appointed his fate to the kingship.

SAVOR, SWEET.

Gen. 8:21. And the Lord smelled the sweet savor. Compare Exod. 29:18; Lev. 1:9, 13, 17; 2 Cor. 2:15; Eph. 5:2.

In the Chaldean account of the deluge (R. IV. 50. 49, D. L. 105. 151, and A. M. 60. 19), after Khasisadra left the ship and offered sacrifices, it is added, as in Genesis, "The gods inhaled an odor. The gods inhaled a pleasant odor." **Ilani itsinu irisha, itsinu irisha tabi.**

Nabonidus says (R. V. 64. 2. 11, 12 and A. M. 36. 24. 25), "Doors of cedar, whose fragrance was pleasant, I erected in its doorway."

SAW NOT ONE ANOTHER.

So the authorized version renders Exod. 10:23, but the Hebrew reads לֹא רָאוּ אִישׁ אֶת אָחִיו, *Lo raoo eesh eth akhiv:* no man saw his brother. Thus Moses describes the intense darkness which God produced in Egypt during the day time when he sought to induce Pharaoh to let his people go out from their house of bondage. And the Assyrian record of the deluge uses precisely the same language to describe the darkness caused by that event: **Ul immar akh akhushu,** Brother did not see his brother. D. L. 104. 106, A. M. 58. 24.

SCEPTRE, GOLDEN.

Esther says (4:11), that whosoever, whether man or woman, shall come unto the king into the inner court, who is not called, there is one law for him, that he be put to death, except such to whom the king shall hold out the golden sceptre, that he may live.

It may seem to the reader of such a statement that the life of some might be sacrificed because the sceptre did not happen at the moment to be within reach of the king. It may, however, reassure such to know that in all the bas-reliefs of Persian kings at Persepolis, and there are many, there is not one in which the king does not hold the long slender sceptre in his right hand. In fact it formed a part of the royal dress, and the king would no more appear on his throne without that than without any other portion of his royal apparel.

SEA TO SEA, FROM.

Psa. 72:8. He shall have dominion also from sea to sea.

Sennacherib in R. III. 12. 3, and Senn. 4. 3 says: **Ultu aabba iliniti sha shulmu shamshi adi tamti shapliti sha ziit shamshi gimri maalki sha kipraati ushaknish shipuua:** From the upper sea of the setting sun (Mediterranean) to the lower sea of the rising sun (Persian Gulf), all the kings of the regions I brought into submission at my feet.

Sargon also has a similar statement in his inscription in Halls II. and V., as numbered on the plans of Mons. Botta; for a translation see R. of P. VII. 27.

SEAL OR SIGNET.

Where we would append our signature to a letter the Oriental appends his seal. So every man except the very poor has his signet, which he either carries in his bosom or wears on his finger-ring. Tamar asked of Judah his signet as a pledge for the payment of money. Gen. 38:18. Jezebel wrote letters in Ahab's name and sealed them with his seal. 1 Kings 21:8.

It is a general impression that seals are used to authenticate the documents to which they are attached, but all are not aware of the extreme care that was sometimes taken in the matter. The seal of the monastery of Mount Athos, on an island in the Ægean Sea, was in four pieces, and each piece was entrusted to a different person. The key that combined them into one was kept by the secretary, so that it required the presence and co-operation of five men before a document could be sealed.

When the writer resided in Mesopotamia he found that custom required a seal to be used with the signature of an ordinary letter, and so he had to provide one to authenticate his own signature, which he still retains. This custom is not confined to men in office, but exists among all classes in the community who use the pen at all. In such a land one sees new meaning in the Scripture statement, "He that hath received his testimony (*i. e.* of Christ) hath set to his seal that God is true" (John 3:33), or, as the new revision has it, "hath set his seal to *this:* that God is true."

It is a pure delight to affix our seal, if only in thought, to any and every statement of Holy Scripture, and when we read it in that state of mind the Word is radiant with a new beauty, for God himself looks out of the page on us and his own lips address us. Let any one read such a word as Isa. 66 : 13, "As one whom his mother comforteth so will I comfort you," with no special apprehension of the truth, and then let him set to his seal that this is true, and it will be as if he entered a new world.

The same practice prevailed in Babylonia and Assyria. According to M. Menant, there were when he wrote as many as 3,000 of their seals in Europe. The British Museum alone had at that time 660, the *Cabinet des Antiques* in Paris 500, and the Louvre 300. P. and C. II. 251. At first they were in the form of cylinders, but afterwards they were made in the shape of cones or spheroids. The cylinder was rolled on the moist clay, as may be seen illustrated in B. and N. 609, P. and C. II. 256. The others were simply stamped, as the matrix occupied their lower surface. The cylinders were cut in limestone, marble, and steatite, or in the harder basalt, porphyry, syenite, and hematite. The others were made of jasper, onyx, and chalcedony, garnets and rock crystal. The oldest of these conical seals yet discovered dates from the reign of **Bin Nirari**, king of Assyria toward the end of the ninth century B. C. P. C. II. 277, query Vul or Rammanu Nirari II., 913-891 B. C.

The engraving on all of them is in the style of intaglio, not of cameo. Some of them, as, *e. g.*, those in P. and C. II. 261, are rude enough; heads and shoulders are represented by drilled holes of equal size, and knee-joints and calves of the legs by the same contrivance. Others again, as on pages 262 and 264, are very creditable pieces of work. These facts in the neighboring nation of Babylonia amply justify speaking of " the work of an engraver in stone, like the engravings of a signet " (Exod. 28 : 11) as early as 1491 B. C., which was as long before the Christian era as the discovery of America by Columbus was after it.

Job speaks of being "turned as clay to the seal," 38 : 14, and Mr. Layard found in a chamber or passage in the south west corner of the palace of Koyunjik many lumps of fine clay bearing the impressions of seals which had been affixed to documents like modern official seals of wax, though the documents themselves had either been burned or perished from decay. B. and N. 153.

The seal of King Urukh, or Ur Bagas, as Prof. Sayce calls him, H. L. 167, once belonged to Sir Robert Ker Porter, then for a long time was lost, but recently it has been recovered and is now in the British Museum. P. and C. I. 38. It is of green serpentine and shows the king on his throne. Two of the legs of the throne are shaped like legs of oxen.

When the writer left Mosul, in 1844, Mons. Botta gave him for a souvenir a beautiful chalcedony seal with the sacred tree engraved on it, surmounted by the winged globe, a priest on one side of the tree and a dagger behind him.

SEAL PRESENTED TO DR. LAURIE.

SEAL SKINS.

Exod. 36: 19. And he made a covering for the tent of rams' skins dyed red, and a covering of seal skins above (them).

The old version reads badgers' skins, but seal skins is more correct, for they belonged to some sea animal, and most probably to the seal.

It would be very easy to refer to Dr. Julius Oppert, the French savant, who quotes Sargon as saying, "I built in the town (of Dur Sargina) palaces covered with skins" (R. of P. VII. 54 and XI. 40); and again, "palaces covered with the skin of the sea calf" (R. of P. IX. 18); also "halls covered with (sea calf) skins" (XI. 36); or, still better, "I constructed palaces of skins of **takhash**," the precise word in the Hebrew (XI. 21); but unfortunately he pronounces **takhash** to be "a very obscure word," and of his sea-calf skins he says, "the assimilation is not quite certain."

So, being thus put on our guard, we look at the only original of his "palaces covered with skins" within our reach and find no mention of skins at all, but only of **shin piri** (ivory), and the same is true of his quotation of "palaces covered with the skin of the sea calf," from the silver inscription of Sargon. Prof. Lyon, S. 52. 19, reads that also **shin piri,** and so we conclude that the whole thing is a mistake.

Indeed, how could it be otherwise, when Moses writes of a movable tent that needed a covering easy to put on and take off, and Sargon described permanent structures that were never to be moved from the place where they were first erected? Similarity of material in circumstances so diverse would have thrown doubt over the inspired narrative more than it would have illustrated the work of Moses.

SEPHARAD.

Obadiah (v. 20) speaks of "the captivity of Jerusalem which is in Sepharad." Till recently the locality of this country was not definitely known, but in the Achæmenian inscription at Behistun the name of Spareta immediately precedes that of Yanna (Ionia) and it is spoken of as "by the sea." Also at Nakshi Rustum it occurs between Cappadocia and Ionia, and so it represents central Asia Minor west of the Halys, or the Greek provinces of Galatia and Bithynia. R. of P. new VI. 8.

SERPENT.

If Paradise lay in the region of the lower Euphrates, we should expect to find not only some trace of the name of Eden and of the tree of life, but also of the serpent, and though the trace is not very distinct still we find it. Among other names of the Euphrates, it is called "the river of the serpent," and as it is not noted for its sinuosity it would seem as though this title was an echo of the narrative in Genesis. Then **Ea,** the local deity of Eridu, was the god who is said to have taught the Babylonians the knowledge of practical arts, and he had a daughter, named **Nina** or **Nana,** who was also spoken of as "the serpent." Have we not here also a trace of the serpent who was "more subtile than all the beasts of the field"? True, the connection is somewhat remote, but still it may claim a place among Assyrian echoes of the Word.

There is a strong temptation to include among them a seal

containing the representation of a tree with fruit hanging on

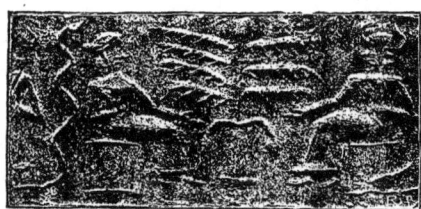

SEAL REPRESENTING TREE OF LIFE AND TEMPTATION OF ADAM AND EVE.

some of its branches and a man and woman seated nearby with a serpent close by standing very unnaturally on its tail. But though this seems a perfect picture of the Mosaic narrative, yet until we have some evidence that it was intended to be this we do not feel at liberty to claim it as an endorsement of the sacred narrative, for it may relate to something else, and there are enough of reliable facts set before us by the monuments, without resorting to uncertain things that after all may fail us. Still the resemblance is so complete as to justify the mention of this fact.

SEVEN.

The number seven is very prominent in Scripture. Seven of every clean beast were taken into the Ark. Balaam ordered the erection of seven altars. Seven priests blowing seven trumpets marched around Jericho seven days, and on the seventh day did so seven times, when the walls fell. Samson was bound with seven withes, and his seven locks of hair were shaven off. The golden lampstand in the tabernacle had seven lamps. Seven baskets of broken pieces were taken up after the feeding of the four thousand, and time would fail to tell of the seven candlesticks, seven stars, seven trumpets, seven seals, seven angels, etc., etc., of the Revelation.

The division of time into seven days is common to Scripture and the monuments. The Assyrian flood lasted seven days. Seven vessels of earthenware were prominent in the sacrifice that followed. Seven gates had to be passed through into Sheol by Ishtar. The witch tied seven magic knots. R. IV. 3. 5. 6. The sick man was anointed seven times with oil. R. IV. 26. 49. Certain prayers had to be repeated seven times, the planets and the demon messengers of Anu were seven, and the god number seven received special honor. H. L. 82.

SHADOW.

In our cold climate it sounds strange to hear the shade spoken of as a thing to be desired or trusted in. But in Isa. 30: 2 we find men trusting in the shadow of Egypt, and in R. V. 10. 64 we find the monuments speak of the good shadow of the gods, *i. e.*, their benign protection. More than that, it speaks of their divine darkness of peace, **ilu rapala shunu sha shalami**; *i. e.*, their divine shadow, which is a benediction to them that enjoy it.

Asshurbanipal says (R. V. 62. 15, and A. M. 24. 2), over all the cities I placed a protection (literally, a shadow).

SHEPHERD.

Rev. 7: 17 assures us that not only in this life, but also in the world to come, the Lord Jesus Christ shall be our shepherd. "The Lamb who is in the midst of the throne shall be their shepherd." The old version read "shall feed them," but the verb is ποιμανει from the noun ποιμην shepherd. It also means to govern, as in Matt. 2:6; Rev. 2:27, 12:5, etc.

Precisely so in Assyrian, from the noun **riu**, or **rium**, we have the verb **riu** with the same meanings corresponding to the Hebrew רעה; though there it is the present participle form that means shepherd.

Thus Sargon styles himself **riu kiinu**, true or faithful shepherd (A. M. 9. 3, and Layard 33. 2, also Prof. Lyon's Sargon, 1. 3). In this last work the verb is found with the meaning "to rule," in 11. 72: "The warrior of the gods, the lord of all, ruled the dwellers in mountain and plain in the four realms (*i. e.*, quarters of the world) of strange tongues and speech discordant." Sargon here is speaking of the god Adar, named also Ninip and Uras, to whom he ascribes the epithet "lord of all," a title which belongs to Christ alone, Acts. 10:36; who has not only all authority in heaven and in earth, Matt. 28:18, but is also our Shepherd, Psa. 23:1.

SHIP.

Isa. 43: 14. The Chaldeans, in the ships of their rejoicing. The Persian Gulf in ancient times extended up so far as to make Chaldea a maritime province, and the Chaldeans a seafaring people, so that what in English is the sailor's "Yo heave ho!" must often have been heard in the ancient harbor of Ur.

It is a corroboration of the above Scripture that whereas Moses speaks of the "ark" of Noah, the writer of the Izdubar legends everywhere speaks of a "ship." It is uniformly its *elippu,* the ship, and not the ark.

SHOULDER PEELED.

Ezek. 29 : 18. Nebuchadrezzar king of Babylon caused his army to serve a great service against Tyrus: every head was made bald, and every shoulder peeled.

One day in Mosul, Mons. Botta told me that he had found a wonderful illustration of this Scripture in one of his bas-reliefs at Khorsabad. It represented the siege of a seaport; the soldiers were at work carrying stones on their heads, and great beams of timber were borne on the shoulders of as many as could well get under them, so that a long continuance of such toil was well fitted to make the heads bald and peel the shoulders of the soldiers engaged in the work. See *Monuments de Ninive*.

SHUSHAN THE PALACE.

Esther 1 : 5, 6. The king made a feast unto all the people that were present in Shushan the palace, both unto great and small, seven days in the court of the garden of the king's palace; there were hangings of white cloth, of green, and of blue, fastened with cords of fine linen and purple to silver rings and pillars of marble; the couches were of gold and silver, upon a pavement of red and white and yellow and black marble.

Loftus describes four masses of ruins belonging to ancient Shushan. The citadel, a mound rising 119 feet above the water in the river and 2,850 in circumference. The eastern platform extensive but not easily defined, because it sinks so gradually into the plain. The central platform covering upwards of sixty acres represents the city; and lastly in the northwest corner is Shushan the palace, a large square mound near the centre of which was a square of 36 pillars. From the centre of one pillar to the centre of the next is 27½ feet, making the whole group about 140 feet square. The pillars are gone, only their bases remain. These are four feet three inches high and rest on blocks of limestone nine feet square. Three of the 36 bear trilingual inscriptions in the cuneiform character. Distant from this central group 64 feet 2 inches on the west, north and east, stand two lines of bases, six in each line, making 36 in all, the same number as the central group, forming a parallelogram 343 feet 9 inches by 244 feet. The central bases are square but the outlying ones bell-shaped, and from fragments the base and capital were reproduced, though of course the height could not be ascertained. Each capital may be readily divided into four parts, and the four together measure 28 feet in height. See Loftus' C. and S. 369.

If the central group of pillars supported a roof, and awnings extended from that to the three outer lines of pillars, in the style of the throne room at Teheran as given in B. and N. 649, Xerxes had a most magnificent hall for his feast, where his guests might look out from their gold and silver couches on the city and country and enjoy the cool breeze, that was not hindered by walls from circulating freely through the hall.

As for the pavement of red and blue and white and black marble, Loftus, 408, speaks of "a piece of *red* sandstone slab" and also of "a broken slab of *blue* limestone;" 415, mentions very archaic sculptures upon a trough of *yellow* limestone, lying in the river near the tomb of Daniel; and chap. 31. p. 416 seq. describes the celebrated "*black* stone" that was found on the palace mound and rolled down to the bank of the river, where it long served as a washing-block, till the offer of 1,400 kerans for it by a Frank resulted in its being blown up by a Seyid of the Beni Lam tribe in the vain hope of securing the gold he thought must be inside of a stone valued so highly; the fragments were built into a pillar in the veranda of the tomb.

These facts are all the more interesting because Mr. Loftus was not thinking of an illustration of the description in Esther when he unwittingly furnished one so satisfactory.

SHUTTING.

Our Saviour describes himself to the church at Philadelphia as "He that openeth and none shall shut, and that shutteth and none openeth." Rev. 3:7. The speaker is evidently one possessed of power that cannot be gainsaid or resisted. It is singular that the acts of opening and shutting should have been chosen to express this idea out of so many other acts that might have expressed it equally well, but it is still more singular when we find in the Assyrian monuments that the common name for governor is **pikhatu,** he who shuts, from the verb **pikhu,** to shut.

The use of the title **pikhatu** is so common that it hardly needs a reference. Take only one. Esarhaddon, 681–668 B. C., says, I appointed my generals to be their governors, or satraps (R. I. 45. 1. 34. and A. M. 19. 5). So both in Scripture and Assyrian the idea of shutting is used to denote an exercise of authority which no man may presume to contradict or disobey.

SILOAM, THE INSCRIPTION AT.

In the summer of 1880 a boy was playing in the pool of Siloam at Jerusalem, and while wading up the channel in the rock that supplies it with water he slipped and fell. His sharp eyes at once detected traces of an inscription on the rock in the semi-darkness, and he informed his teacher, Mr. Schick, who tried to copy it. In the beginning of 1881 Prof. Sayce succeeded in getting a better copy, but six weeks later Dr. Guthe washed out with an acid the lime that had formed in some of the characters, and made a very good fac-simile of the whole. It is not in the round Hebrew characters now in use, but in an old Hebrew alphabet resembling the Phœnician. The language is pure Hebrew, and the writing must have been done in the reign of Hezekiah, who "stopped the upper course of Gihon, and brought it straight down to the west side of the city of David," 2 Chron. 32:30, and also "made a pool and a conduit and brought water into the city," 2 Kings 20:20, unless the mention of "the waters of Shiloah that go softly," Isa. 8:6, written while Ahaz was yet on the throne, throws the date farther back, for that "going

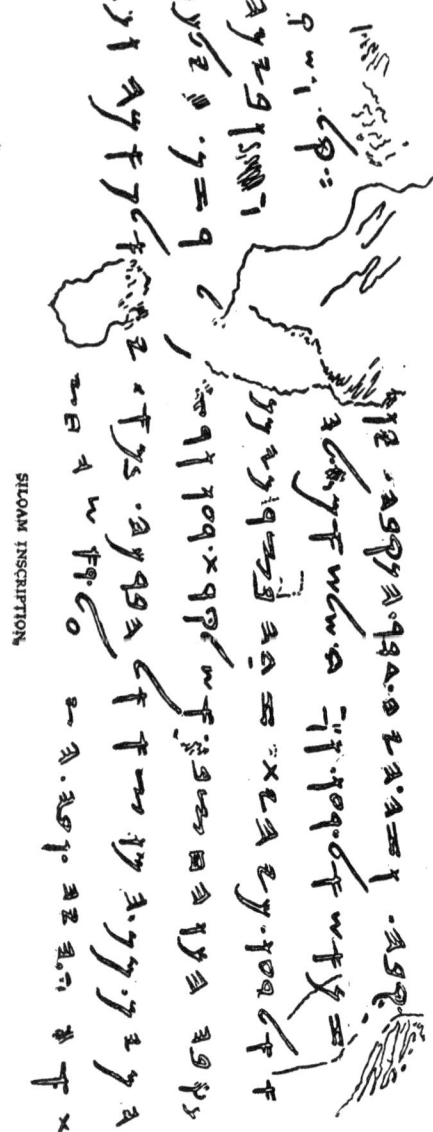

SILOAM INSCRIPTION.

softly" must refer to the quiet flow of this artificial channel in the rock.

The inscription relates to the excavation of this tunnel, which was begun by workmen at both ends, and is as follows: "(Behold) the excavation! Now this is the history of the excavation. While the excavators were still lifting up the pick each towards his neighbor, and while there were yet three cubits to (excavate, there was heard) the voice of one calling to his neighbor, for there was an excess (?) in the rock on the right hand, and after on that day the excavators had struck pick against pick, one against the other, the water flowed from the spring to the pool, a distance of 1,200 cubits. And (part) of a cubit was the height of the rock over the heads of the excavators." Fresh Light 97–107.

The accompanying facsimile of the inscription is from the same work.

The blank spaces show where the writing has been obliterated by changes which time has wrought in the surface of the rock.

In these ancient letters we see the mode of writing that was employed by the earlier prophets of the Old Testament, and they are of great value for the restoration of passages that have been altered by transcribers, especially of proper names that have been misspelt.

SIN AND SINAI.

On the east of the Red Sea Israel came into the wilderness of Sin, between Wady Feiran and that sea, Ex. 16:1, and of Sinai we read that it was moved at the presence of the Lord. Psa. 66:8. What was the origin of these names? It cannot be the Hebrew word *Sin*, for that means *mud*, and however that derivation might suit Pelusium, located in the mud of the delta of the Nile, it is not appropriate for either the sand of Sin or the granite of Sinai. Prof. Sayce suggests (H. L. 50) that both names were derived from **Sin,** the name of the moon god, Sinai having probably been a high place for his worship; so that his shrine may have stood there long before Moses asked leave to go three days' journey into the desert to worship the true God. Ex. 8:27.

Several things favor this idea. The name of the moon god and the desert are the same, and though Sinai was far from Ur, the centre of the worship of **Sin,** yet, on the other hand, a Himyaritic inscription in Southern Arabia contains his name. H. L. 50. Then an inscription on one of the statues found at Telloh, near ancient Eridu, tells us that the stone was brought from **Magan,** which Lenormant and Sayce agree is the Sinaitic peninsula, and in both style and attitude the statues resemble the Egyptian statue of Kephren. H. L. 31 and 137.

Nor should this derivation of these names seem strange when we meet with the names of so many Babylonian gods in Palestine. There was a city called Nebo in Moab (Isa. 15:2, Jer. 48:22). The children of Reuben built a city of that name (Num. 32:38). It is well known that Moses died on Mount Nebo (Deut. 34:1, 5), in sight of the moon city, Jericho—for that name is almost identical with the Hebrew for moon, ירח, *yaraekh.* There was also a city of Naphtali called Beth Anath (Judg. 1:33), in Assyrian, "the house or temple of **Anatu,**" the wife of the god Anu; and the birthplace of the prophet Jeremiah was Anathoth (1:1), *i. e.*, the **Anatus,** just as Ashtaroth was the **Ishtars.**

If this derivation is correct, and there seems no reason to call it in question, then that verse of a familiar hymn,

> "Shine, Lord, on each divine attempt
> To spread the gospel's rays,
> And build on SIN'S demolished throne
> A temple to thy praise,"

has a meaning which its author never dreamed of, and that manifestation of the glory of the Lord on Sinai becomes a symbol and a pledge of the suppression of all idolatry and his taking possession of the whole earth for Christ.

SINGING MEN AND WOMEN.

2 Sam. 19:35. Can I hear any more the voice of singing men and singing women?

Exod. 15:1. Then sang Moses and the children of Israel this song. Ver. 20. And Miriam took a timbrel in her hand. Ver. 21. With timbrels and dances.

Compare 1 Sam. 18:6, Neh. 7:67, and Ezra 2:65.

Esarhaddon (R. I. 45. 52, 53, and A. M. 19. 16) says: **Itti amilu lib zikaru u zinnisu ina ribit nina itiittiik**: with male and female singers, or musicians, in the broad street of Nineveh I marched. There is a bas-relief that represents them as both singing and playing on instruments (B. and N. p. 435.) Asshurbanipal, in Ass'l. 132. 20, 21, says, concerning **Dunanu** of **Sapibel:** "His wife, his sons, his daughters, his women, male and female musicians, I brought out;" and on p. 134, lines 46 and 47, it is added, "With players making music I entered Nineveh with rejoicing." Sennacherib also (R. I. 37. 30, and Senn. 35. 30), among others belonging to Merodach baladan, king of Kardunias (Babylonia) speaks of **amilu lib sal lib,** players and women players. In all these inscriptions **lib** is not the Hebrew לב, meaning heart, but לעב, to play. The Arabic *laub* has the same meaning. See "Music."

SKIES.

Isa. 45:8. Let the skies pour down righteousness.

Psa. 77:7. The skies sent out a sound.

In the Chaldean account of the deluge (D. L. 103. 83, and

A. M. 58. 1) it is written, **ushaaznannu shamutu kibaati**: the skies poured down woes, or destructions.

In both languages the skies, and not any living person, are poetically said to do these things.

SKIN.

Job 19:26. And after my skin had been thus destroyed, yet in my flesh shall I see God.

It is manifest that the word is not used here in the literal sense. So also Job 2:4, "Skin for skin, yea, all that a man hath will he give in exchange for his life." This seems to be a proverb in the sense of value for value. Job. 18:13, "It shall devour the strength of his skin," is rendered in the revised version, "devour the members of his body."

This same word is used in a non-natural sense also in Assyrian.

In R. I. 41. 49, and A. M. 15. 15, and Senn. 119. 49 Sennacherib says that in **Khaluli** the enemy was drawn up in front of **maskiya** (my skin), that is, myself, or my body, as in Job 18:13. So the Hebrew uses also גרם and עצם, both meaning bone, for self, or body. See Job 21:23: one dieth, literally, in the bone of his wholeness, *i. e.*, in his full strength, or in his very wholeness; and 2 Kings 9:13: they took every man his garment and put it under him, literally, upon the bone of the steps, *i. e.*, the steps themselves. In Arabic the word for eye is used in the same way—to denote the very thing, or the substance and essence of a thing.

SLAUGHTER.

It denotes the very bloody character of ancient warfare, which was in fact a mutual butchery, that Ezekiel (9:2) calls the weapons used "slaughter weapons." In Assyrian the soldiers themselves were known by the term slaughterers, or butchers. So Asshurnatsirpal was accustomed to speak of them as **tsabi tiduki**, men of slaughter. See R. I. 18. 47, and elsewhere.

Shalmanezer (A. M. 8. 11) uses precisely the same term in a similar sense. See also A. M. 8. 18, R. III. 5. No. 6. 10, and D. L. 98.

SLAVES.

Gen. 17:12. Every man-child in your generations, he that is born in the house, or bought with money of any stranger, who is not of thy seed.

That there were slaves bought with money in Assyria appears from the following bill of sale:

"— Seal of **Nabubikhti usur,** son of **Akhardise** the Hasean, who assists in his art **Zikar Ishtar** in the town of ——. — Seal of **Tebetai** his son. — Seal of **Silim Asshur** his son, the owners of the woman who is sold.

"The girl, **Tavat Hasina**, daughter of **Nabubikhti usur, Nihti Equarrau** (Nitocris) for 16 drachmas of silver (£2 8s.), for **Siha** (her son) to marry her, she bought her. She will be the wife of **Siha.** The price was definitely fixed.

"Whosoever at any time hereafter will stand before me, *i. e.*, the judge, and will invoke me, either **Nabubikhti usur,** or his sons, or his grandsons, or his brothers, or his brothers' sons, or his representative, or any relative of his, who would claim before me the annulment of the contract from **Nihti Equarrau,** her sons, or her grandsons, shall pay 10 minas of silver. Then he shall be free from his contract. He has not sold.

"**Sahpimayu** the sailor. **Bel sum idin,** son of **Udanani. Ardu Tavat,** son of **Ate.** The man —. These are the three heirs of the woman (Nitocris) on account of the fastening of the hands, and the tying of the knots (legal ceremonies), with **Kermeoni,** the heir.

"In the presence of **Akhardise** of **Nipikalantakar,** of **Muthumhepu** of **Hasba,** of **Ululai.**

"In the month of Elul, the first day, of the eponymy of **Asshur Shadu Shagil.**

"Judged before **Nur Shamash,** before **Muthumpaiti,** before **Ate,** before **Nabu idin akhi,** the chief."

The treatment to which slaves were liable may be seen from the following decision: "If a master saws asunder and kills his slaves, or injures their offspring, etc., his hand must measure out every day a half measure of corn" (in requital). R. of P. V. 24. No. 18.

On the other hand, R. of P. new I. 154–162 gives an account of the trial of a slave for falsely claiming to be a free man, and the only penalty imposed was simply the confirmation of the fact that he was a slave.

Slaves in our own land carried the mark of their condition in the color of their skin. This aggravated their suffering, for if they fled from one locality they were more easily recognized wherever they went. If they remained where they were their condition was more hopeless, and now that they are legally free their color is a constant reminder that they were once slaves and invites a continuance of the feelings cherished towards them in their bondage.

In Assyria all this was reversed. The slave was of the same color, and generally of the same people as his master. If in some cases he belonged to another nation, yet the presence of fellow-countrymen who were free prevented his national features from bringing down upon him the odium attached to slavery, and he could rely on the clannish feelings of his tribesmen to help him out of any difficulty in which he might be involved.

Thus his avenues to freedom were many. Not only might he acquire money and purchase liberty, he could also be set free by his master, or he might prove in court that he was unlawfully enslaved, if that was true. Moreover a man could be taken into the service of the king, and a woman into the royal harem, and in either case this made them free. Indeed a former slave could become an officer of the government, and so exercise authority over his quondam owners. All this tended greatly to mitigate the asperities of slavery.

It is interesting to note the price of slaves. One slave woman was taken as payment of a debt of two-thirds of a maneh of silver (£6.) Another was estimated at half a maneh (£4. 10s). A Persian slave woman and her infant at 19 shekels (£2. 17s.) Sukinnu and her three ... years old daughter sold for 25 shekels (£5. 5s.), and a slave with his wife for 55 shekels (£8. 5s.;) also the slave of a slave for two-eighths of a shekel (2s.) See Social Life among the Assyrians, etc., chap. 6.

SLEEPETH.

There is a curious illustration of that ironical appeal of Elijah to the priests of Baal (1 Kings 18:27), "Cry aloud, for he is a god; peradventure he sleepeth, and must be awaked," in an old hymn to Bel, a hymn so old that it is partly in Accadian. One line reads thus: "What is **Bil** (doing) now? He is resting."

The Accadian hymn must have been written, however, many centuries before that heroic conflict of the prophet with the champions of idolatry.

SLIPPERY PLACES.

Jere. 23:12. Wherefore their way shall be unto them as slippery places in the darkness.

This Scripture was impressed so visibly on the mind of the writer while travelling in the mountains of Assyria that the reader will perhaps pardon some personal allusions.

In 1843, while on my way to Amadia with Dr. Grant, the road passed over a hard, smooth shelf of limestone, with a steep cliff rising on one side and a sheer precipice, I know not how deep, on the other. My horse was unwilling to trust himself to the slippery surface, but there was no way round it; that was the only road. I had just said to myself, "If my horse ever falls I hope it will not be here," when, after a moment's scratching of the horse's shoe on the rock, I found his feet over the edge and my foot held firmly under his side. Dr. Grant extricated me from my perilous position and we resumed our journey.

A still greater peril was encountered by Dr. Azariah Smith in the autumn of the following year. Dr. Grant had died in April, and we had gone as far as Julamerk and Berchullah to learn what was the condition of the Nestorians after the massacre. We were high up the mountain on the east of the Zab, heading for Tehoma. At one point we were crossing the path of the avalanches from the summit on our left, and an unbroken slope of bare clay extended from the peaks above to the edge of the precipice at whose base the river rushed noisily along on our right. Nothing but a line of footprints made while the clay was soft in the spring marked the path. In some way Dr. Smith lost his footing and began to slide down the steep incline toward the brink of the cliff. I looked on in horror, expecting to see him go out of sight to destruction, but just before he reached the edge he succeeded in grasping a small shrub that God had planted there for his help, and our sure-footed Nestorians, accustomed to such work, soon landed him safe out of danger and we remounted our saddles.

If now to the slipperiness there had been added darkness our perils had been greatly increased.

SMALL AND GREAT.

There are some expressions so natural that we utter them spontaneously; the lips seem to speak them automatically. In an age of great refinement they may seem too simple to be used and men seek to express the same thing in more elaborate ways, but in the early ages these were precisely the expressions men loved to use. Among them is the familiar phrase, "small and great." In Gen. 19:1, the angels "smote the men that were at the door of the house of Lot with blindness, both small and great." See also 2 Chron. 15:13.

So Asshurbanipal destroyed with the sword both small and great. R. V. 2. 2. and Ass'l. 44. 49. Sennacherib also took captive 200,150 Jews, small and great, male and female. R. I. 37. 17. and A. M. 12. 12, also Senn. 61. 17.

Small cattle. Isa. 43:23, God complains to his people, "Thou hast not brought me the small cattle of thy burnt offerings." These included both sheep and goats. The Hebrew is שׂה and to this corresponds the Assyrian **Tsiinu**. It is of very frequent occurrence, especially in lists of plunder. See R. V. 8. 114 and A. M. 30. 27; R. I. 39. 19 and A. M. 12. 13; R. V. 9. 5 and 42, and A. M. 31. 4 and 34.

SMOKE OF BURNING.

The smoke caused by burning villages in the East is exceedingly black and dense, because there is such a mass of earth upon the roof that it prevents the wood below it from kindling into a blaze. The writer has more than once seen this in the case of war, both on Mt. Lebanon and in Kurdistan.

Similar scenes are mentioned both in Scripture and in the Assyrian monuments.

Gen. 19:28. The smoke of the land went up as the smoke of a furnace. Compare Rev. 18:18.

Sennacherib (R. I. 40. 68, Senn. 109. 68) says that **qutur naaqmuti shunu kima imbari kabti paan shamii rapshuti ushaktim**: the smoke of their burning, like a dark heavy cloud, covered the face of the whole heaven. And he wrote describing precisely that which his own eyes had seen.

SO, SABAKO.

In 2 Kings we read that Shalmaneser, king of Assyria, the fourth of that name, who reigned 727-722 B. C., "found conspiracy in Hoshea, king of Israel, for he had sent messengers to So, king of Egypt, and offered no present to the king of Assyria, as he had done year by year. Therefore the king of Assyria shut him up and bound him in prison." Mr. Birch of the British Museum says, in a note in B. and N. 158: "The hypothesis originally proposed by Marsham, in his commentary on 1 Chron., p. 457, and subsequently adopted by others, is that **Sabaco** is this So;" and in a chamber marked LXI. of the palace which Layard excavated at the southwest corner of the mound of Koyunjik he found many pieces of clay bearing the impressions of seals—the documents originally attached to them had been consumed either by fire or by the decay of the material on which they were written—and one of these bore a perfectly legible impression of the royal seal of Sabako II. of the XXVth dynasty. The other seal connected with it, on the same piece of clay, was Assyrian. The Egyptian king is represented wearing the red cap, **teshr**, seizing an enemy with his left hand by the hair of his head, and about to smite him with the mace which he wields in his right hand, with the hieroglyphics denoting "the perfect god, the lord who creates, Sabako." B. and N. 157, note. The document to which the seal belonged was probably a treaty between Sabako and the king of Assyria (B. and N. 159), and thus furnishes an interesting illustration of this portion of the word of God.

Unfortunately lines 4 and 5 in the hall marked II. by Mons.

Botta, in the great inscription of Sargon which he discovered at Khorsabad, are destroyed. They appear to have described the great battle at Raphia between Shalmaneser IV. and So, Sabako, or **Sebech,** for the name is written in various ways, but line 6 reads, "**Sebech** trusted in his armies and advanced against me to deliver battle. I defeated them by the help of the great god **Asshur,** my god. **Sebech** fled with a shepherd who was watching his sheep and escaped." R. of P. VII. 29.

SON OF GODS.

When Nebuchadrezzar looked into the furnace where Shadrach, Meshech and Abednego had been thrown by his orders, he was astonished to see a fourth person walking with them, all being alike unharmed in the midst of the fire, and described him as like a son of the gods, Dan. 3 : 25. Is there anything in the inscriptions that throws light on this expression: a son of the gods?

One who was devotedly attached to his god was known among the Babylonians as "the son of his god;" but this could not have been the thought of Nebuchadrezzar, for that meaning does not fit the occasion, and so we must seek for another. The first gods of the Babylonians were without any distinction of sex, but afterwards they were known as male and female. **Anu** had his **Anitu, Bil** his **Beltis** and **Ea** his **Davkina.** These last were the parents of **Shamash,** the sun god, called also **Dumuzi (Tammuz),** the only begotten one, known also as **Bil** or **Bil Marduk** by the Babylonians. Then **Namtar** (the plague demon) is the son of **Bil (Mullil); Adar,** called also **Ninip** or **Uras,** the god of war, was another of his sons. The Assyrians also called **Asshur** "the Father who created the gods" (H. L. 128. 2); and these things shed light on the expression.

Then as to the relation of man to the gods. A hymn to **Ea** speaks of him as the creator of the black-headed race, *i. e.*, the non-Shemitic race from Eridu (H. L. 143). In the story of the deluge Ishtar calls herself the mother of the human race (see also R. IV. 61. 27). So that Nebuchadrezzar may have had in mind either a god or a man who was a son of the gods, most likely the former.

Our interest in this incident is greatly increased by another consideration. When the old Babylonians saw fire devouring like a thing of life, and also ministering to the wants of man, they worshipped it as a god. Afterwards **Gibil**, this fire god, was absorbed in **Shamash**, the sun god, and **Shaul**, another form of **Gibil**, became identified with Bil Marduk, the great god of Babylon. It was most astounding, then, for Nebuchadrezzar not only to find his command disobeyed, but that fire, which was the special servant of his god, had no power to punish the disobedient. It was not only that the furnace heated seven times hotter than usual did not burn up rebels, but that the executioner belonging to his own god had no power against them. Surely he must be a Great God against whose servants the all-devouring fire of Merodach could avail nothing. It was the fact that the angel of this God had power to nullify the force of flames acting under Merodach that led Nebuchadrezzar to say that he was like a son of the gods.

SONS OF ZION.

Jeremiah in his Lamentations (4:2) mourns over the calamities of "the precious sons of Zion." Asshurbanipal often speaks of the sons of Assyria. Thus, R. V. 2. 24, Ass'l 29. 57 and A. M. 48. 25 and 26, he says that Urdamani, son of Shabaku, king of Egypt, gathered his army to fight my troops, **apli matu ilu Ashurki,** the sons of Assyria.

He also speaks of **apli Babil**, the sons of Babylon, in R. V. 4. 92, A. M. 27. 5, and Ass'l. 153, 22 and 25, also 168. 27, showing that the form of expression was common to both Hebrew and Assyrian.

SOUL IN LIFE.

Psa. 119:175. Let my soul live.

Psa. 66:9. Who holdeth our soul in life.

The Hebrew word נפש *nephesh*, rendered soul in both these scriptures, means life as well as soul. The corresponding word in the Greek, πνευμα, has the same peculiarity, and precisely the same thing is true in the Assyrian. Thus Asshurbanipal, R. V. 3. 17. Ass'l. 87. 74, says that **Uaallii**, king of **Minni, ashshu balat napishtishu,** in order to the life of his soul; the identical word in

Assyrian which we had in the Hebrew, and, like it, meaning life as well as soul.

"To the saving of their lives" (souls) is a very common phrase also. See R. III. 5. No. 6. 14, and A. M. 8. 20, also R. I. 42. 18, and A. M. 16. 30, also R. III. 14. 39 and 41, and A. M. 17. 15, and 20, and compare Heb. 10: 39.

These things show that in passing from the Hebrew to the Assyrian and *vice versa* we do not leave behind us the phrases that have become familiar to us in either, and as the *usus loquendi* of the Hebrew has moulded the style of our English Bible it follows that we are at home in many Assyrian idioms.

SPOIL.

Num. 31: 12. The captives and the prey and the spoil. Hebrew שלל.

No one can read very far in the records of Assyrian kings without meeting with the Assyrian form of this word. **Shallatu ashlula**, I carried away spoil, is a universal statement, and constantly recurring in the records of their campaigns. Instead of quoting instances where the expression occurs, take the following detailed enumeration of what their spoil consisted in: Asshurnatsirpal records, R. I. 19. 84–88, that he took away from the city of **Asibi**, silver, gold, copper (various forms of this are mentioned), iron, tin, alabaster, hilts for swords and daggers; the women of the palace, their daughters, relatives, and treasures; **esuquru** stones, chariots, war horses, yokes, trappings of horses, and accoutrements of men, **birmi** (variegated?) garments, **qitu** (linen?) garments, beautiful stands of cedar, perfumes, cases of cedar-wood, red and blue purple, heavy wagons, oxen, flocks, etc.

There are two words to denote spoil, **khubtu** and **shallatu**. Both of them are found in R. V. I. 116 and 117, A. M. 46. 7. 8, and Ass'l. 23. 121, **itti khuubti maadi shallati kabitti**: with much plunder and abundant spoils peacefully I returned to Nineveh.

STARS.

Deut. 4: 19. And lest thou lift up thine eyes unto heaven, and when thou seest the sun and the moon and the stars, even all the host of heaven, thou be drawn away and worship them and serve them.

Babylonia was the cradle of astronomy. It was also the earliest home of the worship of the stars. That people named the leading groups of stars, formed a calendar, and noted and recorded eclipses; they divided the annual course of the sun through the sky into twelve sections, and named each from its most prominent star, and thus formed the Zodiac. Its signs are Accadian, from "the directing bull" of the first to "the fish of Ea," which was the last. The fact that their Zodiac began with Taurus proves its antiquity, for that constellation ushered in the year at the vernal equinox from B. C. 4,700 to B. C. 2,500; but the copy of the great astronomical work of Sargon of Accad now extant, called "The Observations of Bel," makes Aries to open the year instead of Taurus, showing what changes the work had undergone in the days of Asshurbanipal.

However that may be, whether in the days of the king of Accad or of the king of Nineveh, the stars were regarded and worshipped as gods. Babylonian cylinders with their frequent representations of a star show that they were their gods. Indeed the most ancient form of the word god was an eight-rayed star, and this was used as the determinative for deity. The enumeration of the sacred days in the month Elul (September) and the rule of worship for each ordained that on the tenth night sacrifices should be offered to two specified stars (R. IV. 32. 47–50, H. L. 72,) and long afterwards an Assyrian scribe required the king to sacrifice to the stars, to **Asshur** and to **Marduk**. It will be noticed that the stars took precedence of both the god of Assyria and the god of Babylon. See H. L. 396–402.

When God would reveal to Abraham the number of his posterity (Gen. 15 : 5), he brought him forth abroad, and said, "Look now toward heaven, and tell the stars, if thou be able to tell them," and he said unto him, "So shall thy seed be."

And when Asshurnatsirpal would describe the immense plunder he had taken from some captured cities, after enumerating the things mentioned under "Spoil," he ends by calling it an immense booty, which, like the stars of heaven, could not be counted. R. I. 19. 86–88. The metaphor is the same, but how different the object and spirit of its use. In the one case it points to a blessing through which all the families of the earth are to be blessed; in the other it is employed by a robber to set forth the extent and thoroughness of his robbery.

STONES, COSTLY.

1 Kings 5:17. And the king commanded and they hewed out great stones, costly (יקרות) stones, to lay the foundation of the house with wrought stone.

These were manifestly different from what we call precious stones, such as John saw in the foundation of the walls of the New Jerusalem (Rev. 21:19, 20). Their costliness depended not on their intrinsic value, but partly on the amount of labor bestowed on them—in hewing them out of the ledge, squaring and shaping them for the place they were to occupy in the structure—and partly on their size. Stones of ten cubits, such as some of them were, must have been very valuable. 1 Kings 7:9, 10.

The Assyrians also made a distinction between precious stones and the square stones used in building. The former they named **abni nisikti,** and the other **abni piili.** D. L. translates this last *quaderstein,* and so does Prof. Lyon in his Sargon, though in his A. M. he renders it only "a kind of stone." I incline, however, to the opinion that the first will be found in the end to be the true meaning. The wall that retains the eastern approach to the bridge across the river Tigris at Mosul is constructed of these large, square, costly stones taken from the palaces of Nineveh. The stone is different from that used for bas-reliefs and inscriptions on the walls of the palaces: that is a dark-colored sulphate of lime, so soft that it can be cut with a knife, but these are of mountain limestone, much harder, and of a lighter color. There must have been some name to distinguish them, and if **piili** is not that name no other is yet found.

The above also furnishes an illustration of Dan. 2:45: "Forasmuch as thou sawest that a stone was cut out of the mountain without hands." Some read that Scripture as though it had no basis in any actual occurrence, but was an imagination of the prophet and nothing else. But both Daniel and his readers had seen these huge costly stones growing under the hands of the workman as he laboriously cut them out of the mountain ledge, and he seizes on the fact as a fit illustration of that work of God out of which shall grow something larger than any costly stone of Baalbek, or the mountain from which it was taken, for it shall fill the earth.

The summer visitor at Cape Ann, in Massachusetts, may see in the granite quarries of Rockport just such a process going on as the prophet has here made use of to illustrate the work of God in the earth, only, while the **abnu piili** is smaller than its parent ledge, and never grows, the kingdom of God shall not cease growing while earth has one square foot of surface unfilled with the glory of the Lord.

STOREHOUSES.

After Joseph had gathered up the grain of the seven years of plenty and stored it in the cities (Gen. 41 : 48), when the famine came he opened the storehouses and sold to the Egyptians (verse 56), and all countries came into Egypt to Joseph to buy corn (verse 57).

In the precepts of Ptah Hotep, an Egyptian papyrus said to be the most ancient book in the world, the writer speaks of the Larit, a well-guarded collection of magazines for storing away all kinds of provisions, and says: "If thou art employed there, determine from the first never to be absent, even when weary; keep an eye on him who enters; what is consigned to thee is above appreciation." Am(o)nteh, overseer of one, tells us that he never closed his eyes at night. The place was guarded so carefully that only the presentation of the seal of the governor could open the door, and its keepers had authority to strike even an official who did not produce the seal. The tax of the corn raised in the district formed the principal contents of these buildings, and the tomb of Rekhmara shows the peasants bringing the whole of their wheat that the government might take its quota, as the farmers in Turkey do to-day. They empty their baskets in a heap, from which the keeper measures out the share due to the state, so fixed are the customs of the East.

In the same tomb we see foreigners bringing their sacks to be filled with grain, as the sons of Jacob did when their brother Joseph ruled in Egypt. Gen. 42 : 3 and 25. See R. of P. new, III. 1–10.

STRAW FOR BRICK.

Ex. 5 : 7. Ye shall no more give the people straw to make brick as heretofore. Let them go and gather straw for themselves.

Many see no use for straw in making brick, unless as fuel for the brick kiln; but the bricks of Assyria and Babylonia are

BABYLONIAN BRICK. (IN THE LOUVRE.)

more than fifteen inches square and three or four inches in thickness, and chopped straw is mixed with the wet clay to give it firmness and consistence. A friend sent me a brick from Nineveh, and, as it had to come on horseback to Constantinople, to save the cost of freight he chopped off all save the inscription in the middle and then split away part of the thickness of the piece that remained. So my heart of a brick from Nineveh not only shows plainly where the iron used for making the inscription broke the straw on the surface, but it shows everywhere in the mass, which is burned of a red color, the impressions of the pieces of the straw in the interior. Of course the straws themselves have disappeared in the burning, but the outline of every line in them is as sharp and clear as when the brick was first moulded, affording a beautiful illustration of the accuracy of Holy Scripture even in little things, and those, too, wholly secular and apart from spiritual teaching.

A building contract made in the sixth year of Nabonidus reads thus: "It is agreed that twelve manehs of silver (£108) be paid for bricks, reeds, beams, doors, and chopped straw for building the house of **Rimut**." The straw was no doubt for the manufacture of a clay coating for the wall and for the floors.

There is an interesting fact that deserves mention in this connection. Mons. Naville, a French explorer in Egypt, discovered in **Tel el Maskhuta** evidence that the ancient religious name of the city was Pithom (Ex. 1:11), and its civil name Succoth (Ex. 13:20). Here, then, was one of the treasure cities built by Israel for Pharaoh (Rameses II.), and from this point they began their long journey to Canaan. Mons. Naville also found the treasure chambers which they built, strongly constructed, and with brick partitions eight to ten feet in thickness. Some of the bricks had straw and some not; were these last those made after the order, "I will not give you straw. Go yourselves; get you straw where ye can find it"? Ex. 10:20, 11. Prof. Sayce's Fresh Light, 60. It would not be a bad idea should some Sabbath schools that have Biblical museums add some of these bricks to their collection.

STRIKE OR THRUST THROUGH.

Psa. 110:5. The Lord at thy right hand shall strike through kings in the day of his wrath.

To the ears of some in this nineteenth century such words sound strange, but they were not unfamiliar to Assyrian ears.

Asshurbanipal (R. V. 9. 78, and A. M. 32. 29, and Ass'l. 278. 61) says in the account of his war with **Vaiteh**, king of Arabia, Beltis pierced through my enemies with her strong horns: **unaqib nakrutiya ina qarnati gashraati**. Four lines farther on he adds, **Dibbaru**, the god of pestilence, resistance devised, and pierced through (**uraassipa**) my enemies.

Isa. 15:19. Thrust through with a sword.

In those connections where the word sword is used in Scripture, **kakki**, weapons, occurs in the Assyrian inscriptions. Thus R. V. 4. 2, A. M. 25. 1, and Ass'l. 158. 65, **urasipushu ina itsu kakki**:

he thrust him through with weapons. And **Nebubilzikri**, grandson of Merodach baladan (R. V. 7. 35, Ass'l. 239. 57), said to his armor-bearer, in the same words as Saul used in Mt. Gilboa, 1 Sam. 31:4, thrust me through, **rasipaanni**, and in line 61 it is added, **urasipushu**, he thrust him through. But where Saul and his armor-bearer fell separately, each on his sword, the Elamite chief and his armor-bearer thrust each other through, **ina kakki**, with their weapons—probably their swords, or the daggers which they carried in their girdles.

SUCCOTH-BENOTH.

2 Kings 17:30. The men of Babylon made Succoth-benoth.

This would seem to be the name of an idol, for it follows that the men of Cuth made Nergal, and the men of Hamath made Ashima, and the Avites made Nibhaz and Tartak.

While scholars agree in this, and are also generally agreed that this name represents **Zirpanit**, the wife of Marduk, who had a chapel in his great temple of E Sagilla set apart for her worship (see Five Great Monarchies I. 136, H. L. 95, K. A. T. 281 and 282), yet nowhere do I find any explanation of the way in which **Tsir**, the great or exalted one, is transformed into Succoth, the Hebrew for tents. It is easy to see how **banit**, the creator (feminine), slides into **benoth**, daughters. I have somewhere met with a verb **banu**, to shine, from which we might get shining tents, a name given on account of the special splendor of her shrine; but that is nothing more than conjecture. So we must live in the hope that future finds will make the matter clearer.

SUICIDE.

1 Sam. 31:4. Saul took his sword and fell upon it. 2 Sam. 17:23. Ahithophel set his house in order, and hanged himself.

In Ass'l. 135. 56 we read that **Nabudamiq**, when he saw the lifeless head of his king Teumman, stabbed himself with the dagger which he carried in his girdle, as the Koords of to-day carry theirs.

So in Section 29 of the great inscription of Sargon in the palace at Khorsabad we are told that **Urzaha**, king of **Urardi**

(Armenia), killed himself in the same manner. See under "Zimri."

But suicide seems to have been much more rare in Assyria than it is among us, perhaps because sinning against greater light makes men more desperate.

SWIFT DESTRUCTION.

This somewhat unusual expression occurs in 2 Pet. 2:1, but it finds an exact parallel in the inscription of **Tugulti pali sharra** (R. I. 13. 1. 42), which reads, **Tugulti pali sharra, nablu, Hhaamtu ma, Shuzuzu, abuub tamhari.** Tiglath Pileser, the swift destroyer, the one who causes to stand, the storm-flood of battle.

This passage is rendered less correctly in R. of P. V. 18. 24: Tiglath Pileser, the ruling constellation, the powerful, the lover of battle.

SWORD, A FLAME OF A.

Gen. 3:24. And the flame of a sword which turned every way, to keep the way of the tree of life.

In an ancient Accadian liturgy, translated by Prof. Sayce in R. of P. III. 125–129, and again in H. L. 480–482 (for the original see R. II. 19) occur the following lines:

> The deluge of battle, the weapon of fifty heads I bear,
> Which like the strong serpent of the sea (drives) the foe before it.
> That whose light gleams forth like the day,
> The terror of whose splendor (overwhelms) the earth,
> Which in my right hand is made to move mightily,
> The child of battle, the flail of the hostile land I bear.

Bil (Merodach) is the speaker of these words, and the weapon is the sickle-shaped sword with which he is represented as fighting with the dragon **Tiamat.**

See also the English translation of Lenormant's Beginnings of History, 137–145.

SYMBOL OF POWER.

Scripture abounds in symbols. Power is represented by a throne or sceptre, and also by a horn. It is worthy of note that the power thus symbolized is power for good, and not for evil. David calls God the horn of his salvation (Psa. 18:2). Hannah said, "Mine horn is exalted in the Lord" (1 Sam. 2 : 1), and Mary sang (Luke 1 : 69), "(God) hath raised up a horn of salvation for us in the house of his servant David." On the other hand, the Psalmist said to the wicked, "Lift not up the horn," *i. e.*, do not put forth your power to do evil.

The Assyrians used the same symbol for power: horns were laid in rows one above another around the royal tiara, and also around the head-dress of the human-headed bulls, to indicate the greatness of their power, and when they came to describe the use of that power they showed that in their minds it was power to destroy.

Asshurbanipal says (R. V. 9. 75-78, and A. M. 32. 27-30) **Beltis,** the beloved of **Bil** the victorious, the mighty (?) (**kadirti**), the exalted, who with **Anu** and **Bil** rules enthroned, pierced my enemies with her strong (**gashraati**) horns. So even a goddess is set forth as not only pushing but piercing the enemies of her worshipper. It is a sad picture, but quite in keeping with the spirit of the people and their history.

TABERING UPON THEIR BREASTS.

This very unique expression occurs in the description given by the prophet Nahum of the reverses of Assyria (2 : 7): "Her handmaids mourn as with the voice of doves, tabering upon their breasts," *i. e.*, smiting their breasts as one beats a drum. The writer felt sure that there must be some special appropriateness in this imagery, but looked in vain through all the commentaries within reach for any explanation of it. At length he found the following in Dr. W. M. Thomson's The Land and the Book II. 562, latest edition: "The low sad plaint of the turtle-dove may be heard all day long at certain seasons in the olive groves and in the solitary valleys among the mountains." "There is a foundation in the habits of the dove for the phrase 'striking upon their breasts,' for when about to utter its plaintive moan the throat is inflated and thrown forward till the head rests on and tabers on the breast."

A description of the conquest of Erech in the Izdubar legends, K. 3200, says:

Like cattle the people are afraid, like doves the slaves mourn.

TAHTIM-HODSHI.

2 Sam. 24:6. Then they came to Gilead, and to the land of Tahtim-hodshi; and they came to Dan-jaan, and about to Zidon.

The route here is plain enough: from Gilead, on the east of the Jordan, Joab and his captains went either across to the west of the Jordan, and so up through the high lands west of the sea of Galilee to Dan, now Banias, or they reached the same point by keeping on the eastern side of the sea of Galilee and crossing the Jordan at Jisr benat Yakoob; perhaps part of them went one way and part the other, so as to take the census thoroughly. Then from Dan they went down to Zidon.

But how about Tahtim-hodshi? This is the only place in Scripture where the name occurs, and it is the despair of all the commentators. The old versions furnish no help, and Gesenius only says, "*vix pro sano habendum.*" In Robinson's Gesenius it is not given at all, only *tahath* is "the lower part," and *hodshi* a matronymic from a woman's name. The Septuagint, however, gives among other renderings of the passage: "The land of the Hittites of Kadesh," and four ancient MSS. agree in this rendering. The Speaker's Commentary adopts it, and above all others, it seems the most likely to be the true emendation of the passage. There was a Kedesh or Kadesh to the west of the waters of Merom, and that may have taken its name from Kadesh on the Orontes and, like it, been inhabited by Hittites, and that lies directly in the route taken by Joab and his captains.

TALENT AS A WEIGHT.

2 Sam. 12:30. The weight thereof a talent of gold.

Not that a talent of gold was of a different weight from a talent of anything else, but the crown had so much weight of gold in it besides the precious stones.

So Asshurnatsirpal (R. I 25. 73) speaks of 20 **biltu** (talents) of silver, a talent of gold, 100 talents of lead, and 100 of iron; manifestly designations of weight in every case.

In like manner Asshurbanipal (R. V. 2. 42, A. M. 50. 24, and Ass'l. 54. 77) speaks of two lofty columns made of white or pure **zahali** (some sort of metal) 2,500 talents in weight, which he took from in front of a temple in Egypt and carried to Assyria; no doubt by water, down the Red Sea and up the Persian Gulf.

TAMMUZ.

Ezek. 8:14. Then he brought me to the door of the gate of the Lord's house which was toward the north; and, behold, there sat the women weeping for Tammuz.

Who and what was Tammuz? This is an interesting question to such as recall the words of Milton (Paradise Lost I. 446-457):

> "Thammuz came next behind,
> Whose annual wound in Lebanon allured
> The Syrian damsels to lament his fate
> In amorous ditties all a summer's day,
> While smooth Adonis from his native rock
> Ran purple to the sea, supposed with blood
> Of Thammuz yearly wounded. The love tale
> Infected Zion's daughters with like heat:
> Whose wanton passions in the sacred porch
> Ezekiel saw, when, by the vision led,
> His eye surveyed the dark idolatries
> Of alienated Judah."

The name Tammuz in Assyrian is **Duzu**, contracted from **Duwuzu**, which represents the original Accadian **Dumuzi** or **Duwuzi**, the son of life. H. L. 232.

Prof. Sayce finds the basis of the legend in the sun god of Eridu, who was the son of the god **Ea** (H. L. 236) and the goddess Ishtar, his wife—represented by the Aphrodite of Greek mythology, as Tammuz was by their Adonis. The legend is that Tammuz was killed by a boar, and Ishtar went down to Hades to bring him back again to life. The philosophic explanation of the myth is the young and beautiful sun god slain by the approach of winter; and this occasioned an annual mourning over the death of Tammuz, noted for its fearful exhibitions of sensual passion and religious frenzy. Greek writers stood aghast at the violations of social decency enjoined as acts of religious worship. The worship of the fierce powers of nature required from the worshipper a sympathetic participation in the sufferings and pleasures of his gods, involving alternate outbursts of frenzied self-torture and frenzied lust. H. L. 267.

Amos (8:10) says, "I will turn your feasts into mourning," and "I will make it as the mourning for an only son;" and in the account of the descent of Ishtar into Hades occurs the line (R. IV. 31. 2. 55), "O my brother, the only one." See translation of the myth, H. L. 221-227.

"When Macrobius states that Adad meant 'the only one' in Syrian, he implies that Adad was identical with Tammuz." H. L. 231. The story of his fate must have come to Phœnicia in those remote times when Chronos (**Ea**) had taken Yeud, his "only begotten son," and, arraying him in royal robes had sacrificed him on an altar in a season of distress. Philo Byblus 44. in H. L. 235.

One word about the season of this annual weeping for Tammuz. In Babylonia he was the god of spring, and his foe was the summer heat which burned up the entire region; but when Julian reached Antioch in the late autumn he found the festival of Adonis being celebrated, "according to ancient usage," after the harvest and before the new year, in Tishri (October). So too Ezekiel saw the women weeping for Tammuz "in the sixth month," and the feast of Hadadrimmon (Zech. 12:10) was in the autumn. Indeed Macrobius tells us that the Syrians explained the boar's tusk that slew the god as the cold and darkness of winter, and that he returned to the upper world with the lengthening daylight.

The gradual disrobing of Ishtar at each one of the seven gates on her descent into Hades, and the equally gradual reclothing of her on her return, denote the gradual destruction of verdure by the approach of winter, and the no less gradual return of verdure in spring.

TARTAN.

Isa. 20:1. In the year that Tartan came unto Ashdod, when Sargon the king of Assyria sent him.

Here the translator evidently takes Tartan for a proper name. The same is true of 2 Kings 18:17. Gesenius also gave it as a proper name (see last page of Robinson's ed. Gesenius), but the Assyrian inscriptions show that it is an official title, and should be translated "the tartan." It is composed from **tur**, the

TELASSAR.

Accadian for son, rendered **aplu** in Assyrian, and **dannu** (strong), and so means the strong son or strong prince. See Ass'l. 14. 1. and 38. 11. The first of these places speaks of the eponym of Marlarim, the turtan of the city Ku—the other simply gives the word, made up as usual of the two ideograms referred to. Senn. 18 and 19 also gives us another eponym: **Bilemurani amilu turtannu;** the **amilu** being the determinative prefix for a class of men. Prof. Sayce in A. L. and S. 156 derives the word from **tur** and **dannu**, but in H. L. 472, note, he says **turta** (guardian priest) whence **turtanu**, and refers to R. II. 31. 26. Prof. Delitzsch says (Hebrew Viewed in the Light of Assyrian Research, p. 12) that it means commander-in-chief, and is a derivative of **turtu,** law. See Bib. Sacra 1884, 382. We have seen that Marlarim was the **turtan** of Ku—. Iludari also (Ass'l. 98. 6) was, according to one copy, **Bil pikhatu** (prefect), and according to another, **turtan** of Luubdi. Then even the Assyrian general might be in time of peace the ruler of a city, or in old age, when unfit for a campaign, he might retire to that position.

TEAR IN PIECES.

Ps. 50:22. Lest I tear you in pieces.

A terrible expression to our modern ears, and one which we can scarcely bear to think was ever carried out in practice.

The thing, however, was not at all unfamiliar to Assyrian thought. Asshurbanipal, one of the mildest of Assyrian kings, says of **Akhsheri,** king of Minni (R. V. 3. 9. and Ass'l. 87. 67), **indaashsharu pagar shu:** they tore his body in pieces. **Nashar** is an eagle, and the verb corresponding to that noun means to tear in pieces the prey which he brings to his eyrie wherewith to feed his young.

TELASSAR.

Isa. 37:12. The children of Eden who were in Telassar. Compare 2 Kings 19:12.

Telassar is in Assyrian **Tilu Asshur,** the hill of Asshur. G. Smith (Hist. of Assyria, 137) locates it in the mountains southeast (query, west, or even northwest?) of Assyria, in the region of the Assyrian **Bit Adini,** the Eden of Isaiah. It is connected with Gozan (Gauzanitis) or Mygdonia (modern Nisibin), Haran (Carrhae), and Reseph, the **Resappa** of the monuments. The first of these lies along the river **Khabor**. The next in the valley of the **Belik,** and the last, probably a day's march west of the Euphrates, on the road from Rucca to Hums. Still all these helps do not enable us definitely to locate the place. The old version in 2 Kings spells it Thelasar, but the new revision Telassar, as in Isaiah. In Amos 1 : 5 Beth Eden is translated Χαρραν in the Septuagint.

TELLOH.

Telloh is the name of a group of ancient mounds on the Shat el hie (river of the serpent), that flows in a southwesterly direction from Kut el Amarah on the Tigris to Elkut on the Euphrates. It is not far from the Tigris, and only a few miles north of ancient **Eridu** (H. L. 142). To Mons. Ernest de Sarzec, French Consul at Baghdad, belongs the honor of having excavated them and thereby added much to our knowledge of southern Babylonia. They contain a small palace, 172 by 101 feet, after the same pattern as the larger one of Sargon at Khorsabad. Digging down the explorer came to another and older ruin. The upper one was built by King **Gudea** about 2800 B. C. It contains the temple of **Ningirsa,** the fire god. A clustered column built wholly of brick in a most artistic way claims special notice; also a number of statues of **Gudea,** and one of **Urbahu,** a predecessor of **Gudea.** The most striking thing, however, in connection with them is that several of them are made of green diorite from Magan (Sinaitic peninsula), one of the hardest of all stones, and the pose is identical with that of Kephren in the museum of Gizeh—also of Menkara and Userenra, all of them Pyramid kings. They are all made out of the same stone from the same locality, and, what is more remarkable, on the knees of **Gudea** is a tablet bearing a scale of an Egyptian cubit of 20. 63 inches, and not the Babylonian one of 21.6 inches.

Some dates are full of interest in this connection. In B. C. 3800 Sargon of Akkad and his son, Naram Sin, say they conquered Magan. A century later, B. C. 3700, Senefru says he drove out the foreigners from Magan, and between the VIth and XIIth dynasties was a period of weakness in Egypt and prosperity in Chaldea, and during this period **Gudea** worked the diorite quarries and turquoise mines of the Sinaitic peninsula.

See H. L.; also P. and C.; but better than either a paper in "Harper's Magazine," 1894, pp. 190–205, by W. S. Chad Boscawen.

TEMPLE.

1 Sam. 1:9. Eli the priest sat upon a seat by a post of the temple (היכל) of the Lord.

Then even the tabernacle, as well as the more splendid structure built by Solomon, was known by that name. In 1 Kings, chap. 6, the word is applied to the latter.

The origin of this word was unknown until it was revealed by the Assyrian inscriptions. Gesenius sought to derive it from a verb, יכל, to be spacious; still he did not give such a verb a place in his lexicon. But the monuments revealed the secret of its origin. The Assyrians named the palace of the king **Bit rabu,** the great house; but the signs that represent these words had been previously used by the Accadians, who read them **E gal** or **E kal,** with precisely the same meaning, and this old Accadian **E kal** reappears, hardly changed, in the Hebrew *Haikal.* In all three languages it is the great house in which the sovereign lord dwells among his people. It was more than seventeen centuries before Christ when the old Accadian **E kal** was supplanted by the Assyrian **Bit rabu**; but the Hebrew *Haikal* preserves it to this day, as the amber preserves the dead insects enclosed in its transparent mass.

We meet the term very frequently in Assyrian, and often in connections that forbid it to be misunderstood. Thus the expression **Sal nishu ekalisu** can mean nothing else than the women of his palace. See R. V. 1. 51 and Ass'l. 308. 31. Also R. 39. 38 and Senn. 64. 38.

The same meaning appears in Prov. 30:28: "The lizard taketh hold with her hands, yet is she in kings' palaces" (היכל); also in Isa. 39:7: "They shall be eunuchs in the palace of the king of Babylon." And so the temple in Jerusalem was only the great house in which the King of kings condescended to dwell visibly among his people, that in their daily life they might joyfully sing, "For great is the Holy One of Israel in the midst of thee." Isa. 12 : 6.

The temple at Jerusalem consisted of a central building, surrounded by courts and other buildings. G. Smith (Atheneum, February 12, 1876; and Hib. Lect. 436-440) gives an account of a Babylonian text that describes **E Sagilla,** " house of the raising of the head," the famous temple of **Bil Marduk** at Babylon. In that he mentions two courts and a court within a court. The number of temples, however, that were here dedicated to different idols was in marked contrast with the one temple of the only living and true God.

The Jewish temple had a sanctuary and a Holy of Holies. Babylonian temples also contained a shrine, **Parakku.** Prof. Lyon in his Manual translates it "sanctuary," and Prof. Sayce as " Holy of Holies." Hib. Lect. 94. It often occupied the upper story of the **ziggurat,** though sometimes it was content with a humbler position; and, like the inner sanctuary of the Jewish temple, was regarded as the special abode of deity.

TENSES.

The Assyrian tenses are formed like the Hebrew, by prefixes and suffixes; thus:

				Permansive	
1st imp: Sing.		3 m.	ishukan		shakin
		3 f.	tashakan		shaknat (a)
		2 m.	tashakan		shaknata
		2 f.	tashakani		shaknati
		1	ashakan		shaknak (u)
	Pl.	3 m.	ishakanu (ni)		shaknu (ni)
		3 f.	ishakana (ni)		shakna
		2 m.	tashakanu		shaknatunu
		2 f.	tashakana		shaknatina (?)
		1	nishakan		shaknani.

TESTAMENT.

Heb. 9 : 16. For where a testament is, there must of necessity be the death of him that made it; for a testament is of force where there hath been death, for doth it ever avail while he that made it liveth?

It is not proposed to endorse this truth by quotations from the monuments, but only to quote what Prof. Sayce calls "the earliest example of a will extant," known as the private will of Sennacherib. Esarhaddon was not heir to the throne by right, for he was not the eldest son, and his father may have expected another to inherit the kingdom ; but Esarhaddon was his favorite and so he deposited certain treasures with the priests of Nebo to be paid over to him according to the following testament:

"I, Sennacherib, universal king, king of Assyria, have given and bequeathed to Esarhaddon my son, afterwards named **Asshur ibil mukinpal** according to my will, rings of gold (gold was preserved in that form), heaps of ivory, a **gil** of gold (Prof. Sayce says cup; it may be a term used as we use the word plate), crowns (?), and rings other than those before mentioned, all the treasures, of which there are heaps, precious stones of various kinds, and a crystal—the weight of them amounting to one-and-a-half manehs and two-and-a-half shekels," etc.

So Sennacherib intended to provide for his favorite son, but through the murder of the testator by two of his sons Esarhaddon became his successor on the throne of Assyria.

For the original testament see R. III. 16. 3 ; and for a translation made about nineteen years ago, which the learned translator could now much improve, see R. of P. I. 138.

THRONE.

1 Kings 10: 18–20. (Solomon) made a great throne of ivory, and overlaid it with the finest gold. There were six steps to the throne; . . . and there were stays on either side by the place of the seat, and two lions standing beside the stays.

We get a very good idea of this throne from that of Sennacherib portrayed herewith. The six steps of Solomon's throne are wanting, for it is set up out of doors, near Lachish ; but even so, Layard says, "it stood on an elevated platform." There was little ivory in it except in the legs, for it was of wood covered with embossed metal (bronze?). The steps or arms are there (as well as a high back), and are supported by twelve men in three rows of four each. The legs ended in pine-

ASSYRIAN ECHOES OF THE WORD.

THE THRONE OF SENNACHERIB.

cone-shaped ornaments of bronze, and a richly embroidered shawl was thrown over the back and hung down almost to the ground. A highly ornamented footstool furnished a support for the king's feet.

For a description of the throne found by Mr. Layard at Nimrood, see B. and N. 198–200.

In the throne. Pharaoh said to Joseph, Gen. 41:40, "Only in the throne will I be greater than thou;" *i. e.*, in everything else we shall stand on the same level. This seems contrary to universal oriental tradition, for in that royalty always takes the precedence in everything. But if we had arranged beforehand for an illustration of this Scripture we could not have devised one so appropriate as we find in a letter of **Aziru** to his father **Dudu**. He calls him "my lord," the title usually employed in addressing Pharaoh. Nor that only, but he uses the following collocation of names (R. of P. new. III. 70. 35 and 36):

"And thus speak Dudu,
And the king my lord, and the nobles."

So striking was this disregard of the usual precedence that it suggested at once these words of Pharaoh to Joseph in the mind of Prof. Sayce (p. 58).

TIGLATH PILESER.

We are told in 2 Kings 15:17 that Menahem began to reign over Israel in the thirty-ninth year of Azariah, king of Judah, and the reign of the latter is described as very prosperous, precluding the idea of his suffering any trouble from Assyria.

The annals of **Tiglath Pileser** confirm this, for though R. III. 9. 23 only mentions his name, the rest of the line being illegible, yet line 31 speaks of him in such an unfriendly way as to show that he had not submitted to Assyria.

2 Kings 15 : 19 relates that **Pul** (Tiglath Pileser) received 1,000 talents of silver from Menahem, who sought in this way to secure the favor of Assyria; and Tiglath Pileser tells us in his annals (R. III. 9. 50), that he received, among other gifts, those of **Ritsunnu** (Rezin) of Damascus and **Minikhiimmi Samirinaaa** (the Samaritan). 2 Kings 15 : 30 informs us that Hoshea conspired against Pekah, and slew him and reigned in his stead; and Tiglath Pileser tells the story thus (R. III. 10. 26-29) — the inscription is very broken, but we can make out: "The land of **Bit Umria** . . . all the assembly of its people and their property I carried to Assyria. **Paqakha** their king I (?) slew. **Ausii** (Hoshea) I appointed to rule over them." We cannot determine who is said to have done the slaying, but Tiglath Pileser claims the credit of seating **Ausii** on the throne.

G. Smith (History of Assyria, p. 6) gives only two kings of this name: T. P. I., B. C. 1120-1100 and T. P. II., B. C. 745-727; but Prof. Sayce, R. of P. new II. 207, gives three: T. P. I., B. C. 1110, T. P. II., B. C. 950, and T. P. III., Pul, or Poros, B. C. 745.

TOWER OF BABEL.

This goes so far back into the past that if any echo reaches us from that confusion it must be only a distant and muffled murmur, yet Prof. Sayce thinks we have a Babylonian version of the occurrence. Mr. Geo. Smith discovered a fragmentary tablet which said of the leader of the rebellion that "the thought of his heart was hostile" (to the gods), and "he had turned against the father of all the gods." When "he was hurrying to seize Babylon, and when small and great were *mingling* the mound, the divine king of the illustrious mound intervened. Anu prayed to his father, the lord of the firmament. All day long he troubled them; in his wrath he overthrew (their) counsel, in his (fury) he set his face to *mingle* their designs; he gave the command, he made strange their plan." The same verb which Moses used, נבלה v. 7, בלל v. 9., is also used in the Assyrian, and in the same sense of mingling or confounding. Prof. Sayce suggests that **Etanna,** the Titanos of Greek writers, may have been the wicked king under whom this event occurred (Fresh Light, 36.) See H. L. 406 and Trans. of Soc. of Bib. Archæology, 1876.

The monuments make the autumnal equinox the time of the occurrence, for September is "the month of the illustrious mound;" so the mound of Borsippa must have been a ruin when the Accadian calendar was formed.

The building of this is described Gen. 11 : 1-9, and as the tower was built in the land of **Shumir** (Shinar) the reader may look for some confirmation of the record from the monuments. We find this in the materials used, burned brick and bitumen being the articles employed exclusively in all that region. Then the journeying from the east (verse 2) is confirmed by the Accadian tradition that they came from the mountain of the east.

We have not yet as detailed a tradition of the Dispersion from the monuments as we have of the deluge.

TRANSLATIONS, ACCURACY OF.

The question of the trustworthiness of the interpretation of the inscriptions by Assyriologists is one of such vital importance that it deserves thorough investigation. It is easy to indulge in general statements, and say that, while at first the translations were more or less tentative, as words were studied in new connections their meaning came to be better understood. So that, just as the ripe fruit differs from the unripe in sourness and immaturity, so our interpretations of the monuments, by a process perfectly natural, become continually more trustworthy.

But an example will present the matter in a clearer light, and let it be one that makes at first anything but a favorable impression, though the more we look into it the more clearly we see that it set out for the true goal from the first, and could not but reach it in due time. It makes it all the more satisfactory that the same learned Assyriologist who made the first translation also gives us the last.

In his Lectures on Babylonian Literature (p. 78), which unfortunately was published without date, and has not even a preface or printer's colophon to supply the omission, but which appears to date from about 1877, Prof. Sayce gives the following transliteration and translation of R. III. 16. 2.

1 **Abat binat sharri ana**
The prayer of the daughter of the king to
2 **Neshat D. P. Asshuri sharrati**
The lady of the city of Asshur the queen
3 **Ataa Umpiki la tasadhdhiri**
Why Umpiki dost thou not write?
4 **Impuki la taqabbii**
Impuki dost thou not say?
5 **Ulaa iqabbiu**
Thus they say
6 **Maa annitu belat sa**
This (is) the prayer to her lady
7 **Sha D. P. D. P. Serua edherat**
Of Serua edherat
8 **Binati rabitav sha bit-riduti**
Eldest daughter of the harem
9 **Sha D. P. Asshur-etil-ili-yukinni,**
Of Asshur etil ili yukinni
10 **Sharru rabu, sharru dannu, shar kishshati, shar mat Asshuri**
The great king, the mighty king, the universal king, king of Assyria.
11 **Va atti marat dannat bilti sha D. P. Asshurbanipal**
And thou art the potent princess, the lady of Asshurbanipal,
12 **Ibil sharri rabi sha bit riduti**
Son of the great king, of the harem
13 **sha D. P. Asshur akhi iddina, shar D. P. Asshur**
Of Esarhaddon, king of Assyria.

In October, 1890, at least 13 years later, Prof. S. gave the following translation of the same tablet (R. of P. new IV. XII):

"Order of the daughter of the king to the lady **Asshur Sharrat**. Now do not inscribe thy tablet, do not utter thy word, lest perhaps they say, This is the mistress of **Serua edherat** the eldest daughter of the harem of **Asshur etil ili yukinni,** the great king, the powerful king, the king of legions (all), the king of Assyria. Yet thou art a mighty princess, the lady of the house of Asshurbanipal, the eldest royal son of the harem of Esarhaddon, king of Assyria."

A few notes may throw some light on the changes in this last translation, and may help some beginner in Assyrian:

Line 1. The professor in his second rendering reads **amat** for **abat,** and although Prof. Delitzsch does not give **mat** as one of the sounds of that sign, yet it must be so, for this is not a prayer but an order.

Line 2. The determinative prefix here is **alu,** city, followed by the ideogram for the old capital of Assyria, now Calah Shergat, literally, heart city — a very good definition of a capital. **Nishat,** better **belit.**

Line 3. He makes **ataa** an affirmative particle, not an interrogative; **um** is read **dup,** which very closely resembles it; **pi** is the phonetic complement, showing what was the last syllable of the word. **Duppu,** gen. **Duppi,** a tablet; and **ki** is the pronominal termination of the second person singular, feminine.

Line 4. **Impuki** is obscure. D. L. says, under **im, Duppu?** But this is not written, it is spoken. So that Prof. Sayce's rendering is better. It seems to be a form derived from **nabu,** to speak. For **ki** see line 3.

Line 5. **Ulaa** is rightly rendered lest, or, literally, that (they may) not.

Line 6. **Annitu** is the demonstrative pronoun, feminine, this. I am not quite sure about **sa** at the end of the line. It is an ideogram for band and may imply something of superior authority. The writer does not deny this power, but would have it used wisely. The implication seems to be that **Asshur sharrat** had in some way "assumed authority" over the family of the reigning king.

Line 7. **Serua edherat,** his eldest daughter, is evidently the writer of this "order."

Line 8. The reader will notice both here and in line 12 the *usus loquendi* that calls the child of the king the child of his harem.

Line 10. **Shar Kishshati** is equivalent to universal king, or lord of all.

Line 11. **Atti** is the personal pronoun, second, singular, feminine. **Marat,** feminine of **mar,** offspring, and here wellrendered princess, **bilti,** lady.

So the professor was quite excusable in missing the exact drift of the communication at first, because some words were strange, and either **um** was written by mistake for **dup,** or there was no clew showing that it was used as an ideogram rather than a phonogram. Yet, for all that, he was on the right road and was sure sooner or later to arrive at its true meaning, and every new tablet discovered fills up the lacunæ of those we have, and either confirms right renderings or corrects mistakes.

Even the Hebrew has still a large space left for progress in this direction, and the Assyrian has so much more material whence to draw emendation that it would not be strange if it came in ahead of the language that has been studied so much longer at the goal of a comparative perfection.

TRAVAILING WOMEN.

We cannot but be struck with the perfect naturalness with which the Bible mentions such things, and well is it that it does, for so woman in her hour of anguish may know that she has a compassionate High Priest. Heb. 11 : 18.

The Lord Jesus himself spoke words full of sympathy to such, though one would hardly realize it from the form that is given to his prophetic condolence even in the revised version of Matt. 24 : 19. The feeling there intended is no doubt this: "Alas for them who in such a time of trouble are in a condition that renders flight difficult, if not impossible."

The monuments are equally free in the mention of such matters. In the 11th Izdubar Tablet (D. L. 104. 110, A. M. 59. 3 and R. III. 50. 3. 8), Ishtar cries out like a woman in travail; but it is hardly necessary to give examples.

TREAD DOWN, TRAMPLE ON.

The word describes an act implying combined power and hate, haughtiness and brutality. Micah 5 : 5. "The Assyrian shall tread in our palaces." Compare Job 40 : 12; Psa. 50 : 12; Isa. 10 : 6; Zech. 10 : 5; Mal. 4 : 3.

The idea is expressed in a single word in R. V. 2. 30, A. M. 50. 3, and Ass'l. 52. 63, **akbusu**: I had trodden, or trampled on. G. Smith here renders crossed over, thus losing the whole force of the expression. See also R. V. 4. 102 and A. M. 27. 12: Upon the whole of them I trampled. Sargon describes himself (Layard I. 4, A. M. 5. 10) as the strong man, **mukabiis**

kishad aabishu, treading on the necks of them that hate him. See Josh. 10:24; Psa. 18:40.

So Asshurnatsirpal speaks of the god Ninip or Adar (R. I. 17. 3) as **kabisi irtsiti rapshuti :** treading down the broad earth, and Layard, Standard Inscription I. 4, A. M. 5. 10, **mukabiis kishad aabishu, daaish kullat nakruti :** treading on the necks of them that hate him, trampling on all enemies.

TREE OF LIFE.

Gen. 2:9. The tree of life also in the midst of the garden. Compare Prov. 3:18, 9:30; Rev. 2:7, 22:2.

Trees are very prominent among the religious emblems of the monuments. One of the oldest names of Babylon is **Dintirki,** the place, or the land, of the tree of life. This at one time seems to have been regarded as that kind of pine, called *Snobar* in Arabic, which bears a large cone, the kernels of the seeds being cooked and eaten. It is also called the stone pine. See Royal Seal of Sennacherib, B. and N. 160, also 606; also C. G. 85. The winged figures in the bas-reliefs are often represented as holding the cone in their hands; see L. N. I. 71 and 118. At another time it is a palm-tree; see C. G., 2d ed., 112, also B. and N. 604. Again, it assumes a conventional form, as in L. N. II. 233, C. G. 97, and P. and C. I. 63 and 213.

There is a curious representation on an early Babylonian cylinder already referred to, on page 293, of two persons seated under a pine-tree (?) engaged in earnest discussion, with two cones or other fruit hanging within reach of their hands, that would pass readily for Adam and Eve discussing the question of eating the forbidden fruit.

On seals there is often a symbol of the deity over the tree while the priest worships before it. Mons. Botta presented the writer with one of them. See illustration on page 291; another is given B. and N. 606, and still another on page 160.

The Biblical student will not be troubled by the mention of two different sacred trees on the monuments when he remembers that there was not only a tree of life in Eden, but also the tree of the knowledge of good and evil ; *i.e.*, the tree in connection with which that knowledge entered the world : not a tree bearing a fruit by that name, which would be indeed mythical, while all these memorials of the event call for something more than a myth to furnish an explanation of their existence. A myth could hardly supply a foundation solid enough for such very concrete things to stand on.

It is significant also in this connection that Babylonian tradition has placed the garden of Eden near the ancient city of Eridu, and an old hymn has been preserved which says (H. L., 238):

> In Eridu a stalk grew overshadowing. In a holy place it grew green.
> Its root of white crystal extended down to the deep.
> Before the god Ea it grew. Eridu was very fertile.
> Its abode was in the central point of the earth;
> Its foliage formed the couch of **Zikum,** the (primeval) mother.
> Into its holy abode, spreading a shade like a forest, no man has entered.
> There is the home of the mighty mother who walks across the sky.

As Prof. Sayce adds, "This reminds us of the Ygg-drasil of Norse mythology, the world-tree, whose roots go down into the abode of death while its top rises into Asgard, the heaven of the gods."

The cedar, the tree that shatters the power of the Incubus, was to Babylonia what the rowan tree was to Scandinavia. It was used in connection with sacrifice, as in that first one offered by Khasisadra after the flood. It was also used in magic rites performed to heal the sick, and hence was also set forth on the monuments as a tree of life.

The vine also was called **gistin,** a tree of life, perhaps from the exhilarating nature of the wine which it produced; and that proverbial saying about "every man sitting under his own vine" may have had reference to this. The conventional form also of the tree of life in some of the bas-reliefs may have been an attempt to combine in one both the tree of life and the vine. P. and C. II. 99.

TREES.

1 Kings 4:33. And he (Solomon) spake of trees, from the cedar that is in Lebanon even unto the hyssop that springeth out of the wall.

Eccles. 2:4-6. I made me great works; I builded me

houses; I planted me vineyards; I made me gardens and parks and I planted trees in them of all kinds of fruit. I made me pools of water to water therefrom the forest where trees were reared.

Many may have the impression that in these things Solomon was different from all other oriental kings; but many kings of Assyria devoted themselves to the same line of culture. Tiglath Pileser I. (B. C. 1120-1100) lived about half a century before Solomon, and he says in his inscriptions (R. I. 15. 7. 17-27, translated in R. of P. new I. 115): "The cedar, the **likkarin** tree and the **allakan** tree, from the countries which I had conquered, these trees, which among the kings my fathers before me no one had planted, I took, and in the plantations of my country I planted, and the costly fruit of the plantation which did not exist in my country I took (there). The plantations of Assyria I established." It must have required a great deal of care to transport living cedar trees from Lebanon to Assyria, and no less knowledge of plant life to select the soil and climate favorable to their growth. His words imply that he had more than one such plantation in different localities. "Kew gardens," then, existed nearly 3,000 years ago in old Assyria.

Four centuries later Sargon (B. C. 722-705), in describing his city of Dur Sargina, says: "I planted around it an extensive park (or paradise) resembling Mount Amanus (Mount Amanus was their *beau ideal* of a mountain forest), of all the forest trees of Syria, and all its mountain plants." S. 42. 41.

Sennacherib, son of Sargon (B. C. 705-681), seems to have inherited his father's taste for groves as well as for war and building. He says (Senn. 147. 57): "I made large plantations, resembling the forests of Amanus, of every choice plant and reed, the products of mountains and of the land of Chaldea." He tells also of cleaning out and deepening water courses, of developing springs, and other things that denote great attainments in what we would term landscape gardening.

Isaiah says, 41 : 19, "I will plant in the wilderness the cedar, the acacia tree, and the myrtle and the olive tree. I will set in the desert the fir tree, the pine, and the box tree together," and promises that "the desert shall rejoice and blossom as the rose," 35:1. Sargon and his son must have wrought a similar change in the region around Nineveh, but no one who travels over the treeless plain of Assyria to-day finds the least trace of their royal paradise. Their only monuments are the buried ruins of their palaces. These also in the days of their glory were much indebted to trees for their beauty, as Asshurnatsirpal says (A. M. 6. 20–23): "A palace of cedar, one of cypress, one of juniper, one of **urkarini,** one of palm tree, one of **pistachio** and **ladanum,** for the abode of my royalty, for the majesty of my lordship, which is enduring, I erected in it."

TREES FELLED.

2 Kings 3:25 ... and they stopped all the fountains of water and felled all the good trees.

This was a common procedure in ancient warfare, but it was expressly forbidden by the Mosaic law, and the law is so peculiar that we cannot forbear quoting it: "When thou shalt besiege a city a long time, in making war against it to take it, thou shalt not destroy the trees thereof by wielding an axe against them, for thou mayest eat of them, and thou shalt not cut them down: for is the tree of the field a man that it should be besieged of thee? Only the trees which thou knowest that they be not trees for food thou shalt destroy, and cut them down." Deut. 20:19. How different this is from the practice of the Moslem Arab in our day in destroying the banana groves of Africa and leaving their owners to perish of starvation, as described by Mr. Stanley.

Among the many horrid cruelties inflicted by Asshurnatsirpal we cannot expect so small a thing as the cutting down of trees to be noticed, but the monuments show us soldiers in the act of cutting down palm trees. Anc. Mon. I. 475, B. and N. 588.

Egypt also did this. Brugsch Bey tells us that Thothmes III. destroyed Kadesh of the Hittites, and cut down all the trees. Egypt under the Pharaohs, I. 376, in Emp. of Hittites, 17.

TRIBUTE.

Tribute was paid to rulers as an acknowledgment of subjection to them and a means of maintaining their power. When the payer of tribute had gold and silver he paid that, and when he had neither he paid what he had, and so tribute was often paid in kind. Thus 2 Kings 3:4 tells us that Mesha, king of Moab, paid to king Jehoram the wool of 100,000 lambs and of 100,000 rams, or, as it may be rendered, so many animals with the wool.

Precisely so Asshurnatsirpal tells us that he received tribute in kind from his provinces. See his inscription *passim* (R. I. 17-26, and translated R. of P. new II. 128-177). A dozen times at least it is oxen, sheep, wine, etc., and again it is horses, silver, gold, lead, copper, bowls of copper, plates of copper, variegated cloths, linen vestments, cedar beams, treasures of the palace, chariots, riding-horses and their grooms, teams, ivory dishes, couches, yokes and thrones, beads and torques of gold, iron, furniture, images, weapons, couches, and legs of couches, female musicians, etc. Nothing seemed to come amiss. Even a porpoise is mentioned as one item in the tribute received from the Syrian coast. R. of P. new II. 172. 88.

Tribute was not made up of things only, but of service also. The Canaanites who were not driven out from Gezer "were made servants to do task work." Josh. 16:10 and 17:13. So also Solomon "raised from them a levy of bond-servants," 1 Kings 9:21, and 2 Chron. 8:8, "but of the children of Israel Solomon made no servants, but they were men of war, and chief of his captains, and rulers of his chariots and of his horsemen," (v. 9). And Sargon in giving an account of the building of Dur Sargina says, "People from the four quarters, having a foreign tongue, and discordant and mutually unintelligible words, dwellers on mountain and plain, all whom the sovereign warrior of the gods ruled over, whom in the name of Asshur my lord I had taken captive by the power of my sword, I made to speak one language, and caused to dwell in it," *i. e.*, they were the serfs or peasantry; as an Arab would say, they were the fellahin. "But the sons of Asshur who were intelligent I made to keep guard, as they were readers, and feared god and the king." S. 11. 72-12. 74, also 38. 72-74).

Again, Darius made a decree that of the tribute beyond the river expenses be given to the elders of the Jews for the building of the house of God. Ezra 6:8. So also in Assyria, "the city of Nineveh was taxed 30 talents: 10 of it for clothes, 20 more for the fleet, and a fresh assessment of 10"—though there must have been more besides, for it follows—"274 talents in all." R. of P. II. 141.

The city of Calah was assessed 5 talents and 4 and a special tax of 30 for the highlands. The city of Enil 10 talents for the lowlands. Nisibis 20 talents for 600 makakhi, whatever they might be. The city of Alikhu had to pay for 600 royal robes, and 6 vestures of linen, 3 talents for the keeping of the gates, and — talents for the collector, and — again for the chariots, — for the astronomer, 3 for fringed dresses, — for the throne of the palace, and 2 for royal robes of purple, and so on. So the assignment of the taxes beyond the river for the building of the temple was in perfect accordance with Assyrian custom, though one wonders whether this prevision of the use to be made of the tax made it any easier to be collected. Other interesting details may be found in R. II. 53. 2, 3 and 4, and the translation in R. of P. XI. 138, 46. We cannot forbear quoting one, which seems to be an utterance of the collector or treasurer: "We do not receive (*i. e.*, retain for ourselves); what we take we give up."

TRUST IN GOD.

Psa. 40:4. Blessed is the man that maketh the Lord his trust. Psa. 34:8 and Prov. 29:25.

Asshurnatsirpal (R. I. 17. 22) calls Asshur and Shamash **Ilani tiikliya**, the gods of my trust. Sennacherib (R. I. 41. 50 and 51, A. M. 15. 17-19, and Senn. 120. 50, 51) says, I prayed to Asshur, Sin, Shamash, Bil, Nabu, Nergal, Ishtar of Nineveh and Ishtar of Arbela, the gods in whom I trust—**Ilani tiikliya,** as before.

There is no end to such expressions in the monuments; one can hardly go amiss to find them at the beginning of the annals of any king.

TRUST IN HIMSELF.

Prov. 28:26. He that trusteth in his own heart is a fool. Compare Psa. 44:6, 49:6, 52:7; 2 Cor. 1:9, and Luke 18:9.

In the Assyrian monuments frequently, when Asshurbanipal narrates the rebellion of a tributary king, he begins by stating that he trusted in himself, or in his own might. Thus (R. V. 2. 113, A. M. 22. 25, Ass'l. 66. 27) he says: "Gyges, king of Lydia, paid no regard to the command of the god Asshur, my creator. To his own strength (or forces) he trusted, **ana imuk ramanishu ittakil ma**, and made his heart strong." Then follows an account of his rebellion and overthrow in answer to the prayers of Asshurbanipal to Asshur and Ishtar.

So **Tarquu** (Tirhakah) (R. V. 1. 57, A. M. 42. 6, Ass'l. 16. 56) despised the power of Asshur, Ishtar, and the great gods, and trusted to his own might; and then follows the account of his war with Assyria, his defeat and death.

ULAI.

There is a very unusual expression in Dan. 8: 16: "between the Ulai." The Ulai is a river, and in their perplexity our translators have rendered it "between the banks of Ulai." Gesenius would render it, "among the windings of the Ulai." Mr. Loftus furnishes a very satisfactory solution of the enigma (C. and S. 423–431). He was informed by an Arab named Sheikh Mohammed that the Kerkhah (ancient Khoaspes) anciently bifurcated near Pai Pul, and the eastern branch flowed about two miles east of the great mound at Shush (ancient Shushan), and after receiving the Shaour (it is Shapur on the map) below a ford named Umm et timmin, emptied into the Karûn (ancient Pasitigris, *i. e.*, Little Tigris) at Ahwaz. A few days after, riding northeast to Dizful, on the ancient Coprates, now called the Diz or Dizful River, he crossed a depression, about 900 feet in width and from twelve to twenty feet deep, with the ruins of irrigating canals on both sides, and known among the Arabs as Shat el atiq (the old river). A little water from the Kerkhah still flows in the old channel, but is exhausted in irrigation. This explains the language of Daniel as meaning between the two channels of the Ulai—the western, which was the natural bed of the river, and this eastern, which was probably raised by a dam and carried along a higher level for purposes of irrigation. It shows also how Alexander could, according to Quintus Curtius, cross the Choaspes before entering Susa from the west (Lib. 2. 9), and again, according to Strabo (Casauban, 729), cross the same river, going from Susa eastward to Persepolis. Ptolemy (Lib. 6. ch. 3) speaks also of the two branches of the Eulæus (Ulai), and Pliny (Lib. 6. ch. 27) says that the Eulæus surrounded the citadel of the Susians. This ancient branch of the Ulai also explains how Alexander, then at Susa, could embark and sail down the Eulæus. Arrian Exped. Alex. 7. 7.

UNCHANGEABLENESS IN MAN AND IN GOD.

Asshurnatsirpal ruled Assyria from B. C. 885 to 860. Though the kingdom had begun to recover from a long decline before his accession, still he was the founder of the later Assyrian empire. He rebuilt the city of Calah, that had been founded by Shalmaneser I., and enclosed it with a wall five miles in circumference. He built his palace on an artificial mound facing the Tigris, and from it came some of the finest monuments now in the British Museum. His annals fill ten pages, each 21x14 inches, of vol. I. of "The Inscriptions of Western Asia," and contain 389 lines.

He begins with the praises of the god **Ninip**, called also **Adar** or **Uras**, who is described as "the strong one whose command never changes, the leader whose utterance is immutable, the mighty god who does not change his purpose." Compare Psa. 89: 34, "I will not alter the thing that is gone out of my lips."

We might seek to determine whether the Assyrian or the Hebrew utterance was expressed more tastefully, or which was the original, or whether both are independent of each other, but as each simply declares that the utterances are unchangeable it is more important to know the moral character of each.

The spirit of **Ninip** is plain enough. He was the son of **Bil** of **Nipur** (Niffer), known also as **Mullil**, the strong, who was the Pluto of the Babylonians, and as such opposed to the gods of the heavenly regions. His messengers were demons, nightmares and diseases; his wife was **Allat** or **Ninkigal**, *i. e.*, lady of the great place, which is Hades. He was represented by the fierce sun of an Assyrian sky, scorching the earth through the long summer day. He is further described as "the warrior whose battle charge is resistless, the crusher of opposition who tramples down the broad earth, the unsparing one whose onset sweeps down the foe like a flood." It was his father whose anger caused the flood, and who was with difficulty held back by the other gods from destroying the ship of **Khasisadra** and all on board. The mild Merodach was the favorite god of Babylon, but this Assyrian fighter chose **Ninip,** the warrior of the gods, who breathed out threatenings and slaughter.

It is very true that an idol is not a real existence (1 Cor. 8:4 and 10:19), but as God created man in his own likeness so man devises gods after his own evil likeness, and in worshipping them intensifies that evil. So this worshipper of **Ninip** describes himself as one whom none can resist; who subdues the rebellious and treads on the necks of his enemies. He is "the consumer of the violent, the unsparing one"—a favorite expression, often repeated. Four times he speaks of shedding the blood of mountaineers till he dyed the mountains in blood like heaps of wool. He says, "Asshur entrusted to my hands his weapon that spares not;" thus linking in his cruelties with his idolatry, and declaring that in him unchanging meant never swerving from his course of ferocious cruelty. He even styles himself "the mighty monster (vampire); the powerful king foreordained by **Sin** (the moon god); the beloved of **Rammanu** (god of storms) (in 2 Kings 5:18 it is Rimmon), the strongest of the gods, the weapon unsparing, the butcher of his foes, am I."

It would be a relief to know that all this was idle rhodomontade, but while his annals narrate the facts already mentioned under the head of "Cruelties," they are also graven on the stones of his palace as worthy to be handed down to the latest ages. As we think of those pyramids of living men with earth enough above the writhing mass in which to insert stakes for impaling others, unchangeableness of purpose has a terrible meaning; the denunciations of Nahum (2:7–3:4) are better appreciated, as also those words of the Psalmist, " The dark places of the earth are full of the habitations of violence." Psa. 74:20.

We gladly turn from these horrors to study the unchangeableness of God. We have the key to this in those words of Malachi (3:6): "Because I, the Lord, change not, therefore ye, O sons of Jacob, are not consumed." We tremble lest our sins exhaust the grace of God; yet even though we are faithless he abideth faithful, for he cannot deny himself (2 Tim. 2:13). "For what if some were without faith; shall their want of faith make of none effect the faithfulness of God?" Rom. 3:3. How different this Scripture view of the unchangeableness of God from the merciless persistence of the king of Assyria in cruelty under the fancied sanction of his gods! Were they not so familiar we might quote in illustration of the same divine unchangeableness those precious words of the apostle in Rom. 8:32-35 and 37-39. The following, however, may not be so familiar: "They say, If a man put away his wife, and she go from him and become another man's, shall he return to her again? Shall not that land be greatly polluted? But (though) thou hast played the harlot with many lovers, yet return again unto me, saith the Lord" (Jer. 3:1). "Return, thou backsliding Israel, saith the Lord; I will not look in anger on you, for I am merciful, saith the Lord. Only acknowledge thine iniquity that thou hast transgressed against the Lord thy God ... Return, O backsliding Israel, for I am a husband unto you, saith the Lord" (vs. 12-14).

Assyria may furnish many valuable illustrations of Holy Scripture, but nothing more satisfying than this contrast between the unchangeableness of man and that of God. Better acquaintance with God through his word forms our best defence against all the assaults of unbelief.

UR.

Ur of the Chaldees must always be of interest as the native city of Abraham, the father of the faithful. On account of a slight resemblance in sound and some Jewish tradition it has been located in northern Mesopotamia; but the resemblance between **Ur** and **Orfa** does not furnish a very substantial basis for a derivation, nor does the older name of **Orrha** help the matter. The very name, Ur of the Chaldees, points us to Chaldea as the true locality. Was the name Chaldea ever applied to any district north of Mosul? We must look, then, in Southern Babylonia, and two places there have been made to claim the honor. One is Warka; but that is Erech, and therefore cannot be Ur, for they were separate cities and cotemporaneous. The other is Mugheir. At first sight it seems more difficult to make Ur out of Mugheir than out of Orfa; but this is only a modern name given to its principal ruin by the Arabs. This structure is built of large bricks cemented with bitumen, hence called in Arabic "El Mugheir," *i. e.*, "the bitumened." Of course that modern name is no more the ancient name of the city than El Mujelibe or El Qasr is the ancient name of Babylon. Mr. J. E. Taylor, who first explored the ruin, discovered the ancient name of Ur in the cylinders under the corners of its upper story, and that settled the point beyond all question. This is endorsed by the old Jewish names of Qamarina and Khaldiopolis, for each city in Chaldea was dedicated to a god, and Ur was dedicated to Sin, the moon god. Qamarina is derived from Qamr, the Arabic for the moon, and Khaldiopolis is also from Khaldi, the Armenian name of the same planet.

The ruin where the cylinders were found was the temple of Sin, built by Urukh, the oldest king of Babylonia of whom we have any record, and repaired by his successors as late as Nabonidus (**Nabunahid**, *i. e.*, Nebo is exalted) B. C. 556–541.

The inscription which vindicated the historical accuracy of Daniel in making Belshazzar the last king of Babylon was found in this ruin. (See "Belshazzar.") Mugheir is now a verdureless desolation, consisting of a circle of mounds half a mile in diameter and some two miles in circumference, surrounded by a cemetery that has been in use more than 4,000 years. The Euphrates is now six miles away, but in winter the surrounding lowlands are flooded by the river; anciently both river and gulf were so near that Ur was a seaport. These mounds have not yet been explored, but though one part of the place is now an arid waste and another a useless marsh, ancient canals irrigated the desert and drained the marsh, so that the beautiful palm groves that now line the river once dotted the whole region, while the fields, according to Herodotus, yielded two crops of wheat every year, with an increase of two hundred-fold. The landscape in those days must have formed a bright contrast to the bare sand-hills and reedy jungle of to-day, for Turkish mismanagement and neglect make the great river an engine of destruction instead of a power for good.

VEIL.

1 Cor. 11 : 10. For this cause ought the woman to have a sign of authority on her head, because of the angels.

It is not intended to go into the discussion concerning the meaning of this obscure statement; only to enquire whether the following lines in R. IV. 1. 45, translated by Prof. Sayce in H. L. 451. 21 and 452. 22, may not illustrate the text. Prof. Sayce reads, "The god of the man, O shepherd who lookest after the sheepcote, is toward the man whom his god has carried away to the veil;" and in a note says, "The reference is to a sort of monastic vow, whereby a man placed himself under the protection of the deity, and, as in the case of Izdubar, by wearing a veil on his head became proof against all evil spells."

VERBS.

The Assyrian verb has four primary, four secondary, and two tertiary stems:

PRIMARY:

I. 1. Peal, as **Ishkun**, denoting a simple act.

II. 1. Pael, as **Ushakkin**, intensive, causative, or making an intransitive Peal transitive.

III. 1. Shaphel, as **Ushashkin**, causative.

IV. 1. Nifal, as **Isshakin**, passive, rarely reflexive.

SECONDARY:

I. 2. Ifte'al, as **Ishtakin**, reflexive.

II. 2. Ifta'al, as **Ushtakkin**, reflexive.

III. 2. Ishtafal, as **Ushtashkin**, reflexive.

IV. 2. Ittafal, as **Ittashkin**, reflexive.

TERTIARY:

I. 3. Iftane'al, as **Ishtanakin**, reflexive.

IV. 3. Ittanafal, as **Ittanashkin**, reflexive.

Each of these stems has a first and second imperfect.

The first imperfect in I. 1., has **a** after the first radical, and **a** or **u** or **i** after the second, as **ikash shadu**.

The second imperfect in I. 1., has no vowel after the first radical, and **a, i,** or **u** after the second, as **ikshud**.

In the other stems they are distinguished by the vowel **a** after the second radical in the first imperfect, and **i** after the same radical in the 2nd imperfect. The 1st imperfect denotes continuous action, past, present, or to come, and the 2nd is the tense of narration, marking an act as occurring at a point of time.

Both forms of the imperfect may be used as precatives.

Many verbs in Assyrian and Hebrew are identical, as נדן, **nadanu,** to give; גמר, **gamaru,** to complete; קרב, **qarabu,** to approach. Some are almost the same, as נשא, **nashu,** to lift. In one case a curious reversal of the stem letters occurs. In Hebrew ברך, *barak*, means to bless, but in Assyrian the verb is **karab.** Thus D. L. 106. 181 and A. M. 61. 24, in the account of the deluge, we have **ikarrabannashi:** he was blessing us.

VESSELS OF THE TEMPLE.

Daniel tells us that Jehoiakim and a part of the vessels of the temple of God were given into the hands of Nebuchadrezzar, king of Babylon, who carried the vessels into the land of Shinar and deposited them in the treasure house of (Merodach) his god. Dan. 1:2.

The Standard Inscription of Nebuchadrezzar, col. 2. 30-39, says, "Silver, gold, the shining of precious stones, copper, **mismakanna** (palm?) wood, cedar, whatever is precious, a large abundance, the produce of mountains, the fulness of seas, a rich present, a splendid gift to my city of Babylon, into his presence I brought." Of course the whole of it was the plunder of the countries he had conquered, and we may suppose that these vessels of the temple were among the large abundance of those precious things that went into the treasure house of his god, which appears to have been regarded as safer than the treasure house of the king. See also col. 8. 1. 30, and R. of P. new III. 107. and 119.

VOICE.

Exod. 19:19. Moses spake, and God answered him by a voice. Compare 1 Kings 19:12; Job 37:4 and 5; Psa. 18:13; Psa. 68:33; Isa. 40:6, 46:6; Ezek. 1:24, 10:5; Dan. 4:31; Matt. 3:17, 17:5; John 12:28 and 30; Acts 9:7; Acts 10:13 and 15; 2 Pet. 1:17; Rev. 1:12, and 16:17.

These Scriptures point out a very prominent mode of divine manifestation, and it is precisely what we should expect, for God is a Spirit, and therefore invisible.

It is remarkable that, though idolatry deals in tangible images, yet the same theophany appears in the Assyrian monuments, and characteristically in one that dates far back, near to the time when as yet idolatry had not blotted out the memory of the true God.

In the 11th Izdubar tablet (R. IV. 50. 2. 31., A. M. 58. 1, and D. L. 103. 83) we read, "A voice said (**izzakir kuukru**) that in the evening the heavens will rain down destructions" (**kibaati**), and the same words are repeated three times below.

WATER-WORKS.

The son of David who was king in Jerusalem says (Eccles. 2:6), "I made me pools of water, to water therefrom the forest where trees were reared;" and the pools of Solomon (El birak) near Urtas, south of Bethlelem, furnish a good illustration of their construction. A subterranean collection of springs was carefully excavated, the several streams brought together and conveyed underground to a large reservoir, partly excavated in the rock and partly built up with stone and cement; this overflowed into a second one of similar construction, and this again into a third, and from these the plantations were watered. Robinson's Bibl. Res. II. 164–168.

So Sennacherib tells us that he prepared beautiful fountains from the borders of the city of **Kisiri** down to the vicinity of Nineveh (Senn. 148. 59), and Mr. Layard found a tunnel excavated in the rock on the banks of the Zab, south of Nimrood. It was entered by two low arches from the river, whose swift current seems to have lowered its channel during the centuries since the work was done. The tunnel form soon gives place to a deep open channel, also cut in the rock, that extends a mile into the plain. A slab with a cuneiform inscription bore witness to its Assyrian origin. It was doubtless intended for the irrigation of the plains around Nimrood. L. N. I. 83.

Another monument of Assyrian art in the Tigris opposite this city claims a notice in this connection. The Arabs call it the Sidd (dam), also Sakar en Nimrood, and El Awayee (the roaring). It is built of large stones firmly bound together with iron clamps, and extends across the river. Rafts find little trouble in floating over it at high water, but in summer, when the river is low, even they cannot pass in safety.

Accidents often occur here to large rafts, and even with his small *kellek* Mr. Layard was carried over it with some violence in the middle of April, when the river was in flood. L. N. I. 30.

The Assyrians must have used caissons or a coffer-dam in its construction, yet even with all the thoroughness which was thus made possible it is amazing that it has stood so long, and a passage will have to be made through it with dynamite before steamers can go up to Mosul.

This also, most likely, had some connection with the irrigation of the low lands upon the shore.

WAY PREPARED, THE.

Mark 1 : 3. Make ye ready the way of the Lord, make his paths straight.

In Great Britain the roads are marvels of excellence, and in our own land one may guess the age of a town by the character of its highways.

In Assyria the roads along which Sargon, Sennacherib, Nebuchadrezzar and Cyrus marched their armies were mere paths, and, though in some places the wear of centuries has made them plain enough, in others, where the open country invites to change, or snow and mud compel the traveller to turn out of the beaten track, the sultan's highway cannot be distinguished from the path to a neighboring hamlet. These roads are never repaired unless something occurs to make them absolutely impassable. So when some Pasha is expected to pass that way the people are compelled to turn out and prepare the way before him. This is done without wages, the laborers also furnishing their own tools and provisions. This refers to a state of things a generation ago; what change may have taken place in connection with the construction of recent highways in the interior the writer has no means of knowing.

The state of the roads in ancient times may be learned from the Assyrian annals. Tiglath Pileser I. (B. C. 1120–1100) says, "I marched against the people of the country of **Mildis** (Malatia) the powerful rebels. I crossed mighty mountains in an almost impassable region. The best part I traversed in my chariot, and other portions on foot. At the mountain of **Aruma** (Aram: Mt. Taurus?), where my chariot could not go, I left it, and like a lion marched at the head of my army. R. I. 10. 68–76, translated R. of P. new I. 98. Compare also R. of P. new I. 100. 20–25 and 101. 46–51. He also tells us how he managed in the worst places (R. I. 10. 7–9 and R. of P. new I. 96): "in difficult mountains, impassable paths I made passable with picks of bronze."

So also Asshurnatsirpal (B. C. 885–860) tells us (R. I. 21.76 and 77, translated R. of P. new II. 155), "Across the very rugged mountain of **Lara**, which was impassable for chariots and armies, I hewed my way with axes (sledge-hammers?) of iron and pick-axes of bronze." Again, in the 95th line of the same column, he says, "For six days I wrought with the same tools in the recesses of the rugged mountains of **Kasyari** before I could make it at all passable for my chariots and soldiers." We can understand now why in the bas-reliefs we sometimes see a chariot borne on the shoulders of several soldiers over the rocks.

WEIGHING GOLD AND SILVER.

Gen. 23 : 16. Abraham weighed to Ephron the silver which he had named in the audience of the sons of Heth, 400 shekels of silver, current money with the merchant. Jer. 32 : 9, 10. "And I bought the field of Hanameel, my uncle's son, that was in Anathoth, and weighed him the money, even seventeen shekels of silver; and I subscribed the evidence and sealed it, and took witnesses and weighed him the money in the balances.

We call such a document a deed, making prominent the act of sale; the Jews called it the evidence, giving prominence to the proof it furnished of the transaction. But to us the strangest thing about it is that the silver was weighed, not counted. The fact is that in ancient times coins did not exist; neither the early Babylonian nor the Assyrian empire ever had a coin. In the later Babylonian period they began to use them. Till then gold and silver were always weighed. The 300 talents of silver and 30 talents of gold paid by Hezekiah to Sennacherib (2 Kings 18:14) were weights, not coins, and to procure them Hezekiah not only emptied his own treasury but cut off the gold from the doors of the temple.

When Assyrian kings received tribute from other nations they often specified gold and silver among the articles given, but without stating the quantity; at other times they specified only the weight, as in the case of Hezekiah. There is no direct statement in the monuments that they had no coins, for the very good reason that they were not conscious of the want of them; the idea of a coin was unknown to them. The darics coined by King Darius, the Persian, seem to have been among the earliest coins, though Lydia or the Hittites, in northern Syria and Asia Minor, in this matter may have preceded Darius.

It is an interesting corroboration of these things that the names of so many coins designate either the act of weighing—like the Hebrew shekel, from the verb *shakal*, to weigh—or are measures of weight. Thus the talent among the Greeks denoted 57 lbs. avoirdupois, nearly, and among the Hebrews 93¾ lbs. So, too, the mina or pound was a weight of 15.02 ounces—compare the £ sterling; and that again was divided into 100 drachmas, the *dirhem* of the Arabs to-day. So Mexicans speak of the ounce (of silver), all of them pointing back to the time when gold and silver were not counted, but weighed.

WENT UP.

Even this familiar phrase, used so often in connection with going up to worship in the temple, occurs also in the inscriptions. See 2 Kings 19:14 and 23:2; Luke 18:10; Acts 3:1.

Asshurbanipal, after his great victory over the Arabians (R. V. 6. 24), "for the offering of sacrifices went up to **E Babara**, the abode of their lordships, before Beltis, the mother of the great gods, the beloved bride of Asshur," etc.

The origin of the expression both in Scripture and in Assyrian was the elevation of the temple. Jerusalem was higher than the most of Palestine, and the Babylonian temples were built on artificial mounds, and their **ziggurat** (towers) also gave an aspect of elevation to the whole structure with which they were connected.

WHEEL.

Psa. 83:13 in the old version reads, "O my God, make them like a wheel;" but in the new revision, "make them like the whirling dust, as stubble before the wind." So also Isa. 17:13, "They shall be chased as the chaff of the mountains before the wind, and like the whirling dust before the storm;" here the old version reads, "like a rolling thing before the whirlwind."

It is the same Hebrew word that is rendered wheel, whirling dust, and a rolling thing; viz., גלגל. Gesenius renders this (1) a wheel, (2) a whirlwind, and (3) chaff, stubble; anything driven round before a whirlwind. Now it will be noticed that the parallellism in both passages is a vegetable production; in the one case stubble, and in the other chaff. May we not expect to find this wheel and rolling thing vegetable also? Then notice that peculiar rendering of Gesenius: "*Anything driven round before a whirlwind;*" certainly a very unusual definition.

Now turn to Dr. W. M. Thomson's vivid delineation of the wild artichoke broken off from its root and careering before the wind—a round globular mass, about a foot in diameter, so thick with leaves and branches that it is like a ship with all sail set, but so dry and light that it rolls and bounds before the gale like a huge soap-bubble insured against breakage. See Land and Book, latest ed., I. 212, 213. This is equally noticeable in Assyria and in Syria. Here as well as in her ancient monuments Assyria furnishes a beautiful illustration of the word of God.

WHIRLWIND.

Prov. 1 : 27. And your calamity cometh on as a whirlwind.

This is a very striking and effective figure of speech: one can almost see the calamity whirling over the plain like the dust cloud of the storm.

This is a favorite figure in Assyrian, as we would expect it to be with such a fierce race of warriors, only their storm vocabulary is so copious that there is a great variety in the terms used. Thus Asshurbanipal says (Ass'l. III. 88, and R. V. 3. 34), **kima tiib mikhii izzi**: like the onset of a mighty storm. Again (R. III. 14, 44, and A. M. 17. 25), he repeats the same, and adds **kima imbari askhuupshu**: like a black cloud I prostrated him, *i. e.*, with the shock of my attack. Again (Ass'l. 56. 74), They swept it (Thebes) like a whirlwind or tempest, **abubis**. The word used in R. I. 35, No. 3. 13, is **abubanis**.

WIND.

Ezek. 12 : 14. I will scatter toward every wind all that are round about him to help him.

This is a common expression to-day, and I think I have found a corresponding expression in Assyrian. In R. V. 6. 64 Asshurbanipal says, Their gods and their goddesses I gave **ana zakiki** or **zaqiqi**. G. S. in Ass'l. 230. 98 renders this, into captivity; but D. L. 140 renders **zaqiqu**, wind, and as that is the latest so it is most probably the true rendering here. Thus we have the phrase in Assyrian as well as in Hebrew and in our own familiar speech.

WINE.

The Hebrew name for wine is יין, which Gesenius says means fermenting, effervescing, from the verb יין, to boil up. The Arabic term is *khumr*, concerning which it is enough to say that *khumir* means leaven. The Arabic for unfermented wine would thus be un*khummir*ed *khumr*. The same things might be said concerning the Syriac *khamro* or *khamra*.

The Assyrians gave it the name of **karanu** or **kurunnu**, and the verb **karanu** means to heap up; so that the Assyrian term points us to the froth that heaps up on the surface of wine during the process of fermentation or when it is poured from vessel to vessel. The estimation in which it was held may be inferred from the mention of it so often in the annals of Asshurnatsirpal and Shalmanezer II. Among the articles received as tribute from the various provinces of the empire the mention of it is too frequent to call for any specific reference. It takes its place with the gold, silver and copper, the herds and flocks, and the various manufactured articles that found a place in the royal treasury.

Then, though the tree of life was originally a *conifer* among the people who migrated from the high mountains of Elam and southwestern Persia, yet afterwards both the palm-tree and the vine were admitted among the representatives of that tree of Eden, and the reader will remember that wine was made from the palm-tree as well as from the vine. So early did man mistake the transient excitement of stimulation for the vigor of a true vitality—a confusion, alas, that the world has not yet outgrown. He is a genuine benefactor who enables the young to discriminate between things so radically different before it is too late to avoid the consequences.

The prophet Ezekiel enumerates among the commodities traded in by the merchants of Tyre "the wine of Helbon" (27:18), and in a Babylonian wine list, copied from a bilingual tablet and printed in R. II. 44. 3. 9, we find **karanu khulbunu:** wine of Helbon. Nebuchadrezzar also in one of his inscriptions (R. I. 65. 23) makes mention of the oil of the same country, **shamnu mat khiilbunum;** so that Helbon must have been famous for both wine and oil.

WITNESSES.

Deut. 17:6. At the mouth of two witnesses or three witnesses shall he that is to die be put to death; at the mouth of one witness he shall not be put to death. 1 Tim. 6:12. Thou hast professed a good profession before many witnesses.

The reason for this beneficent law is obvious. One witness may be prejudiced, he may even be the bitter enemy of the one accused; but when two or more witnesses agree in the same testimony there is not so much danger from that source. Then, even if a witness is kindly disposed toward the accused, the requirement of more than one witness guards against the error that may arise from mistake or forgetfulness.

Among the Assyrians we find a larger number of witnesses required, perhaps because they were less trustworthy in that country, perhaps to secure greater accuracy.

It is also worthy of note that while the Hebrew legislation mainly had regard to matters of right and wrong, or to acts viewed in their moral relations, the Assyrian witnesses testify mostly to the correctness of pecuniary transactions, or they guard against the repudiation of bargains.

The largest number of witnesses the writer has observed on any document is sixteen. These testify to the sale of a piece of land in the town of Dindu on the 28th of Tebet (December), in the 10th year of **Marduk idin akhi,** king of Babylon (R. of P. IX. 96–99); and the smallest number is four. In one case they testify to a sale of slaves (R. of P. XI. 95), and in another to the lending of 40 *tetradrachmæ* (Do. 106), and in a third to the payment of some cattle or money instead (Do. new IV. 99). Other cases, in which the number of witnesses varies from five to nine, may be found in pp. 92–96 and in Vol. I. 140, 141, Vol. VII. 114–116.

Five witnesses testify that in a time of famine during the reign of **Shamash shum ukin,** king of Babylon, **Remut** lent to **Mushezib Marduk** and **Kulla** his wife the sum of 50 shekels to purchase necessaries. And the beautiful thing about it was that the debt was to be paid, not on such and such a day, but when the land again became fertile, and that without interest, for none is mentioned. It is pleasant to find the record of such kindness among so many things that were just the opposite. (R. of P. new IV. 97. See also p. 105.)

WOMAN, CONDITION OF, IN ANCIENT TIMES.

The glimpses we get of the condition of woman in the times of the Old Testament suggest both grievous wrong and great suffering. God created one woman for one man, but men in the hardness of their hearts soon set aside the divine order of things and set up another of their own, full of impurity and violence, and of course full of distress and degradation. The first intima-

WOMAN, THE VIRTUOUS. 353

tion we have of polygamy is in Gen. 4:19; but we are not told when or how it originated. The inspired historian seals up the humiliating record from human eyes; though now and then he allows the seething mass to flash out into the light. In 1 Sam. 27:19 we are told that David made a raid upon the Geshurites and saved neither man nor woman alive. Was it amid that bloody extermination or previously that he added Maacah, the daughter of the king of Geshur, to the number of his wives? We know not which would call for the severest reprobation: the extermination of the people of one already his father-in-law, or the compelling her whom his sword had left sole survivor to be the wife of the slayer of her parents and her people. 2 Sam. 3:3. And what a record that is of David's son and successor (1 Kings 11:3): "He had seven hundred wives, princesses, and three hundred concubines." What pen can do justice to the wretchedness of these thousand blighted lives!

Unfortunately the Assyrian monuments endorse to the fullest extent this shameful record. From a single expedition of one of the kings of Assyria (Asshurbanipal) we cull the following unblushing statements. Baal, king of Tyre, sent his own daughter and the daughters of his brother as concubines. R. V. 2. 56 and 57; also A. M. 21. 6 and 7. The same thing is said of Yakinlu, king of Aruadda (R. V. 2. 65 and 66; also A. M. 21. 13 and 14), of **Mugallu,** king of **Tabali** (R. V. 2. 70 and 71; also A. M. 21. 17 and 18), and of **Saandasharmi,** king of Cilicia. R. V. 2. 78 and 79; also A. M. 21, 22 and 23.

In the light of such facts it is safe to affirm that, so far as concerns the present life, the gospel has conferred no greater temporal boon on the race than the lifting up of woman from being trodden under foot to that position of equality for which she was created; and the spiritual blessings in the same line of things are as much higher than the temporal as the heaven is higher than the earth.

WOMAN, THE VIRTUOUS.

The portrait of the virtuous woman as drawn in Prov. 31 is too long for quotation here, but another portrait of the same object may be found in R. II. 35, No. 4; and that the reader may compare the two here is a translation of it, from R. of P. XI. 159, 160:

> The woman who being married has caressed no man,
> Who in her husband's absence does not paint herself,
> Who in her husband's absence takes not off her clothes,
> Whose veil no free man of pure race has raised,*
> Who never moistened her teeth with an intoxicating drink.

The rest, unfortunately, is wanting.

The character of the Hebrew woman was far superior to that of the heathen around her. No doubt it was the excellence of her Jewish mother-in-law that led Ruth to choose Jehovah as her God. But woman never attained her highest glory till Christ came. Mary, however good she may have been when she became the mother of Christ, far excelled that goodness under the influence of daily communion with him in her home; and ever since, Christ has been leading a larger number of her sex to higher attainment in the divine life, so that in the millennium woman on earth may become a worthy likeness of woman in heaven.

WORD, THE.

John 1:1. In the beginning was the Word.

Of course we cannot expect anything from Chaldea or Assyria to rise to the height of this great argument, or betray any knowledge of so great a mystery, and yet we are startled to find the following lines in the third tablet on the Creation, translated in R. of P. (new) I. 137. 19-28:

> Then they set in their midst his word unique.
> To Merodach, their first-born, they spake:
> May thy destiny, O lord, go before the god of heaven;
> May he confirm (?) the destruction and creation of all that is said.
> Set thy mouth, let it destroy his word.
> Turn, speak unto it, and let him lift up his word (again).
> He spake, and with his mouth destroyed his word;
> He turned, he spake unto it and his word was recreated.
> Like (the word) that issues from his mouth, the gods his fathers saw it.
> They rejoiced, they approached Merodach the king.

Psa. 119:74 and 147. I hoped in thy word.

Asshurbanipal says (R. V. 3:127), I trusted in the word of **Sin,** my lord.

* Before slaves and men of low rank Eastern women do not wear a veil.

Isa. 55:11. So shall my word be that goeth forth out of my mouth: it shall not return unto me void, but it shall accomplish that which I please, and it shall prosper in the thing whereto I sent it.

In R. I. 17. 4, Asshurnatsirpal describes **Ninip (Adar)** as the mighty one, the word of whose mouth does not bend or change.

WORDS.

When a ruler took the oath of office he was said to utter his words before the Lord. So Jephthah, Judg. 11:11, and Josiah, 2 Chron. 34:31. The inscriptions use the same term to denote covenants of allegiance. So Asshurbanipal (R. V. 1. 119) complains that the kings whom he had set over Egypt **la itstsuru mamit ilani rabuti**: did not keep the word (or oath) of the great gods. The noun is from the verb **imuu,** to speak.

Words smooth as butter: Psa. 55:21. His mouth was smooth as butter, but his heart was war. His words were softer than oil, yet were they drawn swords. Comp. Psa. 62:4; Prov. 5:3, 4.

These scriptures are very expressive, and there is something in the inscriptions which corresponds, only as one word is somewhat doubtful the meaning does not strike one with the same force. In R. V. 3. 80, 81, Asshurbanipal says, **shaptiishu itammaa tuubaati shaplanu libbashu qatsir niirtu**: his lips spoke pleasant things, but underneath, his heart binds yokes, **niirtu. Niru** is a yoke, **niirtu** may be the feminine or the plural, or it may be a word having an entirely different meaning.

WORLD, GOD OR PRINCE OF THIS.

2 Cor. 4:4. In whom the god of this world hath blinded the minds of the unbelieving.

John 12:31. Now shall the prince of this world be cast out. Comp. 14:30 and 16:11.

There is no question that both of these titles refer to Satan, the great enemy of God and man, who alienates the world from its Maker, and seeks to use it in his war against God.

It is a curious coincidence that **Mullil,** the lord of Sheol, answering to the Pluto of the Greeks, is also called the lord of the world. See R. I. 9. 3, 4. In line 3 he is called **sharru gimir,** king of all, or universal king, and in line 4 **bil matati,** lord of countries, or lord of the world. See H. L. 146.

WORSHIPPER.

In Acts 19:35 the town clerk of Ephesus says to the excited populace assembled in the theatre, "Ye men of Ephesus, what man is there who knoweth not how that the city of the Ephesians is temple-keeper of the great Artemis?" He means to describe the city as wholly devoted to the worship of that goddess, so that its inhabitants gloried in being even hewers of wood and drawers of water in her service.

Similar expressions occur on the monuments. Cyrus in his inscription, discovered by Mr. Hormuzd Rassam in 1879 at Babylon, calls that city **palukha ilu Marduk,** the worshipper of the god Merodach (R. V. 35. 7 and A. M. 39. 24). In the 17th line he speaks of Nabonidus as **la palikh shu,** not his worshipper; in the 23d line he claims for himself the honor of having daily looked after his worship, and in the 26th line he says, "For these things Marduk, the great lord, rejoiced in me, **Kuraash** (Cyrus), his worshipper; and in the last line he calls himself in his prayer to Merodach "King Kuraash, thy worshipper," **palikh-ka.**

Asshurnatsirpal, 883–859 B. C., styles himself "the exalted prince, worshipper of the great gods." Layard I. 13, and A. M. 6. 3, 4. "Worship him, all ye gods," Psalm 97:7, is quoted, Heb. 1:6, thus: "And let all the angels of God worship him." It finds an illustration in the India House inscription of Nebuchadrezzar, 1. 55–62. See R. of P. new III. 108. "The Quarter of Assembly, the chapel of the Fates, wherein at Zagmuku the opening of the year, on the eighth (and) the eleventh day (Marduk), the divine king, the god of heaven (and) earth, the lord of heaven, taketh up his abode. The gods of heaven and earth with awe submit to him; they bow, they take their stand before him."

WRONGS OF WOMAN.

Just as the continuance of the human race is provided for in the existence of sex, so the well-being of families, communities and nations—other things being equal—may be measured by the degree of their conformity to the law of God concerning the relations of the sexes. No one can promote human welfare in this life more effectually than by promoting morality, and no one can strike a more cruel blow at human happiness than by pursuing the contrary course. One of the earliest and most bitter fruits of the first transgression was wide-spread immorality. In the expressive words of Scripture, "All flesh corrupted his way upon the earth" (Gen. 6:12). Man, because he was the stronger, made a slave of woman, and ruthlessly sought his own gratification at her cost. The things in which God had fitted woman to make the largest contribution to human well-being man's selfishness made the means of her greatest suffering. Others might look on and pass by on the other side, but God looked down with divine compassion and struck at the root of the evil when he said, "Thou shalt not commit adultery" (Ex. 20:14): Thou, whoever thou art, young or old, rich or poor, man or woman, shalt not break this law; so impartial was the law of God. And its penalty was dealt out with even-handed equity to both parties in the transgression (Lev. 20:10. Deut 22:22.) In that impartial way alone could justice be done.

In quite a different key are the following Accadian laws: "If a woman is unfaithful to her husband, and says to him, 'Thou art not my husband,' into the river they throw her." Those sacks sunk in the Bosphorus, then, with their living occupants, were only the carrying out of a very ancient law. But when, on the other hand, "A husband says to his wife, 'Thou art not my wife,' half a maneh of silver he weighs out in payment." R. of P. 3. 24; and compare "Social Life Among Assyrians," 46.

Why so great difference in the penalty meted out to those equally guilty before God? Is it said, no mention is made of unfaithfulness on the part of the man? It is to be feared that the omission is not so much a proof of his innocence as of the existence even at that day of the spirit which counts that a mere peccadillo in a man which is a capital offence in a woman; and it may be that some laws in Christian communities to-day are administered more in the spirit of that heathen law of Assyria than of the holy and beneficent law of God.

A sensitive spirit may shrink from reading Deut 22:13-21,

but whoso is wise and understands it knows the loving-kindness of the Lord. He makes the parents of the wronged one the agents of her deliverance, well knowing that none would feel such interest in righting the wrong, and then wondrously makes the same means which rescue the innocent make more sure the punishment of the guilty. For though he is "full of compassion and gracious, slow to anger, and plenteous in mercy and truth," yet "he will by no means clear the guilty." Ex. 34:6, 7. I have not yet found an echo to this law in Assyria or Babylonia, though I would rejoice to find there such a disposition to right the wrongs of woman.

YAHUA OR YAOOA (JEHU).

The name of the destroyer of the house of Ahab finds a place in the obelisk of black marble which Mr. Layard discovered at Nimrood. The Assyrian form of the name is **Yahua**, with a very slight sound to "**h**," if indeed there is any. Shalmaneser II. (B. C. 860-825) erected the obelisk and inscribed on it the annals of his reign in 190 lines of cuneiform writing. Five rows of bas-reliefs illustrate the annals, and the second row pictures the bearers of the tribute of Jehu to the Assyrian king. The bas-reliefs run round the four sides of the obelisk, and the inscription reads, "The tribute of **Yahua**, son of **Khuumri** (Omri). Silver, gold, bowls of gold, cups of gold, pitchers (or pails) of gold, lead, sceptres for the hand of the king, and staves (or shafts for spears) I received." R. III. 5. No. 6. 64, and A. M. 8. 27. Also R. of P. V. 41, par. 2, and R. of P. new IV. 52, par. 2.

The term son (son of Omri) is used here in the broader sense of descendant. Shalmanezer does not seem to have known the manner of Jehu's accession to the throne, but supposed that as he occupied the place of Omri he of course belonged to his family.

This tribute was received B. C. 842, while the king of Damascus was being besieged in his capital, and neighboring monarchs felt the need of securing the favor of his powerful assailant.

This obelisk illustrates the inaccuracy of writers in minor details. Prof. Sayce (R. of P. V. 27) gives its height as five feet.

Morris Jastrow, Jr., in the January Century, 1894, p. 408, says "about seven feet;" and the writer of "The Buried City of the East," London, 1851, gives it as "six feet six inches." As it stands in the British Museum that question can be definitely settled at any time by any one who will take the trouble to measure it. It was doubtless a *lapsus pennæ* that led Rev. V. Scheil, in R. of P. new IV. 17, to say that the obelisk was found at Koyunjik instead of Nimrood.

A very good view of the obelisk is given in the Century for January, 1894, p. 400, and the first line of inscription, p. 401, reads, "The presents of Yaooa, son of Khumri, silvers," *i. e.*, bars or ingots of silver.

YEAR OF THE KING.

There are many eras in use by different nations: in India the era of the Kaliyuga, 3101 B. C.; in China one dating from 2700 B. C.; in Persia the era of Yezdijird III. from 632 A. D. The Hejira of Mohammed dates from 622 A. D.; the Roman era from the founding of Rome, *circa* 750 B. C.; that of the Seleucidæ from 312 B. C., and many more. But it is a part of the homage which Christian nations render to Christ that all history is made to date from his incarnation. Whatever has taken place since then took place in such and such a year of our Lord; whatever occurred previous to that event occurred in such and such a year B. C.; so that the whole of human history is made to sustain a relation to his appearance on the earth, and Christians never feel that they fully understand other eras till they have translated them into this Christian era.

And yet the Bible never uses that era unless in the purely personal record of his going up to the temple in his twelfth year (Luke 11 : 42), and entering on his public ministry when he " was about thirty years of age. Luke 3 : 23.

The Scriptures usually record events as occurring in a certain year of the reign of a certain king. Thus, "In the fourteenth year of King Hezekiah, Sennacherib, king of Assyria, came up against all the fenced cities of Judah and took them." Isa. 36 : 1. Again, "In the third year of the reign of Jehoiakim, king of Judah, came Nebuchadrezzar, king of Babylon, unto

Jerusalem and besieged it." Dan. 1 : 1. And, "In the first year of Darius, the son of Ahasuerus," etc. Dan. 9 : 1.

In precisely the same way Shalmanezer II. (B. C. 860-825) says, "In the first year of my reign (**paliya**), I crossed the river Euphrates in the time of flood and marched to the Mediterranean Sea"—sea of the setting sun he calls it. A. M. 7. 23. So on the next page he tells what he did in the sixth and eighteenth years of his reign; and such quotations might be made *ad libitum*.

There was one chronological arrangement peculiar to this people, and that was the so-called eponym, or, as they called it, **limmu,** each year being known by the name of some ruler who gave the eponym for that year. Thus in the reign of Sennacherib we read, "First of the month Tisri, **limmu Tekiya,** ruler of Damascus." That was B. C. 694, and B. C. 691 has its eponym from **Bilemurani,** ruler of Carchemish. See Senn. 15. 17.

It would seem as though Luke the evangelist had heard of this system of denoting the year when he wrote (3 : 1), "Now in the fifteenth year of the reign of Tiberius Cæsar, Pontius Pilate being governor of Judea, Herod being tetrarch of Galilee, and his brother Philip tetrarch of the region of Iturea and Trachonitis, and Lysanias the tetrarch of Abilene." There was no eponym to be mentioned, but he recorded the names of all the rulers in the region so as to make the date unmistakable.

YOKE.

Matt. 11 : 29. Take my yoke upon you. Hos. 11 : 4. I was to them as they that take off the yoke on their jaws.

The ox yoke lies at the foundation of this figure of speech, which seems to have suggested itself to all nations in describing the oppressive governments of ancient times. The use of it is very common in Assyrian. Asshurbanipal (R. V. 7. 19, Ass'l. 238. 44) says of **Nabu-bil-zikri,** grandson of Merodach-baladan, He has thrown off the yoke of my lordship, **izluu niru bilutiya,** and charges **Vaiteh** of Arabia with the same crime. R. V. 7. 87. Ass'l. 256. 101. In the 88th line he says that the god Asshur had appointed **Vaiteh** to bear his yoke, **ishudu abshuani**—another word for yoke. So he says of **Ummanigas,** king of Elam (Ass'l. 129.

105), **izbata niriya**, he took my yoke; the very expression used by Christ. He says the same of **Tammaritu**, another king of Elam. Ass'l. 206. 49. And the god Asshur says to Gyges in a dream, Take the yoke of Asshurbanipal, king of Assyria, the beloved of Asshur, king of the gods, lord of all; or more fully, Take the yoke of his lordship, reverence his majesty, and bow down to his dominion. Ass'l. 74. 17.

ZAPHENATH-PANEAH.

When Pharaoh had made Joseph ruler over all the land of Egypt he called his name Zaphenath-paneah (Gen. 41 : 45), and Dr. Brugsch makes out of it the Egyptian title, *Za pau nt pa aa nkh*, which he interprets to mean " governor of the district of the place of life;" *i. e.*, the district in which Israel afterwards built Pithom and Ramses, where also was the land of Goshen. " Fresh Light," etc., 50.

ZIDON, KINGS OF.

Jeremiah 25 : 22 speaks of "all the kings of Zidon," a somewhat tantalizing expression, as it gives us to understand that there were many of them, but does not even give us their names or the time when they lived; nor have we very much that may satisfy our desire to become acquainted with the ancient dwellers in this primeval city. They have all gone, and their records with them. Now and then, however, a ray of light struggles out to us from their tombs, though we are accustomed to associate darkness only with such places. On the morning of January 20, 1855, the sarcophagus of king Ashmunezer was discovered in its rock-hewn chamber. It was of black sienite, very hard, and highly polished, and its lid bore a perfect Phœnician inscription twenty-two lines long. This may be characterized as above all things intensely human. When he lived we do not know, nor at what age he died, but after giving his name and lineage he breaks out in the passionate cry, " I am snatched away before my time, like the flowing of a stream," and the disappearance of some of the streams in the adjacent mountain in subterranean caverns gives forcible emphasis to his words. He then gives utterance to intense desire that no one disturb his last resting-place, a feeling akin to the one so universally expressed on

Assyrian monuments concerning the name of their builders. See Thomson's Land and Book, 1882, II. 642-645. The February number of the Century Magazine for 1893 gives us some other sarcophagi from the same quarter, the discoveries of Khamdi Pasha, curator of the Ottoman Museum at Constantinople; and as we gaze on the matchless beauty of the finest of them all we can well believe that the discoverer was completely overwhelmed when his eyes first fell on its wonderful elegance. The people that provided such receptacles for the bodies of its kings could not have been lacking in any external refinement.

ZIMRI.

1 Kings 16: 18. And it came to pass, when Zimri saw that the city was taken, that he went into the castle of the king's house, and burnt the king's house over him with fire, and died.

Towards the close of the Assyrian Empire everything seemed to be in a state of decay. All social activities were like the motions of a clock almost run down and just ready to stop. Nineveh was destroyed, after a siege of over two years, B. C. 606, but the Assyrian chronicle, as Prof. Sayce calls it (R. of P. new II. 120), stopped at B. C. 704. The Assyrian eponym canon held on till B. C. 666, and, after a lacuna of two years, till B. C. 659. The splendor of previous Assyrian palaces was wholly wanting in the structures erected by the latest kings. Geo. Smith, in his "History of Assyria from the Monuments" (p. 198), makes **Asshur ebil ili** the last king; but Prof. Sayce (in R. of P. new II. 208) says that Esarhaddon II. was the last. Greek historians call him Saracus, and say that when an unusual flood in the river Tigris had destroyed a portion of the city wall, despairing of holding out any longer he collected his wealth, his wives and concubines together into the palace, and, setting it on fire, perished in the flames.

POSTSCRIPT.

The reader of the Word is sometimes tempted to take offence at the straightforward way in which it speaks of matters over which modern refinement draws a veil, or passes them by in silence; but it may relieve such to notice that some are mentioned only by way of condemning and forbidding crimes that have already been committed; so that the world is purer for the courageous prohibition. They will be surprised also to note how many of these utterances proceed from lips that do not belong to the people of God.

Such an instance is the vile speech of the Rabshakeh of Sennacherib, 2 Kings 18:27. It would not be difficult to match it from the inscriptions of his royal master (see R. I. 42. 18–21, and A. M. 16. 10–15 and 31–33), but the less said on such themes the better; only let the guilty in this matter bear their guilt, and the word of God receive due honor for dealing faithfully with everything that pollutes and is polluted. All goes to bring to pass the glorious result when "there shall in nowise enter into the city of God anything unclean, or he that maketh an abomination" (in word or deed, or even in thought). Rev. 21:27. The sun is not defiled by the carrion whose corruption it mercilessly exposes, and so, notwithstanding its fearless rebuke of all that is vile, "The precepts of the Lord are right, rejoicing the heart. The commandment of the Lord is pure, enlightening the eyes. The fear of the Lord is clean, enduring forever. The judgments of the Lord are true and righteous altogether." Psa. 19:8, 9.

APPENDIX.

THE INSCRIPTION OF ASSHURNATSIRPAL FROM THE MOUND OF BALAWAT (BIL ABUD).

Mindful of his own lack of help in studying Assyrian, and before he had heard of its translation by others, the writer transliterated and translated this inscription, hoping thus to induce others to enter on this fascinating study and avail themselves of the more abundant helps that are now to be found in this department.

The history of this inscription is soon told. Asshurnatsirpal was king of Assyria B. C. 886–858, and recorded the annals of his reign at length in the palace which he built at Calah (Nimrood). These fill 389 long lines, extending completely across the broad pavement of his palace hall. This inscription at Balawat contains only 49 lines, and they are so much shorter that it takes the first 20 of them to repeat almost word for word the contents of only 6 lines of the larger inscription: col. 2. 126–131 ; in R. I. plate 23.

Layard published the larger inscription, which fills 10 folio pages (R. I. 17–26). Mr. Hormuzd Rassam, a native of Mosul, who assisted Mr. Layard, continued in the service of the British Museum after Mr. Layard had returned to England, and in 1878 discovered the Temple of Makhir in the ancient mound of Balawat, 15 miles south-east from Mosul and not very far from Nimrood. In that temple he found a stone coffer containing two inscribed tablets of alabaster—a beautiful illustration of the two tablets of the law engraven on stone and laid up in the ark within the Holy of Holies, in the Tabernacle. These were duplicate copies of this inscription, and are published in R. V. 69–70. They have been transliterated and translated in Transactions of the Soc. of Bible Archeology, VII. 59 seq., and also translated by S. A. Strong in R. of P. new IV. 80–85. The writer has not seen the former. The latter came to hand after this was prepared, and though there are some renderings in it which may be preferable he has concluded to let his translation stand as it is, and leave Assyrian scholars to make their own choice between them; for it is by each one bringing his contribution that we are to reach the perfect translation yet to come.

OBVERSE

REVERSE

OBVERSE—TRANSLITERATION.

1. *Det.* Asshur-natsir-pal | sharru rabu-u | sharru dan-nu | shar kishshati shar *matu* Asshur |
2. apal Tugulti Adar | sharru rabu-u sharru dan-nu | shar kisishati shar *matu* Asshur | apal Raman Nirari |
3. Sharru rabu-u | sharru dan-nu | shar kisshati shar *matu* Asshur | ma |
4. it-lu | qar-du | sha ina tu-gulti Asshur bili-shu |
5. ittalla-ku-ma ina mal-ki pl. | sha kibrat irbit-ta |

6. sha | nin-in-shu la ishuu | sharru sha ishtu i-bir-ta-an |

7. naru Diqlat a-di | *shadu* Lib-na-na u tamti |
8. rabi-ti | *matu* Laqii | a-na si-khir-ti-sha |
9. *matu* Su-khi | a-di | *alu* Ra-pi-qi ana shipi-shu |
10. u-shik-ni-sha | ishtu | rish i-ni |

Lines 1-21 of this inscription are nearly identical with part of the Standard Inscription of Asshurnatsirpal (R. I. 23. 125-131); a translation of them may be found in R. of P. new II. 161. 125-131.

Line 1. The upright wedge at the beginning is a determinative; *i. e.*, a sign pointing out the class of nouns to which the following word belongs. This one determines it to be a masculine proper name, as the sign **sal** would point it out to be a feminine proper name. See A. M. 17. The next sign is **Asshur.** Either thus or with the determinative **ilu** (god) it is the god Asshur; with **alu** (city) it would denote the city of that name, now Kalah Sherghat, and with **matu** (country) it would mean Assyria. These last are also written **alu Asshur ki,** and **matu Asshur ki ; ki** meaning place or country. **Natsir** is an ideogram ; *i. e.*, it represents an idea or thing, and not merely a sound. As the latter it would be read **bab** or **pap**, and **kur** or **gur**; as an ideogram it may stand for **akhu,** brother, **nakru,** hostile, **napkharu,** the whole, or, as here, some form of the verb **natsaru :** in this case the participle, **natsir,** keeping, protecting, A. M. 18. 32. **Pal** is also an ideogram, and as such may mean either **mu,** water, or, as here, **apal,** son. A. M. 24. 210. As a sound it represents the vowel **a.** The name **Asshur natsir pal** means Asshur preserves the son. **Sharru** (king) is written ideographically ; phonetically it would be **man,** or **nish. Rabu** is a phonogram, and the **u** is written out to show that it is the nominative, **rabu,** not the genitive, **rabi,** or the accusative, **raba. Dan,** in **dannu ;** D. L. gives nine sounds to this sign, 21. 172, and A. M. gives eleven, 14. 146. The context determines which of the eleven is to be used. **Kishshati** is an ideogram; as a phonogram it is **shu.** The last sign is an ideogram for Assyria.

Line 2. **Apal** is an ideogram meaning son of. Also **Tugulti,** meaning reliance, or help, or servant, and the next sign is an ideogram for the god **Adar** or **Uras,** known also as **Ninip.** The name means Uras is my reliance, or helper. Both

APPENDIX.

OBVERSE—TRANSLATION.

1. Asshur-natsir-pal, the great king, the mighty king, the universal king, the king of Assyria,
2. Son of Tukulti Uras, the great king, the mighty king, the king of all, the king of Assyria, son of Rimmon Nirari,
3. The great king, the mighty king, the king of all, the king of the said Assyria,
4. The strong potentate who by the help of Asshur his lord
5. Has marched around, and among the rulers of the four quarters (or regions of the earth)
6. Found none that could resist him. The king who from beyond (*i. e.*, to the east of)
7. The Tigris as far as to Mount Lebanon and the Great Sea (Mediterranean)
8. Has subdued at his feet the land of Laqi throughout its whole extent,
9. And the land of the Shukhites as far as the city of Rapiqi
10. From the head waters

Ramanu and **Nirari** are ideograms. "Ramanu is my helper." Nirari has not the meaning of reliance, like Tugulti.

Line 3. For **ma** at the end see A. L. and S. 70 and 127, and A. M. 35. 18. Here it marks the end of a sentence.

Line 4. **Itlu** (exalted) from **ilu**, to be high, here means ruler, and agrees with the adjective **qardu** (strong).

Line 5. **Ittalla** is ideogram for **dudu**, and **ku** is a phonetic complement. A. M. 26. 5. **Ma;** see line 3.

Line 6. It is very unusual to divide lines as in this inscription, and its arbitrary nature is seen in the occurrence of a division in the middle of the word **shanin ;** the second **in** is a phonetic complement as in line 5 ; **ishtu** is an ideogram. Prof. Sayce renders **ibirtan** fords (R. of P. new II. 127), but the *Worterbuch* in D. L. gives *jenseits*, on the other side.

Line 7. The two signs at the beginning form the determinative for rivers or bodies of water. The Assyrian ideogram for Tigris is a pen picture of its arrowy speed. **Tamti** is an ideogram, and **rabiti,** line 8, agrees with it.

Line 8. **Laqii** corresponds nearly to the modern Pashalic of Orfa, north of the land of the Suri. Soorea, on the west bank of the Euphrates above the mouth of the Belik, recalls the name of this tribe. **Bit khalupi,** one of their cities (R. of P. new II. 142. 75) is now Helebi, below the Belik. In Black's General Atlas (1876) it is printed Zelebi.

Line 9. The **Sukhi** are the Shuhites of the book of Job. They dwelt west of the Euphrates, between the Belik and the Khabor. Their city **Rapiqi** was on the north-western border of Babylonia.

Line 10. **Rish ini,** head of the fountain. We say head waters. **Ishtu** is ideogram for **ta.**

11. *naru* | Su-up-na-at | a-di | ni-ri-bi |
12. sha *matu* Kir-ru-ri | a-di | *matu* Kir-za-ni |
13. ishtu i-bir-ta-an | *naru* Za-ba shupali |
14. a-di | *alu* Til-ba-a-ri sha il-la-an |
15. *matu* Za-ban | ishtu *alu* Til-sha-Ab-ta-ni |
16. adi | *alu* Til-sha-Za-ab-ta-ni |
17. *alu* Khi-ri-mu | *alu* Khu-ru-tu *matu* Bi-ra-a-ti |
18. sha *matu* Kar-du-ni-ash | a-na mi-its-ri |
19. mati-ya u-tir u rapshati pl. |
20. matati Na-i-ri | a-na pa-kha-ad gim-ri-sha |
21. a-bil | a-lu shu-u | a-na esh-shu-ti atsbat |
22. *alu* Im-gur *ilu* Bil | shum-sha | ab-bi |
23. E | kur shi-i | ina li-bit | E-kul-ya)

Line 11. The **Suupnat** is the Sebbeneh Soo, that enters the Tigris near Osman Khoy above Diarbekir, after passing through Maiafarikin (the separation of the waters) and Sheikh Butman. **Niribi** is from **iribu,** to enter; but as a pass is lower than the mountains on either side it came to mean lowlands, as it may here.

Line 12. The region described here takes in the whole width of the Pashalic of Diarbekir as far east as Kûrdistan. **Kirruri** lay between Rawandiz and Erbil (Arbela).

Line 13. The lower **Zab** is still known as Zab el asfal. It was the *Kapros* of the Greek.

Line 14. **Illan** or **illaan,** above.

Line 15. **Zaban** was the district to the south of that river.

Line 16. **Zaabtani** reminds one of Zebdany, between Damascus and Beirût.

Line 17. **Biraati** (fortresses). An abundance of them may have given the district its name; but the determinative **matu** shows that it was the name of a district.

Line 18. **Karduniash** is the well-known name of Babylonia.

APPENDIX. 371

11. of the river Supnat even to the entrance
12. of the land (or low lands) of Kiruri and to the land of Kilzani
13. From the other side of the lower Zab
14. As far as the city of Tilbari, which is above
15. The land of Zaban. From the city of the Tel (mound) of Abtani
16. Even to the city of the Tel of Zabtani
17. The city of Khirimu, the city of Kharutu in the land of Birati (and)
18. (a province) of Karduniash to my own territory
19. I restored and the extensive
20. Provinces of Nairi, in all their subdivisions,
21. I brought (back). This city anew I took hold of,
22. I called its name the city of Imgur Bel (the delight of Bel)
23. Its temple I built in connection with (with the brick of) my palace.

Line 20. **Nairi** (river country) in the days of Tiglath Pileser I. lay towards the head waters of the Tigris and Euphrates. In the time of Asshurnatsirpal it belonged to a region more to the southwest.

Line 21. There seems to be an error of the Assyrian artist here. He has just spoken of the country of **Nairi**, and here he refers to "that city." Was he copying from the Standard Inscription which here says (col. 2. 131), "I took hold anew of the city of Calah," etc., and here the same expression is used of **Belabud** (Balawat). The verb is not **aksud,** I took, in the sense of captured, but **atsbat,** I took hold of, with an idea of making improvements.

Line 22. **Abbi,** from **nabuu,** to speak, to name.

Line 23. This line reads literally, "That temple with the brick of my palace I erected." This may mean, I used the same bricks, stamped with my name, in both of them, or, I built them both on the platform of the same mound that was paved with those bricks; either way the meaning is, I built it in connection with my palace.

REVERSE—TRANSLITERATION.

1. lu-u | ad-di tsalam | *ilu* Makhir | bil-ya |
2. ina lib-bi lu-u u-shi-shib | ana shadu Lib-na-na |
3. lu-u | a-lik | *itsu* gushuri pl. | *itsu* i-ri-ni |
4. *itsu* shur-man | *itsu* dap-ra-ni | a-kish |
5. *itsu* gushuri pl. | *itsu* i-ri-ni—ili E-kur-shi-i |
6. u-tsa-bit | *itsu* dalti pl. | *itsu* i-ri-ni |
7. ipu-ush | ina mi-tsir | si-par-ri | u-ra-ki-is |
8. ina babani-sha pl. | u-ri-ti | E-kur-shi-i |
9. u-si-im | u-shar-rikh | ilu Ma-khir | bilu rabu-u |
10. ina libbi u-shi-shib | *abnu* na-ra-a | ashtur | ina E-kur-shu |
11. ash-kun | rubu | arku-u ina sharra-ni pl. |
12. apli-ya pl. | sha Asshur | i-na-bu-shu | E-kur |
13. shii | i-na-khu | *abnu* na-ra-ya | ta-mar-ma |
14. ta-sha-su-u | an-khu-sa ud-dis | shum-ka ki shum-ya |
15. shutur | ana ashar-shu | ti-sa | Asshur bilu rabu-u (rubu) | *ilu* Ma-khir |
16. a-shib | E-kur-shi-i | ina ni-shi | inaa-shu-nu | ki-nish-ish |
17. us-tu-lu-shu | shum-shu | zir-shu | ina matu-shunu | lu-ki-nu |
18. sha *abnu* na-ra-a | i-ma-ru-ma | an-na-a mi-na |
19. i-qa-bu-u | *ilu* Ishtar | bi-lat | qabli | u takhazi |
20. *itsu* kakki-shu pl. | lu-u | tu-sha-bir | *itsu* kussi-shu |
21. lu ti-kim-shu | sha *abnu* na-ra-a | i-ma-ru-ma |
22. i-sha-su-u | shamni pl. | i-pa-sha-shu | lu-niqu aqqi |
23. ana ashar-shu | lutir-ru | Asshur bilu rabu-u | tuq-ri-bi-shu |
24. i-shim-mi | ina takhazi sha sharra-ni pl. | a-shar |
25. taq-ru-ub-ti | am-mar | lib-bi-shu | u-sham-tsa-ma |

The words in italics are simply determinatives. See p. 96.

Line 1. **Lu.** This is a particle of asseveration. A. M. 35. §18. It seems to be an antique form of the verb expressing completed action. **Makhir;** there is not much known about him save that he was the god of dreams.

Line 2. **Ushishib,** shaphel from **ashabu** with causative meaning.

Line 3. **Irini,** cedars. In Hebrew and Arabic the cedar was אֶרֶן and ארן was the pine-tree.

Line 6. **Dalti** is an ideogram.

Line 7. **Ipush** is an ideogram, also **siparri.**

Line 8. **Babani** are the doorways, or openings for doors. **Daltu,** the frame of boards that closes them.

Line 10. **Abnu** is here a determinative. **Ashtur** is an ideogram. The masculine pronoun **shu** is here used with **E kur** instead of **shi,** the form in line 5.

Line 13. **Tamar.** This and the following verb are in the second person singular.

Line 16. **Nishi inaa-shunu,** literally, in the lifting up of their eyes; so in Hebrew

APPENDIX. 373

REVERSE—TRANSLATION.

1. I placed an image (and so) the god Makhir my lord
2. I caused to dwell in it. To Mount Lebanon
3. I went; beams of cedar,
4. of cypress (or pine) and of juniper I cut down.
5. Beams of cedar upon (the roof of) this temple
6. I laid firmly. Doors of cedar
7. I made, with a covering of copper I bound (or enclosed) them,
8. In its portals I set them up. This temple
9. I made beautiful. I made it strong. The god Makhir, the great lord,
10. I caused to dwell in it. A written tablet of stone in this temple
11. I placed. O thou future ruler among the kings
12. My descendants whom Asshur shall call to the throne, (when) this temple
13. shall decay, my memorial tablet thou shalt look (up)
14. Thou shalt recite (it), its decayed portion restore. Thy name like mine
15. inscribe (in it) (and) restore it to its place. Asshur the great lord and Makhir
16. dwelling in this temple, let them with kindly feeling together
17. regard him, and let them establish his name and his posterity in their land.
18. (But) he who shall look (up) my tablet and injury to it of any kind
19. shall order, let the goddess Ishtar, the queen of battle and of war,
20. break in pieces his weapons, and let her take away from him his throne.
21. He who shall look (up) this my memorial tablet,
22. Who shall recite (it), anoint its **kisalli** with oil, offer sacrifice,
23. And then restore it to its place, the great god Asshur shall hear his prayer.
24. In the battle of kings, the place of fierce encounter,
25. The desire of his heart, he shall cause him to find.

the lifting up of the countenance is used in the same sense. Num. 6 : 26 ; Psa. 4 : 6 ; 42 : 5, 11.

Line 17. **Ustulu-shu,** from **natalu,** with pronominal suffix.

Line 18. **Mina.** Mr. S. A. Strong, in R. of P. new IV. 84. 41, seems to derive this from **manu,** to count, for he renders it "in plenty." Is it not better to take it as the neuter interrogative pronoun (see D. L. IX), and render "whatever," or "of any kind"? **Ishtar** in line 19 is set down as **alu,** god, masculine. (Attention is here called to what in our view is an irregularity: **Alu** is god; goddess would be **Ishtar**—also her name.)

Line 20. **Kakki** is an ideogram; **tushabir,** feminine, agreeing with **Ishtar,** so also is the next verb, **tikim,** in line 21.

The spirit of the last line is most thoroughly Assyrian. The king regards the hottest of the battle as the most desirable place, and that once found he has no doubt as to the issue. **Ammar** means, literally, the filling up.

INDEX.

	PAGE.
Abbreviations in this volume	6, 7
Abednego	9
Abni piili	311
Abraham	9, 10, 218, 257
" why he blessed Melchizedec	203
Accadian folk-lore	131
Accuracy of translations	328
Adrammelech	10, 11
Adultery impartially condemned	357
Ahab	11
Alphabet	12
Altar	12–14
" golden, of Bil	14
Amazons	159
Ameni	123
Amenemhat	156
Amenophis IV.	43, 55, 88, 181, 184, 202
Amraphel	54
Angel, Destroying	14
Anointing, Prominence of	15, 16
Ansan, Anzan	74, 79, 80, 111, 112
Ansar and Kisar	71
Apparel, Royal	16
Appiryon	17
Apple of the eye	17, 18
Appropriation of tributes	337
Ararat, Mountains of	93
Arel	13
Arioch	19
Ark (shrine)	20
" Chaldean	93
Arpad	21
Arrows	21
" Divination by	237
Art, Hittite	162
Artemis	159
Artichoke	349
Asherah, The goddess	22
Ashkenaz	138
Asses	23
" white	24
Asshurbanipal	28, 29, 48, 68, 132, 180, 226
" prayer of	250
Asshurnatsirpal	16, 18, 72–74, 123, 127, 133, 365–369
" his time for war	273
Assyrian, The (Isa. 52:4)	24
" language	25
Atonement, Vicarious	269, 278
Atys	159

	PAGE.
Baba's record of famine	123
Babylonia, Fruitfulness of	342
" Literature of	9, 10, 68, 84, 85
Balaam	26, 27
Balawat	12, 35, 36, 363, 365
Banks	27
Battlements, round-roofed	27, 28
Beasts of the field, and wild	28, 29
Beautiful gate	31
Beer	106
Bel	15, 29
Belshazzar	4, 31, 48, 124
Benhadad	11, 148, 281
Bethel	32
Binding and loosing	32, 33
Bisik Siparri	75
Bit Yagina	204, 205
Black-headed race	14, 79, 307
Bliss, Mr.	181
Blue	64
Body, nailed to wall	33
Boscawen, W. S. Chad	323
Botta, P. E.	5, 12, 16, 38, 65, 121, 291
Bound hand and foot	34
Bow down	34
Bowels, Cometh forth out of	35
Brass, Doors of	35
Brazen sea	36
Breaches	37
Bricks, Assyrian	313
Bridle	37
Brightness	38
Bring back	39
Brothers	40, 288
" The two	247, 248
Brugsch Bey	156, 159, 160, 335
Bulls, winged and human-headed	97, 142
Burial, outside of cities	135
" of kings, in cities	136
Burn with fire	127
Burna Buriyas	88, 202
Bury alive	72, 73
Butter and honey	42
Caillou Michaux	187
Calah	42, 43, 68, 234, 337
Campaigns, how often	273
Candelabra	241, 242
Caphtor	12, 138
Cappadocia	43

INDEX. 375

	PAGE.
Castor-oil plant	145, 146
Cauls	44
Caves	281
Cedar	44, 45, 279, 333, 334
Cemeteries	46, 135, 136
Century Magazine	359, 362
Chain of gold	48
Chaldean story of Deluge	89–91
" " agrees with Genesis	91
" " differs from "	92–95
Chaldean learning	189
Change of gods	48, 49
" " name	9
Chaos	70, 71
Chariots	51–53
Chedorlaomer	54, 55
Cherubim	98
Cheyne, T. R., Rev.	155, 156
Children desired	55
" eaten	56
Cistern	57
Cities, ancient	57–59
City and country	59–61
" thy	61
" and tower	62
Clean and unclean beasts	63
Clothed with cursing	64
Coffins	47
Coincidence, Wonderful	181
Coins invented by Hittites	162, 348
Colophons	68, 108, 259, 262
Colors	64–66
Commandment, Second	66
" to destroy	96
Concubine	67, 68
Confidence, Self-	337
Copied out	68
Count	69
Covenant	69
Cover the face	70
Creation	70
Creator and Father	71
Creatures, Living	195
Cremation	135
Cruel	125
Cruelties	72–74
Cumulative evidence	4
Cuneiform writing	25, 26
" " extent of use	74
Curse of Jericho	74, 75
Cursing	75
Cut themselves	77
Cylinders	290
Cyrus	77–81, 111, 243
Dagal	81–197

	PAGE.
Dagon	81–83
Darkness	83
Deciphering inscriptions	4–6
Dedication	84
Delitzsch, Prof. Friedrich	18, 67, 108, 114, 202
Deluge	84–96
" Duration of	94
Determinatives	96
Destruction by command	96
Devils (Shidi)	97
Devise evil	98
Dial	98, 99, 168
Diarbekir	73
Divorce	99, 100
Dogs	100
Doom of the heathen	178
Dove	90, 94, 134, 317
Dragon	71, 104
Dream, doubled twice	101–104
Dreams	105
Drink-offering	105
Drought	106
Dualism	118, 119
Duisratta	25, 197
Dur Sargina	38
Dust	106
" on head	107
Ea	67, 83, 141, 292
Earrings	108
E Dabara	11
Ebed Tob	176, 202, 203
Eden	108, 109
" rivers of	100
Education	109
" of women	110
" honored of God	10
Egibi, Sons of	27
Elam (see Ansan)	111
Ellasar (Larsa)	19
Elohim	112
El Shaddai	112–116
Elul, Hemerology of	283
Entering of gate	116, 117
Eponyms	43, 262, 321, 360, 362
Eras, Chronological	359
Erechite lament	50
Eri Aku	19
Eridu	108, 109, 168, 383
Esarhaddon	51, 133, 134, 165, 200, 202, 224, 300, 325
Eternity	117
Evening and morning	11, 87
Evil, Whence	118, 119
" Merodach	120

INDEX.

	PAGE.
Eyes destroyed	121
Face	121
Faith and grace	122
Famine in Egypt	123
Fast, Proclaiming a	123
Father, God our	258, 259
" Creator	71, 72
Fear	124
Feast, Women at	124, 125
Feet	125
Fertility of Assyria	280
Filial duty	125
Fire, Burnt with	127
First-born	128
Flaying alive	34, 72, 73, 129
Flesh of men eaten	129, 131
Foot-marking	131
" stool	132
Fore-ordination	132
Forgiving	133, 134
Forms, Grammatical	146
Forsaken of God	134
Foundations	41
Fountains	135
Fresh Light, etc.	12, 21, 112
Funerals	135
Furnace	136
Ganneau, Mons. Clermont	207, 208
Gashmu	137
Gate, City	137
Genealogy, Without	203
Genesis 10	138
Gibil	49
Gladness and joy	138, 139
Glorify God	139
Go before	140
God and Lord	143
" of gods	145
Gods, animal	67, 141, 142
" bird	66, 67
" fish	67
" many	143
" prevaricating	95
Goeth	143
Goings out	144
Gold much used	144
Golennischeff, M.	17, 44
Gourd (Jonah's)	145, 146
Grant, Dr. A.	214, 304
Graves	46, 47
Greaves	147
Grotefend	5
Groves, mistranslated	22
Growth of idolatry	48, 49

	PAGE.
Gudea	322
Gula	64
Guthe, Dr.	297
Gutium	54
Gyges	103, 105, 125, 194, 338
Hadadrimmon	148
Haikal (temple), origin of word	323
Hallowed be Thy name	225
Hamath	148
Hanameel	149
Hands, Lifting up of	191
Hannah and Samuel	149
Haran	150
Harper, Prof. R. T.	6
Harps	151
Head	152
" Carrying off	152
" Lifting up of	191
Hearing	107, 110
Heart stirred up	152, 153
Heaven	154, 169
" Moslem	95
Hebron and Hittites	154, 156
Helbon, Wine of	351
Helmets	157
Hezekiah, Prayer of	249
Highways	157
Hilprecht, Prof. H. V.	79
Hittite art	162
" chariots	163, 164
" dress	162
" gods	159
" inscriptions	158
Honor, for obey	164, 165
Horns	22, 316
Horse	165
Hosts, Lord of	166
Hours	167
House of fathers	168
" " my royalty	282
Idols	108
Immortality	168, 169
Immutability in Assyria	339
" " God	341
Impalement	34
Incantations	170, 171
Incense, altar	14
Individuals, God judges	178
Inscriptions, numerous	171
" accurately translated	328–330
" dates of	172
" languages	172
" material used	172, 173
Isaiah 10	173, 174

INDEX. 377

	PAGE.
Ishtar	266
" descent into Hades	190
Israel	174, 175
Ivory palaces	175
Izdubar (Gisdubar)	32, 85, 232
" tablet	36, 89, 331, 345
Jastrow, Morris, Jr.	359
Jehovah	175, 176
Jehu	358
Jeremiah	149
Jerusalem	176, 202, 203
Joseph	48, 248
" Knew not	184
Judge	177
Judgment, Righteous	177, 178
Justice	179
" Royal	253
Kadesh, Battle of	160
Khamdi Pasha	362
Khammuragas	19, 111, 264, 284
Kharran	82, 150
Khasisadra	31, 32, 45, 85, 89, 92, 95, 279, 333, 340
Khorsabad	12, 65, 66, 121, 201, 256
King of kings	180
Kings and priests	201, 256
Kingdom against kingdom	180, 181
Kirjath Sepher	181
Kisallu	13, 16
Kiss	182
" Oriental	183
Klein, Dr.	207
Knees	183
Knowledge of the fathers	184, 185
Koyunjik	84, 108, 185
Kudur Mabuk	19, 20, 54
" Nankhundi	39, 50, 54, 111
Lachish (Tel el hesy)	57, 181, 186, 187
Lagamaru	54
Lakhma and Lakhama	71
Land and the Book, The	3, 349, 362
" Growth of, at Ur	109
Landmarks	187
Languages	188
Larit	312
Larsa	19
Lassen, Prof.	5
Layard	65, 66, 84, 241, 242
Learning of the Chaldeans	10, 189
Lending without interest	252
Length of days	195
Libations	105
Library of Asshurbanipal	6, 68, 85

	PAGE.
Libraries	10, 68
Life, Spiritual, from Christ only	120
" Tree of	255, 332, 351
" Water of	189, 190
Lig Bagas	19
Light of the world	190, 192
Lilith	192
Lion	193
Litany	193
Literature of Babylonia	9, 10, 68, 84, 85
Liver, The—the seat of emotion	194
Lobdell, Henry, M. D.	145, 146
Loftus, W. K.	19, 46, 47, 295, 296
Long life	195, 196
Look in the face	196
" on " "	197
Looking-glasses	197
Lord of all	198
Lyon, Prof. D. G.	13, 82, 117, 122, 257, 324, 343, 344
Madaktu	57
Magan	88
Majesty	199
Mamit	26
Manasseh	200
Mariette Bey	156, 159
Meal-offering	278
Meat and drink	200
Mediterranean Sea	289, 360
Melchizedek	201–203
Menahem	326
Menant, Mons.	290
Mene, Tekel, Upharsin	203
Merathaim	204
Merodach	30, 49, 62, 71, 78–80, 101, 104, 128, 204
" relation to other gods	49, 79–80, 141
Mesha	208
Methuselah	205, 206
Milk of sheep	207
Mirrors	197
Mitsraim	128
Moabite stone	207–209
Monotheism	87, 206, 210, 211, 220
Months	211–213
Monument	214
Moon, Worship of the	215–218
" in Accad set before the sun	216
" Temple of, in Ur	30, 216, 218, 342
Mordecai	218
Morning star	218
Moses in the ark	219
" used other writings	85–88
Mount of congregation	220

INDEX.

	PAGE.
Mountains	220
" God and	116
Mouth for command	222
Muezzim, Basis for the	257
Mullil	15, 355
Music	222–224
Nabonidus	31, 32, 49, 60, 78, 80, 117, 133, 139, 150, 243
Nabopolassar	42
Nahum, picture of chariots	53
Name, Assyrian idea of a	225
" Number of	236
" of God	224–227
Names, Meaning of	228
" Origin of	228
" Men's, of which God is a part	228–230
Nana	39, 40, 50
Naville, Mons.	314
Nebo	29
Nebuchadrezzar	30, 45, 133, 145, 153, 230, 231
" " astonished at furnace	308
Nergal	14, 15
Newman, Prof. F. W.	163
Nimrod	232
Nimrood	232
Nineveh, Extent of	233–235
Ningirsa	322
Ninip, Names of	11, 285
Nisakku	202, 256
Nishit ina	18
Nisroch	235
Nitsir	93
No return, Land of	274
Nouns	235
Numeration	91
Oannes	83
Oil, Anointing with	16
" Mollified with	210
Omens	236, 237
Oxen not offered whole	13
Padan Aram	238
Paine, Prof. J. A.	25
Particles (grammar)	238, 239
Patesi	202, 256
Pathrusim	138
Peace, God of	176, 240
Pentaur	155, 164
Perrot and Chipiez	12, 16, 36, 41, 125, 242
Persian gulf	109, 289
Pethor	73, 240, 241
Petrie, Dr. Flinders	181

	PAGE.
Pharaoh Necho	9, 48, 227–276
Phœnician alphabet	12
Phrases, Scripture	4, 34, 35, 65
Pikhatu	33, 297
Pinches, Theophilus G.	44, 50
Pine-tree and cone	332
Pitch	241
Place, Mons.	65
Plaster	241, 242
Polygamy	100, 353
Polytheism	243, 263
Poor in spirit	244
Porch before the house	245–247
Potiphar, Wife of	247
Potter's vessel	248
Power, Symbol of	316
Prayer, Hebrew and Assyrian	249, 250
Precative	146, 147
Presents to kings	251
" of Hezekiah to Sennacherib	252
Prices of asses	253
" " grain, houses, oxen, sheep	253
Priesthood	254
Priests' dresses	279
Priest-king	201, 256
Procession, Musical	223, 224
Psalms	257, 260
" Penitential	260–262
Pul	262–264, 327
Pyramids of living men	72, 73
Queen of heaven	265
" on throne	265
" Semiramis	265
Queens in Arabia	264
" " Babylonia	264
" " Egypt	265
Quti	79
Rab Mag	266
Rabshakeh, The	266, 363
" " as linguist	268
Rainbow, after Deluge	95
Rain fire, etc.	268
Ramses II.	25, 160–162
Ramsey, Prof. W. M.	44
Rassam, Hormuzd	11, 12, 35, 36, 79, 218, 356
Raven	268, 269
Rawlinson, Sir Henry	5, 6, 30, 74, 189
Records used by Moses	88
Redemption	269
Refuge, God a	115
Religion, National, in Assyria	78
Religion, Local, in Babylonia	78
Repetitions, Vain	270

INDEX.

379

	PAGE.
Reprobates	134
Rest	58, 270, 271
" The gods also	58, 272
Retribution	178
Return not	274
Righteousness	274
Rimmon	275
Ring (bracelet?)	275, 276
Rites	277–279
River of Egypt	280
Rivers	280
Roads	346
Rocks of Assyria	280
Ropes on head	281, 282
Royal house	282
Sabako	306
Sabba	119
Sabbath	282–285
" belongs to God	282, 283
" date of Sabbath tablet	284
" day of rest for the heart	283
Sacrifices	278
" human	269, 278
Sakar en Nimrood	346
Sakkut and Chiun	285
Salt, Sown with	286
Samaria peopled from Assyria	286, 287
Samuel	150
Sand, Building on (see 233)	41
Sanctified from womb	287
Sargon, his justice	179, 253, 254
" and Isaiah	4, 287
Sattuku	277
Savor, Sweet	288
Sayce, Prof. A. H.	21, 42, 44, 83, 92, 100, 104, 109, 110, 114, 118, 124, 138, 147, 156, 159, 161, 181, 205, 206, 210, 220, 283, 297, 299, 362
Saw not one another	288
Sceptre, Golden	288
Schools	109, 110
Scripture and the monuments	86, 87, 91–96, 269, 270, 295
Sea to sea, From	289
" Upper and lower	80
Seal	289–291
" of Sabako	306
" " Urukh	291
" skins	291, 292
Seals all intaglios	290
" Number of	290
Seamen in the ark	93
Season for campaigns	272
Semiramis	265
Sepharad	292

	PAGE.
Serpent	292
Seruaed herat	110, 111, 329
Sevens	293
Shadow	294
Shakkanaku	202, 254, 256
Shalmanezer II.	11, 36, 51, 161
Shangu	202, 254, 256
Shanu	103
Shars	91
Sheep, Milk of	207
" Price of	253
Sheil, Rev. V.	359
Shem, Ham and Japhet	138
Shepherd	294
Shidi	67, 97, 142
Shikaru	106
Ship	294
Shoulder peeled	295
Shumir and Akkad	80
Shushan	111, 295
Shutting	297
Siloam, Inscription at	297, 298
Silver sky, Land of the	169
Sin, Temple at Ur	30, 78, 217, 218, 342
" and Sinai	299, 300
Singing men and women	222–225, 300
Sippara	10, 11
Skies	300
Skin	301
Slaughter	301
Slaves	302
" condition and prices	303
Sleepeth	304
Slippery places	304
Small and great	305
Smith, Azariah, M. D.	304
" George	85
Smoke of burning	305
So (see Sabako)	306
Son of the gods	307
Sons of Assyria	308
" " Zion	308
Sorcerer, power of	26, 27
Sorcery	170, 171
Soul (life)	308
Spoil	309
Stand before	29
Star worship	310
Stones, Costly	311
S. S. Times	79, 83
Storehouses	312
Straw for brick	313
Strike through	314
Succoth Benoth	315
Suicide	315
Swift destruction	316

	PAGE.
Sword, Flame of a	316
Symbols	316
Tabering	317
Tablets	84
Tadukhepa	25, 55, 197
Tahtim Hodshi	318
Taklimu	278
Talent as a weight	318
Tammuz	319
" two seasons for mourning	320
Tartan, The	320
Tear in pieces	321
Teie	25, 197
Telassar	321
Tel el Amarna tablets	55, 74, 88, 97, 181, 184, 202
Tel el Hesy	181
Tel el Maskhuta	314
Telloh	88, 322
Temple	323
Tenses, Assyrian	324
Testament	325
Thothmes III.	159, 160
Throne of Sennacherib	325, 326
Thrust through	314
Tiamat	70, 71, 104
Tiglath Pileser I.	51, 74, 185
" " II.	21, 174, 205, 215
Timin (corner stone)	75
Toora 'd Jeloo	221
Tower of Babel	62, 63, 327
Towers in cities	62
Traditions of the Deluge	87
Trampling on	331
Translations, Accuracy of	328
" with notes	328–330, 336
Travail	331
Tread down	331
Tree of life	255, 293, 332, 351
Trees, Culture of	334
" felled	335
Tribute	335, 336
Trust in God	337
" " self	337
Tubal and Meshech	138
Ulai, Between the banks of	338
Ummanaldas	177
Unchangeableness, etc.	339–341
Ungodly heaven, An	95
Ur of the Chaldees	78, 341
Urukh	215, 291

	PAGE.
Vaiteh	100, 125, 137, 140, 251, 314, 360
Van Lennep, H. J., D. D.	77
Veil	343
Verbs	343
" Hebrew and Assyrian	344
Vermilion	64
Vessels, Sacred	91, 344
Vine	124, 333
Visions	105
Voice	345
Wady el 'Arish	280
Wages	253
Ward, Dr. W. Hayes	11
Warka (Erech)	46
Water-works	345
Way, Preparing the	346
Weighing gold and silver	347
Went up	348
Wheel (artichoke)	349
Whirlwind	350
Winds, To the	350
Will of Sennacherib	325
Wine	350
" in the ark	95
Witchcraft	170, 171
Witnesses, Number of	351
Wolfe Expedition	3
Woman in Babylonia	100, 110, 126, 352
" The virtuous	353
" Wrongs of	356, 357
Womb, Sanctified from the	287
Word, The	354
" Thy	258
Words	355
World, God of this	355
Worshipper	356
Wright, Rev. W. W.	158, 159, 160, 164
Writing in the days of Moses	88
Yahua	358
Yavnan	138
Year of the king	359
" Return of the	272
Yoke	360
Zaphenath Paneah	361
Zidon, Kings of	361
Ziggurat	63, 226, 247, 324
Zimri	362
Zimrida	181, 182
Zodiac of Babylonian origin	310

www.ingramcontent.com/pod-product-compliance
Lightning Source LLC
Chambersburg PA
CBHW071225230426
43668CB00011B/1310